# HOME
*and*
# AWAY

Library of Congress Cataloging-in-Publication Data

Simon, Scott.
    Home and away : memoir of a fan / Scott Simon.—1st ed.
        p. cm.
    ISBN 0-7868-6415-X
    1. Sports—Illinois—Chicago—History. 2. Chicago Bulls (Basketball team)—History. 3. Chicago
Bears (Football team)—History. 4. Chicago Cubs (Baseball team)—History. 5. Simon, Scott. 6.
Sports spectators—United States—Biography. 7. Journalists—United States—Biography I. Title.

GV584.C4 S56 2000
796.323'64'0977311—dc21

                                                                                            99–049282

Designed by Vicki Fischman

FIRST EDITION

3   5   7   9   10   8   6   4   2

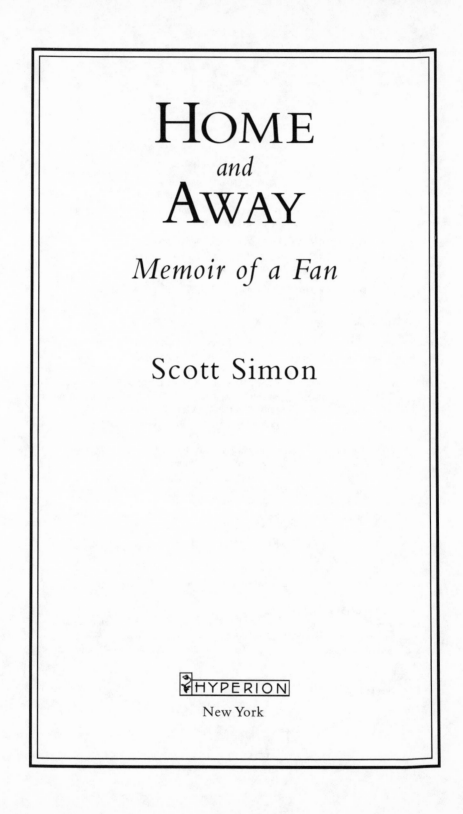

# HOME
### and
# AWAY

*Memoir of a Fan*

## Scott Simon

**HYPERION**

New York

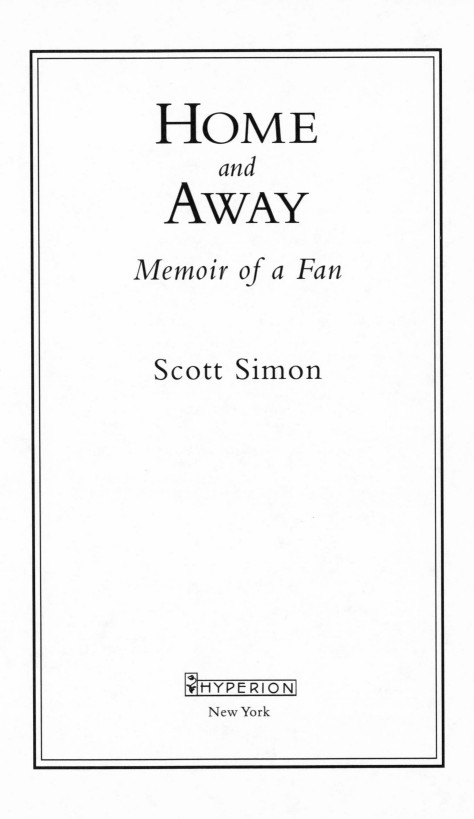

# HOME
### *and*
# AWAY

## *Memoir of a Fan*

## Scott Simon

**HYPERION**

New York

Library of Congress Cataloging-in-Publication Data

Simon, Scott.
    Home and away : memoir of a fan / Scott Simon.—1st ed.
        p. cm.
    ISBN 0-7868-6415-X
    1. Sports—Illinois—Chicago—History. 2. Chicago Bulls (Basketball team)—History. 3. Chicago
Bears (Football team)—History. 4. Chicago Cubs (Baseball team)—History. 5. Simon, Scott. 6.
Sports spectators—United States—Biography. 7. Journalists—United States—Biography I. Title.

GV584.C4 S56 2000
796.323'64'0977311—dc21

                                                                              99–049282

Designed by Vicki Fischman

FIRST EDITION

3   5   7   9   10   8   6   4   2

*For Sparky*

# *Acknowledgments*

A man's friends, family, and colleagues pay the price of a personal memoir. It's hard to decide what's harder to suffer: a writer's repeated absences, or his preoccupied immersion in his own thoughts. I apologize for both.

Ken Hom, the Senior Producer of *Weekend Edition Saturday,* along with Senior Producer Peter Breslow and editor Gwendolyn Thompkins, worked hard to keep our program the best weekly news show in America. Clearly, my own efforts are not critical to its continued distinction. I have been blessed to share my professional life through this period with a wonderful staff that has included Sarah Beyer-Kelly, Alicia Montgomery, Julia Holmes Bailey, Susan Schuyler Engel, Brigid McCarthy, Vashtai Van Wyck, Raquel Dillon, and Daniel Schorr. NPR Associate Managing Editor Barbara Rehm offered time off that allowed me to complete this project and attend to family business. Managing Editor Bruce Drake approved the project, along with NPR's former chief operating officer Peter Jablow. Our technical director, Shawn Fox, charitably extended his commission to include tutoring me in computer technology and taking me along to Detroit Red Wings games.

Kee Malesky, in NPR's library, proofread and improved every page of this text. Any reputation NPR authors enjoy for producing polished manuscripts is a deception Kee promotes by her own skill and scrupulousness. Her colleagues, Alphonse Vinh and Caleb Gessesse, kindly answered urgent calls for information. Tom Goldman, NPR's deeply talented sports department, has been helpful to a visitor who loves to stray into his territory. Doug Fabrizio at KUER in Salt Lake City was helpful in tracking down the trail of the last basketball Michael Jordan ever lifted in professional competition. Jay Cruz of San Juan kindly shared his devotion for the Santurce Cangrajeros, and his feeling for the great Roberto Clemente.

My longtime Saturday morning cohort, Ron Rapoport of the *Chicago Sun-Times*, was unfailingly available with sound advice and friendship; as was his wife, Joan Rapoport. David Halberstam, of course, has already published a much more accomplished and complete book about Michael Jordan and the Bulls. It was a pleasure to bump into him in our travels, and I am glad to at last have a forum in which to thank David and Jean Halberstam for their years of friendship and inspiration.

The people whom I have interviewed over the years, either for NPR or this book specifically, are quoted herein. I thank them for their time and thoughtfulness. Contrary to any impression, I was not taking notes during my childhood and adolescence. My memories, like those of many people, I imagine, tend to blend my own incomplete remembrances with the impressions and anecdotes of others. No doubt over the years, some of those anecdotes have been polished to shine. While I share some of my father's disinclination to tamper with proven material, I have occasionally had to adjust an old anecdote to conform with history. I have tried to check the core of anecdotes against available records (for example, I do not remember the specific number of wins and losses that Charlie Grimm cited in talking about his managerial record in 1948. But I remember that he remembered it to the exact digit, and have included those numbers in recollecting his monologues here).

Leigh Haber, executive editor of Hyperion, lent her pivotal support to this project and her editorial talents to shaping the resulting material. And, there would simply be no book without the good heart and wise guidance of Jonathan Lazear.

I am at a loss as to how to ever thank Luc Longley. His friendship, and that of his family, not only afforded me a front-row seat in a fascinating world, but affiliations and insights that have enriched my appreciation for sports—and life. It is heartening to see such good fortune awarded to a man who shares it so selflessly. At the same time, it should not be assumed that any opinions or experiences ascribed to a member of the Bulls traces back to Luc. On the contrary: I have been circumspect about passing on any stories he imparted to me personally.

The final sections of this book coincide with pain and loss in my family. To say that Tish Valva, now the Executive Producer at WBEZ in Chicago, has become regarded as a member of our family implies a minute distance. There is none. Tish is a member of our family.

Dr. Pauline Maki gave unstinting support, boundless understanding, and love to myself and my family. My debt to her is precious and permanent.

My cousin, Annette Simon, is our family's leading artist, genealogist, and herbalist. I am fortunate that the planets have revolved and churned to deposit two itinerant cousins into the same metropolitan area at the same time. Annette's help in the most mundane of personal errands that can accumulate was indispensable; and her companionship a joy. Any mitigation in thanks to my mother, Patricia Newman, is occasioned only by the fact that I hope one day to dedicate another book to her.

I write this note of thanks while on assignment with my long-time collaborators, Leo del Aguila and Peter Breslow. They have been awfully tolerant of my insistent habit of pointing out each Chicago Bulls symbol we see on a hat or T-shirt in beleaguered locales around the world. It is a blessing to have them as both colleagues and friends.

The personnel in the Periodical Room of Chicago's Harold Washington Central Public Library were skillful and courteous in locating copies of old newspapers, so that I could check my recollections against the statistical record. Their encouraging courtesy would gratify my late stepfather, Ralph Newman, to whom this book is dedicated. When Ralph was chairman of Chicago's Public Library in the late 1960s and early 1970s, he campaigned for the city to build a new downtown central library—a place that could not only contain an information revolution, but serve as a vital gathering place. But at the time, Chicago, like most major cities, was contending with revolutions more immediate than libraries. Finally, in the 1990s, a splendid new central library was completed, and named after the late Mayor Harold Washington.

A number of people in the library remembered Ralph's activism and suggested that the new building should visibly commemorate his contribution by having a section or room bear his name. It was one of the few times I ever sensed that Ralph actually hankered for an honor. But there were objections. Ralph had once been convicted of back-dating the appraisal deed for papers Richard Nixon donated and took off as a deduction on his income taxes (a case that I take up in an extended footnote in a later chapter—it was just a footnote in Ralph's distinguished career). One city council member (I take some pleasure in pretending to forget her name) asked, "How can you name a part of the library after a convicted felon?"

Ralph, who pleaded not guilty but was convicted and did not appeal, was puzzled and hurt by such sanctimony. The infraction for which he was convicted was unpretentious by local standards. Chicago has a long tradition of encouraging incriminated men and women to remain active in community affairs. In fact, Ralph was too nice to mention—but I am not—that the entire central library is named for a convicted felon (the late Mayor Washington was convicted for income tax evasion).

The scholars, school kids, retirees, and solitary searchers who are welcomed to the library today are the direct beneficiaries of Ralph's determination that Chicago should have a central library to match its other ambitions and attainments. I hope that the library will one day reconsider inscribing Ralph Newman's name in a place that will honor the service he gave to the city that he cherished.

—SSS
August 1999
Pristina, Kosovo

# Contents

# HOME
*and*
# AWAY

## Chapter 1

# SPUTNIK BY THE BAY

There was a time when I was Billy Pierce, the high-kicking left-handed pitcher of the Chicago White Sox (211 career wins, 169 losses). But being only about two and a half feet tall, my impact on the game was small. I had another name, too, but no use for it. When my mother called out, "Time to get to bed, Scotty," I reacted with elaborate inattention, as if she must have been calling to a stranger. Within a few moments, my heedlessness would force her to track a trail of toys to find me at play in our apartment. "What did I say about bed, young man?" she would demand with a mother's mock reproach. And I'd demand back, "What did you say my name was?" "Ohmigosh, *Billy*," my mother would rush in to add, "*Billy*, I almost forgot. Big game tomorrow. Time to get to bed, *Billy*." Once (this is a childhood story that may explain too much) I was standing below our kitchen counter as my mother defrosted the freezer when a couple of ears of frozen corn, flinty as bricks, rolled off the ledge and rang my head. *Bong! Bong!* My mother leaned down with alarm and took hold of my shoulders. "What's your name? What's your name?" Blinking back tears, I answered. "Billy Pierce." If I had replied with the name she'd given me, she would have feared brain damage.

I liked Billy Pierce because my father did. I could tell he admired certain traits in Billy Pierce and I wanted him to find them in me, too. My father said that Billy was stylish, nervy, and classy (the words he also used to distinguish Adlai Stevenson, Jack Paar, and Edward R. Murrow). *Stylish* for the way Billy would raise his right foot high as he stepped into a pitch, adding some force to his throws and baffling a batter's view, and *nervy* for the way he'd throw a curve when he was three balls down in the count and the bases were full.

"Goddamn, Patti, did you see that?" he'd call out to my mother as he watched some game, and she bustled about elsewhere in the apartment.

"No, dear."

"Goddamn threw a curve to Kaline with the bases loaded, and got him to chase it." When my mother sent back no reaction, my father would turn to me, where I sat on the floor to watch my father watching the game.

"Nervy, Scotty, Billy's *nervy*. Bold." He'd shake his head in admiration, a different sort of waggle from the ones he would award me for looking clownish. "Gutsy. A classy guy, too." *Classy* was a word that was taking shape in my mind, between my father's work (he was a wandering comedian) and Billy Pierce. Classy guys were gentlemen. They shook hands, remembered your name, and stopped to say hello to children. Classy guys reached for the check and tipped more than the minimum. They said please, thank you, and—when it came to it—I'm sorry (as in, "I'm sorry, Patti, okay? I'm sorry").

My father's best friend, Jack Brickhouse, whom I called Uncle Jack, was a classy guy who was the play-by-play announcer for both the Cubs and White Sox. We came to see Jack at the park one Saturday, and he said he had a surprise. Uncle Jack took us through a winding tunnel that emptied out near the steps leading down into the dugout, right up to the bench where only players could sit. There was a man at rest there, a morning's sweat gleaming on his raspy chin, like drizzle drying on the infield grass. He raised a reflexive smile at Uncle Jack.

"You know who this is, don't you, Scotty?" I had a suspicion. The man I revered, it turned out, spoke with a slight sibilance, a delightful suggestion of Daffy Duck.

"Hey, *Ssscotty*. How are you, A*ccce*?" Ace was a baseball nickname, I knew even then, for a team's best pitcher. Meeting the flesh-and-blood ace I knew only as a flickering, small screen, black-and-white figure, I guess I got too full for a four-year-old; and began to cry.

"Hey, Scotty." My father stepped forward. "You know how much you love Billy. Say hello to Billy." But Billy Pierce had already looped one of the liveliest arms in the American League lightly around my shoulders. "Say, I'll bet you're a pretty good pitcher," said Billy Pierce. "Let's take a look, Ace." My father and Uncle Jack had sweet rolls in their hands (in those days, locker rooms stocked sweet rolls and cigarettes for players' snacks, rather than vitamin bars and zucchini strips) and took off a corner. "Okay, Ace, stand up straight to get the signal," admonished Billy Pierce. "Now, give us a pitch." But what did I really know about pitching? I stood up straight, my shoulders braced against Billy's knees, shaking my head and scowling for a signal, the way I'd seen my father mimic pitchers. I paused, picked up my right hand, squeezed the sweet roll horsehide, and then—kicked out my right leg, Billy-like. And stopped. The confectionery sphere stayed in my hand. What, after all, did I know about pitching? *Be stylish, be nervy.* But from above, I heard the friendly rumble of the three most eminent men in my world, laughing pleasingly. "You taught him well, Ern," Uncle Jack said, while Billy Pierce rubbed an encouraging hand over my head, the way he might rough up a baseball, and my father beamed to see something in me that so clearly traced back to him. "Attaboy, Ace!" he said. "Atts-aboy!"

In those days, we were on the move. But wherever we landed, we were Chicagoans Abroad. Years before any other civic characteristic signified the city in my mind—fierce winds, mob hits, or fractious politics—I grasped that my parents and I came from a place marked in my mind by Billy Pierce, Ernie Banks, Minnie Minoso, and George Halas. City of Broad Shoulders, White Sox, burly Bears, and hapless Cubs.

We lit out for San Francisco, on one of the last cross-country trains. For years, my parents would delight in their recollections, "We sure saw the country, didn't we? We sure saw things!" But I mostly remember the french toast in the dining car, and taking a bath out of a bowl. When bedtime came on our first night out, I campaigned to be tucked in to the upper berth. But my father wouldn't allow it.

"Oh no, Ace, don't you know what can happen up there? The train stops in the middle of the night. You get *thrown* through the window, and the glass *cuts you* to ribbons. Or, you pop out through the curtains, hit the floor, and *crack your skull* wide open, just like an egg." My father had served with the British Army in North Africa and played a card my squalling could not match. "Listen, pal, I've seen men with their skulls cracked open. I've seen their brains spill out, all over the ground, just like scrambled eggs. The buzzards eat them for breakfast. Do you want that to happen to you?"

They tucked me in to the bottom berth and I nodded off, twitching with visions of cartoon buzzards eating scrambled eggs off Santa Fe railroad china. Within a few minutes, my father poked his head and arms into the berth, and shook me gently; it might have been the first time I had seen him become shy. "Hey, pal," he said in a low tone. "Hey, Ace. How would you like to sleep on top?" He had brushed his teeth, washed his face, patted himself down with Lilac Vegetal, tied himself in to his drawstring pajamas—and then found he was too large to squeeze into the upper berth. "Great view up there," he said. "I'll bet it's a lotta fun."

"But—but—you said—"

"Oh, I know, but Mommy and I will tuck you in real tight—"

"that my skull would crack open—"

"Hey, Ace, *don't worry* about that. You know we wouldn't let *anything* happen to you! It'll be a lotta *fun* up there. Trust me." We might have crossed into Nebraska by the time I was nervy enough to let myself be moved. When we arrived in San Francisco, my mother insisted that we set off on a tour of that dreamscape, riding up Nob Hill on a clanging cable car and descending into Chinatown, where I gnawed on my first egg roll, speared through a chopstick like a Popsicle. Near dusk, we boarded the ferry that passed within hailing distance of Alcatraz.

"They call that The Rock, Scotty," my father explained. "They lock people up there and they can't get out."

"Who do they lock up there?"

"Bad people. People who hurt other people." He began to find rhythm in the routine. "People," he went on, "who don't laugh at Daddy's jokes. People who don't root for the Cubs or the White Sox." My mother began to laugh (can I say girlishly? She was in her mid-twenties) as she overheard my father's little list of scoundrels and low-lowlifes. "Little boys," he concluded, and we all began to giggle, "who don't go to bed when their parents tell them to."

When we landed in San Francisco, we ran into rough times. My father, who was after all a comedian, was berated by the city's leading columnist for being funny. *Funny*, rather than *witty*, which was more to the worldly taste of the columnist and the cut of the city's culture. The columnist derided my father for telling mother-in-law jokes, dialect stories, and wearing polka-dot bow ties, calling him The Big Wind from Chicago;

which only made me feel all the more like an offspring of a hometown I was too young to recall.

My kindergarten classmates didn't read newspaper columnists, but their parents did. Several of my schoolmates sneered at me for being *a Chicagoan* (apparently a drear identity in dazzling San Francisco). The teasing bewildered my mother, an Irish Catholic who had married a Jew. She had faced enough anti-Semitism to cautiously prepare me for the chance that someone might taunt me as a kike or yid. But—*a Chicagoan?* One day, a cluster of older kids put me up against a corner of the schoolyard.

"You know Al Capone?" they demanded. The name meant nothing to me. I reacted with fatal hesitation.

"You gotta know Al Capone," said the apparent ringleader (I don't mind recalling that his name was Brad). "Al Capone is the most famous person in Chicago, and he's bad."

"I know Billy Pierce!" I shot back into uncomprehending faces. "I know Billy Pierce!" Apparently, my tormentors didn't. To conceal their embarrassment, they tied me against a tree with a jump rope. A strange, solitary kindergartner encircled by first and second graders—fighting back seemed futile. Crying left them unmoved. But fear inspired an early form of passive resistance: I wet my pants. Brad and his cohorts stepped back, disgusted, shrieking, wailing, wiping their hands desperately on their shirts as if kindergarten pee was radioactive. The older boys and their girlfriends ran away, appalled and pinching their noses, which, however, still left me lashed to the tree, my legs turning cold and clammy. Within a few minutes, a teacher came by. But she apparently deduced that having yourself tied to a tree and peeing in your pants must be some crafty new tactic to avoid class. She took me inside to be upbraided by the principal, a kind woman who saw at once that something more dismaying had taken place. I was sprung from class and sent home. I suppose the trauma of the ordeal should have left me saddened and wiser. But aside from a damp pair of pants, I felt triumphant: nervy, classy. A few jerks who didn't know who Billy Pierce was got scared off by a little bit of pee-pee. Bullies ought to be made of sterner stuff.

My father's attackers were not so easily routed. *Clown, fool, silly*—words that only delight a five-year-old son—began to attach themselves to his name.

"Minor leaguers," was my father's biting explanation. "Minor leaguers, that's what they are here." It was 1957, and though reports abounded that Brooklyn's Dodgers and New York's Giants were scheming to head west, San Francisco was still minor league territory. "They think they're so classy out here," he complained. "So, so, so—what can you say?—lah-dee-dah and all. But at the end of the day, pal, they're still minor leaguers."

Saturday mornings, after he came off work and had a nap, my father would take me to a movie theater down by the wharves that showed nothing but cartoons. Old Popeyes and Mickeys that had been threaded though so many times, there were small, dark scars scratching the frames. My father would lay his head back, laugh with me through the first cartoon or two, then fall deeply asleep; the snorts of his snoring as colicky and comic as Goofy snoozing in his sleeping cap.

"Pssst: yer father's snoring," another adult would hiss, "*Plllease!*" Gently and urgently, I'd touch his wrist. "Uh, Dad?" He would awake in a cartoon state, all banging elbows and clanging cow bells as he shook stars out of his head. "Huh!?!?!? *Huh?!?!?!* Oh, sorry, pal, just resting my eyes . . ." Years later, when I began to cover wars, I would remember seeing some of the young sailors on shore leave who would come to watch the cartoons—they were after all not much older than us chortling children—and I think it touches me more today to remember how young those seaman looked, in little boy bell-bottoms, the hair on the back of their sunburned necks as short and fine as a kitten's. If they couldn't get laid on shore leave, they could at least laugh at Daffy.

After the cartoons, my father would steer us on a walk through the streets of North Beach leading away from the wharves and try to teach me how to read the lettering on license plates of tourist buses that churned their motors along the docks. Once, he pointed to a building at the end of a runway and announced, "Look, Scotty, that's DiMagge's place."

I knew that Joe DiMaggio was considered the greatest ballplayer of his time, and his time was just a few years past. DiMaggio had retired from baseball in 1951, married Marilyn Monroe, moved out of that marriage after just one season, left Hollywood, remained devoted to Marilyn, and came back home to San Francisco where, it was said, a number of the men working along the wharves still remembered, "Joe? Helluva bocci player. *Helluva* bocci ball player."

Once, we walked inside DiMagge's place. He wasn't there—rarely was, they said, except maybe late at night, for a nightcap, and early in the day, before they opened, to run over the receipts. But the place was cool and dark and creaked like a ship when you walked over the flooring into the bar. I had a Coke. My father had something added to his, probably so he could, straight-faced, later profess to my mother, "We just had a couple of Cokes."

The man behind the bar recognized my father; and my father expressed his appreciation with a joke.

"I'm sure you've heard this," he began, "but in case you haven't: Man walks into a bar with his dog, and the bartender says, 'Sorry, buddy, we don't let dogs in here.' "

"Lemme guess," the real-life barkeeper interrupted. "The dog says, 'And at these prices, I'm not surprised'?"

"No, no," said my father. "This is another story. The man says, 'But sir, my dog can talk.' The bartender says, 'Don't test my patience, buddy,' and the man says, 'No, no listen,' and says to his dog, 'What goes on top of a house?' The dog barks, *'Roof, roof!'* Well, this just irritates the bartender, who says, 'Buddy, get your dog outta here!' And the man says, 'Wait, wait, listen to this,' and turns down to his dog to ask, 'What holds a tree in under the ground?' The dog thinks for a minute, then barks, *'Root, root!'* Well, now the barkeeper is really getting angry. 'I'm warning you, buddy,' he says, 'don't make me call the cops!' And the man says, 'Please, just one more chance,' and turns down to his dog and asks, 'Okay, don't disappoint me now. Who was the greatest homerun hitter of all time?' Well, the dog knows that one easy, and barks, *'Ruth! Ruth!'* But the barkeeper isn't impressed. He gives the heave-ho to the man and his dog. So then, the two of them are out there on the street. The man is embarrassed. The dog can tell that his master is humiliated. So the dog looks up at the man and says, *'Hmmm. Perhaps I should have said DiMaggio?'* "

The man behind the bar leaned over, laughlessly, and tapped my glass. "Son," he said amiably, "I'm cutting you off. Your dad needs help with his jokes."

"Sliding, Joe was like velvet," my father began to recollect. "No dust, no muss, no fuss, just *bing*, like he was sitting down on a pillow, take your base. DiMagge was the greatest in the world, lemme tell you."

"Better than Billy Pierce?" My father was caught for a moment between truth and kindness; and, after a moment's contemplation, conjured up a reasonably truthful form of kindness.

"Billy's a pitcher," he said finally. "Joe was an outfielder. Can't compare."

"What if Billy pitched to Joe?"

"Oh. Well, I guess it would be about even. Joe just makes it all look so easy," he continued. "Nice 'n' easy does it all the time. You never saw Joe sweat. He glided over to catch fly balls that would make other people trip over their feet." My father stepped down from the bar stool and knotted his hands, as if holding on to the end of a bat. "I mean, most players, swing out, *ooomph!*, like they're chopping down a tree." And here, with intentional clumsiness, my father lunged out with a phantom ax. "But Joe," and then my father straightened up tall, squared his shoulders, and braced his stomach visibly. "Joe made it all look easy. Fluid, elegant. He never gritted his teeth, never frowned, never smiled when he hit a home run, because he didn't want to rub it in to the pitcher. Class, that's the word for him, even today. *Class.* He makes it all look easy, nice 'n' easy." Even then, I could detect that my father passed on this appraisal with a performer's envy. Once, when I was flushed with a fever, my mother had folded me into their bed, and I pretended to be asleep when my father came back from some kind of show. He sat down heavily, lit a cigarette, threw back a drink, as he did when no one was watching, and then stood up to let his shiny jacket slide down from his shoulders. His shirt, I could see even in the smoke and gloom, was dark and slick with sweat. His sweat caught the light like a wound.

One Saturday morning we passed a confectionery shop showing candy baseballs and bats in the window. Back on the street, my father tossed a small, sugar-white marzipan baseball toward the stance I had struck up with a miniature, orange marzipan bat at my shoulder. "Steeerike one!" he called out. "Steeerike two!" And then, before he could work me to a full count, my father said, "Let's eat the equipment, Ace, before they can catch us."

On succeeding weeks, we delved deeper into the stock of the shop and discovered some real treasures that were stored farther back. The candy maker also made life-size marzipan dog turds and beige-and-orange splotches of candy vomit. The confectionary discharges looked impressively lifelike when sprinkled with sugar crystals that glinted under the counter light. My father and I giggled as we gamboled down the street, biting into marzipan dog turds and hoping to be overheard.

"Gee, Dad, these are great!"

"Sure are, son. And best of all, you can just pick 'em up off the street." Ho-ho, all you lah-dee-dahs. Once, we bought a third turd to bring back in a sack to bite in front of my mother. "Look, Mother, what we found on the street!" She was not at all fooled, but mildly, generously amused, laughing and looking on, lovingly and a little helplessly, at the couple of clowns dancing in the doorway. "My boys, my boys."

The puddles of candy vomit, while artfully accomplished, seemed somehow not as delectable or diverting. There must be tenured scholars in Chapel Hill and Madison who have researched the reasons as to why candy turds are funnier than candy vomit. But my father had a routine in mind when we brought home a confectionery vomitus and laid it on the bathroom floor of our hotel room, splashing the ersatz spew lightly with water for added verisimilitude.

"Okay, Ace," he said in a hush, "go tell Mommy."

We had rehearsed my part—he used to call me "my little trouper"—while walking home. "Mommy, Mommy, come quick!" I called out, "Daddy's sick!" Tender concern sprang to my mother's face. Without hesitation or question, she rushed toward the bathroom where my father stood unsteadily, holding his stomach and contriving to look green.

"Oh, that's all right, my little boys," she said gently, so gently and sweetly that my father and I swapped quick, guilty glances. "Don't worry. Come on out of there. Mommy will clean it up." But my father held my mother off with his hand, waving her back from the mess at his feet.

"Oh, don't worry, honey, I'll get it." And then, my father reached down with professional poise, picked the marzipan vomitus up in his fingers—and took a bite.

My mother shrieked: high, shrill, a curdling Hitchcockian screech that seemed to change direction in her throat and turn into laughter: helpless, hopeless, weakening, wonderful.

Our stay in San Francisco lasted a little less than a year. But it was the year in which I first began to mark my life as a fan. One night, during the World Series between the New York Yankees and Milwaukee Braves (which began right after morning cartoons in San Francisco, in the days before nighttime World Series games played for prime-time audiences), my parents bundled me up in the middle of the night to stand with them on the roof of our hotel to watch the Sputnik satellite trace a line of light in the sky. It was like trying to glimpse a worm wiggling through a plate of spaghetti. I doubt I actually saw it. But I remember the mood on the roof. It was one of the first times outside of a funeral parlor that I was expected to share an adult sense of sobriety.

The Cold War was on, and the Russians had captured the high

ground of outer space. They had an atom bomb, half of Berlin, and could now wink down on us from the heavens in which the Soviet socialist state did not believe. Who could say there wasn't a bomb aboard that small, glimmering gnat of a star? Sputnik may have been the smallest mite in the night sky, but it cast a shadow on the world to which we had become accustomed. All at once, there seemed something mad and misplaced about New York and Milwaukee purporting to play a *World Series.* The weight of some new world seemed to be sliding toward those grim men with gray faces on the Red Square reviewing stand, smiling down mirthlessly at their missiles, as if they were beholding prize orchids.

"It's very small," said my father, pointing up and squinting at some speck he thought to be Sputnik. "No bigger than a basketball, really."

"How does it stay up?" I asked. A thoughtful pause ensued, as the tumblers in my father's mind spun around and clicked. He turned to my mother and laughed. "Well . . . I guess . . . I just . . . don't . . . know . . ." I tried to throw him a suggestion.

"Could Joe Di hit a ball all the way up there?" My father seemed relieved to see a way out. "Yep, he sure can," he said quickly. "I'll bet Joe could hit one up there." A scientific imprecision, to be sure, but a valuable reassurance at the time. The Russians might be able to send basketball-sized orbs around the earth, but they needed huge, brutish rockets to propel them, baring flames and blaring thunder. Joe DiMaggio could do it without straining and sweating, no muss, no fuss, nice 'n' easy, swinging a slim wooden bat with an uppercut toward the stars.

I hope I have reached the point in life at which I no longer have to believe that every scrap of wisdom uttered by my father turned out to be a nugget of gold. He was a warm-hearted, quick-witted, friendly, and funny man who, like the rest of us, was also often foolish and wrong. He had a delightfully effective way of disarming his own advice by adding, "What the hell do I know? I can't even figure out how to make people laugh." But I think that jokes can endure longer than wisdom (that may be why many of us cannot recall all Ten Commandments—the list cries out for a joke; often, we just add our own). One of the most persistent insights my father ever passed on is that jokes work best on a rhythm of three: *one, two, three,* and throw the punch line, as in *roof-roof, root-root, Ruth-Ruth,* and then, *Hmmm. Perhaps I should have said DiMaggio?* In a moment in that year in San Francisco, with Sputnik spinning on overhead, Willie Mays and the Giants packing up at the Polo Grounds for the trail west, and my mother, father, and myself trying to find life's punch line, I realized that my father could make my mother laugh in a way that unlocked something between them that was precious and astounding. I probably even felt a little left out the night I overheard that laughter in our bathroom. My mother's howls and cries, shrieks and smiles, chiming off the chipped hotel shower tiles: we're alone, in love, adrift, and alive.

*Chapter 2*

# I'M A FAN

I am a fan. Fans don't get much respect. In literature and pop culture, advertising and conversation, we are often seen as the anonymously clamorous: bug-eyed and beer-swollen, inert perennials who come to life only as we cheer and jeer the exertions of those who are stronger, fitter, more graceful, and bold.

When Michael Jordan and the 1997 edition of the world champion Chicago Bulls trouped onstage for a rally in Grant Park (carting up five gold trophies then, a display that seemed to bristle with as much hardware as a May Day parade in Havana), Jordan's gracious words still made me cringe a bit—in self-recognition. "We dedicate this trophy to you fans here in Chicago," said Michael Jordan. "You fans, who work your butts off each and every day, then get home and watch us work for a couple of hours, so you can have some entertainment, and something to be proud of." Cringe, also, because I *was* proud. When I had traveled to my first war, in the Central America of the early 1980s, people would often ask me where I was from in America. At the word "Chicago," many would train their index fingers on the distance like twin tommy-gun barrels and squeeze an imagined rat-ta-tat-tat into the horizon. "Ah, Chee-cago! *Al Capone!*" It did not make me proud to know that

the name of my city had become a catchword for violence in an El Salvador rife with death squads. On the other hand, it seemed vain to start
a name game. "What about Saul Bellow? Jesse Jackson? Hugh Hefner?"
But when I went to Rio for the Earth Summit conference in 1992, I
met street kids in the mountainside slums spilling down into the city
who began to bounce on hearing the word. "Shee-cago! Shee-cago!"
they shouted, bounding up from the teeming streets, "Michael Jordan!
Bools! Bools!" You don't forget the sight of a street of small boys throwing themselves at the moon, wanting to Be Like Mike.

I imagine my wince at the rally was as simple as this: I wanted
Michael Jordan to think well of us. A few years before, I had been standing up for halftime when the Bulls played the then Washington Bullets
in the old Capital Center. As the players came off the court, I heard a
man bellowing from the railing above; "Michael! Throw me your sweat
band! Throw me your sweat band!" I turned back to see a man about my
age standing with his small son. Taking the father in at a glance (button-
down blue oxford shirt, suit coat doffed, a burgundy tie discreetly dotted), he was wearing the after-work uniform of a K Street lawyer or
lobbyist (certainly, in the $95 section, he was sitting in those seats). I
imagined the man had planned a night for his son to remember when
he grew older. *Remember, pal, when we saw Michael Jordan play?* Except
now, the son was watching the cords in his father's neck redden and
swell as he squeezed his son's hand. "Dammit, Michael, throw me your
sweat band! Throw me your sweat band!" What would the boy remember of that night? And then, a slight scuff in my own throat reminded
me: just a few moments before, I had been another grown man whose
neck was reddening and straining as I shouted, "Michael! Michael! Way
to go!"

It was the season after the Bulls' first championship. Jordan was
then somewhat accessible in the locker room after a game (before that
first championship, MJ shared the celebrity ranks of Larry Bird and
Magic Johnson; after another, he got classed in the same company as the
pope). Jordan had always dressed alone, away from the team, before
meeting the press. He seemed to believe in an old show-biz bromide my
father had always urged: dress for the gig you want, not the one you
have. Jordan always arrayed himself as a chief executive (he had also been
warned that the incentive for someone, even one of his teammates, to
sneak a snapshot of MJ UNROBED! was too great to tempt). But he
would occasionally wander out while still knotting one of his gorgeously opalescent Italian ties, his bare head gleaming with sweat and

suffused with television lights. I had been conversing with Coach Phil Jackson (who cited Talmud, Jerry Garcia, Buckminster Fuller, and Chief Joseph to explain the triangle offense—of course he listened to National Public Radio), who made an introduction. While shaking hands with a quaver I cleared my throat to ask what was and will probably always be the only question I ever pose to Michael Jordan.

"Excuse me. Do you mind—may I ask? When you leap like that toward the basket—with everyone watching you—what do *you* see? Do you see *us*?" It was not an incisive or astute inquiry, but it seemed to stop Michael Jordan long enough for him to tug a gold collar pin into place.

"Oh yes," he said. "I do. I look down and see all of you." And then, he puffed his eyes up, comically. "And you should *see* some of the things I see." Power brokers begging for his sweat band, 20,000 sets of vocal cords tightening into braids like the ropes on a sail mast. Of course, Michael Jordan had an advantage in keeping a sense of decorum: he didn't watch Michael Jordan play.

These are the recollections of a fan. I was a fan before I ever became a reporter and enjoy slipping off a reporter's skin to be a fan now. Fans can cheer, jeer (though I don't like jeering), and indulge in the daydream that the fortunes of the teams and players we cherish are in some small ways fastened to our own.

One Wednesday night a few years ago, I was wedged into the middle seat on an airplane between a man with a fat file case on his lap and a woman wrestling with a day-old copy of *The Wall Street Journal*. A little after 7:30, the pilot's dry-plains twang crackled through the microscopic speakers overhead: *"Uuh, 'scuse me, ladies and gennlemen. Jest wanted to tell you . . . heard word up here . . . Cal Ripken Jr. has just broken Leew Gay-rigs's record . . . Tew-thousand, one-hunnert-and-thirty-one con-secutive games. We'll keep you posted."* And then, about 200 people riding an air-conditioned tin can over Lake Moultrie through the dark of the night put down their file folders and plastic cocktail glasses and wadded-up newspapers—to applaud.

We were fans. By the time I landed at Washington's National Airport, other fans had laid down their laptops and sample books, or stood with an elbow on their rolling trash carts or floor brushes to look up at Cal Jr. on the airport television screens. A grown man with a receding gray crown of hair, jumping up from the ball field like a boy to slap hands with fans and hug his friends, his family, and the men on the opposite team. "Goddamn," said a score of people, shaking their heads.

"Goddamn, that's something. Isn't that something?" Not a small number of eyes, including my own, were glistening. You can tell yourself: it's just sports, nothing real; it has nothing to do with your life, no resonance in the real world of living, dying, and struggling. And you'd be right. Then, something happens. *MJ leaps! Mac swings! Flutie scores!* And inside, where your body cannot kid you, something takes over and it feels real. It's not like tearing up at your wedding, sobbing at a funeral, or choking up at a child's first steps. It's closer to seeing Caesar stabbed; or watching Emily Webb in *Our Town* so wistfully, tearfully, exclaim in Act III, "Oh, earth, you're too wonderful for anyone to realize you!" A play that rubs something real. By the time I reached my apartment, the folks in my profession were being heard. Pundits, analysts, and social critics who rarely awarded their attentions to a sports story except, perhaps, to try to make the rest of us feel foolish for caring too much. *Overblown! Overpaid! Overdone!* They pointed out, accurately, that tens of thousands of overworked and underpaid teachers, firefighters, homemakers, and nurses had all worked 2,131 consecutive days and more, for much less remuneration, and not even a scintilla of the recognition that was accorded Cal Ripken. And they worked not at games, but jobs truly valuable, life-giving, and occasionally dangerous with no off-season.

They were right. But I just didn't want to hear it, at least not then. In times when sounds have been reduced to bites and attention is paid in short bursts before people are polled, it was warming to see so grand a reward not for just a few minutes, a day, or even a season of dedication, but a professional lifetime. Maybe this is why so many people who work as hard or harder, for less money and glory than Cal Ripken Jr., seemed to join in his recognition, not resent it. People with raw calluses and inflamed feet seemed to see a little of themselves leaping in the brilliant green field. *Local Hero. Favorite Son. The Pride of Baltimore.*

Like all romance languages, sports can be twisted by hopeful or counterfeit hearts to say something they don't. When a sallow and sleepless President Nixon roused himself from an inconsolable night to seek out war-protesting students stirring on the national mall, he could bring himself to banter only about football and baseball. Nixon was not a fan, so much as a user—of people, of loyalties, and finally, least consequentially, of sports. It was a way of passing words with wounded soldiers in veterans' hospitals, so as not to speak about the war that put them there.

But my own record is not distinguished. A few years ago, I was on a reporting trip in Cuba and seeking an interview with Fidel Castro.

Our crew's government *responsable* (a minder, essentially) was also a sports fan, and spoke of Fidel's love of baseball. He recommended that we attend an artist's reception at a restored seafront hotel at which El Jefe, it was rumored, would make an appearance. "I'll tell him you're a baseball fan, too," said our government keeper. "You'll get to talking, and we'll"—I didn't exactly appreciate the *we'll*—"get the interview."

The reception started at about six. By 6:15, we had seen all of the artwork, literalist, greeting card watercolors of restored Old Havana that nevertheless contained an element of non-Marxist whimsy: they didn't show all the women working as prostitutes in Cuba's distressed economy. By 6:20, we had eaten as many salt crackers with olives and queso blanco as seemed wise and had jots of rum imprudently diluted with a local cola that was a Dutch-Cuban co-production. We chatted to exhaustion. "I notice that you use a lot of, ah, coral color in your work." "Coral? Well, actually that is pink." "Ah yes, I see that now. So it is." At about 8:20, the leader of the Cuban Revolution arrived and cast his eyes over the easels as rapidly as if they were NO PARKING signs. But before he could stride out, someone from the government's propaganda ministry spoke into Fidel's ear; our minder was motioned over; after a moment, so were we. "So," Castro began without so much as a handshake, "do you think anyone will beat Babe Ruth's record?" Of course, Roger Maris already had, in 1961; but Fidel was busy building the revolution that year. I knew he meant—would anyone else ever hit sixtyone? I should have answered, "I don't know, El Jefe. But will you release Elizardo Sanchez and other human rights activists from prison?" Instead, I said, "Canseco or McGwire, if they stay next to each other in the same batting order." I was, of course, half right on the baseball, and all wrong on the politics.

It is always tricky to use sports metaphors in politics, and especially tricky to see any moralizing stories for politics in sports. But a few may be valid. In his classic essay, *The Light and the Dark*, the accomplished sports writer and radical critic C. L. R. James reflected on how cricket was the one enterprise in colonial Trinidad that attracted blacks, Hindus, and Asians literally to a common ground. "Cricket had plunged me into politics long before I was aware of it," wrote James, who hoped a shared enthusiasm could move fans to perceive common injustice. "When I did turn to politics, I did not have too much to learn." Americans who saw Cuba's outstanding national baseball team split two games with the Baltimore Orioles in the spring of 1999 could glimpse something of the talent that Fidel Castro's forty-year revolution has nourished. That so many of Cuba's most prized and cosseted athletes were willing to risk their lives to leave the island also showed something of the human treasure Fidel was prepared to suppress to keep his grasp on power.

Most of these recollections trace my life as a fan through Chicago's major sports teams, baseball, football, and basketball, the Cubs, Bears, and Bulls. It is also a partial catalog of loves: friends, family (lineal and spiritual), the confluence of faith, theater, and politics; and finally, overall, Chicago. A few passions would not fit the frame, but may merit some attention.

There is no hockey here, even though I think Wayne Gretzky and Mario Lemieux may have been the most remarkable athletes of these times. They moved like Michael Jordan—but at lethal speed on cold, hard ice, balanced on skates sharp as sabers.★ But I have never made much of an emotional connection with hockey and depart from Chicago fealties here to root for the Montreal Canadiens.

Like many Americans, I grew up playing soccer. But only until somebody brought by a bat and ball, football, or basketball. We called it soccer. But the game we played might have been better called run, kick, and fall over. My lack of feeling for soccer has occasionally tested my pretensions to appreciate other cultures.

Once, when my engineer, Manoli Wetherell, and I were reporting from besieged Sarajevo, we stopped to watch a few moments of a football (soccer) match beamed down by satellite into the European Broadcasting Union. We were war weary and deeply dulled. We struggled to enjoy watching men in short pants from Leeds flail after a ball slipping through the dexterous feet of men from Verona (or maybe it was Haarlem versus Liege). After several minutes, Manoli turned to me with a withering grimace. "You know," she said, "sometimes I just want to shout at the players, 'Use your hands, man! Just pick the ball up with your bloody hands!' "

Stints in England have made me a mild fan of the fabled Manchester United. But that's had more to do with the team's personality than the game they play. Manchester, like Chicago, is a proudly gutty, gritty Second City. United is a team of international repute, like the Chicago Bulls. They sell paraphernalia in their signature colo(u)rs around the

---

★Actually, Bebe Neuwirth may be a more complete athlete than all of them. She displays all the moves of Jordan, Gretzky, and Lemieux—while singing and dancing. Not even the most extravagant fan of *Space Jam* would make such a claim for Michael Jordan.

world (red and black, also like the Bulls, and that's no coincidence). But United's appeal has grown so huge, these days it's like rooting for Rupert Murdoch—who, at this writing, is trying to acquire the club for a billion dollars. A long soccer kick arching into the goal has all of the loveliness of a Ken Griffey Jr. home run. But while I admire and even try to identify with Manchester—and Brazil's engaging World Cup teams, with their single-named stars—I don't have the fan knowledge or fascination to appreciate what I'm seeing as a game. I find myself wandering and wondering—why *not* pick the damn thing up?

In the summer of 1999 I went to Kosovo while the massacres sewn into the ground were being unearthed. One Sunday afternoon we went to the site of a mass grave in a town called Lukare. Villagers and soldiers from Britain's Irish Guards were turning up the ground along a roadside with small garden shovels, so they would not scratch or crack the hard block of a human skull. The fifteen bodies they found that day were not deeply buried; the men who had put them there had apparently been working in haste. The sad fact is: shoes and shirts last longer than flesh. All that remained of the men dug up were bone and mud and flies. The soldiers placed a delicate pile of possessions on the collapsed chest of one man: a black wallet, a plastic watch, a half-crushed pack of Serbian cigarettes. A dark-haired woman in a red shirt came forward and asked the soldiers to bring the man's black coat around on his shoulders. When they did, she recognized her husband. Her face stiffened as if she was trying to scream; and when the scream froze in her throat, she sobbed.

The very next night, we went to the city's first postwar league soccer game: team Pristina against Tetovo, Macedonia, in the Pristina stadium. For a decade, Albanians had been banned from playing on the capital's official team. Albanians stayed away from the soccer stadium, which was considered Serbian imperial territory. But soccer itself became a form of clandestine protest in Kosovo. Albanians organized small, covert games in their neighborhoods that were sometimes discovered and broken up, like political meetings, by Serb police. There was a man to our right who sat through the first few minutes of the game with his arms around the shoulders of his two young sons; after about fifteen minutes, he sent them off to buy snacks, while he sat down and wept. "They tried to kill us," he said. "Burn us. They threw us out of work. Everything, they did to us. And now." He could only manage to flick his hand toward the field. "And now, we're here." The crowd cheered passionately when Pristina scored, even as their enthusiasms were imprecise. The new club had been quickly stocked with unknown

Albanian players, appearing in league soccer for the first time. But with no electricity in the stadium to power a loudspeaker or a scoreboard, fans cheered them on without knowing who they were. When Pristina won 4 to 3, fans rushed onto the field with flags and drums and raised sweaty players from both teams onto their shoulders. Children turned cartwheels around the edge of the grounds. Boys and girls clambered onto the laps of British soldiers in red berets who were guarding the soccer grounds—British paratroopers had become the favorite visiting club of Pristina kids. The crowd clamored, danced, and cried as the night sun smoldered for a moment over the stands. I turned to see a man holding his happy young son in his arms and exchanged a confiding glance. "My boy, he won't remember the game," said the father. "But he will remember all this. Just a few weeks ago, we were hiding in a basement, afraid." But that summer night in the Pristina soccer stadium, Kosovars became hometown fans; and I guess I did, too.

Like a lot of Americans, I love Muhammad Ali. But I have grown to hate boxing. Ali's flash, dance, wit, and poetics, on his toes and onstage, so astonished and charmed they beguiled and bewildered us about the facts: boxing is intended to beat a man senseless. I have grown to believe it is about as much a sport as dueling. Of course, the nicest people in the business are the boxers.

I was inclined to be in Ali's corner from the first. He was engaging and truly pretty, sleek and sly, politically clever and, for much of his career, a Chicagoan, making his home in a southside neighborhood of mansions alongside The Honorable Elijah Muhammad.

Ali's athletic supremacy is so widely acknowledged today we can forget that at almost each step of his career, Muhammad Ali was underrated. His verbal frenetics, fight analysts said, were mere head feints to conceal his fear. He couldn't hit hard enough, they said, to defeat Sonny Liston. But he did, twice within fifteen months. He wasn't strong enough to stand up against the steam-shovel hands of George Chuvalo. But he did, winning in fifteen rounds in Toronto. He was so light on his feet, he would never be able to get up from a real punch. But he did, when Joe Frazier became the first opponent to dump him on his backside, at their first fight, at Madison Square Garden in 1971. Ali stood up, took the loss, and never lost to Joe Frazier again. He was too old, tender, and distracted to withstand withering broadsides from the steel-beam arms of the young George Foreman. But he beat him, too, in eight rounds, in the middle of the night, in the heart of the old Congo.

My favorite writers of the time, Norman Mailer and James Baldwin, were floored, as it were, by Ali. He seemed the essence of cool, the lion of pride, the embodiment of artistry, voodoo, hip, and the Age of Aquarius in one indomitable, dazzling star. "I'm sooo bad," he declared from a stage in New York, "I make medicine sick!" *Baaad*, and grand. A man with so much animation and intellect to spare, he could spontaneously toss off the one slogan of dissent that would stick with the American public. *I ain't got no quarrel with them Vietcong.* Wasn't that what you meant to say, Senator Fulbright? And then, as he aged and his deftness declined, he displayed almost the most unexpected skill of all—class. I was in the late-night crowd who greeted him when he stepped slowly off an airplane at Chicago's Midway Airport in February of 1978 after having lost a 15-round decision to Leon Spinks. The magnificent and aquiline Ali profile had been swollen. A group of women, overwhelmed, held up a sign painted on the rearranged insides of a brown box. WELCOME HOME CHAMP. Ali came over slowly, smiled shyly, took a pen from a photographer, and drew a line through the A and scrawled a U over it. "Here you go," he said in a friendly wheeze. "That's what I am." Of course, he was never less so.

And yet, there were more than a few touches of cruelty to be found in Muhammad Ali. His conversion to Islam was utterly sincere. So we must take as sincere some of the witless, weird, and insulting remarks he made, citing Elijah Muhammad, about black women. When Ali taunted Sonny Liston as "the big ugly bear," and Joe Frazier as "the big ugly *go*-rilla," drawing the word out like a backwoods white bigot, a man so acclaimed for clever rhetoric was tickling the fantasy stereotypes of peckerwoods. But even if we exonerate Ali from using such slurs as prefight ballyhoo—how do we account for the taunting and thrashing he gave former heavyweight champion Floyd Patterson on the night of November 22, 1965? For twelve rounds, Ali taunted, thrashed, and danced over Floyd, instead of putting him down, with a crushed jaw but unbroken dignity, in the first round. Ali jabbed Patterson, pushed him back, punched him down and picked him up, only so he could smite Patterson time and again in the kisser that had kissed Eleanor Roosevelt. Ali had no quarrel with them Vietcong. What grudge did he hold against Floyd Patterson?

If I knew of a boxer before Ali, it was Patterson. In September of 1962, he came to Chicago's Comiskey Park to defend his heavyweight title against Ingemar Johansson. I was just old enough to read all about it in the newspapers. Floyd was, in fact, Eleanor Roosevelt's favorite pugilist, as she no doubt called boxers, a card-carrying ACLU–NAACP–ADA–Noo Yawk liberal. He was routinely described as *sensitive* in an age when that was a code word for *Liberace*. He said hitting people was "not a good thing to do." He confided that he got scared in the ring. He told magazine reporters that when he was a boy, he used to ride the A-train through Queens and Manhattan, and back to Brooklyn, just to be by himself, alone among multitudes. He knew of a tool shed in a tunnel of the High Street station, and he would crawl into that shed and sit for hours, alone, hiding, at rest and peace in the reassuring dark and shriek of the subway. When he lost to Johansson, he donned a disguise and drove through the night, back to his training site in upstate New York. For a couple of days, the papers had no clue of his whereabouts. When it was finally reported that the former heavyweight champion of the world had been so mortified by his defeat that he had tried to hide in a fake beard and glasses, my mother read the stories and shook her head consolingly. "Poor dear," she said. "Poor, lost baby." Patterson earned such sympathy. When he defeated Johansson in the rematch just a few months later, Floyd ran over to the floored Swedish fighter as soon as he had been counted out—and kissed him, by way of comfort and condolence. A couple of years later, after Floyd had been humiliatingly deposed by Sonny Liston, and then Liston was so shockingly defeated by Ali, Patterson was the one fighter who came into Liston's locker room to put an arm around him. Ali was the greatest; but Patterson, at least to me at that time, seemed the best.

I got to meet Floyd in the fall of 1984, when reporting a series on brain damage in boxing. American, British, and Swedish medical associations had issued similar reports saying that 80 percent of the people who engage in organized boxing suffer some form of brain damage. For some, the damage would manifest itself simply in isolated memory lapses or speech problems. For others, the effects would be even more dire and degrading. The doctors seemed smug, the promoters unmoved. The most appealing people were the boxers.

This included Mike Tyson. We gave him a lift in the back seat of our rented compact from Gleason's Gym in Manhattan up to New Paltz, New York, where he was then trained by the illustrious—all you had to do was ask him—Cus D'Amato. I do not drive. Our producer, Tony Brooks, did the driving, while the unfailing Manoli Wetherell navigated in the front. I sat in the back with Mike Tyson. It was like trying to share a phone booth with a baby grand piano. When he spoke, it was in an unexpectedly high and mild voice—a Brahma who spoke like a member of the Vienna Boys' Choir. "Oh, I was a wild kid down in Brooklyn," Mike said, "but boxing, boxing's the best thing that ever happened to me. Made me a man, not a punk. Gave me discipline, something to shoot for." In 1984, he told us he was twenty. But when Tyson became a criminal defendant, his birth date was recorded as 1966, which would have made him just eighteen. I don't recall the fact now to reprove his integrity. Athletes, it seems to me, have the same right to lie about their age as actors and mothers. What it means is that greedy men in the fight game had put him into the professional ring to make money for them at the age of fifteen. It does not excuse subsequent felonies to note that Mike Tyson never really had much of a chance to develop decency.

José Torres, the former light heavyweight champion and fast friend of Norman Mailer, was then the New York State athletic commissioner, a dedicated Cuomo Democrat and skeptic about brain damage in boxing. The 1984 presidential campaign was in full cry. Torres, a genial and funny man, noted that a number of former boxing champions had all endorsed President Reagan for reelection. "I tell you," he said, "the only thing that makes me think that boxing leads to brain damage is the fact that Joe Frazier, Muhammad Ali, George Foreman, Ken Norton—they all endorse Reagan. I tell you, if one more boxer comes out for Reagan, I'm gonna call for the abolition of boxing myself."

We met Floyd Patterson at his home near New Paltz. It was an airy, spacious place, made comfortable with tasteful Swedish furniture— Johansson's influence again?—that could accomodate a heavyweight's frame. In a front room overlooking a run of woods, Floyd made a sweeping gesture toward the graceful, resplendent trees turning tawny in the autumn on his acres, and the forest of plaques stretching across his sun-washed walls.

FLOYD PATTERSON
WESTCHESTER COUNTY HUMANITARIAN OF THE YEAR 1978
NAACP OF YONKERS MAN OF THE YEAR 1967
BOYS CLUB OF KINGSTON
THANKS FLOYD

"Oh yeah, boxing leads to brain damage," he said. "Look at all this. I'm brain damaged." He was certainly not. He might have been prophetic. Floyd was training amateur boxers in a gym he'd built in a barn on his property. Juvenile officials in Brooklyn, Queens, and Yonkers would bring by troubled and truculent kids to shake a strong hand and see a street kid who had turned his life around.

"That eighty percent?" he said. "Okay, maybe it's true. The thing is, if you're going to get into the ring, you can't tell yourself you're in that eighty percent. 'Eighty percent?' you say to yourself. 'Those are the punks. Me, I'm a fighter, I'm no punk. I'm in the twenty percent.' " Head gear, he said, of a favored liberal reform proposed at the time, would do no good; in fact, it would do more harm. Floyd knew cranial physics. "See, the problem is, you get hit, and your brain sloshes around in your head, slapping up against your skull. *Thwap!* Okay? Imagine Joe Frazier ringing on your brain like that. Okay, put on leather head gear, and you just add another pound to snap back your neck, another pound of pressure on your brain. *Boiiing!* Got it? Head gear is to cut down on cuts. Keep Ali pretty when he trains. But it just exacerbates brain damage. You got only so much brain fluid in there. It's not just the fights. What will a kid have in a career nowadays—fifty, a hundred fights? It's the training, *thwap-thwap-thwap* every day, bending your head back, sloshing your brain. So you can get out of the fight game when you're thirty, thirty-five. But one day it can catch up with you."

There are brain specialists who say that what Muhammad Ali says about his slurred speech and stiff movements is true. Parkinson's Disease can strike people who have never been hit in their heads—although to watch Ali bend and wave, smile and sign his name so haltingly, as if all of his wiring had turned into string, it strains a layman's belief to think getting persistently hit by the strongest men in the world wasn't at least an aggravating factor.

Floyd Patterson has become another kind of heartache for those who have cherished his gentleman's qualities, his good sense and good heart. He was appointed New York State Athletic Commissioner in the late 1990s. Reporters who would come to call on him would confide that his mind seemed to be fading. In March of 1998, Commissioner Patterson was asked to appear before a state legislative committee investigating the license of "ultimate fighting" matches. Floyd stumbled, misspoke, meandered, and forgot—forgot the size of the boxing ring, forgot the names of fellow commissioners, forgot who he had fought to win his first championship (Archie Moore, in 1956, Chicago). "What are we talking about?" he asked the commissioners. "I'm lost." Before the story could make state newspapers, he resigned, sixty-three years old, financially secure, widely admired, and the very last boxer, Muhammad Ali included, you would ever figure for a hard-luck story. I root for the boxers. But not for what they do: to each other, to themselves. I cannot be a fan of boxing.

Over the years, I have developed a fascination for the Santurce Cangrejeros (Crabbers) of the Puerto Rican League. When the league began in the 1930s, it often included Negro League players, including the great Josh Gibson, who were of course excluded from American major league baseball. And in the early 1950s, the Cangrejeros were able to deploy perhaps the best outfield of any team on the planet: Willie Mays was in center field, and Roberto Clemente in right.

I had an esteem for Clemente that was all the more profound because he had no ties whatsoever to Chicago. He was daring and proud on patrol in right field for the Pittsburgh Pirates, throwing himself against the bricks in Forbes Field's corner, daunting with the ball in his hand, tempting a runner to stretch his luck around third, and dauntless at the plate. He was the second Latin American to win a Most Valuable Player title, in 1966★ and was fierce, proud, and somewhat touchy in asserting his heritage (and, paid the price of that, too, in beanballs, catcalls, and snide sureties about the talents and limitations of Latin players).

Roberto Clemente was the subject of the only psychic experience I might have had. I spent New Year's Eve of 1972 at a party at a friend's house. Several of us spent the night. Sometime during the night, I awoke from a nightmare: I had dreamt that Roberto Clemente was dead. Clemente dead? Preposterous. In 1971, he had set a new record for hitting in twelve consecutive World Series games. Just a few months before, he had closed out an outstanding season with a pennant and a .312 batting average—at the age of thirty-eight. I went back to sleep with an image of seeing Clemente next summer, picking a hit masterfully off the grass at his feet, and slinging a throw into third to keep a runner in check. When I joined our group for breakfast the next morning, a radio was on and my friend Wendy was gentle. "I don't think you've heard yet," she said, judging from my mood. "Roberto Clemente died in a plane crash last night." He had been flying from San Juan into Managua with a load of relief supplies for victims of the ruinous Nicaraguan earthquake. My grief was briefly attenuated by amazement. Why had I dreamed of his death? I checked the particulars quickly. The crash had occurred in the middle of the night, after we had all retired. No radio or

---

★Clemente is now so exalted he is often misidentified as the first. But Cuban-born Zoilo Versalles of the Minnesota Twins won the 1965 MVP award.

television had been left on while we slept. Anyway, the news seemed to be just coming in. They had not been able to locate the wreckage until dawn. I had not dreamed or had any premonition of my own father's death. Why Roberto Clemente?

But in death, Clemente's name became part of Chicago. At the time he died, the Board of Education had been circulating a community ballot of names proposed for a new northwest-side high school. The area was heavily Hispanic. To accommodate all interests, the list rambled on with Mexican, Cuban, and Puerto Rican personages, from Benito Juarez to José Marti, Lolita Lebron to Che Guevara. Che's adherents organized (Communists have always been the only group on the left with much of a gift for that). In a lengthy and diffuse field, his name began to lead the ballot. Board of Education officials were horrified. They had included Che's name to demonstrate openness. But they really, truly, did not want to have to name a public high school after the idol of Latin American revolution. And then, Roberto Clemente died. As a superb old pol professed in Edwin O' Connor's *The Last Hurrah*, "That brings us to man's best friend, the compromise." The Board of Education perceived an immediate, overwhelming outpouring of grief and declared there was no further need to take the pulse of public opinion. The national pastime, baseball, came to the service of Chicago's civic pastime, politics. Roberto Clemente High School was proclaimed.

Santurce, I learned, is the sprawling, historically poorer, landlocked community just behind the seaside resort hotels and high rises along San Juan's Condado Beach. Baseball, and the image of Clemente, is possibly even more important and poignant in Santurce, where he became a local hero and was scouted by the Pirates, than in the rest of Puerto Rico. Not so long ago, I fell into conversation with the bellman of a Puerto Rican hotel while checking in. He had noticed Cubs and Bulls traveling stickers on my suitcase and said he was a fan of both Michael Jordan and Sammy Sosa (both, in fact, had been recent guests in the same hotel, Sosa passing through on his own relief mission to the Dominican Republic). It was the middle of the Puerto Rican League season, and I asked how the year was going for Santurce. The Cangrejeros, he said, were his team; and they were in a three-way tie for first place with Ponce and Mayaguez. I told him I had asked the hotel concierge to ask about getting tickets to a game in Santurce; but concierges, said the bellman, tended to be "French guys or Spanish guys, who don't know about Santurce."

So later that week, bellman Jay Cruz and his brother-in-law and nephew took me along to a doubleheader in the downtown stadium Santurce shares with the San Juan Senadores. It was not a good night for the home team. Ponce, with a superb rotation of three different pitchers, won the first game to claim first place. Then, they took the second to extend their lead. But it was a wonderful night to sit under the stars, tickled by a sultry sea wind, sipping a beer with friends at a baseball game. We talked about families, New York and Chicago, the outrageous price of hotel room service, and the Puerto Rican plebiscite. Jay was on winter break from grammar school when Roberto Clemente died and said it was something like John Kennedy's death in the mainland United States—everyone remembered where they were. Jay said his father cried while telling them that a great man had died, and when they went to church for a special service, boys and girls wore their Santurce T-shirts and caps; a few even brought along bats and mitts. It was the only time priests and parents permitted baseball gear in the church. But that day, Santurce T-shirts seemed like vestments. Jay's brother-in-law, Eduardo, remembered the priest turning to the boys and girls in their baseball livery and saying, "Maybe none of you will be as great a player as Roberto. But all of us can try to do the great things he tried to do for others." Jay said he sensed much of the same nobleness in Sammy Sosa. But where Clemente, with his sharp Belafonte profile, had had to burst a trail through bigotry, Sammy could be soft and genial. "I think maybe it's in our culture, if you don't mind me saying. You show everyone how well you're doing not just by buying a lot of cars, but helping others. Treating everyone as your brother."

On the way out, there was a souvenir stand. Jay and Eduardo bought me a framed portrait of the great Clemente at rest, on one knee, in the on-deck circle, fastening a sharp gaze on the sky that looked as if it could stop a fly ball—or a hawk—in midflight. I bought my own Santurce cap. And then Jay noticed a pair of Cangrejeros boxer shorts, little smiling crabs prancing on their pincers along a baseball bat. He held the shorts up in front of his chest and smiled. "You know, Scott, we lost tonight. But you can still hit a home run for Santurce." The shorts went home in my suitcase. And each week during the Puerto Rican League season, I check the standings for Santurce.

I regret leaving out all but a few recollections of Bill Veeck, who owned the Chicago White Sox in the late 1950s, and then again in the 1970s. When he died, a predictable line appeared in the tributes: "They don't make 'em like that anymore." Well, they never did. He was a compelling and remarkable figure in any field, who stood by his friends, lived by his principles, tried to improve himself, and didn't scrimp on fun.

Bill was the man who integrated the American League (he signed Larry Doby and reimbursed the Negro League Newark Eagles for his contract; more than the magisterial Branch Rickey gave the Kansas City Monarchs for the rights to sign Jackie Robinson), installed the first exploding scoreboard, brought the great Satchel Paige into the majors when Paige was at least forty-eight, and sent a midget up to bat (Eddie Gaedel, who wore number 1/8 for his one turn at bat, and walked). Bill never wore a tie, was never without a cigarette during his waking hours or a beer from noon on, and never swore.

Bill Veeck had one of the most absorbing and valuable American lives of the century. He grew up as the son of the man who ran the Chicago Cubs, and as an adolescent drew the duty of sobering up the great and cranky Hack Wilson each game afternoon by lowering him into a tin tub of ice cubes. Bill sold Cub box seats to Al Capone, who always paid in cash, hundred dollar bills. "For years," he insisted, "I always thought that they were called C-notes because only Al and Ralph Capone had them." A bright, lively, and inquisitive youngster, Bill was sent off to first-rate boarding schools and raised hell until he was thrown out of them. As a young adult, Bill planted most of the ivy that today rises along Wrigley Field's brick walls. ("Actually," he said, "it was a variety of vine called bittersweet. But who wants to grow something on your walls called bittersweet? Only a trained horticulturist could tell the difference, so we called it ivy. Then, we planted ivy around the bittersweet, and it grew out. So today, it's ivy.") By the age of twenty-eight, he had bluffed, beguiled, and inveigled his way into buying the then minor league Milwaukee Brewers, taking the El up from Chicago and beginning the season by spending his last ten dollars on a ten A.M. toast of what made Milwaukee famous to Charlie Grimm, who joined him as manager.

Veeck owned the Brewers during World War II, and tried to sign black players but the commissioner of baseball rejected Bill's wartime expression of liberty for all. Bill went off to war himself, as a marine, and he lost most of his right leg when a weapons warehouse exploded on Bougainville. Many soldiers would call that a war wound. But Bill Veeck made the wooden leg lashed on to his knee into a comic prop, scrawling notes on the stump and carving a hole out on the shin for an ashtray. He liked to approach bank vice presidents for loans by patting that stump and saying, "I believe you already have my collateral." Bill spent two hours a day soaking his stump in a hot bath and devoted most of that time to reading: widely, deeply, indiscriminately. Bruce Catton, Colin Turnbull, books on native American weaving, Christopher Wren's architecture, and novels by Joyce, Roth, Pearl Buck, Richard Wright—and Harold Robbins. The examples are not apocryphal—I actually talked about all of those, and more, with Bill Veeck. "It never hurts you to read anything," he used to say. "Nothing is so bad you can't learn something from it. Except, maybe, one of my books."*

His wound was the reason I called Bill Veeck the first time for a story. There was a movement to pardon Iva Toguri, a Chicago shopkeeper who had been an American-born drama student in Japan at the time of the attack on Pearl Harbor and became one of the voices of English-language propaganda broadcasts—Tokyo Rose. Knowing Bill had been a marine in the South Pacific, I sought out his reaction. He answered his own phone. "I don't think we ever thought of Tokyo Rose as an enemy," he said. "She wasn't Tojo. She got us through some lonely times. If they can make a hero of Werner von Braun, it's okay with me if they pardon Tokyo Rose."

After the war, Bill bought the Cleveland Indians, signed Satchel Paige, and won a World Series. Paige was elected Rookie of the Year but declined the "honor" on a point of pride. But for segregation, he would have been in the major leagues thirty years before; or at least five years before, when Bill Veeck first tried to sign him.

Bill was especially close to Paige, whom he admired as a matchless showman and kindred soul, a kidder and conniver who shared a love of the game and the game of life. Any personal differences in personal deportment were resolved with a common capacity for self-mocking laughter. Bill, a confirmed family man and dedicated Catholic convert, recollected how he used to leave tickets for each game in the name of "Mrs. Satchel Paige." Each game, a different woman would claim them. "I went to Satch and said, 'You know, Leroy, we don't want con artists or sharpies getting hold of your tickets. What does your wife look like?' And Satchel scratched his head and said, 'What day you talking about, Will? I'm not exactly married. I'm just in great demand.' " Paige, as Bill used to point out, was the one great star of the Negro Leagues who had to take a pay cut to play in the major leagues. Paige became a co-owner of the Kansas City Monarchs and typically pitched three innings in each game, day after day, so the promoter could paste up banners:

---

*His 1962 autobiography, *Veeck—as in Wreck*, written with Ed Linn, is considered a classic.

## Satchel Paige and the Kansas City Monarchs
## 1:00 p.m. Comiskey Park 35th & Shields

"You can't treat Satch like any other player," Bill used to tell exasperated managers. "He's not like any other player. No one comes out to see any of our other players, do they?" Bill used to hold trains for Paige, an hour, two hours, making co-conspirators of the porters, who would tell the station master there was a problem with this or that, a smoking wheel, or a wheezing radiator. At length, Paige would finally stride out with languid grace onto the platform, looking like a million dollars—a 1948 million dollars—shimmering in a silk suit and silver cufflinks, doff his fedora to the porters, and shine his golden smile on his waiting, weary teammates. "Gentlemen," he would declare, "let us ramble!"

"I don't believe in treating people special," Bill once said. "But I believe in treating special people special. Once in a great while, God gives us a Satchel and says, 'This one's just for fun. Take care of him.' I hope I did."

But a good number of his fellow owners reviled Bill Veeck. They called him a clown, a purveyor of stunts, not a sportsman. He was the first owner to call for free agency for players, telling a federal court that athletes had the right to make their own best deals for their talents. When he co-wrote his autobiography in 1962, Bill was convinced he was dying. Infection was chiseling away bits of his right leg, a quarter of an inch by a quarter of an inch, year after year. Eventually, the creeping contagion cost him his knee. When he took a breath, he sounded "just like Jack Benny's old coughing Maxwell." He began to get headaches that gripped his brain like a barrel stave. Doctors diagnosed cancer and said the sickness had overtaken his lungs and spread to his brain. When *Veeck—as in Wreck* came out, the book's last words were read as an epitaph:

*Sometime, somewhere, there will be a club no one really wants. And then Ole Will will come wandering along to laugh some more.*

*Look for me under the arc lights, boys. I'll be back.*

And then, he lived. The sickness wasn't cancer, but constricted blood vessels that slapped Bill with headaches when he coughed, which for all he smoked, was quite a lot. He had sold the White Sox after they won the pennant but lost the World Series in 1959 because he needed the money to close out his life. With life so providently restored, he angled, he ached, to return to the show. He was comfortable without being wealthy. The game had already been taken over by rich men and gray corporations who owned clubs as an accouterment and write-off, not their own livelihood. Bill wrote a little more, hosted a couple of local talk shows, and dabbled, where he could, in sports. He took over the Suffolk Downs racetrack on what amounted to a dare, and ran it just long enough—two years—to gain the store of experience to write a book whose title was derived from the amount of droppings that had to be shoveled each day from the paddock: *Thirty Tons a Day*. He tried to buy the Washington Senators and failed; buy back the Cleveland Indians and was frustrated again. Finally, in 1975, he put together a huge and unwieldy roster of investors to buy the Chicago White Sox once again. His years of absence from the game had only increased his legend—the man who made scoreboards burst into bright lights and sent midgets up to bat. This time, Bill Veeck had fellow travelers.

I used to take the Elevated train down on summer evenings to watch Bill's White Sox arriving as the first lights snapped on over old Comiskey's green seats. To say that you could find him at his desk suggests that he had an office. In lieu of an office, Bill commandeered a table in the public dining room, pulled out a telephone, and encircled himself with a kind of trinity: a beer, a cup of black coffee, and a smoldering cigarette.

"Evening, Mr. Veeck."

"Evening."

"Read anything special today?" I once asked. He replied with a friendly, houndlike wrinkling of his bald brow and forehead.

"Ah, yes. Let me think." He had a manner of speech that broke sentences into discrete beats, a voice at once grinding and gentle, simmered, brewed, and cured. "Interviews with authors. The *Paris Review* series, I think. Mailer. Miller. Lillian Hellman. William Carlos Williams. Now there's a poet. Allen—the guy who wrote *Howl*—Ginsberg."

"Learn anything for your own writing?"

He laughed in a wheeze and tapped on the edge of his beer. "Maybe I don't do enough of this."

When the telephone rang, it wasn't an interruption: these were Bill's office hours, and by plan he answered his own phone. It could be a scout, an advertiser, a player's wife, or, not infrequently, an importuning fan.

"Hello? Yes. It is . . . Of course . . . Ah, Hazen, I believe. Hazen Shirley, in fact. So you see, Kiki was kind of an improvement. . . . Oh, seventeen or eighteen years. From the late twenties to the mid-thirties

. . . Yes, and too young, he was barely fifty . . . No trouble. Good-bye." Then, Bill would look up at his visitors. "Fan. Two guys in a bar. Settle a bet." They had apparently asked What was Kiki Cuyler's real name? How long did he play? How long was he with the Cubs? Is it true he's dead?

Once—twice—three times—I was with him when the phone rang and a caller asked, "What time is the game tonight?" Every time, he would answer without pause. "What time can you be here?" And each time, I laughed as if it had been the first time. Indeed, I'm pretty sure my laughter increased with each telling, because of my heightened appreciation for Bill's comic timing. "Oh, that's such an old line."

"But a great one, Mr. Veeck. Right up there with, 'And at these prices, I'm not surprised.' "

"If you like it so much, you can have it," he said. "My little gift. Use it in good health." It was August of 1977, and Bill Veeck's White Sox of Jorge Orta, Oscar Gamble, Ralph Garr, and Wilbur Wood—a rookie, a retread, an aging road runner, and an orotund knuckleballer—were running just a surprising few games behind the first place Kansas City Royals. And since then, I have.

One late summer afternoon, I came to the park for a story and encountered a group of neighborhood youngsters who made it their occupation to sneak into the park early in the morning, before security guards arrived. They watched the field groomers and the seat sweepers at work, then the peanut, beer, and ice cream bar vendors count out their wares until batting practice began. Then, they were thrown out for the game. Wilbur Wood, the old knuckleballer (I call him old, but he was about thirty-seven at the time, which doesn't seem so old anymore), huffed 'n' puffed in from running to get loose in the outfield and called out to a boy of about seven or eight.

"Whehvya beeen?" he asked in a broad Bahstan accent.

"At my grandma's," said the youngster. "On the west side."

"Back home now?" asked Wilbur Wood, and the boy nodded.

"Well, don't disappeah like that again," said Wilbur Wood. "We missed yah." And in the middle of the day, fireworks went off in Comiskey Park in the young man's face. When I told the story to Bill Veeck just before the game, he pretended mock horror. "Wilbur. Imagine. Encouraging truancy among youths." He tamped the ash of a cigarette against his coffee cup saucer. "You know," he mused, "I have never had the pleasure of sneaking in to a ballpark. I began to work at the ballpark when I was a kid. Just never stopped. Which is not to say," he said with a last throaty laugh, his thick glasses and gargle of a chortle giving him the look of a frog prince, "that people haven't been trying to throw me out for forty years."

I wanted Bill Veeck to be the commissioner of baseball. I wanted Bill Veeck to be the U.S. Ambassador to the United Nations (practiced in Spanish, well-read in Latin American and European politics and history, and personally acquainted with Fidel Castro, Willy Brandt, and Pope John Paul II, he actually would have been an inspired choice). I wanted Bill Veeck to be president of the United States. He deserves to be the subject of a musical comedy—a jock-rock opera—an epic novel, instead of a subordinate character in another man's memoir. I was a fan of Bill Veeck above his team, which made my relationship to his team count for less in my emotional makeup. As Bill himself used to say in some exasperation over the smug professions of his fellow owners, "What fan comes out to the ballpark to see an owner?" None since Bill Veeck.

Bill Veeck saw, as I suppose my father did, some similarities in the codes of sports and show business. You played hurt. You played to win, or win acclaim, but accepted defeat, or denunciation, with class. "Remember, Scotty," my father used to say, "don't worry about an audience walking out on you. It's when they start coming *toward* you that you have a problem." Professional athletes and professional show people have to believe utterly in what they are doing, no matter how many times they have done it; they have to display conviction, even as fervor flags. I have also tried to find in this an imperfect inspiration for good journalism. A good reporter has to rediscover a sense of conviction to avoid being jaded about doing one more story about suffering, injustice, or the Westminster Kennel Club Show.

I have an old friend, Chuck Faso, a Franciscan priest who performs masses a dozen times a day in a downtown Chicago church. Mass-o-ramas, if you please, every twenty-five minutes in the morning rush, then the evening rush. "Let us declare the mystery of faith, thank you, thank you, you've been a great audience, drive safely." I asked once, "How do you manage sincerity a dozen times a day?" He answered, "How did Gielgud manage to say, 'Tomorrow and tomorrow and tomorrow creeps in this petty pace from day to day,' so sincerely for fifty years? You have to be present in that moment." Not pretend. Present.

I once took in a game at Boston's Fenway Park with a nice man, a labor union official, whose father had recently died after a long siege of Alzheimer's. "It wasn't as sad as I feared," he said between pitches. "In fact, some times were quite joyful. He relived moments I thought were lost forever. Once, we were driving along, listening to a Red Sox game, and someone hit a home run, and the crowd went wild. I looked over at Dad, who was smiling. 'Hey, great,' he said, 'Williams just hit another one.' And you know, I really envied him. In his mind, he could still enjoy seeing Ted Williams play."

I am the son of the funniest man and the most beautiful woman in Chicago—although my father felt that my mother won both titles after she was once asked, "What's it like to be married to the funniest man in Chicago?" and she replied with a skillfull deadpan, "I wouldn't know."

Outsiders often find it difficult to trace my family and the ties that bind us. I grew up accompanied by a compelling assortment of irregular, unrelated uncles and aunties, with Jewish, Catholic, and agnostic allegiances all abounding in the same group of people we considered family. We think of this as being as American as cheese enchiladas. My father's family descends from Spanish Jews, my mother's from Irish Catholics. Both sides came to North America through Montreal, but like many on this continent, we despair of tracing our ancestry back much further and frankly, don't much care. Neither side seems to hold much promise of a monied inheritance. Both the Sullivans and Simons seem to have been city folks, whether Belfast or Toledo, Montreal or Chicago. And both sides seem to have earned their way in this world by the sweat of their smile instead of their brows—jesters, sellers, jokesters, hucksters and, to be sure, a few cons.

My old friend Robert Siegel has said that he can imagine one of my ancestors, perhaps an Ernesto Simone, as the lounge act aboard the *Niña, Pinta,* and *Santa Maria,* telling anxious jokes to the Spanish Jewish serfs who, to escape the persecution of the crown, professed Christianity and then signed on for a sail expected either to plunge off the edge of the earth or run hopelessly aground:

> *Thank you, thank you, gentlemen. You know, a funny thing happened to me on my way to the New World. Hey, this place sure doesn't look like India! Aaaaa-choooo! Did someone say Jews? No Jews out here, Santa Maria! Oy vey—whatever that means. But, seriously folks . . .*

Both sides of my family have seemed to be ecumenical believers. Under Jewish law, I was born a gentile because my mother was Catholic. But tax laws, draft laws, or Talmud, neither family line has been much observant of technicalities. I became a member of the Society of Friends (the Quakers) from the time I was in my middle-teens. I was especially affected by the silence of Quaker worship: the idea that we open our souls with silence, to try to hear that of God which is instilled somewhere inside.

My religious curiosities were nourished by a varied group of friends in high school who took me to Buddhist, Baha'i, Baptist, Congregational, Greek Orthodox, Lutheran, Mennonite, Methodist, and African-Methodist, as well as Catholic and Jewish services. Modern Quakerism is considered a religious society, rather than a religion. It does not insist on exclusivity. When I have attended Quaker meetings in Chicago, New York, Washington, Boston, San Francisco, North Carolina, Dallas, or Miami, there are always an awful lot of Catholics and Jews in the room. The mix, of course, is my spiritual foundation. Quakerism has been a faith that has permitted me to both honor the independence of my parents, and the faiths that embrace both sides of my family.

There is also no doubt of this: pacifism, which is critical to Quaker belief, has been fundamental to my affiliation with that faith. When I began to attend Quaker meetings in about 1968, the lunatic destruction of the War in Vietnam seemed a powerful testament to the logic of pacifism. But so did the brave gains of the American civil rights movement. I became a pacifist not only because I hoped the war would be over, as it was, before I could be killed in Vietnam. I also didn't want to kill any Vietnamese. To invoke the phraseology of a great philosopher, I didn't have any quarrel against them Vietcong.

But almost as powerful was the feeling that Martin Luther King's audacious movement demonstrated that violence, oppression, and hate could be turned back with peaceful means—the means we had to learn. Pacifism did not mean passivity. As Gandhi warned, even peaceful change would exact losses. But in a world that had refined so many techniques for mass murder, I wanted to enlist in a faith that took a chance on trying to bring about change with peace.

My pacifism was never absolute. I doubted that the world could have conjured up a pacifist response to Adolf Hitler; and in fact, about half the draft-age Quakers in America served in the armed forces during World War II. I hope I would have been among them. Later on in my life, when I covered wars, I saw nothing in El Salvador, Nicaragua,

Israel's West Bank, Grenada, Ethiopia, or the Gulf War to convince me that aggressive, even dangerous, organized nonviolence wasn't wiser, craftier, more effective than war. But then I went to Sarajevo (and later, to Kosovo). I could see no pacifist response that would halt the genocide there. The good and brave people were being slaughtered by the bigoted and cowardly ones. The violence of the victims could not be weighed on the same scale as the violence of the aggressors. I became outspoken before Quaker groups, urging military intervention. I said I would rather be inconsistent in my faith than morally immobile. I did not want to sanction massacres with Friendly, even-handed silence. Against expectation, quite a few Quakers agreed.

Four years after my father, the comedian, died (and about fourteen years after he and my mother were divorced), my mother married a man named Ralph Newman, an Abraham Lincoln scholar and bookseller. People would wonder: how does a woman who was married to a comedian wind up married to a Lincoln scholar? But if you knew the scholarly ambitions of the comedian, and the comedic ambitions of the Lincoln scholar, it did not seem incongruous at all. Ralph had once been a minor league ball player, second baseman for the Tucson Toros when Tucson was a much smaller city. We at first embraced one another for my mother's sake, but with the natural suspicions. No doubt about it, sports was our first language. Shortly after Ralph married my mother, in the summer of 1972, he took me along on a Civil War Roundtable trip to Springfield, Illinois. When he introduced me as his son to a dear and doting state librarian, she looked from his well-kept silver hair to my then long, scraggly locks, his second baseman's schnozz to the Irish pug I inherited from my mother. "Yes," she said sweetly. "I see the resemblance."

"You know," Ralph turned to me with a twinkle, "I don't know which one of us should be more insulted."

He took me along on a conducted tour of Lincoln's second-floor law office. "And here," said the guide, "is where Mr. Lincoln composed poems for Anne Rutledge—"

"Crap, crap," Ralph muttered.

"And here," she continued, "is where Mr. Lincoln first told his law partner, Bill Herndon, that he would one day free the slaves—"

"Crap, crap," Ralph groaned, then turned to me with a real revelation. "Say, let's go grab a pizza, go back to the room, and watch the

World Series." It was 1972, Oakland against Cincinnati, and Pete Rose led off the game with a home run and ended it with a run-scoring single. "Gotta hand it to Rose," Ralph said in some wonderment. "Son of a bitch, but gets the job done. Like that son of a bitch Nixon, I guess." By the end of the night, I thought my mother had made a brilliant choice.

There are numerous references in this narrative to various uncles and aunties. Most of them were not blood relatives, but doting adults, friends of my mother and father, who stepped happily into those roles as we moved around the country, away from much of our family. I have felt blessed and privileged that they were there. As more American families rove and move and, sadly, come apart, I gather that this accumulation of uncles and aunts is becoming more common. But I don't pretend that the assortment surrounding our family was in any way typical—a fact for which I am grateful. I could absorb an awful lot of amazing information just by being around.

My Auntie Chris, for example, my mother's best friend, was a staunch Iowa Republican, while my mother was an inborn Chicago Democrat. When President Kennedy came to Chicago in October of 1962 to campaign on behalf of Congressman Sidney Yates for the U.S. Senate, it was Auntie Chris who got tickets.* A man she was seeing at the time was a railroad executive. He was politic enough to buy tickets to a rally sponsored by Mayor Daley on behalf of the president; but Republican enough not to want to go. So Auntie Chris took me. I was ten years old and ecstatic at the chance to see the man I wanted to become, from his Ha-vahd accent to his brown pompadour and sensational spouse. I had stopped looking in the mirror and imitating Billy Pierce's high-stepping delivery. I had started to slick down my hair to bend it to the right, and pierce the air with my right hand as I spoke. "Aaah, hello, Muthah. Aaahsk naaht—what I waant for breakfast. Aaahsk what your country cahn doo for breakfast . . ." The night of the rally, smoky McCormick Place shivered and rang with thousands standing on chairs, clapping their hands and stamping their feet in laudation, "JFK! JFK! JFK!" Auntie Chris stayed seated with elaborate calm and unconcern. "I'm sorry," she said to me between applause lines, "I just don't agree with the man at all."

---

*In the early 1970s, I worked for Mr. Yates, who in 1962 had lost narrowly to wily old Senator Everett Dirksen, the Republican leader in the Senate. Mr. Yates regained his seat in Congress and retired in 1999—one of the classiest guys ever to serve there.

The next day, the White House said the president was returning to Washington on account of a head cold. Auntie Chris was suspicious. "He looked fine to me. Head cold. He was probably giving the slip to some dollie." She may, of course, have been more than half right. But of larger global concern was the fact, soon announced, that the president had seen evidence of Soviet missiles in Cuba. He declared a blockade. Within little more than a year, of course, President Kennedy was assassinated. My mother and I, Aunties Chris and Jeri, sat weary-eyed for days in front of the television set, crying, watching, and crying some more. When Jacqueline Kennedy led the amazing procession of eminent mourners, from a high-hatted Charles de Gaulle, down to a bewhiskered and embroidered Emperor Haile Selassie, along Constitution Avenue, Auntie Chris momentarily set aside her grief to share some hearsay. "You know," she said, "it's a great tragedy for her children. But Jackie's better off without him. He has a girlfriend right here, you know. She's also Momo Giancana's girlfriend. The Kennedys have always been mobbed up. I've seen her. Beautiful girl. Looks like Elizabeth Taylor. She's not the only one, either."

"Oh, Chris, please stop all that Republican mumbo-jumbo!" pleaded my mother. "The man is being buried right now. Stop all that nonsense." All that Republican mumbo-jumbo and nonsense, it must be said, that turned out to be more or less true. After the president was laid to rest on the television screen, my mother took me over to Holy Name Cathedral to say a prayer. I was eleven years old, heartsick—and hungry. My mother and I stopped in at Eli's Stage Delicatessen, right off of the nightclub district on Rush Street. It was unnaturally, mournfully quiet. A man was standing alone at the counter, picking at a corned beef sandwich. My mother recognized him; but he was definitely *not* an uncle. She had met him around one of the Rush Street clubs. She introduced us. I looked up, aghast and amazed. I knew the name from newspapers. He was, as the papers always delicately phrased it on advice from their attorneys, "an organized crime figure."

"Patti, you look great," said the man. "What a terrible day. Terrible day." He looked down and patted my shoulders. "How'ya doin', Scotty? Nice kid, Patti. Looks like you."

"Yes, Marshall," said my mother. "We've just been over to the cathedral to say a prayer for our president."

"Oh, terrible tragedy, terrible tragedy. What's this country coming to?" I tend to believe that in the absence of stunning new evidence, Lee Harvey Oswald acted alone to kill President Kennedy. But as an old

Chicago reporter, I cannot entirely dismiss the idea that Sam Giancana's crime family, feeling rejected by their former confreres among the Kennedys, may have settled their disagreements in their traditional manner. When the Church Committee on Assassinations was convened in the mid-1970s, the name of the man I met in the Stage Deli was mentioned as the Chicago mobster who drew up plans to thwack Jack Kennedy. He was fingered by a man named Johnny Rosselli, who told the story to federal prosecutors, perhaps to negotiate his own immunity. But he never had the chance to testify before the full committee, because Mr. Rosselli was discovered accidentally sealed into an oil drum near the bottom of Biscayne Bay. That doesn't prove someone wanted him to stay silent about the Kennedy assassination; just silent about *something*. But when the details of mob testimony began to appear in the news, my editor reviewed some of the names being bandied about and happened to ask about the mobster I remembered, "Know anything about him?"

"Oh, I think I can vouch for him. He was eating a corned beef sandwich at the time of Kennedy's funeral. And oh yeah, I think he had a crush on my mother." My alibi for the man was not widely accepted.

In Frederick Exley's searing and masterful 1968 novel, *A Fan's Notes*, the drunken protagonist of the title despairs of his own dullness and exclaims that it is his doom "to sit in the stands with most men and acclaim others. It was my fate, my end, my destiny, to be a fan." You want to say to him sometimes, "It doesn't have to be fate. Think of it as *fun*." Sports is not life, but it's also not quite make-believe. The grace and nobility, exultation and despair, can be real—and then we can move on. Sports stories can be memories and daydreams by which we mark our growth, like a parent's pencil strokes inching up the unseen insides of a doorway.

After one of the first long baseball strikes was settled, I took the El back down to Bill Veeck's Comiskey Park to talk to some fans who had returned to the stands. Most were unforgiving, as the players went through the paces of practice, declaiming the pinstriped Sox as greedy, stingy, or lazy-ass. I asked a youngster, a boy of about seven in a sleeveless T-shirt soiled with Comiskey grass stains—he had been chased away from rolling on the field—what he had done over the weeks of the strike.

"Played. Goofed around with my friends."

"Read any books?" An NPR reporter's question for sure.

"Maybe." I retreated.

"Watched some TV?" This response was more emphatic.

"Yeah."

"Well." I set it up for him. "Have you learned through this strike that you can live without sports if you have to?"

"Sure," said the youngster evenly. *"But I don't want to."*

Here's looking at you, kid.

*Chapter 3*

# DON'T KNOCK THE ROCK

I became a fan before I knew much about any game. Up to the age of six or so, any semblance of comprehension was strictly mimicry: *DiMaggio made it look easy. Mantle? Great, but he's got bad wheels. Williams can pick out the stitches on a fastball, but he won't take his bat off his shoulder in the clutch.* I could sound like one of those child evangelists parroting Bible verse. I picked up the cadence of being a fan, chapter and verse, from my father and my Uncle Jack, dozing in the drone, hum, and mumble of late summer games settling in on the radio dial as dusk moved west. *Pierce looks fierce tonight. Got the Moose and the Mick on strikes. And here comes Yogi!* That's the game I grew up loving.

Football was already spreading house to house ("Starr. Taylor. TOUCHDOWN!"), as television aerials poked a new profile into American cityscapes. Before certain left-minded social critics found football's popularity to be a growing imperialist infection, football was often considered more progressive than baseball. Football, after all, had integrated a generation before major league baseball. It was played by men who were, if only superficially, college material. Baseball was still a game best played by bushers, rustics, rubes, and Dem Bums.

But baseball was still that sport most bound up in America's identity. It was a time in which European sociologists proclaimed that to know America, one had to know baseball (which wasn't wrong, but conferred intellectual cover on an awful lot of sillier suppositions about the social import of sports). Americans spoke baseball. Today, how many people refer to a tight predicament as *a squeeze play*? And among those who do, how many know that the phrase derives from sneaking a bunt down the line, hoping to *squeeze* a runner across? Today, it's the vocabulary of basketball—*slam dunk*—that needs no translation.

With a few local exceptions (the Packers in Wisconsin, the Celtics in Boston, the Colts in Baltimore) American fans didn't signify the gains and losses of their own lives with football and basketball teams. Many of the franchises in other sports would rove and relocate, Lakers, Rams, Warriors, and Cardinals, moving from Los Angeles to Cleveland, Minneapolis to Los Angeles, Chicago to St. Louis; and left little trace. But when the Dodgers left Brooklyn for the West, it felt like they shot a hole through the heart of the borough.

The Cleveland my family moved to in 1958 was major league territory. Not only the Indians, who had won the World Series in 1948 and a pennant in 1954 (winning 111 games, a record that would stand until the 1998 Damn Yankees), but Cleveland itself. The city was booming, expanding, and boastful, first after New York and Chicago in skyscrapers and business bustle, and second only to New York in the American League (finishing second an amazing and frustrating *five times* in the decade after their world championship).

Cleveland lacked San Francisco's civic majesty. What place doesn't? But Cleveland took us in, after a battering in San Francisco. And it was in Cleveland that my father took on part-time work that deprives me of any right to complain about the tiniest blights on a fortunate childhood. He became the field announcer for the Cleveland Indians. Not, like Uncle Jack Brickhouse, the play-by-play announcer often referred to as a team's radio and television *voice*. My father was the anonymous, unseen basso buffo crackling and rasping in stops and starts over the ballpark speakers, so that the echoes could die between words:

> *Now pitching-g-g.*
> *For Cleveland-d-d.*
> *Don-n-n!*
> *Mossi-i-i!*

*In center field-d-d.*
*Larrry-y-y!*
*Doby-y-y!*

And—no member of our family will ever earn more applause than these few words when heard in Municipal Stadium:

*Now batting-g-g.*
*In the fourth position-n-n.*
*Number Seven-n-n.*
*The right fielder-r-r.*
*Rrrocco-o-o!*
*Rocky-y-y!*
*Colll-a-veeeto-o-o!*

I don't imagine that my father had left school for vaudeville to wind up, in his prime performing years, unsung and unseen. But his esteem had never been higher with his son. I had a father who worked at the ballpark. When he said, Larry, Minnie, *Rrrocco,* the names rang with authority. "I was talking to 'Cat,' " he'd tease, speaking of the Indians' strong right hander, Jim "Mudcat" Grant.★ "He says you'll make a pretty good pitcher. After you grow big enough to sit at the table without a phone book, of course."

Because Cleveland had taken us in from San Francisco—because the Indians had rescued us from the taunts and mockery of minor leaguers—I became their fan, unruffled by any feelings of disloyalty toward Chicago, which was, after all, not so far away. Or at least, I became a fan of those Indians of 1958 and 1959 my father hailed by name at the stadium: Minnie (Minoso, who had come over from the White Sox), Vic (Power), Jimmy (Piersall), Jim "Mudcat" (Grant), Larry (Doby), Lil' Billy (Martin—but did anyone call him that to his face?) and Number 7, the right fielder, Rocco—Rocky—Colavito!

(About that name, Indians. I don't like it, all old affections aside. While not as repugnant as the outright racial epithet of the Washington Redskins football team, the team name offends many real-life Indians regardless. As the club approaches its 100th anniversary, why not revive a name they wore before becoming the Indians in 1914? A name that

---

★Nicknames like Mudcat were one reason why, within a few years, a number of African-American athletes would take Muslim names.

ennobles Cleveland's role in immigrant and labor history: the *Cleveland Molly McGuires*. The chance to exalt labor history might not move management. But consider the merchandising opportunities of a team called *the Mollies*.)

At the cusp between five and six years of age, the fine points of all games were enigmatic to me. But baseball has a singular feature to enthrall the unfamiliar: the home run. Or, to quote Uncle Jack, "That's hit . . . back . . . back . . . Hey-hey!" There is no other everyday occurrence in American sports that conveys such a distinct excitement: the sharp crack of the bat, the suspenseful seconds as the ball rises, and the final, exultant roar. The home run needs no embroidered explanation to be appreciated: *somebody hit the ball where no one else can touch it*. Even when badly or cheaply accomplished, the home run is beyond criticism. It scores. It contributes. It counts. And in the late 1950s, Rocky Colavito, not some Damn Yankee, had the highest home run percentage in baseball.

To show me something more of the game, my father unwrapped baseball cards and laid out a team in proper position on our living room floor, lining up the outfield along the sofa.

"Okay now, pal. Minnie Minoso plays over here in left," as I remember one of his opening monologues. "Jimmy Piersall is right in the center, see? That's why they call it center field." In vain, he shuffled through a small deck, looking for Rocco Colavito. "Well now. Wally Moon of the Dodgers is a right fielder, just like Rocky. So let's put him there." Moving down a couple of feet over the coffee table, my father dealt out the infield from the hand available. "Eddie Mathews of the Braves plays third. The ball can really get down here fast from a right-handed hitter, Ace, so that's why they call it 'the hot corner.' Ken Boyer of the Cards plays third better. But he doesn't hit as many home runs as Eddie. We'll keep him around for the late innings, when they have to stop a run. Hey, look. We got Little Looie at short! He's from Venezuela. The White Sox saw him play in Cuba. But I can't find a Nellie Fox. Ken Aspromonte of the Senators is somewhere in here. He goes at second. Who do you want to put at first base, Ace? Moose Skowron—or Stan the Man?"

"Mooose!" I bellowed, "Mooose!"

"Stan's a better hitter," my father pointed out, turning over his card—the only incentive I had at the time to learn how to read. "Lookit, Stan hit .337 last year. Moose? Just .273."

Moose's card showed a man in his late twenties named Bill "Moose" Skowron, glowering with what would come to be known as a Nixonian five o'clock shadow. Moose wore his Yankee pinstripes against a blood-red backdrop, his bat cocked high behind his right ear. Glowering at whom? I later wondered, the bubble gum company photographer? (Sixteen years later, I would watch Watergate scandals and news friends would wonder what the hell I meant when I referred to Richard Nixon's Moose Skowron glower.) I was just beginning to read and could pick out at least one word in the twaddle of official statistics running on the card's reverse side:

WILLIAM JOSEPH SKOWRON B. DEC. 18, 1930, **CHICAGO, ILL.**

That was enough to make me root for William Joseph Skowron; that, and the way crowds around the league called out his name. So I persevered with my father, "Mooose! Mooose!"

"Okay, Ace," he laughed in surrender, "you get Moose."

There was a small yard, covering about the same space as a two-car garage behind our apartment building. In the spring, my father took me downstairs, put a flat child's mitt onto my left hand, and hit ball after ball to me over the ground. "Okay, pal, don't bend now. Go down almost like you're sitting down. Kneel, even, if you gotta." My father squatted down in a long tweed overcoat, vaudeville-style, looking a bit like a circus midget wearing the ringmaster's tails. "Get down here, like this. You gotta keep the ball in front of you," he said. "That way, if it takes a bad bounce, you can still pick it up and make a play. Remember that, Ace. Always keep the ball in front of you."

A generation later, I spent a night during the 1986 World Series at a country bed and breakfast, returning from dinner during the final innings of the sixth game. A small group of us watched on a snowy screen in the innkeeper's remorselessly rustic front room. Boston was ahead of the New York Mets, just a single pitch away from winning their first world championship since 1918.

But then ...

Mookie Wilson slapped a ground ball into what turned out to be the most porous spot in the Boston infield: the dirt beneath first baseman Bill Buckner's corroded knees. Quicker than Buckner could screw down his joints to bring down his glove, the ball bounded through, tying the game. All around the gingham-curtained salon, people gasped, as if seeing Jack Ruby burst into the TV frame. Bill Buckner, a good and sturdy player who did not deserve the infamy that followed, turned his head helplessly to watch the ball dribble out of his grasp and into the first line of his obituary. And after twenty-nine years, I astonished myself by announcing aloud, "You gotta keep the ball in front of you." A fellow traveler nearby seemed impressed and nudged his companion. "That's right, you know."

Drifting into sleep that night, I replayed the error in my head and smiled at remembering who had told me, "You gotta keep the ball in front of you." That must have been what my father meant all of the times that he said, "Someday, you'll understand."

For Halloween of my first-grade year, I became Rocky Colavito. Among that vintage of admirable Indian also-rans, Rocco was the leading man. He was then in his mid-twenties, iron-armed, Bronx-born, with wide, darkly handsome, operatic eyes, and a swarthy chin. It was this last feature the mothers in our neighborhood seemed to seize to render their five- and six-year-olds Rocky, dappling mascara or an eyebrow pencil across their sons' jaws until their chins looked like Brutus's stubble in Popeye cartoons. My mother, however, was probably the only local mom who had been in a summer-stock company with Grace Kelly (my mother, in fact, had more than a touch of Kelly's own cool beauty, but warmed with large, dark eyes). My mother recalled her summer stock skills to char a cork with a lit match and smudged my chin with the fine charcoal residue until it looked smoky; until it looked Rocky.

The Rock had a signature flourish that we Little Rocks sought to mimic. Striding up to the plate, Rocky stopped just outside the batter's box and threaded his bat below his shoulders behind his back. So cinched, he would *twwwist* once left, then *twwwist* right, to unbuckle his spine. Was Chubby Checker taking note? Years ago, I found myself unconsciously doing the same with an umbrella while waiting for a taxi in New York. *Twwwist left, twwwist right, twwwist left, twwwist right*. A passing stranger called out, fan to fan, "Hey, man, don't knock the Rock!" Even in New York, the encounter must have seemed cryptic.

In 1958, Rocky actually had a better year than Mickey Mantle. He hit just one less home run (42), but had 16 more runs batted in (113). Perhaps more pointedly, he was the only Indian player of the time that fans in other cities found worth booing. Yet for all the baseballs he struck against outfield seats, a faint suggestion of the absurd clung to

Rocky Colavito. He ran down balls in right field like a deer; but deer are not known for their fielding dexterity. His throwing arm was quick and powerful—*a cannon*, sportscasters called it. But often, a cannon that misfired. Rocky would rear back as a runner rounded third base toward a score at home, the buzz of the crowd rising at the onrushing drama of a strong throw, a sure slide, and a staunch tag all colliding, like Caesar, Brutus, and Cassius, in a single dramatic instant. *Rocky throws!* And the ball would soar—sometimes above the catcher's head. The crowd would quiet quickly, as if a plug had been pulled on a phonograph. *Et tu, Rocco?*

Even as he stood in the batter's box, the ground on which he had to be acknowledged as artful, Rocky faced down jeers. His swing didn't have the elegance of Joe DiMaggio's, who would sweep away a pitch as if he was unfurling a matador's cape off his shoulders. Rocky Colavito swung more like a man trying to break down the door of a burning building. He was often compared, disadvantageously, to DiMaggio. But Rocky actually finished his career with more home runs (374 to DiMaggio's 361, although Rocky played in 105 more games).

Most comically, news photos of Rocky's dauntless swings sometimes seemed to show him with his eyes squeezed closed as he struck the ball. Years later, a doctor at the Cleveland Clinic (physiology, clearly, was not his field) loyally assured me that the science of a baseball swing was such that by the time a power hitter made contact with a pitched ball, his swing was too far gone to be altered anyway. *So his eyes might as well be closed,* said the doctor, if the hitter felt it lent an extra eyelash of power. Still, it was not a photo that flattered. Just a couple of years later, when I played sandlot ball with some of my cousins, they would jeer when I swung and missed. *Why don't you close your eyes, Scotty, like your hero Rocky?*

So Indian fans home and away would take up a cheer to choke off the taunts and chortles: "Don't Knock the Rock! Don't Knock the Rock! Don't Knock the Rock!" He had strength (once, in Baltimore in 1959, he hit four home runs in a single game, the last glancing off his knuckles—and landing 415 feet away), his own style, more than a touch of class, and, in the crunch, nerve. Almost more impressive than the number of the Rock's home runs were his 1,150 runs batted in; that was just 387 fewer than Joe DiMaggio's, and Joe didn't have to hit against Yankee pitching—or follow Cleveland hitters. You don't bat home more than a thousand runs without knowing how to turn pressure into energy. During the years when no club could reliably beat the New

York Damn Yankees, Rocky Colavito could at least, occasionally, beat the Yanks at their own game. He was Cleveland's Bronx Bomber.

Because I was tall for my age and seemed sociable but solitary by temperament, my father had it figured that I ought to be a pitcher. He set about to show me the fine points before the basics, applying the approach of a great natural showman who wants to play Mercutio but doesn't know how to fence. *Hey, no sweat, I'll fake it.* My father showed me the feints and flourishes: how to lean down and squint to catch the signal from the catcher, one finger for a fastball, two for a curve, three for a change-of-pace, though it wasn't clear what kind of change-of-pace you could develop in a pitcher who couldn't heave the ball above an undistinguished dribble. Ah, but I looked the part.

"Okay, Ace," my father would call out, "let's see that scowl." I'd pinch my face down into a comic grimace. "That's great, Ace. Just like Sal 'the Barber'!"

"Sal the Barber?" It was not a name, like Mudcat or Rocky, that was marked in my mind.

"Sal 'the Barber' Maglie," said my father, "a National Leaguer. 'Cause he throws so close to their chins. Scowl now, Ace!" I tucked my lip into my chin and reddened; impersonating my father imitating the Barber. "Okay now, here's the sign. One finger. Fastball."

"Don't tell me!"

"One finger, straight down. Got it?"

"Got it. Here goes!" Winding up from a standing start, I whirled and jerked a pitch down into the ground. One bounce. A second. Then, the ball rolled an inch or three to stop on a patch of brown soil sprouting a small anthill. My father sprinted out from a catcher's crouch to trap it.

"Hey, attaway, Ace," he exulted. "Just get it up a little higher now!"

On weekend days and some nights when the Indians were at home, my father would take me along to Municipal Stadium, the overly enormous oval in which the team played. In the hours before the game began, with lazing outfielders waving their gloves at overlying batting practice balls, and the grounds crew soaking and softening the soil around first base (the Cleveland fielder there, Mickey Vernon, was forty years old), the park had the feel of an abandoned battleship in dry-dock along Lake Erie.

The stadium roiled with 80,000 gray-green seats, by far the largest amount in the major leagues. Quite uselessly so. It would take the entire population of Toledo to make the park appear full. *Toledo, Spain.* Batting practice home runs would often wing into the seats high up, which had not held baseball fans for years. *Thwwwack!* they would smack into a back rest, jerking the seat down into place; as if a ghost had just sat down in the bleachers.

My father would come out onto the field to find out about the lineups of each team. A few times, he took me in tow. Rocky, the Mick (Mantle), Yogi (Berra), the Splendid Splinter (Boston's Ted Williams)—I suppose I saw the shoes and knees of all of them when I was six.

"Mick?" my father would call out pleasantly. "Like you to meet my son," and Mickey Mantle's smile, mild and blond as corn silk, would break out on his face. Two players in particular were notably friendly. Jimmy Piersall, the center fielder, and Billy Martin, the second baseman. Perhaps not coincidentally, they were also the two most verifiable mental cases on the club.

The story of Jim Piersall's audacious struggle against mental illness, in a time when both treatment and public sympathy were limited, has been told in books and movies. When he was breaking into the big leagues with the Boston Red Sox in the early 1950s, the emotional demands of a browbeating father launched Piersall into lunatic displays. Once, he hit a home run and ran around the bases backward, third to home, climbing the backstop like a long-legged spider. By the time Piersall came to Cleveland in 1958, therapy, medication, and greater public understanding had tamped down some of his personal flammability. He was enthralling to watch on patrol in center field. Jim would drift in, to tempt and taunt a batter to dare to lash a ball over his head. The crack of the bat, he used to say, sent a sound that signaled where the ball would carry (his manager didn't mind if he heard *those* kinds of voices) and Piersall would turn around like a circus cyclist to flag down the ball from over his shoulder, then wheel 'round to throw a strike back into the infield. Where other players might bluster and posture, *Don't you dare,* Jimmy Piersall sneered and cheered, *Dare me, I dare you.*

I remember him at rest near the batting cage, down on one knee, waiting to take his turn at batting practice. In spring, he often wore turtleneck jersey shirts under his uniform (his teammates said he fretted about defending himself from colds) and had a thin, sharp, dark face, which seemed to hone his attentions like a knife's edge. Once, my father had introduced me by name; and thereafter I made a point of trying to walk by Jimmy when he knelt at my eye level, because he had once called out, "How ya' doin', Scotty?" and actually waited for an answer.

Billy Martin was a hard-eyed, hawk-nosed man who asked visitors to count the scars on his hands to show how people would slide into him with their spikes high. When I was later able to read and learn more about Billy's career as a barroom brawler, I wondered about how many of those scars had actually been drawn by a slide. Much of Billy Martin's famous churlishness seemed to retreat around children. Once, my father had been walking through the locker room before a game, and Martin stopped him by name. "I didn't even know he *knew* my name," Dad said later. "I kept thinking, 'Ohmigod, I mispronounced his name. He's gonna stuff me in the laundry hamper. Wait a minute. How do you mispronounce *Billy Martin?*' " But the man who had once—more than once—punched up the Copacabana was almost shy as he reached into his locker and took out a couple of battered, bedraggled gloves, one of his own and one that had belonged to Jim Grant. "They were gon . . . throw 'em away," Martin muttered into his shirt. "Figured, maybe, you know, could, well, kids or sumpin'." My cousin Marc got Cat's glove, and I got Billy's.*

One afternoon, Annette Funicello came out to the ballpark. She was, to be gentlemanly about it, the most womanly of Walt Disney's Mousketeers. She came to the stadium on a tour to promote her hit single, "Joe-Joe, the Dog-Faced Boy," and my father stopped her as she came through the press box shaking hands.

"Ohmigod. My kid. Ohmigod. My kid, he's in love with you. I bet you hear that all the time. My kid, he's in love with you. If—I mean, if I could—get him on the phone—would you say hello?"

Annette Funicello turned out to be a nice teenage heartthrob and said she would. The telephone rang in our apartment as the television droned on with an after-school ballgame. "Scotty!" called my mother. "Daddy's on the phone. You won't believe who wants to say hello to you. It's Annette. You know, from the Mickey Mouse Club. Annette!" Of course I knew—and cringed. I imagined my father's rendition of my feelings and got embarrassed in absentia. "Oh, you know," I could hear him saying. "He's just a kid. Just six. They get these, oh you know, funny crushes at that age. Anyway, if you could just say hello . . ." My father, I sensed, would portray my ardor as feckless, childish adoration. I knew it

---

*Which my cousin's dog ate a few weeks later. Whenever I contemplate why I didn't become a major league ballplayer, I like to think it was because my cousin's dog ate my mitt.

was something deeper. Something adult and wise. Something more real than, say, the crush I carried for Miss Ryan, my kindergarten teacher with effulgent red hair.

Abashed, I cowered in the corner of our doorway, across from the telephone table, my mother holding out the receiver at the end of the cord. I could hear my father's pleadings, strained into a puny, tin voice, crinkling out of the ear piece.

"But Scotty! It's Annette!"

"No, no!" Tears brimmed in my eyes.

"She wants to say hello to you!"

"No, no!" I clawed at the air, as if holding off a ghost—or, my imaginary friend.

"But Scotty!" my father rather pointlessly pointed out, "you *love* Annette!" More smoothly, my mother turned away toward the wall to whisper. "Tell her thank you, Ernest. But I think he's just a little itty-bitty s-h-y, you know?"

But my father returned home with Annette's record that night, autographed in lipstick and sealed with an imprint of her pursed, piercing red lips. "*To Scotty*," she had written in teenage girly, curlicue script, "*Love, Annette*." Her inscription contained four of the ten or so words I could read at the age of six. I read them, forlornly, over and over, hoping to discover something more.

Sometime during that second season in Cleveland, my father, forlornly, moved out of our apartment. Urgent, harrowed voices, hushed before I could hear all but a few words; tears turned down before they thought I could be awakened in the middle of the night—I suppose I heard all of that. But through their wounds and turmoils, my parents remained impeccably respectful of each other, and kind to me. They were, to use a word I try to avoid ascribing to sports stars, heroes. My mother was a brave woman, just beginning to draw on her courage; my father, a brave man who was getting broken down by his problems. He moved into a small hotel room downtown, a hurt, merry man watching four walls closing in. But every time I spent the night, I drifted happily off to sleep under the flat, greenish glow of *The Jack Paar Show*, flickering with laughter, my father beside me in the room's only chair, dozing, drinking, drowsing, browsing through *Variety*, *Life*, *Look*, the *Economist*, *Sporting News*, and Spiderman comics. "Morning, Ace," he'd say in the day. "Garry Moore is looking for a summer replacement. The Tribe is trading for Granny Hamner. There are potential Castros all over Latin

America. He actually speaks English, by the way, but won't with Americans because he's not sure of it. Minnie Minoso is the same way. You ought to see the pictures of Elvis with his hair cut." Years later, I read Hugh McIlvanney's profile of the great Manchester United striker, George Best, and was struck by a sentence in which Best, who had left the game because he could not handle drink as expertly as Arsenal or Liverpool, warned his admiring chronicler not to be too taken with Best's conversational fluency. "You see," he explained, "drunks are reading to go to sleep while the rest of you are sleeping." When baseball season started up again, my father would often keep on a late-game as a kind of vigil light and awaken me in the morning with the news. "We got 'em last night, Ace. Six to two, Rocky hit one. We got 'em. Coffee?"

When I asked my mother why we were living apart, she had an answer that avoided a lot with an overall wisdom. "Daddy's sick," she said. "He needs to get help." My father, challenged with the same question, had an identical answer. "Daddy's sick, Ace. He's got to try and get well. I need your help, too." We all got assignments. My mother looked for work, my father went into a hospital, and I was sent off to spend the summer with my aunt, uncle, and an assortment of cousins in Washington, D.C. Obviously, my assignment was the best: to play with my cousins, house to house, yard to yard, until dusk. I had never lived in a house and rather wondered what a bush was for, if not the wall for a home run. *Back, back, hey-hey, scccrunch! Way to hit the azaleas, Rocco!* My aunt came out to find dents from our backsides in the bushes. "Why don't you play in the streets," she laughed, "like other kids?" It was not only the most wonderful summer of my young life—I'm not sure I've had a better one to this date. My cousins were fun, my aunt and uncle considerate, and the neighborhood kids were solicitous after a talk with their parents. *The Simon kid? The strange one? Don't bug him. He's been through a lot.* I had, of course, been through nothing. The summer ended, but my father's sickness persisted. He was cleverer than his doctors. So when my mother arrived to take me home, my aunt, her azaleas notwithstanding, generously offered to take me into her family for the school year.

As second grade opened, the Indians had settled into second place. The Chicago White Sox, however, were bound for the World Series. Our teacher took us into the lunchroom on the series' opening day to see the first inning of the first game beamed in, in ashen black and white, from Chicago. The White Sox won that day, an 11 to 0 laugher, to make Chicagoans Abroad proud. My father came home from the hospital to my cousin's house for a visit. I had won two goldfish at a fair in school by pitching a Ping-Pong ball into a fishbowl, and named them Patti and Ernie. My father bent down to peer at them through the glass. "Which is which?" he wondered. "Which is the funny one and which is the pretty one?" The big one, I told him, was Ernie, the smaller one Patti. "Closest we've been in years," he said, with a W. C. Fields curl. My mother was working as a secretary in Chicago at the Civic Opera House. Sometime during the series, a wrapped shoebox arrived in the mail. She had taken the subway down to Comiskey Park during her lunch hour and purchased a White Sox pennant and a small, kid-sized cap. She had written in Catholic schoolgirl, curlicue script:

*"For my two loyal little boys. Love, Mommy"*

Over the next few days, I would see my father put the note away in the box, then fish it out to read it, over and over; hoping to discover something more.

The rest of the World Series was not so enchanting. The Los Angeles Dodgers (the preface sounded funny and unfamiliar then, so close to their arrival from Brooklyn) won the next three games, lost one more from lack of attention, then captured the last to win the World Series. Consolingly, my father reminded me that Rocky Colavito had a splendid year and would have an even better one the next. It was the first time I marked the phrase. "Next year," he added, "will be better for me, too. Better for all of us."

My father came out of the hospital, looked for work, found it, went back to drinking, and lost it. One day in the spring, he took me into a hilly local park where we searched for a flat stretch of ground on which he could hit ground balls to me: the palliative of the times for childhood turmoils. "Attaway, Ace," he called out between balls. "Keep it in front of you now!" My pick-up, he said, was improving. "Into the hole now, turn, and throw!" He was breathing heavily, as if he was trying to pull a trunk up a staircase, and sweating through his shirt. "Flip the ball, bat it down, way to go, way to go." Dad lit a cigarette and stroked out another ball, playing for time. During the last few grounders, I could feel blood churning in my ears, bracing the body for bad news. My father found a couple of swing seats and brought them together so that our knees knocked. Then, he lit a cigarette and pressed his right hand to my right shoulder. My throwing arm.

"Listen, Ace," he said finally. "They traded Rocky." Even up, to the Detroit Tigers, for right fielder Harvey Kuenn. Rocky had won one half of the home run title with 42, Harvey Kuenn the batting title with an average of .353. The way Cleveland's general manager, Frank Lane, had weighed the tables of statistics, he was willing to trade home runs for average. I could tell that my father thought the swap was incomprehensible. He tried to explain it in that voice that took over when he was fumbling to tell someone that he had been late because of car trouble—or a subway accident—or an unexpected phone call.

"Now, Ace, I think that what Frank figures is that in that big ballpark in Cleveland, Harvey Kuenn can get even more hits. Whereas Rocky, as he gets older—well, who can tell how many more home runs he can hit? I think that's what Frank is trying to do . . ."

But a spout blew up inside of me. The sobbing made me shiver, like a drenched dog in an alley on a cold night. Under ordinary circumstances, it might have been the occasion for a conscientious father to instruct his son that baseball, after all, was only a game, and part of that game was the comings and goings of trades. But my father understood at once—he must have felt it himself—that while some of my crying was for Rocky, much was for all the other comings and goings we had seen. His talking trailed off as he threaded an arm around the chains of the swing and rocked with me, back and forth, back and forth, as I tried to hide my head under his shoulder, along with the smell on his shirt of aftershave, cigarettes, and sweat. "Next year will be better, Ace," he said, repeating the refrain of the inconsolable and heartsick. "Next year will be better, wait and see, wait and see." I replied with just about the most terrible question a child can ask: "Promise? Do you promise?"

A substantial digression here on the subject of the man who made that trade, Frank Lane. He was simply one of the most capriciously malevolent public figures of the era, and I am not forgetting that the era included Mao Tse-tung and Roy Cohn. Frank Lane was a bigoted, crab apple–faced braggart (and, professedly, a religious man) who pretended to candor by saying *fuck* a lot and gloating about his drinking. He insinuated his way into contracts with club after club by flatulently flattering the rich men who owned baseball teams and ridiculing the players to whom they paid so much (and then, much less so) money. To this innate disdain, Frank Lane added his own dripping dollop of personal ridicule.

"Sympathy!" he used to exclaim to players who complained of injury, bad bounces, or exhaustion. "You'll find sympathy only in the

dictionary—right between shit and syphilis." One famous spring training, he had heckled Minnie Minoso for looking over a pitch that was
called for a third strike. "You look like a big sack of shit with a cherry on
top!" Of course, sensitivities about racial epithets were different in those
days. But never *that* different.

He was known as Trader Lane, and earned his sobriquet by trading
ceaselessly, compulsively, pointlessly, 242 trades in seven years. Nowadays, there would be a support group for a man so plainly addicted. He'd
trade on a dare, trade out of spite, trade on a hunch. More than once, he
traded the same player twice in the same day to different teams, and
awoke the next day to defend his mistake provocatively, with the motto
of a man with a problem. "Of course I knew what the fuck I was
doing!" Frank Lane looked to outsiders for help because he was, at least,
shrewd enough about himself to distrust his own judgment. If a player
came up in his system, as did Rocky Colavito, Frank Lane marked the
man down as discounted goods.

Mostly, Frank Lane traded "just for the hell of it. *Just to shake things
up,*" emphasis mine. Once, he hatched a plan to trade the entire roster of
the Indians, down to the trainer, for the entire roster of the Chicago
White Sox, "just to shake things up." The commissioner's office called a
halt. But he succeeded in a mid-season swap of Cleveland's manager, Joe
Gordon, for Detroit's Jimmy Dykes, for no greater reason than that Gordon had begun to be confused by all the trades; many nights, he scribbled
into the batting order the name of a player who had been sent away that
afternoon. Marriages were strained, houses lost, children uprooted, all on
Trader Lane's whim. *Just to shake things up.* He was a clever man, but not
wise enough to know the difference between motion and energy.

He also seemed to have an insecure man's resentment of stars.
When he became general manager of the St. Louis Cardinals in 1955,
Lane tried to trade Stan Musial. Of course, if you set out to remake a
team, a star is often the most salable commodity. But what other player
could match the value of Stan "The Man" Musial to St. Louis—the club
and the community? Where other general managers might see the
chance to rebuild a franchise around the best left-handed hitter in the
National League, Frank Lane saw a rival for acclaim.

Most Americans of my vintage grew up being induced to despise
Nikita Khrushchev.* But after the trade of Rocky Colavito, I found it

---

*Or in Brooklyn, Walter O' Malley.

more compelling to work up contempt for the Frank Lanes of life. Years later, when Bill Veeck owned the White Sox on his last turn, he told me, "Frank had a drinking problem. His problem was, he would drink and make trades." Barroom louts deride those who decline to match them drink for drink. Frank Lane ridiculed players who did not smoke, guzzle, swear, or brawl as "chocolate sodas." When Rocky Colavito stayed on after games to sign autographs, amiably instructing youngsters to stand in a straight line, one by one, so he could lean down and say, "Thank you," to each one of them, Trader Lane muttered darkly, "That chocolate soda crap doesn't cut much ice with me." He was a man who understood the world only through machination and ploy; goodness had to be some kind of ruse.

On the other hand, superior performance on the field wasn't the sort of stunt to impress him much either. After Rocky Colavito shared the 1959 home run title with Harmon Killebrew of the Washington Senators, the Rock sat down to talk about his contract with Frank Lane, in the days before athletes hired professionals who could manage to match general managers mendacity for mendacity. Colavito expected a small raise, if Lane couldn't bring himself to part with outright praise. Instead, Trader Lane flung Colavito's forty-two home runs back across his desk, into Rocky's face, as if they had been a shameful feat. "You're no help to this team," he barked. "You hit just two-fifty-seven. As a matter of fact," Frank Lane wound up, "I oughta cut your salary!" Even as a negotiating tactic, the tirade was ugly.

Rocky Colavito signed for a salary just half of what Mickey Mantle had earned for hitting .285. But Rocky exacted what he took to be a promise: that he would not be traded. The Rock wanted to remain in Cleveland. His picture was tacked up just a shelf below that of St. Francis or Pope Pius XII in the Italian markets of Murray Hill. His family was settled and comfortable. Trading a raise for a promise seemed not such a bad deal. But Frank Lane was not the kind of man to take fairness lying down.

With a bully's fine touch for the tiny details of inflicting pain, Lane made the Kuenn-for-Colavito trade the very day before the 1960 season opened. Rocky Colavito had singled and was standing on first base, in front of 30,000 fans, at an exhibition game in Memphis. Joe Gordon, mortified, called him in from the field to deliver the news out of camera range. The greatest Indian of his time was dealt away and sent off without an ovation, in a minor league town. *Just to shake things up.* Protests and demonstrations broke out at Municipal Stadium. My father showed me a photograph on the front page of the sports section of what looked like a scarecrow in flames. "They call that," he explained, "burning someone in effigy. It's better than burning them in person. Except maybe," he said with a rueful little chuckle, "not this time." It is inviting in these times to loathe athletes for an excess of greed and a lack of loyalty. "Loyalty," said Wade Boggs on leaving the Boston Red Sox for the New York Yankees, "is what you keep pets for." Occasionally, I remind myself how Frank Lane and other sports executives used to swap players with the immature whim of adolescents trading bubble gum cards. We can forget why athletes had to organize to protect themselves.

Many, not all of them baseball fans or even Clevelanders, began to date the decline of the city to that trade. By the end of the 1960s, Cleveland's middle-class core would defect from the city to the suburbs or sunnier climes, leaving the city with just half the people it had in 1950. Joblessness and crime would grow hugely; civic debt would swell into default. By the 1990 census, Cleveland would be smaller than Columbus—Ohmigod, a *minor league town*. Earnest and wise Clevelanders began to grumble about the Curse of Rocky Colavito. *Those that would trade the Rock make the gods angry.*

The Colavito-for-Kuenn trade amounted to a draw. Neither Cleveland nor Detroit would win the pennant they sought in the exchange. If Frank Lane's shaking things up had a discernible purpose, it was to create some new alchemy in Cleveland. But the Indians without Rocco Colavito lacked the spark of glamour. Good players—Vic Power, Tito Francona, Harvey Kuenn among them—lacked a star's spark among them to catch fire. The Indians without their Rock became all tinder, no kindling.★

The Rock actually returned to Cleveland in a trade in 1965. He was loyal, he was loved, and they wanted him back. He played well, too, raising his average to .287 and hitting 26 home runs. But during those years, the Indians were smitten by improbable injuries; the afflictions of the city multiplied; and much of the town had become more infatuated with Jimmy Brown and football's Cleveland Browns. The joy of baseball would not return to Cleveland until the 1990s, when the revival of

---

★By the way: Roger Maris had come to the Damn Yankees in a trade from the Indians. He was traded away by Frank Lane. You can add another insupportable speculation to life's imponderables: if Roger Maris had been kept by Cleveland, might the 1961 Maris-Mantle home run chase that finally toppled Babe Ruth's record of 60 have been a Maris-Colavito competition?

downtown and the ascension of the Indians became independent improvements that still seemed inextricable to many fans.

Frank Lane, however, would flee the scene. After his trades helped lead the Indians from second to fourth to fifth place, he still possessed the admirable, lunatic self-esteem to ask for a contract extension. But even rich owners have episodes of lucidity; Lane was refused. So, Frank Lane treated the remainder of his contract with the same disdain as a promise to Rocky Colavito. He signed to become general manager of a better team, the Kansas City Athletics—another one of life's brutes who seemed to rise each time he fell. Frank Lane boasted that he had traded more than a thousand players in his career. When Lane died in 1981, Terry Pluto of the *Akron Beacon-Journal* could count just eight people at his funeral. All of those players Frank Lane had moved about like dented canned goods, and not one of them came to say good-bye. To their merit, not one of them even came to tap dance on his grave.

Of course, it's a delusion for a fan to trace civic decline or personal disappointment back to the fortunes of a sports team. But part of the condition of being a fan is surrendering enough of your critical senses to feel at least a little exultation and frustration at their wins and losses. I suppose this is also one of the cathartic properties of theater. Who wants to announce to himself, at the moment Tybalt and Mercutio begin to duel, "They're only actors, you know. Don't worry, it's just a play." In a way, I was fortunate that I did not need to see Rocky Colavito traded to learn that life entails loss, and that love is not always enough. But I was also lucky to learn, in the moment that my father held me clumsily, closely, on that squeaky swing, that though I was young and hurt and sad, I could do something to help just by holding on to him for help, when he must have felt that the world was opening up below.

## Chapter 4

# CUBBIE LOVE

Being a Chicago Cubs fan defies metaphor. Nevertheless, over the years I have tried quite a few. *It's like rooting for the Italian army. It's like campaigning for Harold Stassen. It's like raving about your Edsel.* If rooting for the New York Yankees is like rooting for U.S. Steel, then rooting for the Cubs is like ... well, you see the point? No metaphor improves on, *it's like rooting for the Cubs.* They are the devotion that defines despair. They are the love that evinces the triumph of hope over experience.★

The Cubs last won a World Series in 1908. Over that century, the world endured two world wars, launched men and women through the sky and among the stars, devised vaccines, invented bluegrass music and frozen orange juice, unlocked the atom, and cloned mammals. *And the Cubs still lose.* When mad scientist Theodore Kaczynski was captured,

---

★Boston Red Sox fans, incredibly, often compete for this characterization. But as Bob Costas has said, the Cubs are farce, while the Red Sox are tragedy. The misfortune of the Red Sox is that they climb so close to the summit, only to stub their toes (or flub a ground ball) and fall down. Cubs fans would settle for simply coming close. It is a measure of the desperation of the fans of both clubs that there could be this kind of contest over who is entitled to greater despondency.

tried, and convicted for sending murderous bombs, social critics tried to fathom what could drive a man so smart to despair so great he committed such wicked crimes? They looked at his relations with his parents; wondered if he had been the bespectacled egghead, ostracized in school; theorized that he had been rejected in romance or unsure of his sexuality. But sometimes, the best answer comes first: the Unabomber had grown up just outside Chicago. *Oh no, Cubs country.* Loss has become the Cubs legacy, an American tradition alongside Der Bingle singing "White Christmas."

The irony is that the chunky Cubs red **C** pinned on a peacock-blue crown has become, along with the Yankees monogram worn by Ruth, Gehrig, Mantle, and Maris, one of the most recognized baseball emblems in the world. "I don't understand other American sports," a teenager in Sarajevo who fiercely followed the Bulls and basketball told me. "The Chicago Cubs I have heard of. They play baseball, yes?" Some direct questions simply cannot be answered yes or no.

A man who belonged to my Quaker meeting in Chicago used to sing to the world:

> *Do they still play the blues in Chicago?*
> *Whenever baseball season rolls 'round.*
> *When the snows melt away—*
> *Do the Cubbies still play*
> *In their ivy-covered burial ground?*\*

"Oh, jeez, did you see them last night?" Steve Goodman whispered across several shoulders at a meeting. He had stayed up late Saturday after playing at his club to watch the Cubs lose to the Dodgers on the West Coast.

"Naw. I couldn't stay up."

"Lost in the eleventh. Looked terrible. Bonham got shelled. Say, I think I have tickets to the Cardinals series."

An hour of silent Quaker worship passed before feet stirred and Steve ambled over. "Carmen Fanzone was into the club the other night." A utility player, mostly third base, who was also a utility trumpet player along Lincoln Avenue.

---

\**A Dying Cub Fan's Last Request,* by Steve Goodman (Red Pajama 1001, 1981).

"Did he play the horn?" I asked.

"Naw," said Steve Goodman through his quick cunning grin. "He picked it up and dropped it." Steve, a longtime leukemia patient, would die in 1984, making his song pinch in the memory:

> *Give me a double-header funeral in Wrigley Field*
> *On some sunny weekend day—no lights.*
> *Have the organist play the National Anthem, then*
> *a little Naa-na-na-na, Naa-na-na-na, Hey-hey, good-bye*
> *Make six groundskeepers carry my casket*
> *And six umpires call me out at each base.*
> *It's a beautiful day for a funeral—hey, Ernie!**
> *Let's play two today!*

The national image of the Cubs as cuddlesome incompetents probably began with the September 24, 1948, cover of the *Saturday Evening Post*. Norman Rockwell's *Bottom of the Ninth* showed a line of chagrined Cubs slumping in the dugout, while fans in the seats above smirk, jeer, and blow raspberries. In the foreground, the Cubs' batboy stands forlorn, his cap askew, his forehead screwed up into his scalp in wonderment.[†] Behind him in the dugout, a battered old glove hangs like a dark brown cloud above the head of a man who is holding his huge right palm against his cheek, as if trying to contain a tootache. His eyes are huge, houndlike, amazed, and imploring.

That man was Charlie Grimm, the Cubs' manager, and the club's former first baseman. And because he had married an old friend of my mother's, a former nightclub singer I called Auntie Marian, I got to call Charlie Grimm "Uncle Charlie." (Charlie had been a left-handed banjo player as well as first baseman and would perform in Rush Street clubs after a day at the park—one of the advantages of day baseball.) He liked Rockwell's picture without feeling flattered.

"Rockwell was a great artist, of course," he told us at a holiday dinner in the early 1960s.

"He didn't paint you very well," Auntie Marian interjected. "I've

---

*Ernie Banks, the most luminous Cub. Much more will follow about Ernie Banks. His motto remains, "What a beautiful day for a ball game! Let's play two today!"

[†]Anecdotal evidence suggests that the bat boy depicted was Walter Jacobson, who today is a well-known Chicago television reporter specializing in political commentary. His expression is unchanged.

never seen you hold your hand against your face like that. That's Jack Benny. Rockwell made you look like a basset hound."

"A great artist," Uncle Charlie continued. "You can recognize everybody. I see some of the stuff they call art today in apartment building lobbies. I want to ask, 'Who spilled the ketchup around here?' But Rockwell painted so beautifully. You can count the loops in the towels behind us. You can see where a kid's tooth is growing in. What an artist. But he wasn't accurate. Bad as we were, and we lost ninety games that year, the fans didn't really boo us." Charlie laughed behind his huge, ham-slice hands. "Maybe they should have. Maybe they should have. Ninety losses was a record. They asked me to move up to the front office the next year, and hired Frankie Frisch to replace me."

"Well, he did a whole lot better, didn't he?" Marian chimed in. "Ninety-three losses!"

When Uncle Charlie cradled the gravy boat at Thanksgiving dinner, it seemed to sink inside his hands. Only the tip of the ladle handle was visible, like a last plank from a lost deck. When he brought out a mincemeat and a pumpkin pie in each hand to present to the table, they looked small and cookielike, cupped inside the broad, red, battered palms that used to spear the pegs of Billy Jurges and Stan Hack. "I'm just a hard-assed old ballplayer," he used to say after venturing an opinion about Lyndon Johnson, the Beatles, or Dick Gregory. "What the hell do I know?"

And yet, Charlie was one of the first men I knew who left an impression of delicacy. Swollen as his hands could seem, Uncle Charlie was the guest dispatched to excavate the inside of the Thanksgiving turkey carcass for congealed morsels, which he brought out with a banjo player's precision picking. After rinsing and drying, his fingernails gleamed: he was the first man I ever met who got regular manicures. He also had an odd and charming sensitivity about obscenity. Charlie would call himself a *hard-assed old ballplayer*, or a *lard-assed old son of a bitch*—but the likes of Leo Durocher would, at worst, be only "an old SOB like me." Profanity was fair game only against himself.

Uncle Charlie had played a strong first base for the Cubs for nearly ten years, then managed the team three more unconsecutive times for a total of fourteen. He brought them to a pennant three times. The last was won in 1945, with a roster of players too old or unsound to be drafted. "And mind you," Charlie used to say, "they were drafting one-eyed mules in those days. Give you some idea what we had, God bless 'em!" Charlie had loved that team. "Rejects and four-F's," he said, "who got a chance and won a championship. God, I loved them!" But that last pennant had been the last indeed for the Cubs; and Charlie had never been able to win the World Series.

For years, the surmise among scholars was that Uncle Charlie was the man Leo Durocher had in mind when he said, "Nice guys finish last." Superficially, the facts fit. During Uncle Charlie's steward-ship after 1945, the Cubs were certainly last. And Uncle Charlie was, without contest, one of sport's nice guys, cordial and kidding with reporters, lenient and loyal to his ballplayers, who minted him a nick-name: *Jolly Cholly*.

But in his 1976 autobiography, Leo insists that the actual nice guys finishing last he had in mind were Mel Ott's New York Giants, who fin-ished fifth in 1948, before Ott was replaced by . . . Leo Durocher. Leo also insisted, with the solemnity of a senator, that his words had been wrenched out of context. He said that he had merely observed of the Giants, "(They're) nice guys, who'll finish last. Nice guys"—emphasize a pause here—"finish last." That he was merely expressing a specific pre-diction about the baseball season, not casting out some general principle for life. But it was hard to take Leo at his word—any of them. His clari-fication was delayed by more than a decade, after Leo the Lip had slid into Bartlett's between John Betjeman and W. H. Auden. Uncle Charlie said he had never been seriously offended by the possibility that the quote had been aimed at him. "What would Leo," he laughed, "know about what it is to be a nice guy?"

It's difficult to say when ineptitude becomes endearing in a franchise. Several ingredients are necessary. No team really wants to acquire them. During the years in which the Cubs were building their reputation for imaginative inadequacy, the American League's St. Louis Browns and Washington Senators were often equal bumblers. But the Senators and the Cubs at least had a few remarkable individual players on which fans could fasten (Phil Cavarretta, Andy Pafko, and eventually Ernie Banks for the Cubs; Roy Sievers, Camilo Pascual, and Harmon Killebrew for the Senators). The St. Louis Browns had none. Still under the inspired promotional influence of Bill Veeck, the Browns might have persevered into new levels of appalling ineptitude. But St. Louis was too small a place to split between an outstanding National League team in the Car-dinals and the artlessness of the American League Browns. The Brown-ies moved on to Baltimore—and perennial excellence—as the Orioles.

The Senators once approached storied proportions of deficiency. They could even see caricatures of themselves high-stepping across Broadway in George Abbott's 1955 musical, *Damn Yankees*. A chorus line of slumping Senators in wrinkled, sad gray woolens sang, "You've gotta have heart!"

Washington had other critical ingredients: national prominence and a sturdy sense of civic self-importance that outlanders could mock. The phrase Senators' fans turned over from history to acclaim their team's inexpedience—*Washington: first in war, first in peace, and last in the American League*—flattered the city for its omnipotence while it twitted the Senators for ineptitude. In contrast, the Cleveland Indians endured almost a generation of disappointment. But the real-life losses of the city were simply too genuine to treat the team as affable buffoons. Even sports fans can shrink from laughing at a downed target.

But the Senators moved on to Minnesota in 1960. Only fans in a city that sees itself as vital can make a joke into a heritage. The losing legacies of the Mets and Cubs, White Sox and Red Sox, don't dent the local self-image. In fact, it might make some of the swagger New York, Boston, and Chicago carry easier to accept. A man might resent Chicago for its grime, crime, and braggadocio. But who can dislike the Cubbies?

Still: they have been pretty terrible.

The humiliation of finishing 27½ games out of first place in 1948 set a new low-water mark for the next year. The Cubs finished 36 games out of first place in 1949. Uncle Charlie spent most of that year in the front office. Almost twenty years later over the holiday table, he would hold up his hands and say, "They were never meant to carry a briefcase. Just a bat, glove, and banjo." In 1950, the Philadelphia Phillies "Whiz Kids" won the National League pennant. The Cubs of that year were nick-*maimed* the Whiff Kids for striking out a record 767 times. The next year, they negotiated an extensive trade that sent their best hitter, Andy Pafko, their best fielder, Wayne Terwilliger, and two other players to the Brooklyn Dodgers for four players it would be difficult to locate today without the aid of the International Committee on Refugees. The trade, said the *Sporting News*, was such a steal it should have appeared on police blotters. The newspaper speculated that surely, there must be more to the trade—money, or players to be named later. There wasn't. The Cubs finished 34½ games out.

Anecdotes dotted their descent into caricature. On a June afternoon in 1955, the Cubbies put two balls in play against the St. Louis Cardinals. One is considered customary. Umpire Vic Delmore put the second ball into the hands of catcher Sammy Taylor as the Cubs protested that a called ball four on Stan Musial had actually been a tipped second strike. But when a national audience saw shortstop Ernie Banks and second baseman Tony Taylor prancing like mating herons around second base, each confused as to who should try to tag out Musial with what, it seemed to convey the quality of Cubness: innocent incoherence. In the mid-1960s, the club acquired a pitcher named Bill Faul, who hypnotized himself before starting a game. Opposing pitchers would try to break his trance by dangling pocket watches from the dugout and chanting, "Tick-tock, tick-tock, tick-tock." But it was scarcely necessary. Faul couldn't hypnotize hitters and was eventually released. Also in the 1960s, owner P. K. Wrigley decided to replace the traditional position of manager with a rotating college of coaches. The analogy to Clown College was inescapable.

More seriously, there was the trade with the St. Louis Cardinals early in the 1964 season in which the Cubs acquired two good pitchers, Ernie Broglio and Bobby Shantz. Unfortunately, they traded Lou Brock, a promising outfielder who would go on to set base-stealing records, help win two World Series, and hook slide into the Hall of Fame. Then, there was even a real tragedy: Ken Hubbs, an exceptional defensive second baseman, became Rookie of the Year in 1962, the first Cub star since Ernie Banks. But after accepting his award in the off-season, Ken Hubbs died while flying a small private plane. He was twenty-two. "Shows you," Charlie Grimm said in rueful sadness, "ballplayers should be in bars, where they belong."

Some stars managed to shine amid the murk. Hank Sauer, an elk-nosed, Mauser-armed left fielder who ran as if suitcases had been tied to his shoes, was the National League's Most Valuable Player in 1952, hitting 37 home runs and batting in 127. And then, in 1953, Ernie Banks arrived: complete with elegant, reedy wrists and an elegaic smile that would make him one of the most delightful figures in American life.

As the 1960s progressed, the play of the Cubs continued to appall—but their appeal, improbably, seemed only to expand. Part of the charm, of course, was where they played. *Beeeauuutiful Wrigley Field,* as Jack Brickhouse pronounced at the beginning of each broadcast. After Ebbets Field and the Polo Grounds had come down, Fenway Park in Boston and Wrigley Field stood apart as great neighorhood ballparks.

Wrigley's umber brick walls, upholstered in ivy, gave the field the elegant look of a jewelry box lined in green silk. Its small dimensions and closely nestled seats made the park seem as friendly and familiar as a sandbox. Home runs launched over the left–center field seats could easily poke a hole in apartment windows along Waveland Avenue, just like the home run stroke of any twelve-year-old in a city sandlot. *Hey, Mom, look what Willie Mays sent through the window today! Can I keep it?*

By the 1960s, night baseball and reserved seats had become standard; but not at Wrigley Field. Even if the Wrigleys could no longer dismiss night baseball as a fad, they could hold on to their own sense of standards and play all of their home games in daylight. At Mr. Wrigley's insistence, too, thousands of seats were held back each day to be sold just before game time. Fans, he felt, should not have to plan to make games weeks in advance, like a dental appointment.

Whatever their defeats and antics on the field, the clawless Cubbies and their cuddlesome ballpark came to be seen as a living diorama of what the national pastime should be. As modern baseball began to offend many fans with incomprehensible salaries, inconquerably vast, souless stadiums, and overbearing out-of-town owners uprooting fabled franchises for tax breaks, the Cubbies seemed a club with a sense of place. And of principle. The team lost, frequently and comically. But only baseball games, not fans, who still turned out to cheer in the cheap seats and the curvacous grandstands. If baseball, only occasionally, could be mistaken for real life, rooting for the Cubs could take the shape of real love. For many, even those—especially those—who did not follow sports, the Cubs and their Friendly Confines became a dream scene of what baseball would be in a decent world.

And there was something more. The club sold Cubs games at *beeeautiful* Wrigley Field as congenial family entertainment. But I began to see the Cubs, playing day baseball in their beautiful little bandbox, as a pastime that invisibly linked solitary souls on summer afternoons.

On one of those afternoons, when I was about thirteen, my father arrived to pick me up at a bowling alley. Cluckish and clownish, we youngsters were loitering through the last frames. My father installed himself on a stool in the tavern that bowling alleys used to tuck behind the shoe room, thin pine walls gilded with drab league plaques and hazy photographs. I came back there to find him, half an hour later. My father was one of a half-dozen customers, sitting alone on their stools, staring down into their drinks, then up at the television screen blinking with the seventh inning from Wrigley Field. Uncle Jack Brickhouse intoned overhead in isolated sentences:

> *Vic Roznovsky coming up.*
> *Flied out, ground out, last time up.*
> *Maloney shakes off a sign.*
> *Steps off the rubber.*
> *Vic steps out too.*
> *Two down, nobody on, Cubs down by three . . .*

My father looked up, ensnared and surprised. He couldn't back down a stool or two from the vodka and tonic dwindling in front of him, a tell-tale lime bobbing among melting chips of ice. "Hey, pal," he said finally, inclining his head toward the screen. "You know, just watching the Cubs." I said nothing; my father pressed on against the silence. "Want a Coke or something?" he asked finally.

"Naw. Billy, Danny, Avi, and me are having some over by the lane before we go."

"Need some money?"

"Nawww. Mother gave me some."

"Want some more?"

"Don't need it." Finally, I threw him a line. The son of a comedian ought to be able to set up his own father when the audience begins to turn. "Is there a score?" My father brightened slightly.

"Reds up by three," he said with relief. "But next inning, Beckert and Kessinger lead off."

Over the years, cable and satellite broadcasts have made the Cubs a fixture of late afternoons across several time zones. Many times, I've wandered into a bar to borrow a phone or ask for directions and seen, at some other place in the world, another half-dozen strangers perched two and three seats apart from each other at four o'clock in the afternoon: an idle hour, a dwindling drink, and a Cub game droning on overhead to lighten the aloneness.

Only a few days after the Los Angeles Dodgers of Koufax, Drysdale, and Wills defeated the Minnesota Twins of Oliva, Killebrew, and Quilici in the World Series of 1965, the Chicago Cubs announced they had hired Leo Durocher as their manager.

He was considered the most un-Cublike of men: bullying and irascible, a gambler and gam-chaser, his words famously quotable and impossible to believe. Durocher possessed what amounted to a genius for expressing malevolence within the rules. He didn't hit or spit at umpires; instead, he cultivated a technique for kicking dirt over their shiny shoes. "Hey—I never touched him!" He roared epithets from the bench that could be intricately sexual; but not racial. He could also be better than his truculent reputation—or at least, apply that reputation toward worthy goals. Leo was unschooled, but a proficient rhetorician. It was his clever words that quelled a revolt among the Brooklyn Dodgers during spring training in 1947. Jackie Robinson was set to arrive. Some of the Southern-born players on the team were circulating a petition, threatening to quit if Robinson became a Dodger. Leo convened a late-night argument in the hotel kitchen, lit a cigarette with a gold Dunhill, heedless of spilling ashes on his silken Sulka gown, and lectured the players in language they might not have heard from, say, Eleanor Roosevelt. "Listen," he told them, "I don't care if this guy is white, black, or green, he's gonna put a lot of *fucking money* in our pockets. Take your petition and *shove it up your ass*. We haven't won *dick*, and this guy can take us to the World Series." The offending players shoved the petition up their asses, gratefully.

Leo had won three pennants and a World Series with his teams. But he hadn't managed since the Giants left for San Francisco and the Dodgers set out for Los Angeles—without him. He'd worn out his reputation for motivating players by wearing too many of them out during late-season drives for the pennant. Durocher moved to the West Coast himself. It twinkled with the prospect of opportunity for a man who had once been married to the actress Laraine Day, and had become golf chums with George Raft and Frank Sinatra. Leo made cameo appearances on NBC's *Game of the Week* ("Maybe I shouldn't say this, fellas, but . . ."), and a Los Angeles radio show. But when the Cubs called, Leo was usually spending afternoons alone in his den, prowling, proud, and perhaps a little lost, looking forward too much to the day's first martini.

The Wrigleys asked Charlie and Marian Grimm to pick Durocher up at the airport. They welcomed a fierce, balding, biting man who had landed in Chicago wearing a last-minute sunburn and a powder blue Beverly Hills jumpsuit. In their car on the way downtown, Leo puffed himself up a bit next to his luggage in the backseat, growling, "I don't need this job you know, Charlie. I was earning more money than I ever did in baseball out in Hollywood, and I barely had to lift my dick. Hell, I was a young jerk, Charlie, you were a young jerk. But not like these young snots today, who get more in a bonus than you and I ever got for hitting three hundred."★

They took him to Eli's on Chicago Avenue to get the dust of the West Coast out of his mouth. Leo lined the swizzle sticks along their table like broken bats from the dugout rack. "You know, Charlie," Leo went on, "Mr. Wrigley is such a fine gentleman. Best owner in the business. He said to me, 'Leo, we really need you.' Well, Phil Wrigley doesn't blow smoke up your ass. If he really needs me, I want to help him."

Eli's was a kind of thermal springs for the sports, show, and political faces of Chicago. Diners began to send over drinks, desserts, signed cards from aldermen, and models saying, "If I can ever do anything . . ." Durocher excused himself to make his way to the men's room; when he returned, there was a round of applause. *Leo! Leo! We're with you, Leo!* "What the hell!" he laughed, while sliding back into his booth, awarding a wave to the crowd. "This is a great town, Charlie. That's also why I did it. Play ball by day, hell around Rush Street at night. A great baseball town and, as you know, Charlie, a great nookie town, too." (Marian was rather more offended by the "as you know, Charlie" than "nookie.") Leo growled on, coming close to gentle. "Hell's bells, maybe the right woman is out there for me, too." When Charlie raised a huge hand at Eli to ask for the check, the owner bustled over, beaming over his ruffled shirt, to say that dinner had been taken care of. As Leo, Charlie, and Marian walked out through the lounge, the piano bar player struck up "Take Me Out to the Ballgame," and then "Chicago." A new flurry of drinks flew over; cocktail napkins scrawled with phone numbers were pressed into Leo's pockets and hands; a local politician stood shyly by, importuning for Leo's autograph. Later, Marian would remember Leo signing a bar card for a fan and turning up his face as they made ready to leave to stop them with an astonishingly frank appeal. "C'mon, you two, don't make me drink alone. I had enough of that. Sit with me a while. Great, great fucking town."

"This is not an eighth-place team," Leo Durocher announced on arriving to take over a company of Cubs that already included: Ernie Banks at first base, who was beginning his career's descent, but still stroking 30 home runs a year out over Waveland Avenue; Billy Williams

---

★Leo never hit higher than .286. But his point was well taken.

in the outfield, beginning to ring an equal number over the climbing ivy in right; Ron Santo, who was beginning to arrive in All-Star territory at third base; and strong, steady arms in pitchers Ferguson Jenkins and Kenny Holtzman.★

"And I was right," Leo had the saving humor to acknowledge seven months later. "We finished tenth."

And yet, a fan could pick up the scent of improvement. Our divided family had moved back to Chicago in separate pieces. Some summer nights after dinner, I would go walking from the apartment on Elm Street I lived in with my mother to range around Michigan Avenue, peer into store windows and theater lobbies, buy the first edition of the next day's newspaper and . . . hope to see Leo Durocher. Leo had taken possession of a corporate apartment in a new building rising above an all-night drugstore at Michigan and Chicago. His girlfriend of the time warned that his after-dinner cigarettes could singe and saturate the rented upholstery with smoke. So Leo went downstairs to light up.

He would talk to anybody. He enjoyed talking. Which is why on some nights in the mid-1960s, a stroller could glimpse one of the most identifiable bald profiles since Yul Brynner, standing in a cantaloupe-colored Rodeo Drive safari suit under an apartment awning, flicking ashes onto the sidewalk and chatting from an old second baseman's spread-legged stance.

*The Babe,* as I can best reconstruct Leo's soliloquies in my mind, *the Babe could hit infield flies that were worth the price of a ticket. I mean, a second baseman would shout, "I got it," and wait and wait, and finally get tired of waiting, and hell if the damn thing wouldn't fall ten feet away from him. Babe would be on second by then, laughing his big ass off.* If Leo was alone, or simply passing time with a doorman, I would usually try to look away, embarrassed at being unmasked as another infatuated gawker. But often, a small circle of people would widen on the sidewalk. If you stepped into that circle, Leo might catch your eye for an instant and admit you to his reminisce with the flick of an eyelid. He would not trifle with proven material. *Mr. Rickey. Best man I ever played for, worst owner ever. He'd get up at four in the morning on his farm and call you. "Leo, what are you doing now?" "I'm skiing, Mr. Rickey," I'd tell him, "I'm walking the dog. I'm sleeping, for chrissakes, it's still dark."* But you see, that's when his brain was best.

---

★The *other* great Jewish left-hander in the National League. His autographed picture was a fixture over the rugeleh in many deli cases along Devon Avenue.

*Who's the best player you ever had?*

*Mays. By far. Best hitter, best base runner, best fielder, best arm, best atti-
tude. I wish he was my own son. Robinson was great, too, of course. He wanted
to stick a bat up my ass. Dusty Rhodes was the greatest for a season, nineteen
fifty-four. He hit, what, three forty-one as a damn pinch hitter, fifteen homers,
most of them with a hangover. Eddie Stanky was the greatest competitor. He'd
take a ball in the ribs to get a base. When he took over the White Sox this year,
he called me to say, "You taught me everything I know, Leo." I told him,
"Well, you're in a lotta trouble, pal."*

*Ernie Banks?* a woman once called out shyly.

*Awww, Mr. Cub, right? A real gentleman. A pleasure to go to the park
every day and know you can write in his name without thinking. Billy Williams,
too. We got a great group of guys here, lemme tell ya. Kessinger, Santo, Beckert,
Jenkins. You can be proud.*

Years later, I read Leo's autobiography.* Those street tutorials, of
course, had been rehearsals. When I interviewed Durocher about his
book, I told him about my fond memories of those tender summer
nights, when you could take a post-dinner stroll down Michigan Avenue
and find Leo Durocher under an apartment building awning, passing the
time with a smoke and a few stories. After all the tales I had heard about
Leo the Lip, Leo the Irascible, Leo the Shoe Wrecker, I confessed that I
was surprised to find him gracious and charming. Leo shot back with a
twinkle; for a moment it was possible to glimpse that Leo that good men
like Willie Mays and Billy Williams had played for so fiercely. "Ya know,
kid," he said, "you can't be happily married as many times as I have without being charming."

Leo Durocher's Cubs climbed to third place in 1967, and again in
1968, each year running behind Bob Gibson, Lou Brock, and the St.
Louis Cardinals. Ferguson Jenkins won 20 games each year (in what
were to be six successive seasons of winning 20 or more). In school on
early spring and late fall afternoons, we heard occasional home run
cheers ride in through the open windows from Wrigley Field; the occasions seemed to be multiplying. The clumsy, cuddlesome Cubs had
become contenders. But for the first time, I almost didn't notice; almost
didn't care.

War raged overseas. Unrest smoldered at home. I enlisted in the stu-

---

*The title, of course, was *Nice Guys Finish Last,* written with Ed Lynn.

dent revolution. With friends, I went to demonstrations and tried to get arrested; put out an unathorized student publication (what used to be called "underground"), and tried to get suspended. *Creative tension* was the tactic in Martin Luther King's strategy of nonviolence. It's not that I had lost any feeling for Williams, Santo, and Banks. But I was trying to earn a place in the heart of an order alongside Cheney, Schwerner, and Goodman. The times changed the proportion of those feelings.

Shortly before Opening Day at Wrigley Field in 1968, Dr. King was shot to death. He was standing on a motel balcony in Memphis, a scarce instant after leaning over the railing to call down to Chicago's Reverend Ben Branch (who was standing, in fact, alongside the Reverend Jesse Jackson), "Play 'Precious Lord' for me tonight, and play it real pretty." Now that his name has become a national holiday, it's easy to forget that at the time he died, King's pacifism was assailed. Frustrated and frenetic city kids mocked him as *De Lawd* for his King James cadences; they scorned his nonviolence as too slender a club to carry against racism. Sponsors of the war in Vietnam impugned his pacifism as naive and useless against violent ideologues seeking to spread their domain. But to pacifists, the most confounding question was not, "Are you willing to die for your country?" Pacifists were. Martin Luther King just had. It was, "Who are you willing to kill for your country?"

Within hours of Dr. King's death, the thunderclap of grief and anger had caught fire in neighborhoods all over America that had been left to rot. The next morning, the subway stop I entered to ride to school each day was patrolled by the Illinois National Guard. The soldiers, of course, were just a few years older than us students. Dan Quayle to the contrary, it was not likely that they had enlisted in the National Guard because they wanted to fight a war; but now they wore gas masks and carried rifles on their own streets. Photographs in the morning newspapers showed Dr. King, in a searing portrait, pealing his prophecy of just two nights before. "I've been to the mountaintop. And I have *seen* the Promised Land. And I may not get there with you. But we will get there together as a people!" Alongside was another scene: smoke plumes snaking up from streetfires in Washington, D.C., gray gashes of ash against the Capitol dome.

At school, the authorities quickly convened an assembly to commemorate Dr. King—and, to try to gather all students together in the same place, to be glanced over and patted down. Anger, injury, and uproar were in the air. I was asked to speak and felt awkward. I followed friends and classmates who each had a personal signature I lacked. *Speaking on behalf of all black students . . . Speaking on behalf of all Latino students . . . Speaking on behalf of the Senn High School Black Panther chapter . . .* A good-hearted assistant principal admonished, "And if we can be sure of one thing, it's that the man we mourn today would not want his death to be the reason for rioting and violence." But it sounded a bit smug on that morning to make speeches that purported to know what was in the mind of a man who had just been shot in his dazzling brain. As we filed out, the first of a dozen or more fire alarms that would be pulled that day sent us into the streets. We laughed at first over missing class, then fretted over the distress outside. No fires were set in our school. But shrouds of smoke drifted in from the blaze of shambling storefronts and apartment buildings clapped hard against the iron ribs of Chicago's west-side Elevated tracks. We had chanted, "Bring the war home! Bring the war home!" But we hadn't foreseen that it would scorch our own streets. Americans were burning Vietnamese villages while America was burning from the inside out. Watts and Chicago's west side, Harlem, Washington, and the heart of Detroit—the defoliation of America's inner cities made a lyric from Martha Reeves and the Vandellas twist in the heart:

> *They're dancin' up in Chicaaawgo!*
> *And down in New Orleans.*
> *Baltimore and DC now.*
> *Don't forget the Motor City! Don't forget the Motor City!*

And then in early June, Robert Kennedy won the California Democratic primary. My mother let me stay up late to watch him claim victory in the Western time zone. The Democrats would meet in Chicago later that summer, and when a lithe and delighted RFK slapped the podium to bid his supporters good night with the exhortation, "It's on to Chicago, and let's win there!" it kindled a kind of civic pride: history and mystery seemed destined to meet in the middle of the country, in the guts of America, the place where we lived. But within an hour, my mother shook me awake. My father, on the night patrol, was calling. Robert Kennedy had been shot. The next day, he died. Another assembly at school, another memorial speech to make. My father said gloomily, professional to professional, "At this rate, Ace, you're going to run out of material."

A long train ride, trundling over the back streets of Newark, Philadelphia, Camden, Wilmington, Baltimore, and D.C. now, brought

Robert Kennedy to be buried alongside his brother in Arlington National Cemetery. It was a Sunday night, as I remember. My mother had brought me downtown to the ad agency where she worked so that I could type and paste up (my mother, come to think of it, did most of the typing) the contents of the next issue of our underground magazine. We watched the graveside ceremony on a television in the reception area, and when the moment came for Robert Kennedy to be carried, in his coffin, across the moss and grass to his grave, my mother and I noticed in the same instant an unmistakably Kennedyesque pompadour among the grim company of pallbearers. It was Robert Kennedy's young son, Joe. "Oh, my God," said my mother softly, in the stillness of a Loop skyscraper late on a Sunday night. "Look at that poor little boy. Just your age, it looks like. And he's carrying his father's coffin."

By the end of the month, I was doing the same. My father died on the first day of summer vacation. I was downtown, buying a blue button-down shirt for my first day of work as a library stock boy ("Because, Scotty," he had told me the night before, "you dress for the job you want, not the one you have") when he stepped into the shower and had a stroke. He was forty-eight. That is too young to die— younger each year, it seems to me now—but not so young he hadn't recommended his own epitaph a few months earlier. My father had been in the hospital, sick from drinking, but insisting he had at least a few other ailments that couldn't be blamed on drink. "You know what's going to happen someday Ace, don't you?" he asked from the crook of his cranked-up hospital bed as we watched the Cubs lose an aimless late season, late afternoon game. "Someday, I'm gonna die. And everyone is going to realize something was wrong. And I'm gonna have them put it right there on my tombstone—" and here, my father chiseled the air in front of him:

SEE? I TOLD YOU I WAS SICK!

Uncle Jack Brickhouse and I delivered eulogies at a memorial before my father's burial. "Ernie was the kind of performer," said Uncle Jack, "who—as we say in baseball—could really *rrreach* back, and put that little extra something on a pitch. Throw that ball a little harder, just a little cuter, than he ever had before." My mother stifled a groan, then a giggle. "Did he have to put it quite that way?" she whispered. But it was the language, after all, in which Jack was most accomplished and sincere. My own remarks chagrin me now: pseudo-Sorensonian cadences and convertible sofa-bed sentences ("My father was a funny man, with a serious mind, who was serious about being funny") that were much too inspired by all the state funerals of the time. My father's showman's instincts had been sound: I had run short of original material. Only when a thickly accented rabbi recited the Lord's Prayer at the service's end was I able to whisper something truer to my mother: "Dad's got his accent down already."

My mother and I wanted to keep my father's casket closed at his funeral. It was, after all, the Jewish tradition. And even though my father had not been much devoted to religious traditions, a closed casket seemed more in keeping with his theatrical ones. As the funeral director had daintily explained, strokes set off small explosions in the brain. A man's face could get left looking lumpy. A man who so envied elegance—in Joe DiMaggio, in Adlai Stevenson, in my mother—shouldn't have to spend his last hour upon the stage looking ruptured and rubbery. When my grandmother Lillian said she wanted the casket open, we objected, playing a son's grief against a mother's. Gratefully, my Aunt Izetta took me aside and made greater sense. "You can't expect a mother," she said, "to believe her son is dead until she sees him."

The lid on my father's casket was lifted for the family with a low, soft *phhht!* of the kind you can hear on opening a can of coffee. My Uncle Ray and I held on to Lillian as she leaned down and lightly, lovingly, pressed her hand against my father's face, then brought her hand back against her cheek, ashen face to ashen face, the mother's hand trying to warm her son's cold forehead, flesh to flesh. "Look, he's not dead," she said finally, "he's just sleeping!" And then, when my father didn't stir, she brushed her fingers lightly through his stiffening hair. "At least they can't hurt him anymore," she said gently. "At least they can't hurt him." And then, my grandmother sank back a step as the marrow in her shins seemed to drain, and her whisper rasped. "Take me instead," said Lillian. "Oh, please, God, take me instead!" And then, she cried it out as a scalding commandment: *"Oh, God, take me instead! Take me instead! Promise, take me instead!"* It was a love so fierce and blunt it was forbidding. Like many grandmothers, I'm afraid, Lillian had become a slightly ridiculous figure to her grandchildren: crabby, bitter, and cranky with incomprehensible demands. There was suddenly a kind of grandeur in seeing her grieve over her son and hearing her impossible proposition offered so guilelessly. I had loved my father deeply. But I knew, without guilt or misgivings, that I was not prepared to love him as his mother did, to her own death.

To find clothes for my father to wear in the coffin, I had to sort through a thicket of unopened brown window envelopes containing unpaid bills and delinquency notices of increasing intensity. His closet also held a miscellany of rubber bugs and beetles, football bubblegum cards, clip-on bow ties in dots and stripes and Aloha prints, unopened aftershave bottles shaped like baseballs, and enigmatic notes on jokes, bits, and routines (Preg? boy says, "Well, if it doesn't throw you— pony?")* scrawled on index cards stowed in empty Benson & Hedges boxes. But in my father's dented silver cigarette box, I found what I knew to be his most beloved belonging: a pair of plastic, costume cufflinks, inset with plastic elephants with red saddles along their backs.

My mother had given the cufflinks to my father on a Valentine's Day years before, after they had been divorced about as long as they had been married, along with a card written in her looping, careful, Catholic schoolgirl script:

*Irish elephants never forget.*

They became his favorite things. He'd try to wear the cufflinks around my mother, shooting a shy smile as he inched up a sleeve and said, "See? See what I'm wearing?" Someone beautiful and funny had loved him once; and in a way, always would. I admired my parents all the more to see a sign of how a flicker of their love and loyalty could still warm their lives, years after another kind of love had gotten cold.

The death of a parent at any time in our lives is, in the parlance of the age, a passage. But when my father died in the dead center middle of the maelstrom of 1968, it seemed the decisive sign that the world would not wait for any of us to grow up. The anguish and the dying, overseas and in our own streets, was going on *now*. When the Democratic convention came to town a month later, I joined the throngs in Grant Park, partly to protest the war, partly to write about it for our underground newspaper, but mostly because I wanted to stand in what

---

*I remember this card because it represented a joke my father had lent to me to perform at Miriam Strilky's bas mitzvah party. It went: "Well, son, Mommy is pregnant. Would you like her to give you a little brother or a little sister?" And the kid says, "Gee, Dad, if it wouldn't throw her too much out of shape—how 'bout a pony?" The joke was received with alarm. My delivery must have been poor.

seemed the hot center of history. Mayor Daley actually gave a judi-
cious greeting to protesters when he opened the convention saying
that their presence at least signified that they saw the possibility of
hope in Chicago. "Some of the protesters may look odd and sound
loud," said the mayor. "But did you see them at the other (Republican)
convention?" Later, the mayor would dismiss the protesters in the parlance of those times as *outside agitators*, imported rabble rousers. All I
know is, I recognized an awful lot of other north-side students and
Cub fans.

When I heard canisters of tear gas clip the tops of trees before
bursting and exploding into sticky, sickly clouds, I went running toward
the spray; but arrived only in time to watch other people retch and run
off. I had a rasp in my own throat—but it was probably from lending
my own voice to singing "We Shall Overcome," "If I Had a Hammer,"
and chanting at the cameras catching light on the other side of the
police lines:

> *The whole world's watching!*
> *The whole world's watching!*

My grandfather on my mother's side of the family was on the other
side, a Chicago police sergeant at a south-side station house. He was
called away from his desk to stand in the cordons around the convention site; but I never saw him, and was grateful. If he had been ordered
into Grant Park, my grandfather might have been one of the police-
men who slipped their service badges into their pockets and began
beating the demonstrators with their nightsticks, as deliberately as
coaches hitting fly balls at batting practice. The welter of lights and
sirens, songs and chants, gave Grant Park the look of a stadium just
before the Army-Navy game. But the crowd wore rags and patches,
the fatigues of a protester's army. The police were withdrawn from the
park. National Guardsmen, closer to the protesters in age, and perhaps
even conviction, were trooped in, bayonets fixed, sharp steel blades
looking incongruous against the teenage tinge of their smooth chins.
It was silly to shout *pig* or *baby killer* at kitten-haired kids from Oak
Park and Wheaton who were deployed to protect the lounge of the
Conrad Hilton.

Sons and brothers were dying overseas; brothers and sisters
were dying in the streets at home. We had grown up enough to discover bigotry, brutality, and fear in our fathers and mothers. Some-

day, if we grew up a little more, we would also be able to detect it in ourselves.

By the time 1968 ended, I had railed against war, signed up for a revolution, gasped at tear gas, mourned martyrs, been singed by grief, and buried my father. I felt I had put away childish things. And by the time baseball season opened in 1969, I wanted a few of them back.

*Chapter 5*

# BEAR DOWN: PAPA BEAR, THE COMET, AND PIC

The Cubs were endearing, and called out our devotion—but not our identity. They were winsome in a city that still saw itself as swaggering. Fans flocked to Wrigley Field for sun and fun, peanuts and Cracker Jack, Cubs versus Cards, not life and death. For the gruff, tough, and gritty ways in which Chicagoans styled themselves, there were the Bears.

The Cubbies were the pastime of sunny afternoons in the ivy-clad Friendly Confines, watching a grassy game as mild and delightful as a schoolyard recess. But the Bears (who, until the 1970s, also played in Wrigley) were the emblems of a broad-shouldered city. Bear games were blood sport on wintry afternoons as gray and cold as concrete, in a brick icebox lined with dead leaves. The Cubs were diversion. The Bears, character. Who did the Cubs play? Feathery Cardinals and flighty Dodgers. *Da Bears* wrestled meat-Packers to the ground, crashed against Giants, taunted Vikings and Lions. The Cubs were weak beer and soft drinks sipped from paper cups. The Bears were bolts of whiskey gulped down straight, no chaser, from pig iron flasks. Snort and paw, dig in and grin, Bear Down—gggrrrhhh! We cheered for the Cubs, but strove to be Bears.

• • •

When my father died, friends retold the story of when I had entered his world two months ahead of expectation, frail, shriveled, and turning purple inside the glass-walled crib of an incubator. My father sought solace in a downtown bar with Uncle Jack Brickhouse and told him that my chances for survival seemed small.

"Oh, Christ, Jack, he's so tiny and ugly. So weak. Can't they put him back until he's done?" Uncle Jack excused himself to make a phone call. Half an hour later, a Bear walked up to the bar and ordered a martini. Said the Bear to my father, "Hang in there."

Uncle Jack had put out a call to George "Moose" Conner, 6 foot 6, 225 pounds, a future Hall of Fame tackle who had the build of one of the girders that held up the Lake Avenue El—an iron pillar in a Pucci suit. He told my father that he, too, had been born a couple of months ahead of time, and that his mother had nestled him inside the top drawer of a bedroom dresser and wrapped hot bricks close to his hatchling-thin limbs.

"But look at me now," he said. "A Bear. Ah, the kid'll be fine. They have lots better things these days than hot bricks. I'll pray for him. Wait and see. One day, he'll be a Bear."

And in boyish fantasies, so we were. Years later, a boy at my day camp would unsheathe his adolescent erection and shake it like some merry eyeless serpent. "Bronko wants a ride, men! Bronko wants a ride!"

He christened his apparatus after Bronko Nagurski, the running back of the 1930s who became just about the first emblem of Bearness. Another boy dubbed his Ditka, after Mike, the already famously pugnacious Bear then playing tight end; often as not in our Chic-awgo accents, the name came out *Dikka*. Other names we thought apt included Willie, for Willie Galimore, the velvet running back, and Rosey, for Roosevelt Taylor, a sly defensive back. And then, there was Richie Petibon, whose name could be shortened for even greater euphonious effect. At the age at which our members were beginning to misbehave with a mindlessness of their own, we hailed them hopefully with staunch, brawny, Bear names.

"Bronko bursts through!" we would exclaim, imitating Uncle Jack's play-by-play. "Willie is open! Dikka scores!" In contests, we would stand with our camp shorts lowered to our ankles, our name-tagged briefs at half-mast around our bald thighs. "Rosey bursts ahead! Willie leaps into the lead! Dikka's coming on strong! Wait—

here comes Petti-bone!"* Cub names, like Ernie, Billy, or Ron, roused images of endearment. Young summer camp braves craved Bear names—gggrrrhhh!

The Bears embodied brawn. For years, they seemed to esteem it above victory. During decades in which pro football's elegance was elongated by the forward pass, the Bears continued to regard quarterbacks who had to throw the ball to advance their team downfield as faintly pantywaist. Real Bears bore down, grinding out first downs with blood and bone, like kielbasa at a Pulaski Avenue deli.

Bear forefathers liked to tell stories about broken tackles and shattered teeth, hard yards gained on cold ground. George Halas liked to tell about the time Bronko Nagurski tucked his leather-helmeted head down and "blasted through two tacklers like they were old saloon doors," churned through the end zone—and then into a Wrigley brick wall. Trotting back to the sidelines, Halas says his fullback told him, "That last guy gave me a helluva lick, Coach."

The inevitably nicknamed Papa Bear was the most identifiable of the founders of the National Football League. He was a prideful man with a pork-pie hat of a face, famously flinty and frugal. In the early 1920s, pro football was often considered a counterfeit caricature of the college game, rogues in overgrown milltowns making a grotesquerie of the games of college gentlemen. Not coincidentally, the league seemed to expand along with the rise of organized crime. NFL franchises found a following in the major cities as the potential take from gambling swelled. The Bears signed the University of Illinois' legendary Galloping Ghost, running back Red Grange, in 1925, and played him just five days out of college, even though the rule then prevented pro teams from so much as speaking to college athletes. No regulation, however, prevented the Galloping Ghost from hiring a gambler to maintain his chastity. C. C. Pyle was a spats-and-stickpin *sportsman* when that was sports page speech for *bookmaker*. Pyle plotted a two-month barnstorming trail for Halas's club that ran along the rail lines snaking through Florida, New Orleans, and then out to the West Coast, stopping to scoop up lush pickings along the way, like Florida grapefruits or Navajo pottery.

Lesser men than George Halas might have permitted success to soften his affection for frugality. But George Halas was a substantial man.

---

*Richie Petibon would one day coach the Washington Redskins—a team with *a really* embarrassing name.

On an overnight train following a rough afternoon game, he pointedly held out a dollar from the cash envelope of his center, Ookie Miller. "What gives, coach?" Miller asked. "You kept the bottle of Absorbine Jr.," Halas told him. "But Bronk used some, too!" "Yes," Halas told Miller, "but you kept it."

Bear players liked to tell a story to rookies (either it never happened, or happened all the time) about a new player making a poor play at a critical moment. Halas, went the story, called the young man in from the field and put his arm around him. The crowd tamped down their boos, and cooed with admiration for Halas. But all the while Halas had his arm around the young man's shoulders, talking softly into his face, the players say he was telling him, "If you ever pull a dumb-ass play like that again, I'll ship your goddamn ass outta here." Whatta guy, Papa Bear.

Out-of-town sportswriters christened the Bears the Monsters of the Midway, in the mistaken assumption that they practiced along the University of Chicago's broad Midway Plaisance. But the nickname stuck because the *Monster* half seemed beautifully assigned. The Bears played the Portsmouth Spartans (later to become the Detroit Lions) in the 1932 title game, which had to be moved indoors because of treacherous weather. The players scrambled, pawed, and clawed on a field sawed-off to just eighty yards, on sod that had only recently been quit by a traveling circus. Bronko Nagurski told reporters that the lions and elephants had left the field soft and fragrant for the Bears and Spartans. The Bears won their second championship that day, 9 to 0.

(When I was a teenager, I met Bronko Nagurski, who was running a filling station in International Falls, Minnesota: a Bear in blue coveralls. He would lean down and enthrall small children by inviting them to slip their fingers inside his gold championship ring. Most could manage four, and the tip of their thumb.)

With Red Grange and Bronko Nagurski, a ghost and a stallion, running out of the same backfield, the Bears of the thirties both galloped and ground their opponents down. By the 1940s, they were a dynasty. The Bears won the last football championship before Pearl Harbor, in a game that is still a record for debacles. They defeated the Washington Redskins 73 to 0. The scoring got so galling that referees persuaded the Bears to run in their extra points, instead of kicking them through the goal posts; after ten touchdowns, the supply of footballs was running out. During World War II and its aftermath, the Bears won three more championships.

But by the 1960s, the Bears were beginning to look a period piece. Halas's Patton-style preference for brawn over finesse, the ground game over an air attack, defense over scoring, often seemed to make the team a throwback in times when Baltimore's Johnny Unitas and Washington's Sonny Jurgensen were electrifying play with audacious and accomplished passing.

The Bears did win a championship again, in 1963, beating, in all senses, the New York Giants 14 to 10. Significantly, the most memorable image from the game is not any Bear pass, catch, or run. It's a photo of Giant quarterback Y. A. Tittle, beaten, bald, gasping for breath, and hiding his head in his hands on the sidelines at Wrigley Field after his last pass had been picked off by the Bears' Richie Petibon in the Giant end zone. Tittle's long, agile fingers are battered, spattered by mud, and crumpled over his eyes. His breath is hardening into an icy gray cloud. Someone is holding his upturned helmet, with two gashes sliced near his 14, next to his knee. A snail trail of blood curling into his hood is on the top of his bruised, bald head. A Giant, bloodied and beheaded by the Bears.★

Tittle would remind reporters over the years that he had actually removed his helmet himself. He was beaten, he was tired, he wanted to go home. He had *not* been, as Bear fans preferred to retell the tale, figuratively decapitated. Record books will bear out that Y. A. Tittle was, by yards, a better quarterback than any Bear of the time; or for that matter, to the present. Still, the newsphoto of Y. A. Tittle has entered the archives of defeat. For Bear fans, it was a living illustration that Bear brawn could overpower glamorous Giants.†

I watched that championship game with some out-of-town cousins, but could not manage much exultation. As we were to feel again in 1968, sports was in history's shadow. The 1963 championship took place just a month after the killing of John F. Kennedy. Mourning was still our mood. And, anger that the men who ran professional football had not canceled their games the Sunday before the president's funeral. The new commissioner, Pete Rozelle, had issued a smarmy statement to the effect that the late president had been a fan. Surely, he

---

★This photo is often confused with a similiar one of a bloodied Y. A. Tittle on his knees titled "End of an Era." It was taken by Morris Berman in Pittsburgh a year later.

†The Giants of Frank Gifford, whose accomplishments and charisma had aggravated writer Fred Exley to envy—and ultimately became central to the inspiration for the book that was to become the classic, *A Fan's Notes*.

would have *wanted* the games to go on. Watching the gash in Y. A. Tittle's head, however innocuous, bleed on national TV still made me twitch with discomfort. It was a bad time to admire a head wound. My cousins offered congratulations, but I stayed cool. A man I idolized had been shot down. I was eleven years old and didn't want to care too much about some damn football game.

Within a short time, my capacity to care about sports would be generously restored. The Sunday afternoons of Bear games became important to me and my father. I would spend most of those days watching with him, in his one-room apartment above a beauty salon downtown. Around noon, he would trudge out to Ruby's Delicatessen, three blocks away, and return crinkling a paper sack packed with turkey and cheese sandwiches wrapped in plastic (kosher dill pickle spears laid diagonally across—the deli coat-of-arms), and twin tubs of potato salad and cole slaw. Packed into the crest of the sack was usually a waxed-paper pouch with chocolate chip or oatmeal cookies, sent along by Ruby himself ("Ruby said to me, 'Ernie, give these to the boy with my compliments. Tell him they're from an old family recipe—the Nabisco family' "). And underneath the sack, folded against my father's arms, the Sunday newspapers, often already flipped to the thick Sunday sports section anticipating that afternoon's game.

"Looks tough today, Ace," my father would say after digesting a column of newsprint. "The Pack. Always tough. Hornung, Taylor, five yards and a cloud of dust."

It was my assignment to cull the newspapers and prepare them to become part of our decor—separate the wheat of news, sports, comics, and arts from the chaff of auto, real estate ads, and the financial pages. The beauty salon owner who rented the place to my father required that 75 percent of the apartment's pockmarked linoleum floor be covered, to soften our footfalls from his customers (most of whom seemed to be already tucked up to their ears in bubble-topped cosmonaut-style hair dryers). My father and I went out to a rug store, but were sobered by the price tags. We continued on to a dime store, where my father estimated the costs of covering the floor with about ten of the all-weather doormats that were on sale. This calculation was also discouraging. But a British officer learns to contrive.

"Newspapers work just as well as carpets, Ace," he announced on the way home. "Paper is the world's best insulator. Besides, if you spill your coffee or something on a rug, what can you do? With newspapers, we can just crumple it up, reach for the *Trib*, and presto-chango, it's like living in the Ritz." Hearing himself, and seeing my face register, *Oh no—he's really serious*—made my father smile, but he persisted. "Plus, you can always learn something new, just by reading the floor."

So we spread newspapers over the floor, favoring the sports pages for their greater appearance of action photos and boldfaced headlines. True to my father's forecast (he picked up an odd-lot of facts from his reading, as if his mind had been rubbed with static electricity), newsprint was a fine insulator of sound and cold. And, unexpectedly handsome, at least when freshly taped into place, as if tiles had been inscribed with intricate tables of scores, statistics, and portraiture.

With the floors now snugly secured, we turned to the windows. The Sunday comics, we thought, lent a festive aspect to the alley the apartment overlooked. ("I thought that place was rented months ago," my father was once amused to overhear from the parking lot, "but the landlord still has newspapers over the windows.") When the sun shined through the windows each morning, it cascaded through a kaleidoscope of Popeye, Dick Tracy, and Li'l Abner. If we wanted to check the state of an overnight snowfall, we had only to turn back a flap on Andy Capp. "Not bad, Dad. Looks like just an inch or so." Once, I was present when the salon owner came upstairs to collect the rent. As my father wrote out his check at a card table, our landlord stood in the doorway and took in the surroundings with amazement. To an outsider, it must have looked something like a sarcophagus, in which the walls and floors had been encased in scrawls of obscure sacredness:

HALAS STAYS WITH WADE MARK TRAIL APARTMENT 3-G MORRIS SETS RECORD STEVE CANYON LECLERC KICKS BEARS PAST VIKES BRENDA STARR

In a way, it is disproportionate to remember the scene of these Bear Sundays with so much delight. My mother had applied so much care and good taste to make our modest one-bedroom apartment into a charming and decorous home. My father had employed only his ever-lasting twelve-year-old's ingenuity to concoct a kind of tree house—but I was a twelve-year-old myself. One night I got up from my father's sofa bed (he was miles away, pitching on a late-movie car commercial) to finish off some leftover cold spaghetti. I opened a drawer to find a fork—and put my hand into a pile of rubber spiders. *Yeeoow!* Alongside, a Harpo-like bicycle horn. *Hee-haw!* Of course, no fork. The only serving utensils around were bent tin spoons that had been "borrowed" from a nearby diner. Once, my mother had admonished my father that it was not healthy for a young boy to eat all of his meals in diners, delis, and after-hours Chinese restaurants. So on one Bear Sunday night, just before I went back to my mother, my father moved magazines off of his one-ring electric stove and fired up a drugstore frying pan.

"Honey," my mother asked carefully the next night as I bolted down her beautifully pink lamb chops, delicately crisp string beans, and a fluffy baked potato, "does Daddy ever cook for you?"

"Oh, sure, Mom. We had a great dinner last night. Dad fried up a whole pound of bacon. We made sandwiches out of it with Wonder Bread, and had some Pepsi and cupcakes, too." A moment later, I could hear my father protesting meekly as my mother laughed and gasped into the telephone. "All right, Ernest, you win! If that's your idea of cooking, take him to restaurants all the time!" As she hung up the phone, she was still shuddering and bewildered with laughter. "Your father," she shook her head in slow, amused amazement. "Honestly, sometimes. *Your father.*"

The season following the Bears' championship and the president's assassination began in sadness. Racing back to beat training camp curfew one night in Rensselaer, Indiana, running backs Bo Farrington and Willie Galimore were killed in an auto crash. Big Abe Gibron, than an assistant coach, awakened their teammates softly in their dormitory rooms. "We lost two of our boys," he sobbed. "We lost two of our boys." They played the season wearing black armbands. Bill Wade set a Bear record by completing 33 passes in a single game, and Johnny Morris caught 93 passes, which remains a club record. But the Bears sank behind Green Bay.

In 1965, good fortune arrived. In the same hour of the same day, the Bears drafted Dick Butkus, linebacker, out of the University of Illinois, and Gale Sayers, a running back from Kansas. They were praised as great. They would prove to be momentous. What are the odds on two bolts of lightning striking at the same place and time? It was like looking up on a Chicago bandstand in the 1930s to see Benny Goodman playing alongside Louis Armstrong.

Dick Butkus embodied Chicago. His bones could be girders for the Chicago River bridges. He was from a south-side Chicago Lithuanian neighborhood, too; a territory of wide, hard streets staunch with steel works and cement factories, church steeples and smokestacks. His teammate Brian Piccolo used to say that in practice he didn't fear running into Butkus's Bearlike, steel-driving forearms so much as his "boiling eyes." *Butt-kiss, kiss my ass.* No doubt in Vilnius or Cleveland there's a man named Butkus who paints miniature portraits on delicate porcelain tea cups. But it sounded like a name forged for a linebacker.

Butkus boiled and blazed; but his talent to amaze was often misunderstood. He was smart as well as fierce. No ferocity is successful if a player is faked out of a play and left to smolder where he cannot catch fire. Dick Butkus followed the ball. In the foggy tangle of limbs and loins that broke after a snap, Butkus could pick up the ball and anticipate where it was headed. When he tackled, he squeezed running backs like foot blisters, until they popped out with the ball and slapped down passes like . . . well, like a Bear batting away flies.

But in time, his ferociousness was taken with affection. In Sylvester Stallone's first *Rocky*, the bulldog Rocky Balboa pulls along on jogs is named Butkus—not because the pug is savage, but endearingly loyal; even cute. In fact, the fame Dick Butkus earned for brawn may have softened his disposition. He appeared in a spate of television ads and found he liked the lights and camaraderie of acting. Eager to extend his range beyond the gnawing and gnashing they wanted for beer ads and snow tire commercials, Butkus consulted drama coaches. For the first time in his life (which is a kind of hilarious confession for a celebrated college athlete) he read some of the great soliloquies, and liked them. He complained to writer Richard Whittingham, "Everybody gets the wrong impression about me. They think I hate everybody and that I eat my meat raw. But I can talk and read and write like ordinary people do, and I actually like to have my meat cooked."

Scarcely the credo of a teddy Bear. But Butkus's on-field image could be cruelly misleading. One Sunday afternoon, when the Bears played the Detroit Lions, a Lion named Chuck Hughes dropped hard on the ground during a pass play and did not get up. He'd had a heart attack. Not brought on by any block or hit, but, according to the autopsy, an enlarged heart. Newspaper photos the next day showed Da Bruiser Dick Butkus up on his toes over the body, waving his hands. The next day, ugly letters began to arrive at the Bears' office, addressed to *Butkus the Brute, Killer Butkus.* But Dick Butkus had been twenty feet away from Chuck Hughes when the photograph was snapped. He had not so much as brushed up against him during the play. He was on his toes, not in some dance, but to signal the referees running back from the failed pass downfield. An opponent had been hurt in a way even Dick Butkus had never seen.

Gale Sayers was the Comet—in all ways. Blindingly fast, beautiful to behold, impossible to grasp—and ultimately fragile. The best tacklers of the times looked like men running after their hats in a windstorm when they tried to bring down Gale Sayers. He often carried the ball in both hands, like a man bringing a ticking bomb out of a house, sharpening his speed with an exceptional talent to stop still, suddenly, on his toes, leaving tacklers grabbing at air from the lurch as he smoothly high-stepped off in another direction (when you begin to think about the punishment that would eventually shut down his knees, you have to figure in Gale Sayers's own speed). The great Jimmy Brown of the Cleveland Browns ran into tacklers and shed them, like tree branches scarcely scratching a truck. Gale Sayers ran around them, whirling downfield as powerfully and unpredictably as a Kansas tornado.

In December of his rookie year, on a Wrigley Field that had been thickened into a slurry by winter rain, Gale Sayers scored six times. It matched an old record set by Ernie Nevers of the (then) cross-town Chicago Cardinals in 1929 and Dub Jones of the Browns in 1951. The last came on a punt that fell into his hands on the 15 yard line. Sayers raced right and then, a step and squash from being run down by a San Francisco tackler, suddenly stopped on his toes and seemed to hover for an instant, on his heels, then surged left past a tableau of tacklers, fooling, felling them with sheer strokes of grace. Y. A. Tittle was by then an assistant coach for the 49ers and told reporters after the game, almost breathlessly, "I wonder how many Sayers would have scored if we hadn't set our defense to stop him." But Tittle was a gracious man. More surprising was George Halas, who did not lavish praise on his players, lest he have to pay for it later in a fattened contract: "I never saw such a thing in my life. It was the greatest performance ever by one man on a football field." Papa Bear sounded (almost) humbled.

The Green Bay Packers and Minnesota Vikings, who shared the Bears' lair in the NFL's central division, usually had better teams. But the Bears of Dick Butkus and Gale Sayers seemed emblems of different aspects of the city I loved. Butkus, the stalwart white southwest-sider, solid as brick and fast to leap at someone who dared to cross into his territory. Sayers, the black, elegant dazzler, agile as jazz, who lights up new territories. At a time when open housing and school integration protests were rubbing the city's sorest spots, the Bears of Butkus and Sayers, Da Bruiser and the Comet, were a team.

On the last day of the 1966 season, on the afternoon that Gale Sayers ran for 197 yards against the Minnesota Vikings, my father dared to open the one conversation he would ever have with me about sex. Inspired by

Sayers's astounding performance, we drove over to a small city park, listening to Uncle Jack Brickhouse rave on, post-game, on the radio. Dad threw out passes, which I fumbled or caught, and ran back to him in an unGale swivel step. *He's at the thirty! He's at the twenty! He's going! All! The! Way! Hey-Hey!* Clearly, my father was playing for time. He threw the ball until we could begin to smell chimney smoke and see bluish television lights glowing in windows as people settled in for the evening news. "Okay," he said, "time to get back to your mother." On the radio, Uncle Jack had gone home to Wilmette. A Sunday night sermon came on, which my father turned down.

"Okay now, Ace," he said suddenly, keeping his gaze on the road ahead. "Mommy says you've been having these wet dreams." My mother, in fact, had seen a damp stain in my bed clothing about a week before. "Is that coffee?" she asked me without conviction. "Yeah. Coffee. That's what it is," I said feebly. But now to my father, I just said, "Yes."

"You know what they are?" he asked.

"I think so."

"Well okay."

With visible relief, he turned back to the radio and found a sportscast. Father and son drove on, in mutual relieved contentment, listening to happy chat about Gale's great game.

Back in my mother's apartment, I was encouraged to go off into the bedroom while my parents, together again in the hallway, spoke with urgent softness. "Well, Ernest," asked my mother, "did you talk to him?"

"Oh yeah, honey."

"And?"

"It went fine, it went fine, it went great. Don't worry."

Later that night, as I lingered over a book report, my mother stood over me with a cup of tea.

"Did Daddy talk to you today?" she asked.

"Sure."

"Did he tell you about everything?"

"Sure. Like, what's everything?" Where my father was timorous and vague, my mother was concrete.

"Like, the sperm, egg, and the zygote."

"Well, sort of. Yeah, mostly. I mean, I've heard about that. Billy, Danny, Avi, Bruce. We talk about it. I don't know about that last thing, though."

"The zygote," said my mother, sitting down on the edge of the bed

with a smile that said, *Your father.* "But let's go back a little ways first."
The next hour or so was informative indeed.

I was getting old enough to be my father's pal, but also his critic. It is
impossible to hide a drinking problem from a prying adolescent in a
one-room apartment. The deception is in all the details. When my father
said, "I feel like a Coke," it was the occasion for him to wring some
small ice cubes from out of a tray in our pint-sized freezer and chime
them into a glass. He'd pour in the Coke, take a sip from the froth, and
then mutter, "Take it in the bathroom." He'd close the door, run the
water, and open the medicine cabinet, where, I knew, on the second
shelf, two bottles from the left, standing among his pills for ulcers and
sleeping and promoting regularity, there was a frost-colored, chrome-
capped plastic bottle on which my father had written, STOMACH MEDI-
CINE. Written it across strips of adhesive tape, in fact, so I would not miss
its medicinal purpose. *For Chrissakes, Dad,* I wanted to ask him, *why not
just put a skull and crossbones on it?* Of course, it was a flask. More than
once, I had unscrewed the top during one of my own reclusions in the
bathroom, sniffed it, sniffed nothing, sipped it, and realized it was vodka.
He kept another in his briefcase, and another I discovered after he died,
in the box in the closet where he stored underwear and socks. Really,
the details are more depressing to recount now than they were at the
time. At the time, I kept the secret of my father's drinking as he agreed
to keep the secret of my splotched sheets. Now, when I know where the
story winds up, I want to reach out, scream out, act up, keep my father—
I choose not to be subtle about saying this now—from killing himself.
But at the time, it seemed something more like a game, father and son
hiding small, scarlet secrets from my mother. *Are you sneaking a drink,
Dad? Yes. Know what that means, Dad? Yes.* Well, okay.

I had a Thursday night routine with my mother, the night before
weekly classroom reports were due and stores and public buildings
were open late. I would take the Michigan Avenue bus downtown to
Randolph Street, where my mother was working as a secretary and
occasional hand model at an advertising company. I'd stroll with a set of
waves past a fleet of gray-steel desks to find her, standing over a type-
writer in brown-eyed bemusement. *Darling!* Mother! *How are you!* Kiss,
kiss. *Are you hungry? Wouldn't you like to run downstairs?* Downstairs was
the Illinois Central Station, where I would roost on a stool inside a cir-

cular diner and inhale a hamburger slathered in mustard, onions, and neon-green relish, onion rings, french fries, and a chocolate milk shake, read the *Daily News*, watch people stride by, and try to place myself inside the overcoats and shoes of people rushing off after midafternoon trains: bearded college boys with bookbags, crew-cut Army recruits struggling under duffels, suburban lady shoppers gripping thickets of green Marshall Field's bags in each hand. One afternoon, I overheard a young woman with entrancing red hair having an emotional conversation with a friend; the words I specifically recall—I had never heard a woman say them, nor imagined that women knew them—were "He can fuck himself." For half an hour thereafter, I contemplated: *Is that possible? Should I ask my father or my mother about that?*

Then, I'd take the steps on a concrete staircase two at a time up to the entrance of the Chicago Public Library. There was a reading room on the third floor, overlooking Michigan Avenue, where you could fill out slips to receive softball-sized spools of microfilm that you could thread on to a machine with a screen that would show you the pages of old newspapers. My mother had taken me into the room one afternoon when I had to write a school report about the Japanese attack at Pearl Harbor.

"I was just about your age at the time," she said. "A schoolgirl. I remember the nuns telling us the next day, 'This means war,' and some of the girls began to cry, because they had older brothers who could be called away. Let's see what else was happening that day," she said, churning through the pages of an old *Tribune*. Maurice Rothschild's store had a sale on suits with two pairs of pants.

"Why would you want two pairs of pants?" I asked, and my mother mused.

"I guess in case you lose one. Let's look at sports," she said brightly. "I remember some story that in Washington, all the generals and admirals were at a football game, and they kept calling them over the loudspeaker. 'General, come to the office. Admiral, you are wanted at your office.' It was so much earlier in Hawaii, you see, and as the news was breaking, all the military people were watching the football game." An old *New York Times* confirmed: the Washington Redskins had defeated the Philadelphia Eagles 20 to 14 that day. But attendance thinned after all the professional soldiers had been called into work after the calamity a world away. "Imagine that," said my mother. "Like us, a lot of them probably had never even heard of Pearl Harbor. Then in one minute, the rest of their lives are changed."

The reading room had red leather seats, crackled and rubbed drab by a multitude of squirming backsides, and elegant old lights hanging down like long willow branches from the towering, dark, peeling ceilings. The bustling women at the archival periodical counter were gracious and efficient, chuckling a bit at taking in slips from a twelve-year-old who would ask, "Do you keep the *New York Post* on file, too? I'm looking for something by Murray Kempton." Now and again, they would send over a high school girl in a blue plaid skirt and tufted white kneesocks. "The nice lady over there," they would say, tossing russet hair behind their ears, "says you might know the answer to something I'm trying to find out . . ." My face would redden in a second, like the cigarette lighter under the radio in my father's car. "Uh, maybe. I'll try." Once, a dark-haired Noreen wearing a pouty daub of red lipstick thanked me by reaching out and squeezing my hand, ever so slightly, no harder than you might pat the head of a canary. But I felt a kind of percolation inside. "So sweet," she said. "You're just my little brother's age." Buck up. Bear down. *Aaarrgh* . . .

The Bears were no more progressive in outlook than other football teams. But George Halas might have been more sensitive than other owners to unpleasant publicity in a city in which he was considered a civic benefactor. Papa Bear didn't mind being called cheap or mean. Tightness and toughness, on the contrary, were useful to his reputation. But he worried that in a city besieged by blood-and-guts disputes over integrated schools and housing, a newspaper or do-good group might notice that when that civic institution known as the Bears played out of town, their black players roomed with other blacks, and whites with whites. It was still the custom of the times. Draft a black star, Ernie Banks, Minnie Minoso, or Gale Sayers, then sign someone to keep him company. The custom could even be bent to seem like common sense. A black star might feel more comfortable if he could confide in someone who knew the same stings of insult and bigotry.

But Halas also liked to be honored at brotherhood banquets, where he would remind the assembled that his National Football League had black players while major league baseball still barred the likes of Jackie Robinson, Josh Gibson, and Satchel Paige. Baseball people, he said, could carry on so haughtily about Robinson only because they had catered to prejudice for so long.

So, just before the Bears were to leave for an exhibition game in Birmingham, Halas sent out assistant coach Ed Cody to tell players that henceforth, they would room on the road according to position: running backs with running backs, tackles with tackles, kickers with kickers. The result, Cody intimated for those who did not grasp it immediately, would be *integration*, just like they saw on the news each night. No quotas, but also no exceptions. Pro football was expanding south, and the Birminghams of the world had to know that the best hotel in town would have to have room for Gale Sayers, as well as Dick Butkus. If a player couldn't accept that, Mr. Halas would try to accommodate him—elsewhere. But if the Bear experiment (and that, sadly, is what integrated roommates were considered in 1967) succeeded, Mr. Halas was sure that all professional sports teams would soon be obliged to follow. Who would keep a player of average skills if he refused to share a hotel room with a star like Dick Gordon or Gale Sayers? Thus did George Halas advance civil rights with the eloquence he commanded best: bluster and intimidation.

But Gale Sayers wondered about rooming with another starting running back. An older player might be annoyed by the special demands of Sayers's catapulting success and celebrity. In the literal crunch, Gale Sayers felt uneasy about coming home, on-the-road, to a player who might feel dimmed alongside the bright lights being shined on Sayers's fleet feet. So Sayers said, "What about Piccolo?"★

He already knew Brian Piccolo as the funny, effusive, and profane running back who had the locker between himself and pass receiver Dick Gordon. Players lockered according to number, the names running: SAYERS 40 PICCOLO 41 GORDON 45.

"Look at me," Piccolo would sometimes exclaim after practice, "a little old Southern boy between two big buck Negroes. I feel like the cream inside an Oreo cookie."

Piccolo was part of the same college draft that had brought Gale Sayers and Dick Butkus to the Bears. Pic, in fact, had gained more yards than any other college runner in his senior year at small Wake Forest College in North Carolina. But pro teams were not impressed by the size of his school, or, for that matter, Piccolo's own size (about 5'11, 200 pounds) and speed. Another one of his monologues recreated the time an NFL scout hid him away in an Atlanta hotel suite on

---

★Today, black or Latin athletes might feel inclined to room with one another in an act of common consciousness. But the issue rarely arises in times of millionaire athletes with contracts mandating private rooms and suites.

the day of the draft, so that the rival American Football League would not find and sign him first. "Anything you want, kid, order it up, it's on the tab," the scout told Piccolo. He hadn't expected to be picked in the first round; or the second. But as the picks proceeded through the seventh, eighth, and ninth rounds, he began to squirm for himself, and the scout signing his food and drink tab. By the time the afternoon ended, 440 college players drafted, and none of them Brian Piccolo, he was mortified. "I would have offered to pay the room tab, too," he told friends, "except that I felt I might never play pro ball and couldn't spend money like that."

But Piccolo was still on the roster for a couple of post-season college All-Star games. The college stars whose pro futures were already signed and secure often played with only half a head of steam; they had little left to prove, and much to risk with an injury. But Brian Piccolo blocked like a man possessed—by anxiety. The North-South game of 1964 was the first time Piccolo encountered the most sensational college runner of the time, and as he said in a recording later turned over to writer Jeannie Morris, "One guy I wasn't impressed with—personality-wise—was the Kansas Comet, Gale Sayers. What an arrogant son of a bitch. I didn't see him speak to a soul the whole week we were together."*

Wouldn't any man look a bit plodding, pudgy, pale, and stodgy standing next to SAYERS 40? Brian Piccolo made everyman's chagrin into a quip against himself. "Oh, touch me," he would call out to friends, "I'm good luck. I'm the running back signed by the Bears after they gave all their money to Sayers. Great career move."

Gale Sayers, as Piccolo began to learn, was hardly arrogant. He was a religious man who felt that his unaccountable grace had to be paid back with hard work and humility. His off-field shyness was a kind of recompense he felt he owed for all the attention he received between the white lines. Sayers soared, smiled, then was silent about it. After games, in fact, it was sometimes Piccolo who captured the locker room by recounting how Sayers's astonishing runs had rewarded Piccolo with playing time.

---

*Piccolo began to reminisce and reflect into a tape recorder early in 1970, hoping to write a book about recovering from cancer. After his death, his wife, Joy Piccolo, turned those tapes over to writer Jeannie Morris, then married to Johnny Morris, a Bear pass receiver who had become a sportscaster, as did Jeannie. Her 1971 book, *Brian Piccolo: A Short Season*, is still a heart-piercing read, the adult version of what was to become the famous television movie, *Brian's Song*.

"Gale will break off some sixty-yard run, come back, and look a little winded. I'll go over to Cody and say, 'Hey, Ed, great run, do you think Gale could use a blow?'★ Ed will go running over to Gale, and say, 'Gale, great run, great run, man. Can you use a blow?' And Gale will hold himself tight and say, 'Yeah, Ed, maybe. Maybe I can use a little blow' So Cody tells Halas, and Halas shouts down the line, 'Piccolo, get the hell in there! Sayers needs a blow!' So I'll go in, they'll run off one play into the line, and I'll get flattened, and while I'm getting up with my head ringing, I hear Halas shouting, 'Piccolo, get the hell out of there! Sayers wants to go back!' "

Superficially, there was much to aggravate their differences. Piccolo was Southern, white, cheerfully profane, and proud of all of it. Sayers was Northern, black, innately shy, and proudly, deliberately humble. More pertinent yet for football players, Sayers was the star, above all others; Piccolo was a sub, at best. Sayers was regarded by the Bears as indispensable, the player of a lifetime. Piccolo was disposable, a player added on a whim.

And yet, the intuition that prompted Sayers to ask, "What about Piccolo?" would be borne out. Each man had a sense of being a stranger in his surroundings; each could still evince a sense of isolation. Sayers had grown up in Omaha, at a time when black families were rare. His singular talent alone put him in lonely company. Piccolo was from a garrulous Italian Catholic family in Ft. Lauderdale, at a time when the city was smaller, and ethnic families still stood out; were still considered, no matter how successful, folks on the "other side of town." Piccolo found companionship in sports after his older brothers left home. His parents were, in a way, *too* inseparable, working and rubbing up against one another at all hours at their successful restaurant—and alarming the town with epic, public quarrels. For all his conviviality, there are portions of the tapes Piccolo left for Jeannie Morris that more than hint at loneliness:

> *From the time I was a sophomore in high school, I was pretty much on my own . . . A close-knit family doesn't always turn out so well. I think being on my own had a hell of a lot to do with my growing up quickly. Either I did it or it didn't get done.*

The sense of being on his own may have helped instill a sense of empathy in Brian Piccolo; and a gift for friendship. At Wake Forest, he didn't

---

★In 1965, "a blow" was more commonly taken to mean "a breather."

major in physical education, a course much favored by athletes for the favors those instructors were believed to be ready to do them. He studied drama, with professors who pointedly made the bluff, congenial jock portray lonely, bespectacled intellectuals and—at least once, in Robert Anderson's *Tea and Sympathy*—a sympathetic, effeminate hero ("Turns out," he said, "I can be a hell of a queer"). He was interested enough in acting to spend the summer after his junior year in a local theater company.

He also applied his empathy at close range. The equipment manager of the team at Wake was something of a tubby fussbudget whom the players enjoyed making the butt of pranks and jokes; Piccolo made him his friend and made the young man's life more bearable. Since high school, Piccolo had been determined to marry a young classmate named Joy Murrath, whose younger sister, Carol, had cerebral palsy and lived in a wheelchair. Like many athletes, he found himself deeply affected by the courage of someone who must struggle against physical limitations. He carried Carol into church on Sundays, took her along on dates with Joy, and helped her swim, her arms locked around his neck, her neck on his back, even during those times he and Joy were on the outs with each other. When Joy Murrath finally accepted an engagement ring—Brian Piccolo gave a ring to Carol, too. If his attentions to Carol were some contrivance to attract Joy, they continued to the end of his life.

Sayers and Piccolo each had other, better friends on the team. But as they began to share rooms on the road, they found themselves getting bound up in each other's lives. Sayers—to a degree that is incomprehensible to today's athletes who avail themselves (and should) of consultants, accountants, and agents—was often on his own in the glare of fame. The team could screen out only so much. When the room phone rang with entreaties for interviews, real and phony, offers for investment, valid and counterfeit, fans beseeching Sayers for autographs and cranks seeking him for their psychoses, PICCOLO 41, off the field if not on, blocked for SAYERS 40. They developed, in a sense, a Moses and Aaron relationship, with Piccolo, who loved to talk, doing what he loved for a teammate who often seemed pained on having to begin a sentence with "I." "Gale can't come to the phone right now, but I know he thinks . . ." Sayers opened himself to Piccolo's warmth and was charmed by his impiety. Piccolo was touched by Sayers's shyness and taken by his decency. Tagging along with the Comet let him glimpse greatness. Sayers and Piccolo had been prize athletes since their teens.

Even as young, second-year pro players, they recognized something rare in each other.

There were other interracial roommates around the league. But because of Sayers's celebrity, none were better known. And because of Piccolo's often scabrous humor, none were better advertised. When reporters asked, in so many ways, "You're a Southerner. How do you feel about rooming with a black man? How do you feel about rooming with Gale Sayers?" Piccolo had concocted and rehearsed an answer that both shocked and mocked in the manner, if not the language, of Lenny Bruce. "Hell no, I don't mind rooming with Sayers," he often said—it was his best-known quote—"just as long as he doesn't use the bathroom." When defensive back Bennie MacRae became the first black captain of the Bears, Piccolo announced in the locker room, "It's about goddamn time one of us soul brothers got a break around here." The Bears' "experiment" gave both the star and the sub an equal stake in making their conspicuous friendship work—and gave Piccolo a value to the team *off* the field he did not always have on. A lesser man might have felt diminished by that.

P̶ic's everyday humor was more profane and picturesque than the movie of his death and friendship could safely portray on television (although Jeannie Morris's book didn't blanch). In the 1960s, Piccolo's raillery could make people shriek and laugh, before they could squirm about laughing. Today, much of it may sound heavy-handed and not particularly funny. His constant nickname for Sayers was Magic—for *Black* Magic, of course. When they ran sprints, he urged his friend to "Move that big old black ass of yours!" And, then, after Gale surged past, he'd call out, "Hey, Super Nigger, you trying to kill this Dago or what?" Quarterback Jack Concannon was *a dumb Mick*, and teammates Ralph Kurek and Dick Butkus were *the dumb Polacks*, even though Butkus, at any rate, was Lithuanian. "You're still a dumb Polack to me," said Piccolo, on being so informed. Once, Brian flayed an official with an Italian name over a call he thought was bad. "Hey, are you sure you're a Dago? You've gotta be a Polack. No Dago would make a call like that!"

Is it necessary to add?—the men so assailed were his best friends on the Bears. His sarcasm was made easier to enjoy by his own self-effacement. Once, Piccolo admired a pair of cufflinks an admirer had sent Sayers, 40 set on a gold base. Sayers sought out the same jeweler and gave his friend a few sets stamped 41. "Oh, thanks Magic, just what I need," Piccolo said. "IQ cufflinks."

It was a sequence of misfortunes that would make Brian Piccolo and Gale Sayers not only roommates, but metaphors for loss, friendship, and determination. In the ninth game of the 1968 season, the game just after Gale Sayers had gained 205 yards against the Green Bay Packers, he was tackled around the knees—cleanly, fairly, it's always pointed out—by safety Kermit Alexander of the San Francisco 49ers. But the ligaments of Sayers's right knee were wrenched out of socket and torn. It is still painful to see replays of the tackle—a comet shot to the ground. And today, we know how that tackle is the first installment in a story that winds through suffering, recovery, shock, and loss, before it ends in death.

Ligament damage is the injury that's often most feared by finesse athletes. Broken bones can be set to knit back together, and even be stronger, Hemingway-style, at all the broken places. But ligaments are fibrous, rubbery, and tricky, somewhere between bone and gelatin. Aaron went in for Moses—and did well. Piccolo caught 7 passes against the Atlanta Falcons the next week, then ran for 112 yards against the New Orleans Saints the week after that, finally, after three years, winning a start in the National Football League. As the season ended, the Bear coaches began to ponder the possibilities of running Gale Sayers and Brian Piccolo out of the same backfield the next year. If Sayers was able to bring back his knee, Piccolo, who ran his patterns and held on to the ball when he was hit, might be the reliable kind of back they needed to give Sayers a breath every four plays or so.

The movie, *Brian's Song*, greatly exaggerates the actual time Piccolo spent pushing Sayers through an exercise regimen to build back the ligaments and surrounding muscle; Sayers spent much more time, of course, with doctors, physical therapists, and professional trainers. But Piccolo's grating, cheerful goad was a part of the program. "C'mon, one more time, Super Nig, crush my Dago ass, one, two, one, two." If friends, meaning only to flatter, referred to Sayers as a great natural athlete, Pic instructed them: "I've never seen a man work harder in my life." When Sayers returned to the field in 1969, he didn't so much as wear an elastic bandage on his right knee, which deeply impressed Piccolo. "Magic," he said, "isn't gonna give that injury equal opportunity."

But 1969 proved to be just about the worst year of Bear history. Halas had stepped down as coach. His successors were acolytes, not head coaches. The team alternated three quarterbacks, choosing, from week to week, between various options of inadequacy. The frustration was heightened by the feeling that between Butkus and Sayers, the Bears nevertheless had the transcendent stars, offensive and defensive, of the times. Sayers's knee was, perhaps, stronger than ever, although the ligament itself had seemed to lose some of the *squish* necessary to run and cut like Gale Sayers. He still led the league in rushing, but this year, it was by serving hard time, bashing into and over runners instead of eluding them.

In a game against the Atlanta Falcons on a blistering Georgia afternoon in mid-November, Piccolo told the coaches that he was gasping for breath and needed to leave the game. They were startled along the sidelines, and even a little scared. Piccolo had struggled for years to play alongside Sayers—and now was asking to be taken out. Back in Chicago, he had an X-ray taken and saw a shadow darkening his left lung and pectoral muscles. "I'm no expert," he told the orthopedic surgeon who was the Bears' team doctor, "but that's not supposed to be there." It was, of course, cancer: an embryonic cell carcinoma about the size of a tangerine. When I witlessly asked Gale Sayers, years later, was it like hearing that someone in your own family had cancer? Sayers shook his head, ever so slowly. "No. It *was* hearing that a member of your own family had cancer."

In the Bears' locker room just before game time on November 23, Sayers spoke about Piccolo. The team knew, of course, that Pic was sick; a troupe had even invaded his hospital room the afternoon before, with a bottle of scotch they hid from the hospital staff—until doctors made them share it. But George Halas's son-in-law, a gregarious retired personnel executive named Ed McCaskey, had called Sayers early Sunday to say that the team was anxious about Piccolo and looked to Gale to say something about the rumors that were abounding in the press. Gale agreed. McCaskey, a warm-hearted man who was a particular friend of both players, drafted some suggested remarks, which Sayers more or less gave with his own annotations: "Yes, it's true. Brian has cancer. He's going to be operated on next week. Who knows if he'll ever be able to play again? But he will always be our teammate. The courage he shows in that hospital is the kind of courage we need on the field. I know it's corny, but we're football players, and let's give Brian our best by playing our best and giving him the game ball!" Big, strong men blubbered without apology, wiping tears away with the edge of short blue sleeves stretched over their shoulder pads. The Bears broke from their locker room, determined and grim. And then they lost to the Baltimore Colts on a last-second field goal, 24 to 21. When the team shuffled and tumbled in to Piccolo's hospital room after the game, carting pizza, beer, but no game ball, Piccolo went into a comic rage at Sayers. "Goddammit, Magic! If you couldn't get me the game ball, why couldn't you at least bring back the goddamn cash?"

The operation was a success—but the cancer spread. The public reports at the time said that the growth had been removed, doctors hoped for a full recovery, and Brian Piccolo hoped to play football again. But even those reports were tinged with qualification. As the season ground down dismally for the Bears, signs that Piccolo's recovery was questionable began to accumulate.

One of the first, interestingly, was that George Halas became generous. He had been known for bullying injured Bears out of seeking a second opinion from some out-of-town specialist. "Whattsa matter?" he would rail. "You don't like the doctors in Chicago? We have the best doctors in the world here. And you wanna go to some small town in Minnesota? Not on my dime, you don't!" But right after the first tests had been taken, Halas called Piccolo in his hospital bed to say that he was due nothing but the best, and the best was at Sloan-Kettering in New York. The team would pay all of the bills for his illness, would pay Pic his full salary, and all available contract incentives, despite, of course, the fact that he had played in only a few games. "Just get well and come back to us," said Halas, who then called Joy Piccolo to say, "You will not want for anything. You are not to worry. We will pay whatever it takes to make Brian well and make you and your three daughters comfortable."

Gale Sayers took an overnight flight from San Francisco to New York in early December to see Piccolo, who had already begun to work his cheerful impudence on the ward. He prowled the halls with his trim athlete's legs—the nurses hailed as he walked by, "Halloo, Sexy!"—repeating jokes, chatting up children, and sharing honey cookies and cannoli sent to him by friends and family. All of that—and Gale Sayers came to visit, too. Piccolo showed him the long, purpling scar running the length of his sternum. "Beats the one on your knee, doesn't it, Magic?"

He was released in January, to begin chemotherapy treatments back in Chicago. Doctors approved a trip for him the next month: Brian took Joy and their three young daughters, Lori, Kristi, and Traci, out to Arizona where he had been invited to represent Chicago in a celebrity charity golf tournament sponsored by an airline. Piccolo looked forward to warming his muscles in some sunlight; and his partner was the Cubs'

Ernie Banks. The two men took to one another at first laugh. Although Banks was not known to ever tell an off-color story, few men laughed harder at risqué jokes, perhaps because few people, save for Brian Piccolo, had the cheek to tell them to Ernie Banks. But Ernie, who was thirty-nine and alert to the fatigue and grinding in his own bones, was alarmed to hear the much younger Piccolo wheeze as they walked the course. The organizers overlooked strict tournament rules to give the aging Ernie Banks a golf cart to drive between shots. After the third hole, when the number of spectators looking on at their Banks-Piccolo team had dwindled, Ernie would pull up to his partner. "Take a seat, ol' buddy, why don't you, and let the folks see us together." Years later, Ernie would learn from Jeannie Morris's book that one night during that tournament, Brian Piccolo had run his hand along his scar and felt a lump bumping up through the flesh over his sternum. Joy Piccolo felt her knees give way. "What is it?" she asked in a small voice; and Brian Piccolo barked out in apprehension and resignation, "What the hell do you think it is?"

The cancer inside Brian Piccolo's chest was growing faster than doctors could carve or burn it away. In March, Piccolo underwent a radical mastectomy. Gale Sayers came out for the surgery, and, when it was discovered that he and Piccolo shared the same blood type—"I always knew you were a brother, Pic!"—donated two pints. Awakening in a haze of pain and fog, Piccolo told the audience at his bedside, and would tell nurses and visitors over the following weeks, "I have a sudden craving for chitlins." But soon thereafter, when he and Sayers were alone, Pic raised up his hospital gown to show his old roommate the trail of scars and sutures encircling a patched gouge in the flesh of his chest above his heart. He looked up, more in wonderment than anger or despondency. "Ain't this a bitch, Magic?" he asked. *"Ain't this a bitch?"*

It was also not enough. Sayers and Ed McCaskey were with Piccolo when doctors came in to say that the cancer had not been stopped. It was growing into his left lung. His lung, said the doctors, would have to be removed. The doctors had asked Sayers and Ed McCaskey to try to prepare their friend for the fact that he would never play football again; but Brian, they discovered, was ahead of them on that score, telling them, "I know there are more important things, aren't there?"

The next month, Gale Sayers flew to New York to receive the George S. Halas Award from the Professional Football Writers Association for the Most Courageous Player of the 1969 season. He had returned from major surgery after major injury to win the rushing title once again. More telling yet, to do so he had become a different kind of runner. Where once he had slashed, turned, whirled, and disappeared, he now had to bash, burst, and twist tacklers off of his shoulders and knees. It was a bit like watching Zorro retooling his skills to become more like John Henry. Skeptical coaches and football writers had often predicted that a runner as dependent on finesse and evasion as Sayers would founder after a major injury. They demeaned his elegance as being delicate, brittle, and too breakable to trust. Such an injury came—but they had discounted Sayers's stamina and gumption. His physical gifts may have been brought down to the nearly ordinary, but he asserted them now with extraordinary determination and skill. The vote of the football writers that year was unanimous.

But an idea had been building in Sayers. There was no doubt now that Brian Piccolo was dying. In the movie, of course, James Caan plays him as doomed, but determined and immaculate; which, to be sure, is easier to watch. Off-screen, however, cancer often doesn't leave people the dignity of looking like James Caan and speaking with the assistance of top screenwriters. Piccolo turned white and red, as the cancerous tumors pinched his liver and heart, perspired and squirmed and swore. A smell of death settled on his room. It was nothing ethereal, but the harsh smell of a man whose insides are dying, inch by inch.

Sayers sought out Ed McCaskey for advice, and he once again helped Gale draft some remarks. It doesn't detract from Sayers's sincerity to note that he had help. George Bush had more help from Peggy Noonan to utter, "Read my lips . . ." The remarks Gale Sayers delivered that night are worth extended quotation, because they have become, along with Lou Gehrig's farewell at Yankee Stadium, among the best-known speeches of modern sports; words grown men and women can weep over without apology, each time the story is retold (or, replayed on a late movie). Sayers began with an impeccable and original gesture: he told the writers that the person who should receive their award as the most courageous man in football was Brian Piccolo. That night, Moses spoke about Aaron:

> *He has the heart of a giant and that rare form of courage that allows him to kid himself and his opponent—cancer. He has the mental attitude that spells out the word courage twenty-four hours a day. You flatter me by giving me this award. But I tell you here and now that I accept it for Brian Piccolo. Brian Piccolo is the man of courage who*

*should receive this award. It is mine tonight. It is Brian Piccolo's tomorrow. I love Brian Piccolo, and I'd like all of you to love him, too. Tonight, when you hit your knees to pray, please ask God to love him, too.*

When Sayers phoned him the next morning, Piccolo, who had heard the words read to him, was ready with a quiet jibe. "Magic," he said, "if you were here right now, I'd kiss you." And Sayers said, "In that case, we'll be over tomorrow." Within three weeks, Brian Piccolo died at the Sloan-Kettering Center. He was twenty-six years old, had gained 927 yards on 258 carries, had three children, and scored four touchdowns. Joy Piccolo told Jeannie Morris that the last words she heard from her husband were when he struggled to sit up in bed, straining at the tubes plunged into his nose and piercing his penis, his gorgeous dark eyes, widening and shining like downy brown velvet as he blinked. "Can you believe it, Joy? Can you believe this shit?"

Huge Bears, their shoulders still immense and shuddering in shapeless black suits, carried Brian Piccolo's body to his grave. After his death, the Bears on field moved from tragedy to misfortune—and then to farce.

The very next year, Gale Sayers got hit on his left knee in a game against the St. Louis Cardinals, much in the way his right knee had been wrenched out of shape in 1968. He was still a young man, but men have only so many miracle recoveries in their bones—or ligaments. Gale tried to return in 1971, but the reports from training camp were not encouraging. When he was put in for a few running plays, fans wanted to look away. He took a pitchout, tried a stutter-step to paralyze the advance of onrushing tacklers—and found his knees did not have the elastic to propel him left or right. Then, he took a handoff to run into the line—and found they lacked the steel to drive him through a tackler. I was watching with my mother, who said it reminded her of the night she and her mother had listened to Joe Louis being slapped through the ropes of a boxing ring by an opponent she could not recall. "We cried like the president had died," she said. "We didn't want to listen, but it was over before we could turn it off." The great Gale Sayers left football that year.

The most famously ferocious of the Bears, Dick Butkus, also injured both his knees in 1970. George Halas, who had been so generous when he understood that Brian Piccolo's pains were in a realm beyond football, ridiculed and resisted Butkus's efforts to find more expert medical care for the damage the fury he brought to the game had inflicted on his own knees. The idea that Dick Butkus, who had played with almost as much pain as he had inflicted, should have somehow turned timorous was, of course, preposterous. But George Halas was a hard man who was becoming bitter. He had made his son, Mugs, the club's president; and then his son pressed him, as only a son can, to change some of his cantankerous ways. Papa Bear had seen his favorite runner broken on his own field; one of the few players he had ever visibly permitted to reach into his heart had died; and now Butkus, a man who seemed to embody his own temperament as certifiably as any son, told reporters that Halas had become cruelly cheap. "He can take what he said," Butkus announced at a fan luncheon, "and shove it." The line was hardly original—Mike Ditka, in fact, had most memorably said, "Halas throws around nickels like they were manhole covers"—but Butkus's delivery was impeccable. He left football for acting in 1973.

Both Butkus and Sayers were inducted into football's Hall of Fame as soon as they appeared on the ballot, which reminded some fans only how far the franchise had fallen. Sayers was presented by George Halas, whose remarks that day also seemed to betray the hand of Ed McCaskey. He was touched, said Halas, to be asked to present Gale Sayers to the Hall of Fame. "I do so with love and joy. I loved to watch him, and he brought joy to so many who watched him play."

A team with two such special talents should have won something more. But Sayers and Butkus really only had about two years in which each was able to play in full health, and the Halases were never able—or willing to pay—to surround them with the sort of support that could make the best use of Sayers's and Butkus's great gifts. The Bears became a kind of burlesque as the seventies wore on. Sayers and Butkus looked all the more like unaccountable blessings as the club signed a succession of forgettable talent at quarterback, named Avellini, Bukich, Huff, and Douglass. My stepfather called me up on a Sunday night.

"Didja see Bobby Douglass today?" (Bobby Douglass, a big viking of a quarterback from Kansas, was the butt of the joke as told that day; but any of the other quarterbacks' names could be inserted to identical result.)

"Not after a while. I couldn't watch."

"He threw another interception. They took him out of the game. He took off his helmet, threw it at the ground—and missed."

In an imprecise way, the Bears' many downfalls and miscarriages even mirrored our anxieties about the city we loved. A city that was such a big, tough, beautiful melange of so much was being stifled by the loudest louts and slowest touts. It deserved better.

The real-life story of Brian Piccolo and Gale Sayers was lamentably close to the success of the treacley movie and book of *Love Story*; for too many people, I thought, who were not necessarily sports fans, and certainly not bred in Bear devotions, it seemed the same story, recast—with more attractive characters at the center. *Love Story* in cleats. *What can you say about a running back who dies at the age of twenty-six?*

But even from the distance of the stands, fans became caught up in a fierce, real-stuff story of two friends, cajoling and contending with professional and actual death. We saw how it softened hard men, gave steel to the tenderness of kind ones, and encouraged people watching to have the courage of their kindness. The Bears fumbled and foundered, made fans wince and wonder. But for many of us who followed them, there was a feeling that when the game got suddenly real, the Bears, of all teams, had gotten it just right.

*Chapter 6*

# BLUE FLU: THE SUMMER OF 1969

For fans and agnostics alike, the 1969 race between the Chicago Cubs and New York Mets (and I wince even now on noticing that I still reverse the final order of their finish) poses a continuing philosophical confoundment: do good teams *win* championships, or do other teams *lose* them? Nineteen sixty-nine was the season that cast the Cub reputation for boobery into bronze. It made a fable of incompetence seem an unalterable fate. It made the finish of any Cub season seem as immutable as the last act of Hamlet. The children of the Age of Aquarius didn't believe in the Domino Theory, unjust laws, land wars in Asia, the addictive power of drugs, and music with no point or beat. We believed that the times, they were a–changin', all you need is love, and dancing in the streets. Who among us could ever credit curses?

Cub fans.

Uncle Jack, a sunburn on his blunt, bald head flashing like an emergency light out of the folds of his polo coat in a late March snow, bought a birthday lunch for me a few days after he returned from spring training. It was several days before Opening Day at Wrigley Field.

"Santo's smacking the ball a ton," he said. "Billy is as steady as ever. Kessinger, Beckert, work together like a Swiss watch. Fergie, Hands, Holtzman—I swear to God, they look as good as Gibson, Hands, and Briles."

"Is anyone as good as Gibson?"

"No," said Uncle Jack after a pause. Bob Gibson and the St. Louis Cardinals had won the National League pennant the year before, Gibson winning 22 games, losing 9, and establishing a new record low for Earned Run Average: 1.12. Denny McLain of the World Champion Detroit Tigers, by contrast, had won 31 games and lost just 6—but his Earned Run Average was almost a full point higher, 1.96. Neither mark has been equaled since.★

"Of course not," he continued. "Nobody's Gibby. But Fergie's his own kind of great. And the Cards need punch. Lou Brock can't run the damn ball home every time. Santo, Billy, Ernie—who else has a heart of the order with that kind of power? The Pirates have Stargell and Clemente. But they don't play in Wrigley Field. Atlanta has Aaron and Cepeda, of course. And Frisco has McCovey and Bonds. But they're in the west, under this new alignment. The Cards could be trouble. Maybe Philadelphia, if Richie Allen gets hot. But—hey, I don't want to jinx it—but hey, I think ol' Ernie Banks is gonna get his chance after all these years."

The slightest shake of his glass was enough to signal for a new bourbon. "So, Uncle Jack," I asked, "if the Cubs get into the World Series, you get to call it?"

"If they're smart," he smiled. "I haven't worked a World Series in ten years. They have to want me."

"They'll want you."

A black-aproned waitress glowed as the ice in a fresh drink chimed pleasantly on a lazy, late afternoon. "This is compliments of the manager, Mr. Brickhouse. Can I bring something else for your son?"

"Not my son," Uncle Jack said with his eyes still fixed on me across the table. "No son of mine could have hair like that. He's the son of my best friend and the greatest guy in the world, Ernie Simon. Do you remember Ernie? Passed away last year, God bless his beautiful soul."

---

★I met Mickey Lolich at a Durham Bulls reunion a few years ago. He didn't flinch in saying that Gibson's record will hold up longer than his old teammate's. "The rules will change back and forth," he said, "but nobody scared batters like Gibson. Did you ever see Johnny Edwards's hand coming out of his mitt after catching him? Looked like it was on fire."

The waitress plainly didn't, but didn't want to offend, so wrinkled her nose in a compromise. "Mmmmm, maybe."

"The greatest guy in the world. And his son, Scotty, is a helluva guy, too, and I love him like a son. Even if he is a Democrat. Even if he is a hippie."

The waitress went off for water, and I leaned over to Uncle Jack.

"You know, Uncle Jack, I'm not really a hippie. Real hippies probably don't follow major league realignment. I'm not even a Democrat, as a matter of fact. I consider myself an urban–radical–pacifist. Kinda like, you know, Dorothy Day." Uncle Jack pondered that for a moment. "Dorothy Day founded the Catholic Worker houses. Kinda like, you know, settlement houses. Like Jane Addams."

Uncle Jack brightened. "Oh hell," he said, "Jane Addams, she was a great dame. We get groups from Hull House out at the ballpark all the time." Then he leaned over more confidentially. "You like women? I mean, you know what I mean?" His concern reminded me: I was demographically a textbook case for what the high school health class manuals still called *deviancy*: the son of a strong, single mother and a troubled, absent father. "I mean," he continued gingerly, "if you're confused about something, I want to help you. Just like your dad would."

And more, I said to myself, than my dad ever could bring himself to. "Yes, Uncle Jack, I like women just fine. Just fine, thank you."

He sat back, manifestly relieved. "Say," he said brightly, "even Durocher has had to give in a little on long hair. Randy Hundley has these mutton-chop sideburns. Beckert's even getting a little shaggy. The boys say it drives the gals wild, and if you don't want us to live like monks, Leo, you gotta let us grow hair." Uncle Jack and I disagreed about Richard J. Daley and Ronald Reagan, bourbon and marijuana, long hair and crew cuts, Jesse Jackson and Bob Dylan; but we agreed on Ernie Banks and Ferguson Jenkins, Wrigley Field and Leo Durocher. If we steered by those names, we could converse with surprising range, and even with a depth of feeling.

"They'll want you," I said, picking up a thread, "to work the World Series. They'd be crazy not to."

"Well, just maybe I can do the job," said Uncle Jack sitting back. "Just maybe. You know, Scotty, we kind of worry about you in that high school." My inner-city public school was just three El stops north of Wrigley Field. That winter it had been frequently emptied by phony fire alarms and roiled by gang riots. "You know, Aunt Nelda and I were talking. I could probably pull a few strings and fix it to get you into New Trier. Best high school in the country, right? Charlton Heston went there. A helluva guy. Ann-Margret went there. What's-his-name, too, Wyatt Earp."

"Hugh O'Brien?"

"That's it. You'd get a great education. Stay with us, if you like."

I was touched, almost to tears. And then contemplated how congenial it would be to publish my underground magazine from the basement of Uncle Jack's suburban house. "What's this, this *trash* Scotty? Do you think they have any of those goddamn words on the SAT tests?" And I would miss—mortifying as it was for a self-styled teenage revolutionary to admit to himself—I would miss my mother.

Besides, I had a profound feeling for my high school. Sometimes, when the class bells rang, I would stand in the hallways and feel, like Saul Bellow's Wilhelm in *Seize the Day* in the bustling subways beneath Times Square, a fat, sentimental love as my classmates surged past: pink-faced kids from Kentucky and Alabama, smooth-faced south-side blacks, second-generation Japanese kids whose parents had spent World War II in the camps of northern California, Chinese kids packing luscious leftovers from the parents' Devon Avenue restaurants, Jewish kids whose mothers and fathers kept their sleeves rolled down on parents' night over the tattooed numbers on their arms. If there was a passing period in the United Nations, I imagined it might look something like this—except, perhaps not so many scuffed, squeaking rubber-soled shoes and Cubs caps.

"Oh, Senn has been good to me, Uncle Jack. And, you know, even if I came home on weekends, like, I think my mother would miss me."

"Damn right she would." But agreeably (and no doubt with considerable relief) he let the proposal drop.

"So, I mean—really now, you're thinking—the Cubs might make it this year?"

Uncle Jack looked at me evenly, measuring me for a confidence. "Yes. I'm saying that. I'm saying that they have a good, goddamn, solid chance, as much as anybody else does, of making it to the World Series."

"I don't think you've ever said that before."

"Not that you would remember. Not since you've been alive. Honey," Uncle Jack called out to the waitress, "you've got a couple of hungry men here." I had left a shower of crumbs from plowing my way through a pile of hard rolls.

"I don't want to jinx it. But maybe we get to go to the World Series this year. Just maybe." Uncle Jack had seen more Cub games lost than any player or Cub executive alive; it wasn't the sort of profession that a man seasoned by so much disappointment would make casually.

"Say," he winked, "I think I might have had marijuana myself back in the fifties. Some blues joint Bill Veeck dragged me into. The musicians were smoking it, and I think I breathed some in. It sure wasn't Lucky Strikes, I know that. D'ya think that made me crazy?"

The morning after Opening Day, a student in our Contemporary History class presented an absence slip with his mother's signature, claiming he had been out of class with a cold. "But I don't mind telling you, Mr. Coorlas, I had the Wrigley Field Flu. Left field bleachers. Cubs won, and I had a beer."

Mr. Coorlas turned his bald head down and shuffled through a litter of absence slips. "Glad to know you're feeling better, Harlan," he said slowly. "Apparently there was quite a spring cold going around yesterday. It happens this time of year."

The 1969 Cubs opened the season by winning their first four games; then eleven of their first twelve, then fourteen of their first twenty; a wonderful and heady outburst of victory that had the unforeseeably unfortunate effect of alerting the rest of the National League to their rise. At the beginning of May, the Cubs commenced an eight-game winning streak. In one three-day run, three Cub pitchers hurled successive shutouts: Ken Holtzman against the San Francisco Giants, 8-0; and then after a quick commute south, Ferguson Jenkins shut down the San Diego Padres 2-0; and then the next night the team's fourth starter, Dick Selma, who had just come over from the Padres, defeated his old teammates 19-0. By the first of June, Chicago's cuddlesome, clawless Cubbies were in first place of the National League eastern division by 8½ games. One day after school, I journeyed into the Loop to buy a *New York Times* and read in their columns the same major league standings appearing in that morning's *Sun-Times*. But I was a Cub fan. Mayor Daley had warned that out-of-town "hippies, yippies, and flippies" were plotting to slip LSD into the city's drinking water. I had to confirm that the Cubs' success was authentic, and not some shared local delusion.

I had an after-school ritual for the El ride home. In a small deli in the iron shade of the tracks underneath the Thorndale station, I would purchase copies of the afternoon newspapers (*Daily News* and

*American*), a rare roast beef sandwich (on pumpernickel, lettuce, tomato, and brown mustard), a package of Suzy Q's (*devil's food cake and a rich creamy filling*), a can of Coke, and one large coffee (cream, three sugars). The El car became my snacker's lounge. I propped open the papers in my lap, unwrapped the sandwich, and peeled back the coffee cup top as the train clacked over the tracks. We passed flapping laundry strung up above peeling porches and open windows disclosing dreamy and dull-faced children looking out at the train as the station stops tolled by: Bryn Mawr, Berwyn, Argyle, Lawrence, and Wilson. At Sheridan, the El tracks twisted into an iron S, trailing like an unsnarling string that led into the Addison station—and Wrigley Field, nestled inside a neon thicket that blinked on in the late afternoon:

CHOP SUEY TAKEOUT CHIROPRACTOR
CHRISTIAN SCIENCE READING ROOM
TIRES-LUBRICATION-MUFFLERS PIE-OH-MY THICK CRUST
BY-THE-SLICE.

Home games were played by day, of course, and were usually over by the time we pulled into the platform. But on a flagpole poking out above:

WRIGLEY FIELD
HOME OF THE
CHICAGO CUBS

The club would hang a blue banner beaming out a white **W** if the Cubs had won, and white flag declaring a dark **L** if they had lost. That spring, it was becoming almost commonplace to see the **W** waving and snapping on my ride downtown; and during homestands, the Addison platform began to bustle with cheery, beery, late-leaving rooters straggling back to the office or factory.

They seemed the team Uncle Jack had sketched out with excitement just a few weeks before. The sturdiest Cub of all, Billy Williams (he would play in 1,117 consecutive games, an Iron Horse alongside Lou Gehrig and Cal Ripken Jr.), prowling over left field and lacing the ball against Wrigley's right field climbing ivy with a singular swing that reminded sportswriters of a thoroughbred's canter. Anchoring third, the solid and passionate Ron Santo (when the team began to lose, adjectives like *solid* and *passionate* lost out in the chorus of the stands to the sobriquet *Pizza Belly*); an agile and rangy Arkansan, Don Kessinger patrolling the gap at shortstop; sure-handed Glenn Beckert turning the double-play ball at second; a staunch Virginian, Randy Hundley, guarding home plate and guiding Cub pitchers. And standing over first base, of course, was the player who had come to embody the Cubs so completely that the team's name had been incorporated into his own: *Mr. Cub*. Ernie Banks.

The first time I met him was in 1977, on the spring afternoon he had been elected to the Hall of Fame. I was almost relieved to see a certain sharpness piercing his exalted sunniness. His election was unanimous, the first ballot in the first year he became eligible—an honor added to an honor. Ernie had spent the hours after the announcement roving from interview to interview as avidly as a touring author. In those times, public radio was more specialty item than a popular staple. I had borrowed Bill Veeck's joke for when listeners called us at WBEZ in Chicago to ask what time *All Things Considered* would be broadcast. *What time would you like to hear it?* So it was astonishing to hear one of the city's signature voices return our message. "Hello. This is Ernie Banks. I'm calling from a pay phone in the lobby of Marina City. Would you still like me to come over for an interview?"

He arrived alone, in a high whirl of congratulations and graciousness that halted elevator traffic; in fact, three of the building's elevator operators followed him into our studios.

"Oh my, what a beautiful group of lovely ladies you have working here!" Ernie announced into general giddiness, squeezing a hand here, chastely kissing a cheek there. "I can see why you work here, Bob," he said to our sportscaster (Bob Greenberg, who was, in fact, blind). "Everyone must *tell you* how *beeauuutiful* these ladies are!" I admired his deft step out of embarrassment.

"Is this a great day, Mr. Banks?" someone prompted, and Ernie delivered as bidden. "Oh, it's a *beeeauuutiful* day for a ball game! Let's play *two* today!"

His cheerfulness seemed genuine; but even deep traits of character can take time off for good behavior. So I was glad when something cheekier revealed itself before taping began. "All those votes your first time up, Mr. Banks," said a bystander. "You must be proud of those great stats."

"They must have added something to mine for suffering," he said with a stabbing laugh. "They're great at giving out the honors that don't cost anything." When an attractive young black woman engineer bent down a bit nervously to adjust his microphone, Ernie kept up a cordial chatter. But when she walked out to head back into the control room, he made a point of inquiring, "Who's that?" Jeanette, he was told, she's handling the recording. "Well then," said Ernie Banks out of his high-watt Mr. Cub smile, "it certainly would be a pleasure to be in her capable hands." God bless, there was a bit of the old goat in Mr. Cub.

He was the last star of the Negro Leagues to be bought by a major league club. When the Cubs brought up Gene Baker for their Los Angeles affiliate to play second base in 1953, Ernie Banks, a slender and dispensable young shortstop for Satchel Paige's old Kansas City Monarchs, was signed too. Cub owner P. K. Wrigley, who was no bigot, but also not much of a progressive, asked his general manager, "What do we need with a second Negro? We already got Baker."

"Baker needs a roommate," he was told.

"So I was signed as a baby-sitter," Ernie Banks has often recollected since. But given so frail an opportunity, he began to dazzle in the field and amaze at the plate. At shortstop, he had what Uncle Jack called *soft hands*—balls seemed to float into his hands and stick to his fingers. Ernie was almost fragile in appearance in the batter's box, with matchstick arms and marionette wrists; a bat in his hands looked almost like an item of self-defense. But his wrists had the elegant strength of a racehorse's ankles. When Ernie Banks turned on a pitch with those wrists, his bat had the snap of a buggy whip. Clyde McCullough, the team's seasoned catcher, saw something appealingly brutish in Ernie's compact swing—"It's like Jack Dempsey's knockout punch," he told reporters. "He's quick and has strong wrists. He can take a little more time to judge a pitch." His second year in baseball, Banks hit five grand-slam home runs, nineteen on the season. By the next year, he had become the hardest-hitting shortstop in baseball history, lashing 44 home runs and batting in 117 runs on a bottom-dwelling ball club. He won the home run race in 1958 with 47, and was the league's Most Valuable Player; then repeated those feats the next year; and won another home run title in 1960.

It was during this time that *Poor* Ernie began to precede his name in the national press—*Poorernie* Banks, in fact, as the refrain ran together, as Mantle, Mays, Aaron, and Koufax reached the main stage of the World Series with their teams. But Poorernie, *Poorernie Banks, such a marvelous player, such a miserable club,* had only fishing to look forward to in October; and, as he used to joke, "It's too cold to go fishing in Chicago in October."

It was also during this time that Ernie began to be associated with the phrase, "It's a beautiful day for a ball game. Let's play two today!" A qualification may be necessary. It's not entirely clear that Ernie Banks coined the phrase by which he has become known; or if, like Jimmy Cagney sneering "You dirty rat!" he simply borrowed it from his own folklore. "It sounds like something I would say," he told me in an interview years ago. "Maybe that's why it caught on." Over the years, he has allowed other stories to stand: that he said it first between two ends of a doubleheader plagued by thunderstorms; that he said it on arriving at Wrigley seven games into a losing streak to face Sandy Koufax and the Los Angeles Dodgers; or uttered—the stories tend to accumulate detail in the retelling—to catcher John Roseboro as Ernie brushed off the dust from a Don Drysdale beanball. But by the late 1960s, *What a beeeauuutiful day for a ball game, let's play two today in the Friendly Confines of Wrigley Field!* had become Ernie's motto, and more: his armor.

"You never once got up and didn't feel like going to the ballpark?" I got to ask him once.

"Oh, sure," he said. "But it didn't last long. If I felt bad or something, then I could always look forward to going to the ballpark. Who doesn't look forward to going to the ballpark?"

"Oh, I think a lot of us might not like it if it meant hitting against Bob Gibson," I ventured. "Or losing all the time." Ernie Banks shook his head with a smile

"Not me. Not me." Really? Really? His smile cracked—into a laugh. "Really, really. Really."

Ernie Banks's most conspicuous characteristic was also, for many, his most incredible: his geniality. His incessant sunniness seemed undimmed by ceaseless loss and perpetual disappointment. The expansion of baseball in the early 1960s opened a new opportunity for the Cubs to post an unprecedented distinction: they became the first team to finish in ninth place. Mr. Wrigley's rotating college of coaches treated their most distinguished player gratuitously, rotating Ernie Banks from shortstop to left field to first base for no apparent reason greater than to demonstrate their authority to degrade the league's most accomplished player. *It's a beeeauuuutiful day for a ball game! Let's play two today!*

(In 1963, Ernie himself attempted something almost as imponderable: he ran for the Chicago city council. As, more incomprehensibly yet, an *independent* in a south-side district during the years that predominantly black wards were the driving pistons of Mayor Richard Daley's Democratic machine. Mr. Cub finished in club tradition—third in a field of four—occasioning the only political observation I ever recall from Charlie Grimm. "For Chrissakes! How the hell did he expect any goddamn votes from White Sox fans!" Perhaps Banks might have improved his chances by running for office in Chicago under the slogan, *It's a beautiful day for an election! Let's vote twice today!*)

You didn't have to be an agnostic or skeptic—merely a Cub fan—to wonder, how could he mean that? Not just for a day, a three-game series, a week, or month, but an entire season? An entire career? Doctor, doctor, tell me: at what point does unrewarded optimism become insupportable fantasy? If you could not doubt Ernie Banks's sincerity—wouldn't you have to wonder about his sanity? And your own? How could a generation growing weary and wary of hearing, *There's a light at the end of the tunnel!* not be suspicious of hearing a daily declaration from the greatest man to play on a wretched team since Robert E. Lee, *It's a beeauuutiful day for a ball game! Let's play two today!*

One of the most shameful school lunchroom debates I can recall from those years concerned the question of whether Ernie Banks was a white man's black man (the term Uncle Tom was being replaced then by *Oreo*, dark on the outside, white on the inside).

The argument was advanced by a friend named George, who had begun to wear a Black Panthers beret, tan military shirts, and a glower to school each day (if George appeared to be imitating Huey P. Newton, my own lengthening locks bore more than a little resemblance to the leader of the Weather Underground, Bernadine Dohrn).

"I tell you this," George said. "Ernie Banks is no Muhammad Ali. He is no Jim Brown. Shuckin', jivin', smilin' for white folks. Making a white man rich with the sweat o' his brow." The times, they were a changin'.

"It's worse than that," said another friend named Alfred. "Ali, he makes white folks scared. Ernie Banks is scared white folks won't like him. 'Fraid they gonna stop paying him all that money." *It's a beautiful day for a ball game!* paled, in all ways, alongside Ali's perceived, *Hell, no, I won't go!*

I am embarrassed to recall that I did not laugh my friends down from their denunciations. Instead, I felt more like the line from

Theodore Roethke's grieving *Persephone*—an emotional onlooker with strong feelings, but no standing, "with no rights in this matter." I was only and merely a fan. Trying to recollect this colloquy so many years later, I am ashamed. Now that I am older and have disappointed myself so many times, I can appreciate and admire the iron in Ernie Banks's indestructible optimism. His smile was his weapon of choice against the catcalls of bigots, the beanballs of Don Drysdale (who was no bigot, but a right-hand pitcher who hunted heads ecumenically), and the defeat of his own dreams. Ernie Banks was his own man as much as Muhammad Ali. Looking back on that conversation between George, Alfred, and myself, I want to shout at the impudent youngsters we were—what the hell did the three of us ever do with our young lives to give us the license to disrespect Ernie Banks? It *was* a beautiful day for a ball game.

But Leo Durocher had grown to see his thirty-eight-year-old star as an encumbrance. Despite the drop-offs occasioned by age, Ernie was still the team's preeminent home run hitter, a superb fielder, and the team's emotional helmsman. But Durocher complained to club executives and even (carefully) a few reporters that Ernie Banks had become a liability. He swung for home runs, ran Leo's refrain, because he could no longer run out base hits; and his fielding average at first base was fattened by the fact that Ernie shrewdly refused to lunge for balls he knew he could no longer reach, letting them by for hits (Banks finished 1968 with 32 home runs and a virtually flawless fielding average of .996—statistics that Leo would have cited in anointing a younger man, "my kind of ball player").

What's more, said Durocher, Mr. Cub was so beloved that Leo could not manage him. If Leo sat Ernie down in the late innings because the Cubs needed more speed on the bases and range at first base, the crowd booed; reporters wondered why Leo would remove the club's best clutch home run hitter. If Durocher rested Banks for a full game—which even Ernie's adherents felt was due—the crowd clamored for him to pinch-hit in the late innings, even if Leo was looking for someone who might scratch his way on base with a ground ball. Durocher told more than a few reporters confidentially that he had told P. K. Wrigley, "Banks was a great player in his time. Unfortunately, his time isn't my time," and the story got around.

On the first homestand in June after school had let out, I went to the game, saw the Cubs defeat the Phillies, and joined Uncle Jack afterward in the Pink Poodle, a pink-walled lounge a stairway down from the press box in which Uncle Jack would often hold forth over late-afternoon drinks at one table, and Leo Durocher at another. Occasionally, but not often, they would run their circles together.

"Leo's problem is that he can't stand anyone who's more popular than he is," Uncle Jack explained. "Of course, that means most of the people in the world. You'll notice that he doesn't have a particularly high opinion of me, either. But he can't stand someone as popular as Ernie because he can't take credit for him, the way he tried to for Willie Mays. All that 'my kind of ball player' crap. Maybe he thinks by his talking behind Ernie's back, the other players will get the idea that Leo knows the team is bigger than just Ernie. But Santo, Beckert, Hickman—they all start thinking, 'Hey, if this guy bad-mouths the great Ernie Banks behind his back, what must he be saying about me?' Hey, Scotty, move a little closer, I want you to notice something." I inched in over my Coke. "You see Leo over there? Just keep an eye out. When the check comes, see if his hand gets anywhere near it." Uncle Jack twinkled as he sat back and a geyser of laughter rose up from Leo's table as he reached a punch line. "As your dad used to say, 'He'd break his elbow if he ever reached for the check.'"

I still sometimes screen a mental movie of that Cub team in those middle weeks of the summer of 1969. Don Kessinger leads off with a sharp single just to the shortstop side of second base. Glenn Beckert, with characteristic and calculating selflessness, moves him to second by rolling a sacrifice bunt down the first base line. (In some versions I like to imagine the great Bob Gibson swooping in off the pitcher's mound, Tim McCarver standing up in alarm behind the plate, and Bill White scooping a handful of grass, this notable trio sharing chagrin and despair over missing the bunt steered so beautifully between their toes.)* Billy Williams is up next—and slices a double off of the ivy in right field, scoring Beckert. Then Ernie Banks approaches, idling his fingers on the throat of his bat as Gibson leans in for the sign from McCarver, shakes the first away, then the second, settling on some variant of his fastball, glaring, sneering, throwing from the stretch, Ernie's wrists flicking out like a lizard's tongue and stinging the ball into the sky above the ivy in left field.

---

*Bill White, of course, would later become president of the National League.

The everyday denizens sitting in the left-field bleachers had, in the parlance of the times, radicalized and organized themselves into The Bleacher Bums. Sunning, shirtless (women as well as men), and garrulous, often hard-hatted and beer-soaked, the Bums revved up the crowd in Cub cheers and hectored opposing left fielders something awful. In principle, Mr. Wrigley kept the price of bleacher seats low; and, in gratitude, park officials tried to hold back seats for those fans, especially retirees, who had come to build their days around afternoons at Wrigley Field. In the summer of 1969, bleacher seats became more prized than box seats. You could watch the game among fans whom the ballplayers knew by name and often acknowledged with a wave or joke, and stand a chance to spear a home run ball off the bat of Ernie Banks—a lot of entertainment for a dollar-seventy-five. Over the years, I have heard about as many people claim to have sat in those six rows of bleacher seats right along Waveland Avenue as claimed to have voted for John F. Kennedy.

In late June, most of the Cubs and a delegation of Bleacher Bums delivered themselves to a north-side studio to record a theme song taken from Uncle Jack's home run call, "Hey-hey!" Ernie Banks, Ron Santo, Ferguson Jenkins, and the rest of the roster (Leo Durocher, a genuine personal friend of Frank Sinatra, wisely declined on advice of the Chairman's counsel) stood stiffly in front of a ring of microphones and sang:

> *Hey-hey, holy mackerel, no doubt about it*
> *The Cubs are on their way!*
> *The Cubs are gonna hit today! They're gonna field today!*
> *They're gonna play today!*
> *Look out world the Cubs are gonna win today!*
> *Hey-hey, holy mackerel, no doubt about it*
> *The Cubs are on their way!*
> *They got the hustle! They got the muscle!*
> *The Chicago Cubs are on their way!*

Managing to ring with both conviction and whim, the recording had a species of charm. That summer, "Hey-hey, Holy Mackerel" became part of Chicago's daily clamor, chiming on the radio in the morning, punctuating game broadcasts later that afternoon, and even insinuating itself into daily conversation:

"Morning."

"Morning."

"Hey-hey, see those Cubbies? Holtzman was humming."

"Hey-hey, holy mackerel! Had the Phils in handcuffs!"

In my summer-school Spanish class, our most original and energetic scholarship of the term (plus the colloquial advice of several Mexican classmates) established a idiomatic translation of what was becoming a civic anthem:

> *Hey-hey, sagrado mackerel*
> *Sin ninguna duda*
> *Los Cachorros estan en el camino!*

"The nice thing about being a Cub fan," the old catcher Joe Garagiola had once remarked, "is that you always knew you could bet on being able to see a bottom of the ninth." But that summer at Wrigley Field, the Cubs had often outscored their opponents by the top of the ninth. At the last out *(Ground ball to short. Kessinger up with it. Over to Ernie. Hey-hey, that's another one!)*, Ron Santo would run in along the third-base line and leap up, clicking his feet together, once, twice, three times in the happy commotion. "Santo's dance!" Uncle Jack would peal. "Santo goes into his dance!" Each Cub victory did nothing to remedy the wrenching rivalries then contending in the city. Nor should they. The issues were important, more urgent than sports. But between blacks and whites, reformers and regular Democrats, hawks and doves, Jesse Jackson and Richard J. Daley—me and Uncle Jack—Ernie, Billy, Fergie, Leo, and Santo's Dance were the key words of a mutual civic conversation.

But reports of squalls began to appear. Agents and flacks flocked freely in the Cub locker room, offering endorsement contracts and personal appearance fees that could incite petty rivalries. The amounts today (one hundred dollars to shake hands at a supermarket, a thousand dollars to endorse a garage-door company) seemed shockingly unpretentious. Larger problems were posed as weeks wore on and several close games disclosed that the Cubs had several stars, but no regular, reliable center fielder.

In a game against the New York Mets at Shea Stadium on July 8, a twenty-four-year-old rookie named Don Young, who was trying to rise to the role, dropped a routine-looking fly ball; then, another. The runners thereby advanced and scored, helping the Mets to a 4 to 3 win.

Young was—well, *young*; and flustered. He left the stadium without speaking to reporters.

But not so Ron Santo. Reporters in search of a studied and generous reaction to some turn of events knew to apply to Ernie Banks—and then often berated themselves for the opaque graciousness of what followed. "Awww, it's a tough break for the kid, I'm sure it won't happen again. We're behind him all the way." But those looking for something more authentically emotional knew to find Ron Santo; and he obliged.

Don Young, said Santo, had left because he didn't want to talk about his poor hitting, not his bad fielding—and a regular outfielder should at least be able to hit the weight of his mistakes. "He's worried about his average," said Santo, "not the team." Looking back on his words in newspaper clips, Santo's reproach hardly reads like a tirade. Don Young, after all, was twenty-four, old enough to know that professional athletes stick around to answer for their mistakes, rather than leave the task to their teammates. Was it uncivil to point out that he was being paid to *catch* fly balls? At least, one of them? That seems a minimal qualification for a center fielder. To make more of Ron Santo's outburst than Don Young's blunders may seem misplaced.

Besides, Santo was as quick to apologize as he had been to anger. He called Don Young at their hotel later that night to make amends (but Young was not taking calls), then made a point of sitting on the armrest of Young's seat on the bus out to Shea the next day, apologizing, consoling, and otherwise being a teammate. The players told reporters that the crisis, if that's what it was, had only engendered a greater understanding. But reporters said the incident redoubled doubts that the Cubs had the mettle to win when winning was an expectation instead of some delightful phenomenon.

And other teams noted—hit the ball to center field. You'll never know who'll be there, and if he can catch.*

On the afternoon of Sunday, July 20, while the Cubs were winning both ends of a doubleheader against the Philadelphia Phillies (1-0 behind Fergie Jenkins in the first game, for his thirteenth victory of the season; 6-1 in the second, with the whip-armed Dick Selma

---

*Don Young hit .230 that year in 100 games for the Cubs, which was not bad, but also suggested considerable room for the team to improve itself in center field. He was out of baseball the next year, and has since also been out of the business of giving interviews.

throttling the Phillies on just four hits), the first human beings landed on the earth's moon. Hours before Neil Armstrong and Edwin Aldrin would step onto an extraterrestrial surface with a slogan Armstrong had conceived for the occasion, his stark, literal astro-speak actually sounded more euphonious in the moment that the lunar landing vehicle descended through a shower of moon dust and set down in a windless plain.

"Houston, Tranquillity Base here. The Eagle has landed."

It was the middle of the afternoon. I was attending some allegedly radical political meeting of the time. It may be difficult to explain now, but I did not have much company when I excused myself to watch the moon landing. On the student left, there was some contempt for the American space program (while the Soviet one could be celebrated as an inspiration to socialist peoples everywhere). American astronauts were regarded as silver-suited, bubble-topped, crew-cut products of the same military establishment bombing North Vietnam (years later, as a reporter, I would meet a few astronauts and began to see their crew cuts as camouflage for free-spirits and fighter-jocks who could sound as seriously aggrieved with the American military establishment as David Dellinger—or Dwight David Eisenhower). Many of us were still challenged and captivated by space flight. But there were sound questions about the rightness of spending so freely to send men to stand on a cold, gray orb when so many men and women sharing this vital one lived in fear, hurt, and want. The Reverend Ralph Abernathy and remnants of Martin Luther King's Poor People's Campaign hitched up a mule team to make a witness of protest outside the Cape Kennedy launch site; and the space program's director, Robert Gilruth, was honorable enough to meet with them. "Reverend," he said, "if not pushing that button [to launch Apollo 11] could accomplish all the fine things you are talking about, then I would not push that button."

Looking back on that afternoon, I now wonder if my standing as a fan made me more inclined to see manned space flight as a human adventure, rather than the imperialist-industrialist-militarist venture some of my political allies saw. Flying into space held the hope of discovering, in one more amazing way, that just as no flight could lift us away from the problems of our world, our world was also larger than its problems.

The plan had been for the astronauts to secure their craft and then, incredibly, turn in for a night's snooze on the moon's surface. But as

Edwin Aldrin told me years later, "Nobody's that cool—we wanted to get out and see the place." So it was in the middle of the earth night, central daylight time, that I sat with friends in an apartment about ten blocks from Wrigley Field, staring at the first, flickering gray pictures of a couple of men on a distant, drab rock stooping, standing, and dancing like silver-suited circus bears in the half-gravity of the moon. We strained to pick out the words in their first static-sizzled speeches. "That's one small step for man," said Neil Armstrong, who felt compelled to provide a keynote; while Aldrin provided a poetic caption for the landscape we could see only in grainy, indistinct pictures. "Magnificent desolation." But mostly, we were deeply silent; remarkably solemn for young smart asses in a smart-ass time. The only smack of the snide surfaced when President Nixon called up a bizarre, self-absorbed congratulations ("Neil and Buzz, this must be the most historic telephone call ever made . . .") after they had planted a wire-stiffened Stars and Stripes to ripple perpetually in the Sea of Tranquillity.

In a moment of majesty, we were chastened by a humbling thought: were all the political and social passions that enthralled us destined to disappear in some future history timeline that would feature just a single hash mark?—"Twentieth Century. Man lands on moon." The Soviet cosmonaut, Gherman Titov, had orbited earth and radioed back a Marxist boast: "I cannot see God up here. Where is he?" Had we pushed out of our world's orbit hoping to find the face of God—only to see it best in the pearly, fragile cladding on the surface of our own singularly vibrant blue earth?

My friend Avi walked me outside to wait for a bus, and together we searched the lightening sky for the moon. Years later, I heard Neil Armstrong say that when he now looks up at the moon, he sees somewhere he knows, somewhere he's been. In the smallest way, I think Avi and I felt something similar that night. We lay down on an empty Lake Shore Drive to wave up at the sky; as if someone might wave back.

"You know, our kids will be living up there someday," said Avi. "In space colonies. They'll get a fresh start. They'll look back on us and wonder how we could have let all this stuff happen here on earth."*

I bought a newspaper at a stand just a step from the bus stop and flipped it back and forth. MAN ON MOON on the front, CUBS OVER PHILS

---

*Professor Avram Cohen is now an economist of note at Toronto's York University. He has three children: Alexis, Madeleine, and Katie Frances. None of them live on the moon—at this writing.

on the back. The season was halfway through and adjourning for the All-Star break.

"We're 23 games over .500 now," the *Sun-Times* quoted Leo Durocher, "60-37, and we've got 65 games left to play. What we've got to do is play 40-25 the rest of the way and I think that should do it."

"Jesus Christ," Avi had said to me as I boarded the 151 heading south. "Man lands on the moon and the Chicago Cubs are in first place. Did you ever think we'd live to see it?"

But by the time Armstrong and Aldrin had returned to earth, the fortunes of the Cubs all-stars had begun to change. On the last weekend of July, during a Saturday afternoon game, Leo Durocher left the dugout in the third inning with the Cubs up by a run over the Los Angeles Dodgers. His steady coach, Joey Amalfitano, suggested that Leo had taken sick on the bench—nothing serious, probably a touch of stomach flu. More important, the Cubs won in the eleventh, staying five games ahead of the New York Mets.

But he was not back by game time the next day; and then the cover story began to break down.

The actual story of Leo's absence was unsensational, and even sympathetic. He had flown up for parents' weekend at a summer camp in Wisconsin. Earlier that year, Leo had married Lynn Walker, the Chicago socialite who used to send him down to Michigan Avenue for his after-dinner smoke. She had a twelve-year-old son, Joel Goldblatt, whom Leo had grown to love, and did not want to disappoint. Leo's own birthday was Sunday, and he did not want his new wife to feel torn between being with her son or her husband. He missed most of Saturday's game; and then much of Sunday's, when the plane he had chartered from a north woods airport got caught up in summer squalls. Could happen to anybody.

Except, as Uncle Jack exclaimed, "Who the hell ever thought that Leo Durocher would disappear to somewheres as innocent as a summer camp? A nudist colony, maybe. Las Vegas, probably. Maybe a shack-up in a roadside motel. But not a summer camp!" The story, though true, was widely mistrusted, the residual distrust of Leo's career as a carouser. Some of the Cubs groused. They had families, too. But like Leo, they also had half the year off—the rest belonged to baseball. They had to explain to their families that holidays and birthdays had to be worked around the occupation that made them prosperous. Club officials grumbled about Leo's judgment. P. K.

Wrigley told Leo that if he ever needed time off, all he had to do was ask—but, he *needed* to ask.

Years later, Leo was tender in talking about the incident. "I figured I let baseball louse up my first two families," he said, "and I didn't want it to happen again."

Uncle Jack chortled at my sympathy. "Baseball didn't ruin those marriages. Drinking, gambling, screwing around did. Laraine Day [the actress, and Leo's wife in the late 1940s and early '50s] wouldn't know where to find Leo if he didn't have to show up at the ballpark."

Questions about Durocher's sagacity seemed to sharpen, perhaps unreasonably, as the New York Mets began to win. On August 7, the Cubs led the Mets by 9½ games. But then the Mets commenced a streak in which they won 22 of 28 games. Tom Seaver and a young Nolan Ryan would come to earn places in the Hall of Fame. Even in 1969, their talents were obvious and imposing. But what to make of Jim McAndrew, the Mets' fifth starter, who won four consecutive games in that period, 1-0, 2-1, 6-0, and 3-0? I know what Cub fans made of it: *magic.*

You can hear the most vicious things about New Yorkers—from New Yorkers. I have spent some of the happiest occasions of my life in New York City, including the periods in which I have lived there, and have never had reason to believe that New Yorkers, pro-rated according to their population, are more likely to be jerks, cranks, turds, or schmucks than, say, people in Des Moines (although New Yorkers may be more likely to be *called* schmucks by friends, neighbors, and close family). On the contrary.

When I first came to New York, as a high school student on college interviews, I stepped off the airport bus at Grand Central Terminal with my arms straining around a battered brown suitcase holding my one stiff blue woolen Midwestern suit.

"Here, let me help you," said a stranger waiting in the terminal. "Can I help you get a cab? Why don't I help you into a cab with this big thing." *Why do people say New Yorkers are so rude?* I wondered. *Practically the first New Yorker I meet wants to help me.* My benefactor scurried around a corner to flag down a cab.

Of course, I never saw that man again. For a few minutes, I worried about him—it was New York, after all; maybe someone less altruistic had mugged him for my suitcase. Then, I shared my concern with the first New York City patrolman I ever approached. At first, he seemed suspicious; a lad so convincingly dumb must be in on the scam, too. Then, on accepting my sincerity, he laughed so hard the abundance of brass buttons on his uniform began to clack as he held in his sides.★

But by the time I left the city a few days later, I had many more stories about New Yorkers who had treated me with unusual, almost epic kindness—and almost compulsive, confiding warmth. Kindness and consideration in the urgent bustle of New York can take dedication and courage. Those New Yorkers who evince such traits, even intermittently, earn admiration.

But when non–New Yorkers treat themselves to such free and easy observations, they are usually characterizing the New York they think they know, bristling and blooming in Manhattan. There are four other boroughs, equally urgent, distinct—and as susceptible to feeling slighted by Manhattan as, say, Chicago or Iowa.

By the early 1960s, the Yankees performed in the most famous landmark of the Bronx, but were usually regarded as part of that same company of civic assets and boasts associated with Manhattan, Broadway to the United Nations, Mickey Mantle to the Metropolitan. Each hour in New York, boats, buses, and airplanes disgorged people determined to become stars. The place was congested with excellence and ambition. *Of course* the New York Yankees were the best baseball team in the world— they were in New York. *Hey, buddy, where the hell else do you think they oughtta put the best baseball team—Kenosha?* New York should have the best baseball team in the world, just as it should have the world's tallest building, best symphony, most original theater, blah-blah-blah (which may be why it was so important to Chicagoans to acquire those, too).

The Cubs were one of two teams in the Second City. But when the Mets began to play in 1962, they became the second team in the First City. The Mets were a team for those fans who had loyally loved the Giants and Dodgers in their old neighborhoods, until those clubs followed the flow of Americans along expressways for the West Coast; a team for those New Yorkers who resented incessant Yankee success even

---

★I had occasion once to tell this story to an audience in New York. It was received, I thought, with unmerited hilarity. I had not noticed that Mayor Rudolph Giuliani was also on the podium, waiting to make his own remarks. "Now I understand, Mr. Mayor," I tried to recover, "that this kind of thing doesn't happen anymore."

"No," the mayor corrected me. "According to the most recent crime statistics, there is a forty-three percent less chance of that happening anymore."

as they had to admire it. The team for those millions of New Yorkers who preferred *not* to root for U.S. Steel.

As intrepid Yankees, Maris, Mantle, Ford, Berra and Bouton won one more World Series, and then another, the Mets won the city's affections with melodramatic ineptitude. "Not at all," said their first manager, Casey Stengel, cast aside by the Yankees, when asked if his players would find it difficult to play an exhibition series in the high elevation of Mexico City. "We can lose 'em at any altitude."

Years before Ronald Reagan was cherished for the practice, Casey fell asleep on the job, visibly catnapping as his Mets stumbled, bumbled, and literally ran into each other on the base paths, like players in a farce who miss their cues. (Stengel was considered the Lovable Ol' Perfessor by fans. But those who played for him often wondered about the pedigree of his loveableness, more than his professorship. Many of his best lines— "Now we got a twenty-year-old kid here named Goslin. And in ten years, he's got a good chance to be thirty"—were at the expense of his players. That—and nine pennants, of course—was the difference between Casey Stengel and Charlie Grimm.) Yankee success had become assumed. Met ineptitude brought mystery back to baseball in New York.

Cub fans, in fact, became almost envious. Why, the Cubs had already been clowns when the Mets had not stirred even a flutter in a Flushing real estate developer's concrete heart. Why lavish so much celebration on a team that had come so late to futility?

They were New York's team, that was why. New Yorkers had to believe even their awfulness was epochal.

The 1969 Mets are remembered as the Amazin' Mets. Like many of the most memorable nicknames (including, in fact, Quakers), it was a moniker that began in belittlement. But in 1969, it was transformed to mean a team that was, amazingly, beginning to win. The Cubs were winning, too, but beginning in August, not at a pace to compete with the Mets.

Tom Seaver and Jerry Koosman were already among the best young pitchers in the game; Nolan Ryan was beginning to get close. But the Mets' position players were mostly players of ordinary talents, exhilarated by circumstance into amazin' achievement.

Even today, reading the names of their lineup card, it is hard to see how a team consisting of Kranepool, Swoboda, and Grote could measure up against Santo, Banks, and Williams. But if you sort over the box scores, you can glean some pertinent surprises. Billy Williams, for example, of Whistler, Alabama, was then thirty years old and widely admired as a future Hall of Fame player. He played almost every inning of every game in 1969, hitting a substantial .293, which included 21 home runs and 95 runs batted in. In left field for the Mets was Cleon Jones, four years younger, from nearby Plateau, Alabama, a career .250ish hitter. But in 1969, playing in 137 games, he hit .340, with 12 home runs. Now, you would never trade Billy Williams for Cleon Jones, not even for a year (by the next year, as a matter of fact, Cleon had relapsed back to .277, while Billy challenged for the Triple Crown by hitting .322, 42 home runs, and 129 runs batted in). In 1969, Billy Williams had a magnificent season. But merely typically magnificent—while Cleon Jones had a year that was, by his standards, magical. The Mets seemed brushed by magic. For every series the Cubs would win two games out of three, it seemed the Mets would manage a three-game sweep. It was frustrating and confounding for the Cubs—to win games, but lose ground.

On September 3, 1969, as the Cubs lead was slipping to just three games, Ho Chi Minh died. The obituaries remembered that the father of Vietnamese nationalism had, as a student and emerging revolutionary in his early twenties, worked as a dishwasher near the docks in New York and had been inspired by the American Declaration of Independence. If American Liberty so galvanized Ho, I wondered, why not the American League? I entertained myself with a reverie: Babe Ruth, known for his gregarious and gargantuan appetites, seeks out an obscure but recommended Chinese restaurant on the Lower East Side. He falls into conversation with a thin, intense, young dishwasher who is on his break.

"Excuse me, Mr. Ruth," says Ho Chi Minh, "you are a very excellent pitcher. But you hit the ball a ton. Perhaps you should abandon pitching for first base, and thereby be able to bat four times each game. Your home run totals will increase considerably, and could even transform the game from a low-scoring defensive exercise into an offense-laden entertainment that can capture the public imagination as never before!"

"Well, say, I never quite thought of that," says the Babe, "but it sure makes sense to me. Mind if I tell you something? A bright kid like you, Ho, is wasting his time diving for pearls in a jernt like this. Go back home and lead your people to their true national destiny!"

"Thanks, Bambino, will do."

"Don't mention it, kid. Say, before you go, could you please leave a little more of those duck slices in the purple sauce, smooshed into a pancake? Tasty buggers."

"A pleasure, Babe."

On September 7, of somewhat greater local interest, Senator Everett Dirksen of Illinois, with his Mixmaster hair style and cheroot-syrupy, road company Shakespearean voice, died. His loss was felt rather more keenly, as during my childhood—about eight months before—I did an imitation of Ev Dirksen in after-school phony phone calls. Clearing and clacking my throat to get a bit of gravel in it, my friends Billy and Bruce and I would dial some number at random.

"Hello mam, thank you for answering," I would rasp senatorially, "this is Senator Dirksen calling."

"Senator, I can't believe it! What can I do for you."

"I just wanted to take this opportunity . . ."—gasp, rasp, gasp—"to thank you for all of your support. I would also like to ask you . . ."—gasp, rasp, gasp—"a question important to our nation's future."

"Of course."

"Is your refrigerator running?"

Click.

That night, as the Cubs struggled to stay 2½ games ahead of the Mets, the old Yankee pitcher Jim Bouton, then pitching for the Houston Astros, reflected in the diary that would become his book, *Ball Four*, about the race for first place between the leagues' reigning losers:

> *The Mets are beautiful. Here they are, virtually tied with the Cubs, and the panic is on in Chicago. Leo Durocher is not talking to the press, and I don't have to be there to know that their clubhouse is like a morgue. And here's the funny thing. The Mets have virtually the same record and they're going crazy with joy. The players are happy, the manager is happy, the fans are happy. Now what's the difference? It's that the Mets won their games at a different stage of the season. The point is that right now they both have an equal chance to win the pennant, yet the Mets are up and the Cubs are down. And the Cubs are down because they think they should be down. Why? If they were as happy as the Mets they'd win more games.*

The Cubs arrived in New York on September 8 for the final games between the two teams of the season. The last time the Cubs had confronted games so crucial, Douglas MacArthur ruled Japan.

The Cubs lost the first game, 3 to 2. Of course, I state that from the

Cub perspective. The Mets won. But the winning run was contested, with Tommy Agee racing in from second base on a single to left field and sliding under a tag Cub catcher Randy Hundley still insists he made. In fact, he still reddens when he remembers, "I made the fucking tag." But the umpires made another call. And even if they hadn't—the Cubs would have had to score another run against Mets pitching.

And then, the next night, magic struck again. Tom Seaver was pitching for New York and a black cat walked past Ron Santo, kneeling in the on-deck circle in the top half of the second inning, and stopped in front of the Cub dugout to hiss at Leo Durocher—a true catcall. "Can't blame a cat for that," Leo said later, one of his most charming and self-effacing lines. Ron Santo said, "I don't believe in magic, but I wanted to run and hide." The Cubs could run, but they could not hide their descent. Tom Seaver didn't need any pre-Halloween hexes to be unbeatable in September of 1969. The Mets won—it had become the time to start stating the scores that way—7 to 1. The Cubs clung to first place by just half a game.

(By the way: no one claimed the cat from security guards after the game. The cat was reportedly turned over to a city shelter, where its fate became impossible to trace. But when I want to renew my disdain for Mets fans, I think of them letting that dauntless cat languish in a shelter, unclaimed and doomed.)

The Cubs motored down to Philadelphia for the next night's game, lost, and fell out of first place. While he waited for reporters to descend on the clubhouse, Leo Durocher fired up his first cigarette since spring training. The Cubs' longtime equipment manager, Yosh Kawano, told him, "Those things will kill you." And Leo said, "That's the general idea."

The press and public in Chicago had already begun to conduct extensive forensic analysis of the Cubs and their downfall. A prominent, or at least self-promoting, psychiatrist, Dr. Harvey Mandel, said that the Cubs seemed to be afflicted with one of the emotional diseases of affluent America—they did not feel worthy of success. They had become so identifiable as lovable losers, they could not see themselves as winners. "The Cubs," Dr. Mandel pronounced, "have an unconscious desire to lose the pennant." Winning invited risks—like a World Series. Losing at least offered familiar comforts.

Looking back on the times, it is easy to dismiss the doctor's diagnosis as southern California psycho-hooey. But then, the Cubs began to play in a way that made a fan wonder—are you sure, Doctor, that's an *unconscious* desire?

The club continued up to Montreal to play the bottom-dwelling

Expos. They had a reasonable expectation of gaining back some ground against the Mets, who were playing Roberto Clemente's Pittsburgh Pirates. Leo had never set curfews for the club—what could he say, *Do as I didn't*? But as the Cubs plunged, Durocher worried about the increasing scrutiny of reporters and, for that matter, club officials. The Cubs began the stand by losing a night game, which would be followed by a day game. Durocher was appalled to learn from his coaches the next morning that thirteen Cubs had not made it back to the hotel by midnight. Leo, whose own psychological insights had the instincts of a gambler, simply shook his head in chagrin in a locker-room speech that day. "Look, fellas, we're playing for a lot of money here. If you guys don't want to win, then there's nothing I can do to help you."

Well, perhaps there was. Jack Brickhouse was foremost among those who believed that many of the Cubs were simply exhausted as the season edged into September. The club had a strong starting lineup, but a less impressive roster of substitutes. Give Billy Williams a rest, and he was replaced by a .211 hitter named Al Spangler. Bench Ernie Banks, and you brought on a spirited walk-on named Willie Smith. If Fergie Jenkins began to flag, you could bring in relief pitcher Phil Regan, an accomplished ball doctor who was rumored to keep an oil slick of contraceptive jelly (prized for its moisturizing properties) secreted under the collar of his uniform. But after Regan, the bullpen was thin. So by the time September struck, Billy Williams had not missed a game; Ernie Banks and Ron Santo had played all but a few. Ferguson Jenkins, Ken Holtzman, and Bill Hands were all advancing on twenty wins—but were often kept in to pitch in the late innings, when their arms might be most susceptible to strain. Uncle Jack thought they were all game and accomplished men who were being mismanaged by Leo Durocher.

"He did it with the Giants and Dodgers, if you take a look," Jack said. "Win a lotta games early, when no one else is going all out, to put yourself ahead. But then, when you need the steam in September, the boiler is bare." Years later, I was impressed to see that a cursory review of the statistics can support Jack's argument. In a managerial career of twenty-four years, Leo's teams—the Dodgers, Giants, Cubs, and Astros—finished first place three times. But *eight* times, they finished second; six times, they finished third. A strong record, but one that can suggest his teams ran out of gas when they most needed to move ahead.

Thirty years later, Ferguson Jenkins declined to cast blame against Durocher. "Sure, I was tired," he recollected. "We all were. But in Leo's defense, you gotta wonder: if he didn't play us all out early on, maybe we wouldn't have had that nine-game lead. And the way the Mets were play-ing, it would have been hard to win more games than they did anyway."

Billy Williams thought that the late-season charge of the Mets is part of what took a charge out of the Cubs. "We were tired in August, sure. But when the Mets started winning more and coming on, we felt more tired. When you're winning, you feel stronger. When you're losing, you feel every ache and pain."

More fantastic theories of the Cubs' misfortune abounded. Many centered on the club playing all their home games in the bright daylight of Wrigley Field. When they were on the road, went this reasoning, the Cubs could not adjust their eyes to stadium lights. When they returned home, day games left the Cubs too free for carousing and kanoodling along Rush Street (a theory that would gain plausibility the next year when Joe Pepi-tone joined the club). Baseball on real grass under a summer sun was a fine thing for public relations, went another theory, but the swelter of playing in the scalding daylight of July and August sweated strength from the Cubs. Perhaps most appealingly original was the complaint of several Cubs that the tightening pennant race kept them up late, watching ball games on the West Coast (watching other clubs *win* ball games).

There were also straight-faced suggestions from doctors that the up and down of playing in daylight one day, and under arc lights the next, threw a ballplayer's body out of synch. Symptoms could include sleeplessness, fatigue, irritability, and *irregularity*. Columnist Mike Royko later suggested a Prunes for the Bruins campaign, in which fans were bidden to send the purgative of their choice to their favorite Cub. An awful lot of Ex-Lax got unloaded by Ron Santo's locker.

As the Cubs sank, the Mets soared. The Cubs began to fall so far, they lost even the chance for one last dramatic do-or-die series. In mid-Sep-tember, President Nixon withdrew 60,000 soldiers from Vietnam and cut the draft by a commensurate amount. My friends and I began to think that the war we so reviled would be over before we could be caught up in it personally.

Leo Durocher also began a kind of strategic withdrawal as the Cubs slipped four games in back of the Mets. He benched some of his veterans, albeit past the point when rest might refresh them. Ron Santo ceased to dance. One began to wonder about the Bleacher Bums—were people with nothing more to do during the day than soak up beer and sun in cheap seats just *bums* after all? Ernie Banks still said, "It's a *beeauti-ful* day for a ball game," but the motto now smacked of a brave show.

Riding the El home after school, I kept my head down inside the *Daily News*, rather than look out at the signifying flags sprouting at Wrigley Field. When we stopped at Addison, only a few desultory stragglers got onboard.

At home, I set aside *Sgt. Pepper*, Martha Reeves, and Laura Nyro and put the Cubs' "Hey-hey, Holy Mackerel" on the turntable, pressing my thumb against the edge of the vinyl to slow down the song until the chorus of singing Cubs began to sound as grave as *The Dirge of the Volga Boatmen*:

> *Hhhhhhey-hhhhhheeeeeeey*
> *hhhhhhhhhoooooooooly mmmmmmmmackerallllll*
> *nnnnnnnnnooooooodoubtaboutit*
> *The Cuuuuuuuuuubs*
> *aaaaaaaaaaaare on*
> *theirrrrrrr wayyyyyyyyyyy*

Ugh.

During the Cubs' September descent, my grandfather, Chicago Police Sergeant Francis Joseph Lyons, went into a southwest-side hospital for thoracic surgery made necessary by diabetic complications that had thickened his circulation. Looking back on that time, I flinch a bit with regret that my grandfather's death—his life, too, for that matter—doesn't occupy more space in my memories of what was precious to me. He was a strong, vigorous man, and, I think, a good cop. But he more or less read my mother out of his embrace when she married my father, a *Hee-brew*, in the argot of the Irish southwest side, and kept himself remote even after my mother returned to Chicago as a divorced single mother working odd jobs and rearing a rambunctious boy in a one-bedroom apartment. A few years before, my mother had taken it on herself to reopen relations; so when my grandfather got sick, I was glad we were able keep an abiding vigil at his bedside.

Late on a Sunday night, my mother and I took a train back into the Loop from the southwest-side hospital in which my grandfather was sinking in the last summer of my high school years. I was reading the sports section of that day's newspaper, which detailed the Cubs' decline in snide headlines. My mother, who had been enthralled by the Cubs' pennant run without fully following it—she called the team, as she would later call the Bears and Bulls, "those darling boys"—asked something like, "So, is it really over for the Cubs?"

"Yes, Mother," I said slowly. "I guess it is. Just a few games left, and they're a few games out." My mother sat with that for a moment, as the train clacked past smokestacks and storehouses in the early autumn dark.

"Well, what if they win all their last games?"

Damn my juvenile self-importance, but I sputtered as if the answer was too obvious to make any claims on my knowledge and time. "Well, they won't. Not the way they're playing. And even if they do, the Mets would have to lose all their games. It's just not possible. They blew it."

My mother absorbed that for a moment, and then said, in absolute and lovely, wide, dewy, and brown-eyed earnestness, "That's not being a real fan. Anything's possible, isn't it?" Subtly and agreeably, we were changing places, or at least trading a few inches of our respective personalities as child and parent. I felt the year since my father's death, and all the public turmoil and travails of the times of which I'd tried to be a part, had purchased me the right to a little adult cynicism. My mother, on the other hand, was willing to give hers back. She knew that cynicism leaves lines, in our faces and hearts. Who wants to go around, squeaking from a wrinkled heart?

In early October, as the Chicago Conspiracy trial then going on at the federal courthouse downtown became the best afternoon entertainment in town (Abbie Hoffman, arriving back in the courtroom from luncheon recess, sees Mayor Richard J. Daley already back in the docket for his afternoon testimony. Curly haired and antic-eyed, Hoffman begins to trudge heavily up the aisle toward the mayor, gunslinger style. "Let's just settle this here, you and me," he says. "To hell with all of these lawyers!"), a couple of hundred members of the Weather Underground revolutionary cell went into a frenzy late on a Wednesday night on the north side, bashing in store and car windows up and down the brownstone-lined streets of North Clark, Goethe, East Division, and Astor Streets. A speaker had urged them to "go where the rich people live!"—but I guess the trains to Winnetka had stopped running. It's often forgotten that the rally was called to commemorate the second anniversary of the death of Che Guevara, and I suppose car-bashing is the kind of commemoration Che himself would have chosen over, say, a yarzheit candle. In my northside Quaker meeting, we fretted over the violence of people we considered friends, continued to condemn the larger violence they were protesting, and, probably, uttered a quiet thanks that the glass-bashing had been a little ways south of our own windows.

Years later, after they had spent eleven years underground avoiding prosecution, I got to know and love Bill Ayers and Bernadine Dohrn, two of the leaders of the Weatherpeople, who had gotten married, started a family, and created a remarkable partnership. They were also ardent Cubs fans. Smash the State—and the Mets. It can make you rethink recent history: Weatherpeople on the rampage while a World Series in which the Cubs should have been playing was going on—Days of Rage, indeed. You don't need to be a weatherman to know which way the wind blows (it carries the ball out onto Waveland Avenue, Hey-hey!).★

The Chicago Cubs' loss of 1969 was a historic civic disappointment. But the seasons that followed were outright failures, unredeemed by any feeling that the Cubs woulda, shudda, mighta won if not for just . . .

The Cubs sought to shore up their weak spots by acquiring the strongest-armed outfielder in the National League, Johnny Callison, and the effervescent if erratic former Yankee, Joe Pepitone. Jim Hickman moved to first base (and had an All-Star year, batting .315 and hitting home the winning run of the All-Star game) to afford a rest for Ernie Banks, and Ferguson Jenkins won another 22 games, Kenny Holtzman 17, winning as routinely as withholding tax. Billy Williams was ascendant. And so the 1970 Cubs beat out the New York Mets by a game—but finished 5 games behind the Pittsburgh Pirates of Roberto Clemente and Willie Stargell.

Nineteen seventy-one belonged to Ferguson Jenkins. He won 24 games (20 or more, six years in succession—and then, a seventh year in 1974, after being traded to Texas), the Cy Young Award over Bob Gibson and Tom Seaver, and—the most stupefying and delightful part of his performance—hit .243, the team's eighth-highest average. "He's not a pitcher," Leo Durocher offered in his highest acclamation. "He's a ballplayer." But the Cubs finished third, this time behind both St. Louis

---

★William Ayers is now a professor of education at the University of Illinois in Chicago. Bernadine Dohrn heads Northwestern University's Legal Assistance Foundation. They take their children on a family vacation to the Cubs' spring training in Arizona every year. I have been their companion on Opening Day at Wrigley Field. Since a number of the founders of Students for a Democratic Society were, like Bill, students at the University of Michigan, I have always wondered if the slogan, "Smash the State," originally meant merely Ohio State.

and Pittsburgh. The refrain was becoming, *Poorernie, Poorfergie, Poorsan-toandwilliams*.

One of those Mays, in which scores of thousands of young protesters swarmed into Washington, D.C., to denounce the war, a sleepless and fitful Richard Nixon bundled himself out of the White House to speak with some of those who booed his name and bled over his policies. The president appeared frazzled and haggard. The protesters, invigorated by their greater youth and conviction, seemed puzzled and appalled, but received him respectfully.

Yet no one was sure what to say. The rhetorical battle between the president and his resisters was never really joined. The protesters talked about war and peace, while Richard Nixon mostly talked sports. He told a gaggle of young protesters from Ohio State that he knew just what they felt, he had grown up in a pacifist Quaker family, and by the way, what a *grrreat* Buckeye team Woody Hayes has in Columbus, just *grrreat*. He told kids from the campus cauldron of Madison, the Yankee Stadium of protest, that the Packers were great, just *grrreat*.

On meeting one young demonstrator from Illinois State University in Bloomington, Nixon asked knowledgeably (he did have a road atlas in his mind for congressional districts, and knew Bloomington sat in that broad heart of the state, southwest of Chicago, northeast of St. Louis, in which allegiances are torn), "Cards or Cubs fan?" And the young protester replied after a pause, "Cubs."

"Oh, the Cubs," said the president of the United States, "I think the Cubs are gonna make it this year." I remember resenting Richard Nixon at the time for making sports fans look like mindless, shoe-sniffing boors who liken war to sports and games to combat. These days, I see in Nixon an inept and awkward father who did not know what to say to his daughter's longhaired friends. So, he says, "How 'bout them Cubs?"

I have needed friends from outside Chicago to point out how remarkable and sweetly absurd it is that the 1969 vintage of Ernie, Fergie, Santo, and Sweet Swingin' Billy Cubs may remain the most beloved among fans (until perhaps the Sammy Sosa/Mark Grace edition). After all, they won nothing, and winning is how we measure worth in America. In fact, as the years progressed, the Cubs' losing ways became reliable comic schtick, and even a political prop. A group of Washington notables, including Ronald Reagan, George Will, and David Broder, became conspicuous members of the Emil Verban Society, a luncheon group ostensibly formed to proclaim loyalty to the Cubs by honoring a second baseman who played 143 games for the club in 1949 and '50. Inevitably, there was puckish publicity—all these opinionmongers embracing a feeble ball club.★

The 1984 Cubs, led by Rick Sutcliffe and Ryne Sandberg, actually got into post-season play against the San Diego Padres and were up, two games to none. I had tried to delay leaving to cover elections in Grenada during that series, and my editor said, "Don't worry, by the time you're back, they'll be in the World Series." But several mornings later I heard a BBC announcer plummily intone, "The San Diego Pad-rays have defeated the Chi-cahgo Cubs, and will play for the World Series of baseball against . . ." In Grenada's post-war recovery, it took a couple of hours to book a call to my editor, who said, "Oh no, I've been dreading this. I don't know what to tell you. Should I put you in for some compassionate leave?"

The 1989 Cubs, the team of Ryne Sandberg and a young Mark Grace and Greg Maddux, were credible opponents for the San Francisco Giants for the National League championship. But credible opponents aren't the ones who play in the World Series. The Greg Maddux who would become one of the dominant pitchers in baseball history was hit hard and lost his two starts. Mark Grace could have been the Most Valuable Player of the series, with 11 hits in 17 at bats. But Will Clark of the Giants had 13 hits in 20 appearances, and the Cubs were eliminated in five. After the series, Greg Maddux became a free agent and the Cubs could not match the blandishments of the Atlanta Braves. Every time I see the great Greg Maddux wearing an Atlanta uniform in a World Series, I imagine I must feel a bit like Norma Jean Baker's first husband on seeing Marilyn Monroe in *Some Like It Hot*.

I think those '69 Cubs survive in the affections of fans more vividly than many championship teams because our devotion is the only reward they can receive, and the best we can award. "Those darling boys," said my mother, "gave us such a fun summer." To be a Cub fan, finally, is to learn something of the vexations and disappointments, smashed promises and diminished dreams that love survives, if you

---

★Emil Verban, from Lincoln, Illinois, was known as Dutch at the same time Mr. Reagan was known as Dutch Reagan, the Voice of the Cubs, on WHO in Des Moines. What if Dutch Reagan had joined the Cub broadcast team in Chicago instead of moving to Hollywood? I can imagine Jack Brickhouse whispering to me in the broadcast booth, "That's Dutch Reagan. Helluva nice guy. Don't get him started on politics, though . . ."

And yes, I am a member of the Emil Verban Society.

want to keep it. Fans of baseball teams who have offered more conventional pleasures—such as *winning*—may not be able to appreciate affections so complicated and involving (well, Red Sox fans can). I have noticed that as others may question the coherence of Cub fans, they often admire our constancy. Losing is part of games; it's not always the same as failure.

In the mid-1970s, I was working for the local public television station in Chicago and had the opportunity to interview Leo Durocher. He had "written," with the accomplished Ed Linn, a reasonably candid autobiography—of course it was called *Nice Guys Finish Last.* Just before the cameras rolled, the director sent word out onto the floor that Mr. Durocher's bald head was shining. Our floor director advanced carefully with a powder puff. "Can I touch you up, Mr. Durocher?" he asked cautiously. And Leo barked, lionlike, "Touch yerself kid, where it counts." And then he laughed and offered his head for camera-ready presentation.

Of course, I asked about that 1969 season, and those that followed before he was fired in 1972. "I didn't have the horses," protested Leo.

"You had Ernie Banks, Billy Williams, Ferguson Jenkins, and Ron Santo," I pointed out. "Kessinger, Beckert, and Hundley. They were considered pretty good horses."

"Ah yes," he said, "but look at them one by one. Ernie. Great player, past his prime. Billy. Great player, but greater the next year. Fergie. Solid, strong, but gave up a lotta home runs before he settled down. Plus, you got, you know, all those national press types yelling 'Leo-this' and 'Leo-that,' yelling for my head, and the Cubs fans crying, 'Why don't we see more of Mr. Cub?' when Mr. Cub is on his last legs. Best bunter on the team, I don't mind saying, and he couldn't get to first if you sent him in a cab. Milt Pappas, now there was a guy, I saved his skin, and he turned on me, just like Pepitone . . ."

In the years that followed, I have interviewed genuine war criminals, corporate cutthroats, confirmed liars, insufferable braggarts, and several species of scoundrels. Leo Durocher, who was a better man than all of them, is the only one I wanted to tell, "Fuck you."

Later, when I admitted as much to Jack Brickhouse, he was surprisingly serious. "No," he said, "you're more original than that. Everybody eventually tells Leo to"—and Jack revised the language here, to encourage me to do the same—"go screw himself."

When my mother and I went to the Brickhouse home for Thanksgiving near the end of 1969, the Cubs' decline was the subject of several jokes over the sweet potatoes, but nothing more. The Bears' season had begun, Uncle Jack was their announcer, and the Bears, led by a valiant but lame Gale Sayers, had yet to win a game (and would win only one, their worst season ever, by the end of the year).

Coffee and pumpkin pie were brought out. Then, it was brandy and cigar time, which Uncle Jack offered me in his study ("so Mom won't know"). He showed me a new autographed framed photograph sent by Governor Ronald Reagan of California. "One helluva guy, Scotty, one helluva guy." So I changed the subject to the Cubs.

"Oh, I don't know what happened. Leo could have managed them better, but at his age, he would have done anything to win another pennant. He just got in over his head. Maybe you can yell at a lot of young players, shake 'em up, put the fear of God in them, and light a fire. But Ernie Banks and Billy Williams are men. Fergie Jenkins, Santo, they're all gentlemen. You can't yell at them. You can't scare people who know how to stand in against a Bob Gibson fastball. Hell, we all missed out on some fun. A World Series at Wrigley—that would have been something to see." I caught myself before I could say, "Well, maybe next year."

"Well, you know why I'm sorry?" I said. "I'm sorry you didn't get to call a World Series again. That's one of my dreams."

Jack's heavy ham slice of a face split with a smile. "You want to know my dream?" he asked.

"The Cubs play the White Sox in the World Series. You can ride the El between the games, Addison to Thirty-fifth and Shields. It goes to seven games, and they play the last one in Wrigley Field. After nine innings, the game is tied. The Sox don't score in the bottom of the tenth, and then the Cubs come up. It's getting close to darkness, of course. And then there's this buzz in the crowd. They look down and see *Ernie Banks* in the on-deck circle! The team brought him out of retirement. And then the Sox manager waves toward the bull pen, and who starts walking out for the mound? *Billy Pierce*, also brought out of retirement. Well, Billy still has good stuff. He throws strike one. Then a ball. Then, strike two. Then, another ball. Maybe another. And then, three and two, Billy reaches back and throws his best stuff and Ernie swings. The ball goes sailing out toward left, right near the corner, and in the dark you can't tell if it's fair or foul. But before the umps can signal either way, you know what happens? *They call the game on account of darkness!* And then P. K. Wrigley and Bill Veeck come out to the pitcher's mound, where someone's set up a spotlight. They shake hands and say, 'Hey, let's call it a tie.' " I felt wrapped up in an uncommon adult tenderness, of the kind I sensed Jack had shared with my father.

"Well, anyway, that's my dream," said Uncle Jack Brickhouse "Do you think I'm expecting too much?" At the end of 1969, it might have cheered us both to know that in San Pedro de Macoris, Dominican Republic, Samuel Sosa y Peralta was turning a year old.★

---

★How useful it would be for this narrative if I had been a solitary recipient of Jack's eloquent reverie. But he was a professional. When he knew he had good material, he refined it before many audiences. On the first night of his visitation after his death in 1998, several of us found we could exchange various versions of Jack's dream. In the late 1970s, he also spun out a version for members of Chicago's Organic Theatre Company, who were then creating the workshop version of their play, *Bleacher Bums*. The play's curtain speech is derived from Jack's World Series dream. Even now, it has the same surefire effect on me as Emily's "Oh, earth, you're too wonderful for anyone to realize you!" soliloquy in *Our Town*.

*Chapter 7*

# THE DEATH OF THE MACHINE AND DA BIRTH OF DA BEARS

The Super Bowl Bears of the 1985–86 season were the team that broke the hex, shattered the jinx, dispelled whatever whammy there was in the world that seemed to curse the fates of Chicago franchises. The 1945 Cubs had wound up in the World Series; but they were a wartime promotion of retreads, retirees, and returnees who had a moment before the real players came back, in real uniforms, from real battles. The 1959 "Hitless Wonder" White Sox who won the American League pennant seemed a fluke—certainly after they were so easily dispatched by the Dodgers in the World Series. The 1963 Bears won a football championship, but in the doleful days just after President Kennedy's shooting, when the national mood was mournful.

But the Bears of the mid-1980s became a kind of national comic repertory, with their own routine, rap song, and nicknames (The Fridge, Buddha, Sweetness, Mac) that could have been minted for a serio-comic movie about the crew of a World War II bomber. During the late 1960s and '70s, American football had been made, by too many, into some kind of overweight national metaphor, a territorial sport of conquest (the *blitz*, throwing the *bomb*, and *driving deep*) for a nation ground down in wars at home and overseas. The Super Bowl Bears of Walter Payton, Jim McMahon, Mike Ditka, Mike Singletary and William "The Refrigerator" Perry may have helped return games to real-life size.

To be sure, I had overblown some metaphors myself. As the Bears of George Halas declined each Sunday in the early '70s (almost always moving national announcers to describe them as *the once-proud Bears*), it seemed to me that the team began to share some traits with the decline of Richard J. Daley's once-proud political machine. Each organization was presided over by an original: two shrewd, prideful men of national reputation, hardened in their ways by accumulating defeats. The analogy came with irresistible ease because while court-mandated reforms had shorn the machine of many of the spoils of politics, in jobs and contracts, politics itself was still the city's most popular sport. I followed it as avidly as baseball or football.

When I was still a student I managed a city council campaign in the 46th Ward on the city's north side, in a neighborhood called Uptown. There were four candidates: a balding, amiable old Vista volunteer liberal who was an assistant to the president of the County Board; a serious, liberal lawyer with clenched hair from the U.S. Attorney's office, running as a spoilsport reform Democrat; and a flame-haired liberal Republican, a former runway model, who was the favorite opponent of the man whose campaign I was mismanaging, the community organizer and Pentecostal minister, the Reverend Charles Henry Geary. "I spend all my life looking for a woman like you," Chuck would coo at his blushing Republican opponent during community debates, "and here you are, running against me for alderman." If my recollection seems too fascinated with hair styles, it may be that in retrospect I recognize that there were few political distinctions between them. Each candidate favored more federal spending for the cities, especially in our ward; more city jobs for all, especially in our ward. And they all advocated a foreign policy for Chicago that called for the Soviets to pull out of Poland, Castro out of Cuba, the British to quit Northern Ireland, the Chinese to keep their hands off Taiwan, and for the Israelis to hold on to whatever they wanted. All the candidates were domestic liberals with different political accents. The Reverend Geary had the most distinctive.

Chuck was part of the Appalachian migration that had come

north to Chicago from Kentucky and West Virginia, to work in the
steel mills and auto factories. But his earthy eloquence, wit, and ambition brought Chuck a place away from the assembly lines. He made
himself an itinerant minister and community organizer. Chuck
chewed plugs of Red Man tobacco, sluicing the juice, like water rising
over the side of a bathtub, through his missing bottom-most teeth
and into a paper cup. At home in his own apartment, Chuck's wife,
Martha Elizabeth, would tell him sharply, "Stop spitting, Charles
Henry! Where in the hell do you think you are, in a barn back in
Horse Branch?" But at community meetings in synagogues and
church basements, and liberal political conclaves in lakefront apart-
ments, hosts would sometimes approach me carefully over a tray of
mushroom caps. "And what kind of cup would the Reverend Geary
prefer for his . . . residue?"

As we went around between assemblies, Chuck claimed to have
overheard a nickname attached to our duo: The Hillbilly and the Freak.
"Shoot," Chuck joshed on our way out, "just smellin' like a goat don't
make you no hillbilly. And just havin' hair like a goat don't make you no
freak." Chuck himself had devised an appealing campaign button: five
stripes of handpainted color—red, black, white, brown, and yellow—signifying Uptown's inspiring ethnic diversity. The button became, for a
time, a popular emblem on many north-side lapels; we even managed to
pin one on the Reverend Jesse Jackson's dashiki, and exulted on seeing
newsfilm of Mr. Jackson wearing it at a speech in Hollywood (however,
few Hollywood liberals were registered to vote in Chicago's 46th Ward).
But the button's emblematic cleverness had a serious shortcoming: the
candidate's name did not appear. Understatment is an imprudent technique in political advertising.

Chuck had a natural charm and good sense that I wish had served
better. Chuck's wit had a streak of John Kenneth Galbraith's sensibility,
delivered with the performance sense of Gabby Hayes. Chuck was genuinely torn, for example, over a question of the time about the desirability of an elected school board. Many reformers thought that mayoral
appointments only gave Mayor Daley's political machine control of the
schools to dispense patronage. Chuck, presciently, worried about equally
political community groups flailing over the spoils. I counseled Chuck
that he might like to say something on the order of, "While an elected
school board may give more direct power to the community, I think we
want to avoid politicizing the education of our children." When asked

in community debates, Chuck replied with greater vividness, "That's like pickin' 'tween the witch's tit 'n' the devil's ass." Over the years, I have had far more occasion to quote Chuck Geary than vice versa.★

We finished fourth (and I invoke the editorial *we* only because I am eager to shoulder the blame) in a field of four. It would have been more cost-effective to spend our campaign funds on five-dollar bribes to potential voters; calculating by that scale, we had a chance to finish third. Our finish confirmed an old Chicago political observation: if you put together a coalition that tries to unite disenfranchised blacks and whites, liberal reformers, Asians and Hispanics, good government activists, intellectuals and community leaders, there's no way they can keep you from winning 20 percent of the vote.

But elsewhere in the city, Mayor Daley's machine was picking up dents. They lost the campaign for States Attorney, the local prosecutorial office. With Richard Nixon still in the White House and appointing Republican U.S. Attorneys, more prosecutions of Daley Democrats for corruption were ahead. Illinois' former governor, Otto Kerner, got sent to prison; then Mayor Daley's city council floor leader, Alderman Thomas Keane. More independents were elected to city council seats. The Mayor still had the parliamentary power to turn off their microphones in floor debate—but the number of reformers was increasing so much, they needed less amplification. Mayor Daley was still unassailable when he ran for reelection himself. Even as voters began to see Daley's machine as decrepit, they esteemed its maker. They felt that reformers might be right on the issues, but soft at the center. But the mayor's minions began to lose to reformers, machine rebels, and the spread of voters to the suburbs. As the 1970s progressed, Mayor Daley became what he claimed to detest most: a charismatic leader. A pol with personal appeal, but no coattails. A charmer exposed in the open field by a lack of muscle up front. It was tempting to see in the mayor's predicament more than a suggestion of a Bear running back, slowed by time and girth, trapped behind his own lines.

Other Chicagoans were certainly better-known around the world. Sir Georg Solti and Muhammad Ali were more celebrated; Sam Giancana

---

★Chuck Geary deserves his own chapter in another book, or his own book. Those interested in seeing him in his prime might seek out a copy of Haskell Wexler's 1969 film, *Medium Cool*, in which Chuck played a guitar-picking Pentecostal minister in Uptown. Chuck liked to buy a ticket when they reprised it at local theaters and hang about near the popcorn—waiting to be recognized.

was more notorious; Ann Landers and Gwendolyn Brooks more quotable; Saul Bellow and Jesse Jackson more esteemed. But in much of the city, Richard J. Daley and George Halas were the face of Chicago for their times, even as their times seemed to be in eclipse.

Once, I saw them at the same time and place, although I can't say I saw them say a thing to each other. It was in October of 1976, when Jimmy Carter came to town as the anointed Democratic candidate for president to march in the Columbus Day parade. Mayor Daley organized a welcome in a downtown ballroom, and George Halas was the elder statesman in a chorus line of civic leaders—a black steel executive, a banker, the head of the Chicago Symphony board—who had been brought in to shake the hand of the man their mayor said would be the next president of the United States. I was a local reporter then and found myself surrounded by national political writers who found the mayor's locutions curious.★

"Now Jimmy Carter is from Georgia," the mayor began, his great, round face at first impassive. "From da great state ah Georgia. And you know, and you know—" a pause here, as if discovering something unexpected—"Georgia, Georgia, dey voted twice for Adlai Stevenson in Georgia!" The room erupted. There was a chiming overhead as the applause died down; chandeliers were still tinkling. A New York reporter, whom I had flattered by recognizing, leaned down to whisper, "Isn't he dead? What gives?" He had perhaps forgotten that Adlai Stevenson of Illinois, despite his classy striped-pants antecedents, had twice been the Chicago machine's grateful nominee for president. At least a few of the men and women applauding in the ballroom might have become federal appointees instead of county functionaries if Stevenson had been elected over Eisenhower. The mayor's beginning was a reminder to his sycophants that even if they found Jimmy Carter too rural, a generation before, Carter's country-cousins had produced for a Chicagoan.

"Yes. Yes. Dat's right. Georgia, dey voted for Adlai Stevenson. And Adlai, we were proud of him. And we miss him every day. And we're so glad, so glad, to have his son, Adlai da Tird"—I'm sorry, but that's what it sounded like—"Adlai Stevenson da Tird, wid us." This time, there was

---

★I don't render the mayor's remarks in dialect because I am trying to make him sound doltish. On the contrary. His words will bear out that Mr. Daley was an exceptionally adroit political speaker. But this is the dialect as most national reporters heard it—and made them wonder what Mayor Daley was saying.

a rather more comprehensible ovation for the younger Adlai, the state's junior senator.

"And Georgia. Georgia. So many great tings come from Georgia. Especially people. And warm springs. Franklin Roosevelt went to Warm Springs every year. And when he died, da train dat brought him back, it came, it came up from Georgia. And Georgia, Georgia voted four times, *four times*, for Franklin Roosevelt!" Most of the men and women slamming their hands together had their first government jobs through the generosity of Franklin Roosevelt and his effusions of federal dollars through Chicago's machine. The mayor had made the progression from Roosevelt to Stevenson to Carter sound as natural as Tinker to Evers to Chance.

"And so," concluded the mayor, now thumping the lectern with the blunt palm of his hand, "I give ta you, da man you're going to give to me, da man who will do, will do fir us, as we will do fir him, da man, Jimmy Carter of Georgia!" *The man who will do for us, as we will do for him,* is about as cryptic as, *If we scratch his back, he'll scratch ours.* But only a man immensely accomplished at talking the special language of politics can make such an unvarnished declaration sound obscure to a raft full of big-name national political reporters.

Chicago and Illinois would do indeed, for Jimmy Carter; who would make his first phone call of thanks to the mayor of Chicago. But just about five weeks later, Mayor Richard J. Daley would drop dead in his doctor's office on Michigan Avenue. By the time I got to the second-floor pressroom in City Hall, the principal beat reporters who had covered the mayor for most of his career and some of his younger acolytes who had been more openly resistant to his iron-fisted ways were holding an Irish wake. Tall stories and short whiskies on tap.

"I tell you," railed a white southwest-side alderman, "the Irish are dead. The Polacks think their time has come, but they don't have the votes. The colored don't have the votes. The Litvaks don't have the votes. The Eye-talians don't have the votes. Nobody has the votes. It's every man for himself."

"Eddie," a kindly reporter said by way of encouraging the speaker to tamp down his volume, "the mayor isn't cold in his grave yet." But the alderman took that as a call to thunder back. *"He would have understood this shit better than anyone!"*

Bob Crawford, the kindest and wisest man in the pressroom, had been driving off with his family for a holiday vacation when he heard the news on the radio. He sat in his hallowed window seat in a far, cramped corner, still in his light driving shoes and a fleecy knit shirt, looking weary and wistful.

"You know what I was thinking about? I was thinking about nineteen sixty-eight. When Robert Kennedy was running for president, the one thing that gave him any hope he could win was that he could win a lot of primaries and then call up Mayor Daley and say, 'Mr. Mayor, we go back a long way. Ask yourself who you'd rather have on the top of your ticket, someone named Humphrey, or someone named Kennedy.' And Daley, you know, was no friend of the war in Vietnam. He thought it was taking too much money away from the cities. After that convention in 1968, that's when he became this big ogre to the kids, 'cause they had long hair, which he couldn't stand, and they taunted his cops. But before that, they might have had a friend in Daley. You know what Kennedy said? He said, 'Daley, Daley is the ball game.' Daley could have made another Kennedy president, stopped the war in Vietnam, and united reformers, blacks, kids, labor, all of them. It's amazing, isn't it? The history that almost happens. What one bullet can change. Daley, Daley was the ball game."

I didn't leave until dawn. Of course, I had stories to file; but I was also having, as one will at Irish wakes, a wonderful time. A light snow fell that night, and by the time I walked out onto Clark Street to begin to tramp a trail through to the State Street subway entrance, flakes were freezing into a sugary film over several ice sculptures in the plaza across from City Hall that Mayor Daley had dedicated just the morning before. There was a nativity scene, a Star of David, a leaping salmon, a Santa Claus, and yes, a snarling Chicago Bear head—fragile forms that would melt away in the first strong sun, while the powerful politician who had inspected them was laid out, almost as coldly, a couple of miles away. As a young student activist, I had worked hard to try to loosen Mayor Daley's iron grip on the city. As a young reporter, I was alert for stories that could bring attention to the corruption, grossness, and heartlessness in the smack of his iron hand. But that dawn, something in the snow striking the stone and steel in the downtown that had been his domain allowed me to see the mayor in softer focus: a towering figure in a cityscape I loved. He was a boss, a builder, and a White Sox fan. Daley, Daley was the ball game.

It is part of Chicago lore that Richard J. Daley was the only man who could bluster George S. Halas. Once, in the mid-1970s, Halas made a show of entertaining offers from suburban Arlington Heights, Illinois, to build the Bears a new tax-supported stadium. City Hall confidants had circulated the story that the mayor had called Papa Bear to say, "I think that's fine, George. You're a businessman. Do what you have to do. I'm a businessman, too. I think moving out there would be a fine thing for you, George—if you wanna call yourselves the *Arlington Heights Bears.* Our lawyers say you just can't take the name *Chicago* with you out there to the suburbs. We'd have to take you to court. That could take years. You know the backlog. Besides, I wonder how many people will come out to see the *Arlington Heights Bears,* George. I wonder how excited the network people will be about broadcasting the *Arlington Heights Bears* coast to coast. You're a fine businessman, George. You make the call." The Bears stayed in Chicago.

The '70s were a dismal decade for the club, in any and all venues. They won 60 games, against 83 losses. Mugs Halas, the son Papa Bear appointed the club's president, reportedly raised his voice against his father as probably no one had since Richard J. Daley.

"I am," George Halas Jr. told his father, "so . . . *sick* . . . of . . . *this!*" Shattered by the confrontation, and more than a little sick of losing himself, Papa Bear authorized his son to seek changes.

But Mugs Halas died, suddenly, in 1979, sending George Sr. into a deeper despondency. In 1981, he received a short, plain, unapologetic handwritten note from an old Bear who had left the team over a contract dispute and was now an assistant coach with the Dallas Cowboys. "I know you have had some bad times," wrote Mike Ditka, "and I just want to renew our friendship. I want you to know that if you ever make a change in the coaching end of the organization, I just wish you would give me some consideration."

In the 1986 autobiography he wrote with Don Pierson,* Mike Ditka talked about the regret he had felt over bolting from the Bears over money. On the one hand, he was entitled to more money; on the other hand, he knew . . .

> *I'll always be a Bear. That's a fact of life. That's how people perceive me. Just like Butkus could never have been a San Diego Charger . . . There were certain people who were Chicago Bears, period. Halas*

---

*Ditka: An Autobiography,* by Mike Ditka with Don Pierson. Bonus Books, Chicago, 1986.

*looked for those kind of people. Maybe he didn't always find them. That's why I was a Bear, and when I left I was still a Bear. And it hurt.*

And, in a frank passage, Ditka talks about seeking solace for that hurt in booze and debauchery. He was signed by a Philadelphia Eagles team that was, for its time, almost as doleful as the Bears; and found himself relegated to a substitute role even in a company of incompetents:

*Basically, every night I would go out. I really drank a lot. I wasn't playing and it was just ridiculous. I was about trying to kill myself with drinking. I was in bad shape. I was a mess. You wonder why you pull muscles. My God, you pull muscles if you're full of alcohol. You pull muscles because it dehydrates you . . . I know I woke up in some strange places, not knowing how I got there or why I was there or who I was with or anything like that. It could have been Alabama as well as Philadelphia. I would go through the day after like I was in a fog, not being able to distinguish between what was real and what wasn't real.*

He got traded to the Dallas Cowboys where, he said, a stern and strait-laced Tom Landry nevertheless took a paternal interest in his problems. Both men burned; Landry was just better at banking his fires. It was Landry, says Ditka, who gave him the chance to recover and another chance to play; and then, when Ditka grew too old to be a bashing Hall of Fame tight end, it was Landry who suggested that his ursine intensity might be best turned into coaching; and made him one of his assistants.

There's a famous Cowboy locker-room story—Ditka insists he does not remember the incident, but says he knows his own nature well enough not to deny it—that holds that Ditka so hated to lose that once, after losing money in a round of gin rummy with some fellow coaches, Ditka swung a four-footed chair into the clubhouse wall—and drove all four feet into the wall. It was during this time, he says, that he rediscovered faith. Tom Landry, of course, was one of football's best-known born-again Christians. Ditka admired his sincerity and constancy, but did not simply borrow the creed of the man who had become his mentor. He says he looked back, for the first time in years, to the Catholicism of his youth in Pennsylvania's coal country. His faith reminded him that life was too fleeting, our talents too fragile, to let them fritter away through indolence. He believed in hard work, good times when you're through, and Bearing down all over again the next day. When you have a talent for temper, you apply that, too. After all, Ditka said he had discovered through his faith, God sent down swarms of locusts, slaughtered innocents, and drowned legions in the Red Sea (plagues against his enemies which, you sometimes get the impression, Coach Ditka would like to diagram for his own use). He wrote with Don Pierson:

> *The Lord isn't out there making check marks when you swear or kick the sideline marker or throw a clipboard . . . If you read the Bible, the Good Lord had a temper, too. Threw a few people around. We all have it, but how do you use it?*

Halas received Ditka's letter and reacted—well, like a lover who gets another chance to rekindle something lost. He called. Ditka instantly flew off to Chicago and took a cab to Papa Bear's solitary bachelor apartment along the lake on North Sheridan Road. They sat at the kitchen table, and when Halas asked, "What's your philosophy about football?" Ditka was able to give him an answer that was at once almost insufferably flattering—and utterly sincere. "To play rough, tough, fundamental, Bear football." Halas was impressed by the fact that Ditka told him, "Let's do the deal right here. No need for agents, lawyers. Write it out on a napkin, let's sign, and let's get started." He might also have been further infatuated by Ditka's willingness to accept the lowest coach's salary in the league. Papa Bear was wounded, old, and lonely, but not senile.

The roster Coach Ditka surveyed was already being improved. A talented defensive line, including Dan Hampton at end and tackle Steve McMichael, was already in place. But most valuable of all for Ditka's early reputation as a man who could build a defense was the draft of a linebacker out of Baylor named Mike Singletary.

Singletary was a round-shouldered bullet of a man who was said to keep a collection in his dorm room of all the helmets he had broken—*his own* helmets, cracked on impact with a running back's chest. The young man who first met the press seemed at odds with his annihilative reputation. What you first saw in Singletary was an affable, moon-faced black man with Asian-accented eyes that seemed as hard and small as shooter marbles behind his thick glasses. Singletary was said to be something of a math whiz, and the story was told about a white coed who once approached him in the Baylor library as he read a calculus textbook. "Oh, I didn't know you people read that," she said, and Baylor's best-known helmet-buster raised an eyebrow at the young white woman. *"You people?"* he said evenly. "Ohmigod," she gasped, "I meant *football players.*" Of course, they got married.

Something in the sharp edge of his eyes and the way he launched himself into tackles, fixed the name Samurai Mike into sports page features about Singletary. But around the Bears themselves, the name never took. Singletary had a calm aspect of command on the field and called out defensive formations in a deep, imposing drumroll of a voice from the linebacker slot. The calm with which he carried himself between outbursts over the ball suggested another nickname for Singletary: *Buddha.*

Singletary joined a Bear team that already was graced with a star who was called the greatest running back since Gale Sayers; by the time he retired, he would be called the greatest of all-time.

Walter Payton, who had been drafted out of Mississippi's Jackson State in 1975. Where Sayers glided and eluded, Walter Payton exploded. Typically, he would begin to break off a run with a flurry of stutter steps, causing advancing tacklers to break left, right, or dare to advance on him directly—then, burst away as they floundered toward his feet. As tacklers tried to bring him down in full stride, Payton would thrust his free arm out from his shoulder into the tackler's face, snapping back their heads and blocking their view. If a defensive back managed to slip that, Payton would finally, in a magic application of adrenaline, put on an extra half-step of speed and attack the tackler with his solid shoulders and bony elbows. "Make them pay for it," as Walter always explained.

Ironically, there may never have been a player that was more often helped to his feet by opposing players; they respected every bruise he left, knowing they made any tackle more impressive. Walter wore a towel in his pants, tucked like a chef's cloth over the front of his belt, that read SWEETNESS 34. His number and an old nickname from high school in Jackson, where Payton won a welter of local dance contests (in fact, his first trip to Chicago was to boogie for a national dance trophy on Don Cornelius's old television series *Soul Train*). But the name "Sweetness" seemed to suit his voice, which was high enough to prickle and itch the ears, like the squeak of a glass being wiped with a dry cloth. "Oh, I knew we had to get seven on that roll-out," you could hear him hold forth in the locker room after the game, in an almost tinny-sounding cartoon voice, "so I knew I had to go *blaaam* when they got to me."

Ditka—who threw compliments around like manhole covers—declared Payton, "The most complete football player I've ever seen."

Over a thirteen-year career, Walter would run for more yards than any other player in history, block with malevolent conviction, catch passes lesser receivers would wave by, throw 8 touchdown passes (he was a lefty, like the great Bobby Layne), and even punted once—for a respectable 39 yards. In The City that Works, as Chicago styled itself, Payton worked hardest. No one did more things better, or with more exuberance. In a vocation usually held to be short-term, Payton missed just one day of work in thirteen years.

And yet, by the time Ditka arrived in 1981, a lament, and even a loneliness, had begun to attach itself to Walter Payton. Journalists began to place him in that exceptional company of Chicago greats—Ernie Banks, Fergie Jenkins, Gale Sayers, and Dick Butkus—who were considered the best of their times, and yet had no championship to show for it. It was an absence that curdled the enjoyment of all other achievements; it questioned, in fact, their value. Didn't the genuinely great players raise the talents of others?

In the early 1980s, opposing players began to shake Payton's hand after peeling themselves off his knees in a tackle. He accepted their hands as a gentleman, but cursed what they signified—that for all of Walter's endowments and deeds, opposing teams had nothing to fear from his Bears. Payton was a gregarious and even prankish teammate, who took some advantage of his celebrity. At the bottom of a pile, he would sometimes reach out and untie the shoelaces of a referee. The referee would often utter an oath as he stumbled, but would usually laugh by the time he recovered his step. What referee could throw a flag on the great Walter Payton for untying his shoelaces? Yet as the seasons progressed, Payton became more isolated. Increasingly, he sat by himself on the team charter, in the same aisle seat just behind the first class compartment, music headphones snapped into his ears to stiff-arm any conversation. Few teammates felt they had earned the rank, in yards, blood, or pain, to approach him.

The Bears of the time suffered a kind of anatomical imbalance. Their defense was always more staunch then their offense. To be sure, it was part of the character that made the Bears distinct. While the rest of the league expanded scoring with the forward pass, the Bears kept their advances on the ground and strove to defend their own lands. The imbalance also kindled resentment between the Bears' offense and defense, and the great Walter Payton and a succession of licorice-armed quarterbacks. The defense found themselves worn down by long afternoons on the field, because the offense could not move the ball. Payton, for that matter, was gaining a historic amount of ground, but carrying more than an equal load. It was exhausting; and, to have so little to show for it at the end of the afternoon was galling.

In the game of conquest that football had become, the Bears were a tank corps without aerial support. Part of their predicament was prolonged bad judgment. While other clubs had the foresight or fortune to draft or develop a Fran Tarkenton, Roger Staubach, or Joe Montana, the Bears were claiming and clinging to Jack Concannon, Gary Huff, Bobby Douglass, and Bob Avellini.

But in 1982, Ditka drafted a quarterback who managed to entice both trouble and opportunity. Jim McMahon, out of Brigham Young University, presented himself in Coach Ditka's office, bearing a beer in each hand. Reporters huddled, then asked, *Whadid ya think of that, coach?* "I thought," Ditka told reporters, "that the kid must be thirsty."

Reporters at first looked at McMahon's personal résumé and found his selection baffling. He had been the nation's leading collegiate passer, but at an isolated school where such achievements were often discounted as signifying future success in the NFL.* He was a blondish, spike-haired Southern Californian who seemed to work at becoming an outlaw in whatever surroundings he found himself. At Mormon Brigham Young, McMahon had regarded nighttime curfews as goals to be exceeded; and campus rules against drinking, smoking, and premarital sex as challenges to his cunning (years later, I had occasion to report a story on the BYU campus and asked a school public relations official how Jim McMahon had managed to avoid suspension. The official smiled confidingly. "We made sure he *didn't* sign the campus honor pledge," he said. "No signature, no violations. Mormons can be creative, too," he said rather proudly). By the time he arrived in the arms of the Bears, Jim McMahon had succeeded in turning himself into a compound mixture of surfer dude and Hell's Angel. One could foresee, without too much imagination, that McMahon's deliberate desperado pose might aggravate the clench-haired Coach Ditka.

But Ditka had detected something else in the game films he had reviewed. He saw a Bear. When McMahon ran out of the protection of the pocket, he threw his head and shoulders against tacklers, running them over for an extra yard, rather than falling down to avoid a tackle (usually a shrewd play, not an evasive one, for a quarterback). Ditka

---

*McMahon and Steve Young, who would be drafted four years later out of BYU by the San Francisco 49ers, would cause pro teams to change that judgment.

wanted to alter the young man's technique without diluting his instinct—to hit, shake it off, and keep on going. Bear down, *gggrrrhhh!* The coach also liked his cunning. A young man who could calculate so many ways to find trouble might also have a few ideas about how to move the ball into the end zone. And, he was impressed by the loyalty McMahon seemed to inspire among his linemen. After he threw a touchdown pass, McMahon usually butted heads and shoulders with the men who had scraped and scrambled in the trenches of the line to protect him from tacklers. From his first practice on the Bears, McMahon made sure that his jersey acquired as much mud and blood as any lineman's. The blotches were battle ribbons in the currency of football.

At the same time, Chicago's brick-footed and barricaded political system was betraying a few signs of modernism. Mayor Daley's immediate successor was a neighbor from down the street in Daley's own 11th Ward, Michael Bilandic. A gentle, basset-faced, late-life bachelor (who, on becoming mayor, became instantly intensely attractive to platinum socialites), Bilandic differed from Daley in two significant respects. He was Croatian, which could seem a compromise between rival Irish and Polish politicians. But more critically, Bilandic lacked the late mayor's political perspicacity. When an extraordinary snowfall froze the city in place in 1979, Bilandic closed down a succession of elevated stations stretching from the last stop in suburban Oak Park into the Loop. Assessed strictly as civic management, the decision made some sense. The largest number of passengers boarded at Oak Park; the number of riders dwindled as the trains nosed over the shattered streets of Chicago's vast black west-side precincts, where unemployment was high. But the injury of closing down those stations could not be excused by statistics. It left residents in neighborhoods still choked with snow (because the plows often got to black residential areas last) feeling isolated, stranded—and insulted.

Bilandic's most conspicuous opponent was a renegade from the old machine, Jane Byrne, a flame-tempered, frost-haired northwest-side pol who had been the city's Commissioner of Consumer Affairs and one of Mayor Daley's political lieutenants. She was not a reformer; but among machine functionaries, Byrne was practically a Bolshevik. She used to descend on the City Hall pressroom to declare impromptu press conferences, during which she'd take after butchers who put a heavy thumb on the back of a scale while weighing a pork chop and motor vehicle inspectors who pocketed a twenty-spot clipped to a license application.

Small-time cons, to be sure, but usually reliable supporters of Chicago's machine. I liked her. Jane Byrne was ambitious and blunt, a flirty filter-cigarette smoker among the El Producto chuggers in City Hall's hall-ways. She'd leave off a pile of her press releases, dispense a passing quote, and take up a station by one of the old chromium ashtrays that used to anchor the Hall's halls.

"Hi," she'd say, accepting a match, "how are you? Whaddya hear?"

"Fine, thanks, Mrs. Byrne. I don't hear anything. What do you hear?"

"Nothing. Nothing." She'd exhale with a smile. "Nothing. Didja ever wonder why you got this request now to make forty more hires at Street and San?"

"Always."

"Well, maybe you should check and see where Vito needs a little hired help. His ward is black, now, and he can't get the captains on the streets, so he has to hire and import them." When one checked her smoke signals, there was frequently a fire below, or at least, some kindling.

She left Bilandic's cabinet protesting that a taxi rate increase had been "greased" by the mayor and the cab company presidents supporting him—a popular issue in poor neighborhoods, where cabs, in those days, were often the only available conveyance for overburdened mothers and senior citizens to make long trips to public hospitals and clinics. When Mayor Bilandic shut down the west-side Elevated stations, Byrne trudged in to rail against the closures, telling the cameras from impassable, impossible frozen streets, "I know what *runs* this city. I know how to make it *work* for everybody." For the first time in Chicago's history, that rhetorical coalition of disenfranchised blacks, disenchanted whites, discouraged Hispanics (she'd taken Spanish lessons from a tutor, and could campaign in short bursts of grammar school Spanish), liberals, reformers, and even a few Republicans, coalesced—around a descendant of the old machine.

The night before the election, Jane Byrne rang up Vito Marzullo, the old west-side alderman, and delivered a short soliloquy. "Look, Vito," she told him, "I think I have this election won, if you give me an honest count. So you tell your boys, if they give me a straight count, even if they're against me, they got nothing to fear from Janie. But if I catch any of your boys stealing from me, Vito, I'll cut their balls off. That's a promise." The old ward heeler was softened, rather than taken aback. "Aww, Janie, don't worry," Marzullo told her, "we'll work it out."

The person who told that story—and told in admiration—was *Vito Marzullo*, not Jane Byrne. As reform went, it was Bearlike.

But once the coalition that would elect Jane Byrne came together, it was a force that could be bent against her. Jane Byrne's reign was incendiary for those of us who covered it, and kept turning to the thesaurus for alternatives: *fiery, blazing, tempestuous,* and *conflagrative.* She brought in a few reformers, and kept on a good many crooks; where Daley had ruled by edict and intuition, Byrne tried to prevail by prevarication and press release.

Nationally, Byrne got portrayed as a liar by inviting President Carter to a fund-raising dinner shortly before the beginning of the 1980 campaign and declaring, while the president fixed her with his famous grin, "If the convention were held tomorrow, I would vote without hesitation to renominate the leader of our party for another term as president . . ." The best-known national reporters who had just flown in from New York and Washington yammered "endorsement" into their telephone receivers and microphones. But for once, Chicago provincialism was a truer guide. The convention was *not* going to be held tomorrow. She had spoken only of *the leader of our party,* and managed never to so much as mention Jimmy Carter by name. It reminded me of the way George Halas used to joust with reporters over which of his flagging quarterbacks would start the next game. Concannon? *He has many gifts, that young man.* What about Bukich? *He's done everything we've asked him to.* Which one, Mr. Halas? *I'll make the decision I have to. Let's not get into personalities, gentlemen.* Some endorsement. Mayor Byrne had all but hired an airship to pull over Navy Pier, blinking a message on the bottom of its silvery stomach: RUN TEDDY RUN. When she ultimately endorsed Edward Kennedy and marched along with him in the St. Patrick's Day parade, she was booed for duplicity; and so she could be duplicitous. But not, I thought, about endorsing Jimmy Carter.

Locally, her best moment came when a series of shootings burst through the tight, cold confines of the Cabrini-Green housing projects. Mayor Byrne and her husband moved in to an apartment there, to bring along the phalanx of police that followed the mayor into a neighborhood that could use it. While the times of her tenancy in the projects could be questioned (reporters stationed outside would note her comings and goings like private detectives on a domestic stakeout: *7:00 P.M., subject arrives home. Visible in window. 9:40 P.M., subject departs, arrives Delaware St. apt. 9:53. Overnight*—a level of detail few reporters found the time or space to lavish on life in the projects for those who lived there full-time), the shootings, indeed, diminished. Her move was derided as a gimmick. But gimmickry can be the poetry of politics. A gimmick that helped stopped shootings seemed worthy and expedient.

I was reporting in India four years later when my editor said, "Get back to Chicago—there's some real ethnic rivalry going on." Mayor Byrne was in a three-way dead-heat in the Democratic primary (still equivalent to election in Chicago) against Richard J. Daley's son, Richard M., who was then the local prosecutor, and a third candidate, a south-side congressman named Harold Washington.

Washington had not been the first choice of black opinion leaders and financiers to challenge for the nomination for mayor. But he was the most available. A bluff, blunt, Bearlike man in demeanor, he could run for mayor in an off-year without forfeiting his seat in Congress. Washington was eloquent, loquacious, and ambitious, but had what most electorates might consider at least a small liability in pursuing higher office: he had served a term in prison for failing to file several years of income tax returns (Harold's birthday, by the way, was April 15). The federal prosecutors who took him to trial always believed that Washington was concealing a small amount of income from a numbers racket wheel he had inherited from his father; as a shrewd lawyer, he could be expected to know that the penalties for *not* filing were lighter than penalties for filing fraudulent returns. He served his months in prison without resigning his seat in the state legislature—Chicagoans are wonderfully understanding about the personal problems of public officials—and then battled his way back into position to win the Congressional seat he had long coveted. He was not eager for the limelight that even a third-place, sacrificial stone of a candidacy could bring to his personal affairs. But other, more prominent and plausible black politicians backed away from challenging Byrne, figuring to wait four years. And Harold began to warm to the limelight.

He was both gruff and elegant, tough and funny, and flattered at finally, after so many years as a neighborhood pol, shining on a platform proportionate to his own self-image. He assailed Chicago's machine as *antediluvian*, and when reporters asked him, in frank ignorance, what he meant by that word, he was playful. "Look it up, gentlemen and ladies. Am I supposed to do your homework for you? You'll find it in the

Oxford Dictionary.* It's in libraries everywhere." He had Chicago mother wit, and a charm to kid on the square. When he did especially well at a candidate's debate, he told reporters, "I may have my annual bourbon." When they asked when he might marry a woman, a school-teacher, to whom he had been engaged for twelve or more years, Harold looked grave. "I expect that after a long and fruitful life in public service, I will be buried here in Chicago." No, no, reporters called out laughingly, *married.* "Oh," he said in mock astonishment, "you said *married?*" So when journalists began to examine his tax case, Harold brushed their questions back with the upper hand he had gained. "They didn't care about it when I was down in the polls, at just a point or two. They didn't care about it when I was an also-ran. You tell me," he asked crowds, "why do the press suddenly care about something that's dead and gone, paid my debt and in my past, when suddenly I stand a chance to become the *first black mayor of Chicago?* The first man to break the grip of this *antediluvian* machine? Could that have anything to do with it?" Many Chicagoans, in fact, seemed oddly reassured by Harold's tax conviction—they took it as a sign that he was not some sanctimonious reformer who didn't understand what made the wheel of life go 'round. No less a chronicler of civic corruption than Mike Royko pointed out that if Harold were to be elected, he would be the first Chicago mayor to go to prison before he was in office, not afterward. Politics is a game in which you can also get points for good timing.

On the plane coming back from India, I read news columns in the *International Herald Tribune* that detailed the common wisdom among pundits: that Harold would come close, but fall short. The precinct army—now split between Jane Byrne, Richie Daley, and Washington—would deliver a narrow victory to another Daley. But I became more impressed by the size of the crowds turning out to acclaim Harold on the south and west sides—and the fact that they stayed late to line up at folding tables organizers had set up in church basements and community centers, to deploy and deliver a burgeoning vote. The Reverend Jesse Jackson, then pondering his first run for president, had shucked his dashiki for beautifully cut British suits, finished off with gold collar pins. The righteous reverend had begun to look almost like the Rt. Reverend Mr. Jackson as he beseeched black voters who were just beginning to grasp the powers they could lever with their hands.

---

*First meaning listed is "before the Flood" of the Bible. But in Chicago, perhaps, that should be "before the Fire" of 1871.

"What time is it?" Mr. Jackson called out; and the crowd chorused back, "It's nation time!"

"What time did you say it was?" And then, the response grew louder, more insistent. "It's nation time! It's nation time!"

"Brothers and sisters," the Reverend Jackson would say, looking imposing and masterful as he preened at the rostrum. "Look around. What do you see? Brothers and sisters who have built this city. When they say, 'This is the city that works!' they're talking about you. Brothers and sisters who clean the subways, run the trains, teach our children, and patrol our streets. Brothers and sisters who are now gonna run banks and city departments. What time is it?" And then, an explosion, with church ladies in floral hats pulling handkerchiefs from their purses, and children in Sunday blue sweaters chiming in as their eyes shined up at the reverend with a kind of worshipful limelight:

*"It's nation time! It's nation time! It's nation time!"*

Between his own virtuosity on air and a growing precinct army on the ground, Harold Washington was beginning to enjoy the kind of balance between the passing and ground games that the Bears were trying to build. He already enjoyed something of Dick Butkus's gift for the straight-faced bluff. I went along one afternoon, the weekend before voting, to a candidate's rally at a north-side synagogue. Harold put on a yarmulke; and if, perchance, that rode so far back on his head it was not visible in photographs, he also looped a blue-and-white silk fringed tallis around his linebacker's shoulders—a late-life bar mitzvah boy. "I have always," he told a hushed and admiring audience, "stood foursquare behind the right of the state of Israel to exist, flourish, and prosper along the banks of the ancient River Jordan."

As he wedged out of a back door, through the widening swirl of gathering celebrity, I had a brief moment before his campaign car could be loaded.

"Mr. Washington," I said, "didn't you sign that letter last year from the Congressional Black Caucus calling for recognition for the rights of Palestinians?" He looked around for his car, and saw it was still half a block away, before turning back to me. "I am in favor of the rights of Arabs," he told me. "And I am in favor of the rights of Jews. I am in favor of Israel. I am in favor of Egypt. I am in favor of all people."

"But," I gasped and grasped, "you don't consider that Black Caucus letter a contradiction of—"

"I consider," he said bluntly, "that that letter was then, and this is now." And as a door was lifted open for him, Harold Washington turned back urbanely. "A good Sabbath to you."

On election night, our engineer, Rich Rarey, and I were stationed at Mayor Byrne's headquarters. But early in the evening, it became obvious that the headlines would issue from elsewhere. Rich and I hailed a cab over to Washington headquarters in a hotel just south of the Loop. An exhilarated crowd was bursting out of the ballroom and surging out into the lobby and the street. Struggling to reach the risers on which the press was set up, Rich and I saw Claude Cunningham, an engineer with our local station in Chicago, the man who had first taught me the rudiments of radio. We were longtime friends; I'm afraid much of our humor had the heavy-handed, black-white byplay of Brian Piccolo and Gale Sayers. So when I saw Claude from about fifty feet away, I sank to my knees and began to crawl toward him, halting at his feet to kiss the tops of his shoes. "I told you white boys," Claude declared with a laugh, "I told you, but you wouldn't listen." By the last ten feet or so, we had quite an audience. A nice African-American man helped me to my feet amid applause. "Buddy," he said, "I don't know who you are. But you sure are a hell of a good loser." Through the thicket of supporters standing tall on their toes, we saw that the next mayor of Chicago had made his way onto the ballroom stage. Harold Washington gleamed and beamed in the sprouting television lights, as broad-shouldered as Butkus, as ebullient as Banks, a rapscallion, an odds-beater, a coalition-builder, and a Bears fan. As cheers and tears burst below him, Harold spread his arms wide, like a Chicago linebacker at the snap, as if to envelop the city, from the west side to the lake shore, in an immense and burly embrace. "I extend my arms," Harold Washington roared, "in love and friendship to *every living soul* in this city!"

Politics aside (which, of course, it never is), Harold Washington's election coincided with heartening, hopeful times in Chicago. The flight to the suburbs was turning, ever so slightly, back. The Loop was once again busy, wrecking and rebuilding. The city's theatrical community, between the succeeding generations of Second Citians, stand-ups, David Mamet, and the Organic and Steppenwolf companies, was winning new national notices for rawness and audacity. Bill Peterson, who had been two years ahead of me in high school, had taken his local production of *In the Belly of the Beast* off-Off-Broadway, where it ran to great acclaim. He discovered that being a Chicago actor carried a cachet in New York, where the talents of Mamet, Malkovich, Sinise, and Mosher had stamped Chicago theater as both visceral and brainy. Some New York actors, he complained, were even trying to pass themselves off as *Chicagoans*, to stand out from the pack at auditions. He encountered a woman at a studio party who claimed, in a pronounced Southern accent, to be a Chicago actress. "Hey," said Billy, "which part of the city you from?" He could see her brain wheels turning. "Uh, south side," she stammered back. "Listen, baby," Billy says he told her, "it's a big fucking town, but it don't go that *far* south!" Politically, the town could still be fractious and savage, nicknamed Beirut-by-the-Lake for all the bloody imbroglios between Mayor Washington and the machine elements he had defeated. But there was also some sense of progress—from a Neanderthal political era to Cro-Magnon.

Shortly after he arrived in City Hall in 1983, Harold received a welcoming letter from George S. Halas. "I hope," dictated Papa Bear, "that things are looking up for both of our teams." Within a few weeks, Halas was hospitalized with cancer. In the fifth week of the season, the Bears lost a game they should have won against the Baltimore Colts, 22 to 19. Fulminating in the locker room afterward, Coach Ditka slammed his hand for emphasis against an equipment trunk—and broke it. Before the next week's game, against the Denver Broncos, he called the team together in the locker room and raised up the cast of his damaged right hand. "Okay men," he said solemnly, "I want you to go out there and win this one for Lefty." The Bears exited, laughing; and won, 31 to 14. Coach Ditka began to wear, as Coach Halas had, a tie as he prowled the sidelines. He hoped it might tamp down his temper. "After all," he told reporters, "I only have one more hand to go." On October 31, George S. Halas died. He was eighty-eight. Mayor Washington ordered all city flags to be pulled down in mourning. Ditka told his team, "I'm not going to tell you to go out there and win one for Papa Bear. He deserves a lot more than one goddamn game. I'm gonna tell you, 'Go out there and dedicate your life to playing as hard as you can, win or lose.' " He made Jim McMahon his starting quarterback, and the team finished even for the season; an improvement. And then, Coach Ditka let his crew cut grow out and tamped it down with a permanent. Iron Mike sitting still for a permanent? The game really was afoot.

Earlier that season, the Reverend Jesse Jackson went south in a camper bus, roving the roads between small and large Southern towns in a campaign to register black voters. Harold Washington's election had given impressive emphasis to Jackson's message—that black voters could organize, deliver, and win political power in even formerly forbidding places. In churches in Chickasaw, Hattiesburg, and Mendenhall, where the pews creaked under the hands of people standing up from their prayers to chant, "Run, Jesse, run!" Jackson offered the story of David and Goliath to put flesh on his aspiration.

"In nineteen eighty," he'd begin slowly and deliberately, "Ronald Reagan won North Carolina by a few thousand votes. There were *tens* of thousand of unregistered black voters in the state. They were *rocks*—just layin' around.

"Ronald Reagan won Georgia by thousands of votes. There were *tens* of thousand of *unregistered* black voters in Georgia. They were *rocks*—just layin' around."

The reverend would roll on with this litany, through South Carolina, Alabama, and Florida, his voice dipping into a gruff growl, and then shooting up into a final, rhythmic flourish: "Get up on your feet! Roll your sleeves up! Dry your tear-stained eyes!" and at this, he sometimes brandished the handkerchief that can be so much an oratorical prop in the humidity of Southern churches. "Grab your slingshot! Pick your rocks up! Say, 'Goliath: it's nineteen eighty-three now.' These hands," and here he held them up over the pulpit, fingers crimped from scores of thousands of handshakes, suddenly looking crumpled and scarred, "*these hands* which once picked cotton, now gonna pick presidents. *Our time has come!*"

Like a great many young reporters, I had ambivalent thoughts about Jesse Jackson. His eloquence was astounding; his energy inspiring. Yet my admiration often was equivocal. He had captured public attention in the hours following Martin Luther King's assassination. While other, more prominent King lieutenants, including Andrew Young and Ralph David Abernathy, had stayed close to their leader's body, Jesse Jackson had flown back to Chicago—to give interviews. In retrospect, their resentment over his upward flight may seem small-minded. Chicago was the mission Dr. King had given young Jackson. With riots already roiling the city, it might have been irresponsible for him to stay by the martyred Dr. King anyway. Adding Jackson's voice to a public chorus of mourners was probably less important than lending his persuasiveness to appealing for calm. But when he stepped, still tear struck, off the plane, Jackson pointed to a series of dark splotches on his shirt, declaring, "The blood of my leader is on my body." Jackson wore the shirt out onto the streets, where he bravely walked through furious and dangerous crowds to appeal for calm, and then kept the shirt on for a round of television appearances in the morning. *Testing, one, two, three. The blood of my leader . . .* Hosea Williams and other King assistants rallied from their grief to wonder, publicly, about those splotches. Jesse Jackson, they insisted on recalling, had been in the parking lot below Dr. King when King was struck down by a shot on the motel balcony. Ralph Abernathy and Hosea Williams had been closest and cradled Dr. King's bloodied head while Jackson was still bounding up the motel's stairs. If that really was Dr. King's blood on Jesse's shirt, they suggested, he must have splashed it on afterward—a repellent idea. If it was not—well, the image of the Reverend Jackson spilling, say, chicken's blood on his shirt to secure a slot on the *Today* show was even more reprehensible.

Over succeeding years, as Jackson pulled away from the orbit of the Southern Christian Leadership Conference and into his own trajectory, he often didn't do a great deal to dispel that possibility. When I managed the Reverend Chuck Geary's campaign, we got a promise from Jackson's office that their reverend would attend our reverend's last major rally. By the time Jackson arrived, about three hours late, the crowd had become smaller and more surly. The Reverend Jackson tried to hush them down a bit (this was in 1971, when Chicago audiences would treat him with awe, but not yet veneration), then finally announced that on his way into the building, he had been told by police that someone had called in a bomb threat.

"These kinds of things," he told the suddenly silent bitter-enders still in attendance, "is always happening to poor folks when they try to organize for their rights. So I want you to stay calm," he said, as some shrieks and tears began to break through the ranks, "keep your heads high, and Brother Chuck and I are gonna link arms and lead you out." In theory, I was organizing the event. I had seen no police instruct the reverend; I had heard about no bomb threat. I rushed up to the podium as the reverends were preparing to depart, Chuck already striking up a chorus of "We Shall Overcome."

"Reverend—" I began, and Jackson leaned down into my ear.

"We're fine here," he said. "We got it under control. You know the City News Bureau number?" I looked up, flabbergasted. "Call them," he continued over his shoulder. "Let 'em know what's happened. Get the papers out here." And, although I had no reason to believe that a bomb threat had ever been phoned in, and have no reason to believe it now, I did exactly as instructed. As I suspect the Reverend Jackson had surmised, it was the best publicity such a dismal rally could manage.

But that had been thirteen years before. There ought to be some kind of statute of limitations on crimes committed during the act of self-promotion. Late in the 1970s, I had spent a day across the lake in grim Gary, Indiana, reporting a story in the schools. The Reverend Jackson spoke to an assembly of the students. I hadn't even bothered to set up my tape recorder—a speech by Jesse Jackson was regarded by editors as just about as newsworthy as another sunrise. There were no cameras or other reporters present; just the reverend, Mayor Richard Hatcher, and several hundred sullen and suspicious students. But I scrambled to put up a microphone when Jesse Jackson began to deliver a talk that no other public figure in America had earned the righteousness credentials to utter in front of an audience of young blacks in a tough, poor town.

"Of course there's racism," said the Reverend Jackson. "We all know that. Racism is a fact. It's like the lake. It's out there. You can't ignore it. We know it's there. But don't blame what you can't do on racism. If you're waiting for racism to go away, it's like waiting for the lake to dry up. Don't wait. You don't have the time. This is the only life we're going to have, until the afterlife. Don't wait for others to change. Do what you can now. Put down your bucket where you are. This is the only life you're gonna have—do what you can with it *right now!*"

When I had sorted through research before joining Jackson on his registration drive through the South, I had rediscovered an astonishing fact: Jesse Jackson was just twenty-seven years old when he became an international figure in the hours after Dr. King's death; a more demanding ordeal of celebrity than what all but a few of the most famous athletes would ever face. The good he had brought into life since had far outweighed even his own self-adulation.

Just a few years after that rally, when I had become a reporter and Jesse Jackson had become a household name, I would see the reverend when he came on to our public television show to be interviewed. He was on-set one night when I did a live piece seeking to explain the economics behind some of the enormous sports salaries then being paid.⋆ The floor director had signaled that I was running late. Stumbling too quickly over my words, I tried to say, "So, as you can see, every time Catfish Hunter pitches, he earns twenty-thousand—" Try saying that yourself, fast; listen if it doesn't sound more like, "every time Catfish Hunter *pisses*, he earns twenty-thousand . . ." Our camera people began to quake with stifled laughter. One of the floor directors actually fell down. Our anchorman held his head in his hands, visibly, perhaps out of despair of not being able to put mine on a plate. And the Reverend Jackson looked up from his seat on-set and delivered, straight-faced into the camera, either the perfect stab at saving my dignity or the final coda of hilarity: "You don't say."

I caught up with his campaign for voter registration at a meeting of Southern Democrats in Mobile in the summer of 1983. After the speeches, the Reverend Jackson and South Carolina Senator Fritz Hollings had held forth at a press conference (Hollings had called out, "Run, Jesse, run!" during his remarks—hoping to encourage Jackson to run for president instead of, say, senator from his home state of South Carolina). Most of the reporters were from the region; many of their questions were prefaced with a flattery more commonly slathered on sports or movie stars than people preparing to run for president. But then someone asked about the weighty gold watch so gaudily visible on the reverend's left wrist, a gold Rolex encrusted with sparkly things. It looked as heavy as a prison manacle.

"It was a gift," said Jackson, looking down at the watch face. "From President Tubman of Liberia. It's inscribed. I have been to Liberia several times, and all over Africa, and he was thanking me for bringing words of inspiration to his people." A man from the *Chicago Tribune* and I brightened at the prospect of some spark of controversy, and began to try to fan it with follow-up questions. Was it wise, Reverend Jackson, for someone who might be a candidate for president to accept expensive gifts from foreign potentates? Would a fair person wonder if the policies of the United States in Africa would be held in hock to a gold watch from the supreme leader of Liberia? Did accepting a watch from President Tubman mean that the Reverend Jackson accepted the president's policies toward rivalrous native groups in his

---

⋆The Chicago Winds of the now-defunct World Football League had reportedly offered Joe Namath of the New York Jets a contract for $485,000. This might be the most seriously dated statistic in this book.

country's interior? No, no, and no, said the reverend, almost wearily. "President Tubman gave me a personal gift. He is a generous man. No endorsement of any policy was so much as implied. You want to talk about American policy in Africa? Talk about why the United States is still supporting racist policies in South Africa. Talk about how Nelson Mandela still languishes in prison while American companies sell soft drinks outside his jail walls. Talk about how the United States is ignoring burgeoning, struggling democratic movements in Ghana, Nigeria, and Kenya. You want to talk about Africa? Talk about more than a watch . . ."

As reporters filed out, Mr. Jackson stood in the doorway to shake each of their hands. "A pleasure, Reverend Jackson," many of them said, "a real honor, sir. You are an inspiration to me. Can you sign this for my mother?" When it came time for the man from the *Tribune* and me to file through, the Reverend Jackson took a hand from each of us and smiled down from his superior height. Three Chicagoans Abroad in the heart of the South. "You men fly down from the Big Windy," he asked through tight lips, "just to give me *shit* about a watch?"

A couple of days later, we were in his campaign van, advancing on Hattiesburg, stopping in small spots unrecorded on road maps. The reverend would arrive, stretch his legs, and give a speech, shake hands, give another, meet the mayor, speak again, have a light lunch, and deliver another speech before boarding the bus and heading back to the highway. It was grueling, engrossing, and emotional. Washington reporters had been skeptical when Jackson had suggested that the possibility that he would run for president might animate voter registration drives. But my skepticism was dispelled on seeing elderly black Mississippi women wearing worn, stained head scarves, gravely take his hand in a small-town square. "I'm seventy-two years old, Reverend Jackson. Never voted. Never could. Then, never wanted to. Now, I'm going to vote—for you."

After so many years, I broached the matter of that rally he had emptied by passing on the news of a bomb threat. Of course he remembered Chuck Geary, he said: great guy, great guy. He remembered campaigning for him; but he didn't recall that rally, and certainly didn't remember that bomb threat. There had been, after all, so many threats on his life. I found Jackson persuasive. That rally had clearly been a larger event in my life than his. Jesse Jackson had seen and made an awful lot of history since then. He was more pointed and impassioned talking about the splotches on his shirt he had proclaimed as being the blood of his leader, Martin Luther King.

"Look," said Jackson, "I'm no gunshot expert. I don't know exactly how it happened. All I can tell you is that it did. Have you ever seen a man shot?" I had, I said evenly, in wars and crime scenes. "Well then you know. It's not neat. It's not pretty. It just spills out all over. I was underneath him, in the parking lot, standing with [SCLC's Chicago music director] Ben Branch, just after talking to him, when the shot rang out. I heard him fall, I heard others shout. I went running upstairs. Yes, others were already with him, already trying to talk to him and comfort him. I—I don't know really—touched Martin's head, gently, just to let him know we were all there, I guess, and there was blood all over the floor and I guess maybe, when I just put my hands up to my chest, almost in horror or something, I got Martin's blood on my shirt. And when I looked down, I noticed it, and said to myself what I said to others later. 'The blood of my leader . . . ' I don't know if I can explain this, really. But to see that blood, felt almost comforting. It was a part of Martin, and you wanted the world to see what they had done.

"Some people," he concluded, "may never accept my story. I can't make anything up to satisfy them. I was there. They were not. And since then, I have tried to do the work Martin wanted done."

We were threading through the great, greening gut of Mississippi, headed toward Jackson, the state capital. "And home of Walter Payton, too. Right, Reverend Jackson?"

Jackson, his tie still knotted hard and tight, was lapsing between snoozing and chatting through the last few miles of kudzu and car washes tangling the passing landscape. "Absolutely," he smiled. "Came out of Jackson State, oh, what, seventy-five I think? You know," he said brightly, "I heard that Walter was a dancer before I ever knew he could play football. Used to hear about 'Sweetness' Payton in dance contests when we came down here back in the early seventies. I guess he won every contest in the world down here. But if his reputation as a high school football player had been any higher, he probably wouldn't have gone to Jackson State." The Reverend Jackson himself, of course, had been recruited out of Greenville, South Carolina, to play football for the University of Illinois. But he left after his freshman year, feeling slighted by coaches and instructors, convinced they doubted the ability of blacks to play quarterback. He transferred to the North Carolina Agricultural and Technical College of Greensboro, where he starred at quarterback, was president of the student body, and then returned to Illinois in triumph, on a quite different sort of scholarship, to study at the Chicago Theological Seminary.*

"In the old days," Jackson said, "if you heard about a good black player in Mississippi or Louisiana, chances are you could get him at Grambling or Morgan State. See, even when the big Northern schools accepted blacks, they wouldn't hear about good black players in the Itta Bena, Mississippis of the world.† Who's gonna tell 'em—their white alumni? Kansas got Gale Sayers only because he was so close by, up in Omaha. But these days, you got a great kid playing in Itta Bena, and next thing you know, recruiters are dropping by, not just from Michigan and Southern Cal, but Ol' Miss and 'Bama. Walter may be one of the last, great pro stars to come out of a historically black college." ††

Payton was closing in on Jim Brown's all-time rushing record. A prideful Jim Brown was already reminding interviewers who came seeking premature congratulations for Walter that he, the great Jim Brown, had retired before he was thirty because there were no records left to set, and he wanted to pursue the movies.

"That might be partially true." I ventured an opinion on football to the reverend that I would never offer about religion or politics. "But Jim Brown wasn't the complete player Walter is. Brown wouldn't block like Walter does." The reverend, of course, had known Brown from various Hollywood fund-raising events; photographed together, they were almost unbearably handsome to behold, brothers in some superior species. "Oh, I tell you, don't you ever tell Jim Brown that he didn't block," Jackson laughed. "*Nothing* burns Jim Brown more. Greatest running back of all-time, maybe, until now, and he goes off like a match, you tell him that." The reverend laughed so hard in rec-

---

*A kinder interpretation is that Jackson's coaches may have thought it would be shrewder to make him into an option-running halfback. If you consider that a good football player like Jack Kemp became a credible candidate for president—what kind of pro player would the Reverend Jackson, a credible candidate for president, have been if he had stayed at Illinois? He would have been eligible for the college draft just after Gale Sayers and Dick Butkus. Could Jesse Jackson have become their teammate?

†For years, I assumed the Reverend Jackson had created the rhetorical device of an apocryphal small town, "Itty Bitty, Mississippi." But just a few years later I was embarrassed to discover that Washington, D.C., Mayor Marion Barry had been born in Itta Bena, Mississippi, and that it was an actual place.

††This calculation was premature. The great San Francisco 49er pass receiver Jerry Rice went to Mississippi Valley State—in, of all places, Itta Bena.

ollection that he slapped his thighs; I'd never seen his face break up with such pure delight. It was a golden afternoon in Mississippi, with the leaves turning tawny outside the bus window, and the Reverend Jesse Jackson kicking off his brogues to tell stories about Jim Brown and Walter Payton.

And then, we arrived in Jackson. The rally was not scheduled until later that night, so Jackson's coordinator decided that his traveling party should first check in at a local chain motel where he had made reservations. A small fussbudget of a general manager came out from behind the desk, reddening. "Reverend," he said, "it's an honor to meet you, sir. But I got to tell you, I don't know what to do. I just don't have any rooms for you." With a couple of reporters in the party, Jackson measured his words as carefully as the general manager. "We have a reservation," he said simply; an assistant rushed up to show the number to the manager, who brought it back to his own sheaf of records, then shook his head with regret. "I don't doubt that you do. No sir, I don't. But something just got screwed up, I guess. I am truly sorry. If I had the rooms, I would give them to you. But I just don't have the rooms. Now, if you'll let me make a call, maybe they have a few at our hotel a little ways from here. I'm sure they can make you real comfortable." I wondered if he meant, "You know, on the black side of town."

If a motel in the state capital of Mississippi in the early 1980s was still determined to keep a segregated clientele, it begs belief to think they would begin by keeping out Jesse Jackson; not only probably the best-known black man in America, but an American whose exclusion could do the motel a significant amount of damage. Most likely, the missed reservation was just an error.

But the shade of doubt made our moods sullen as we got back in the reverend's camper. Jackson sat by himself, in a study, sorting over a speech in a notebook, all the jollity in his manner withdrawn. "Back there," I asked carefully of one of the reverend's aides, "I mean, I've never seen how this kind of thing works before. I'm from Chicago, too. My parents used to get told that we couldn't live in some buildings when someone said, 'Sorry, we're restricted.' But I didn't know what that meant when I was a kid. I just remember my father looking crushed. Was something like that going on here?" The aide, a white man, shook his head. "Who knows? Don't make too much of it, please. It's the last thing we need. We had a reservation, but they said we don't.

They have rooms at this other place. Fine. It's not a wedding party. We can make changes. But no, I don't know what happened back there." Pulling past the town's back lots, I found myself wondering: Jesse Jackson is one of the best known people on the planet. He gets recognized and quoted from State Street to Soweto to Stockholm. He wears a gold watch inscribed by a chief of state. Did the Reverend Mr. Jackson spend himself into utter exhaustion in a hundred different datelines around the world, imploring tough and frustrated youngsters from Gary to south central L.A., comforting and fortifying frail old ladies in floral hats from Chickasaw to Oakland, just to fly down from the Big Windy into Itty Bitty, Mississippi and *get a lotta shit*?

That night, the Reverend Jackson seemed on his best game. The traces of tiredness in his face seemed only to sharpen his appearance. A great gospel choir was his warm-up, and the reverend looked quicker on his feet than most other quarterbacks, stamping and clapping in time:

> *Gonna ride that Glory Train! Gonna ride that Glory Train!*
> *Gonna ride that Glory Train! Gonna ride that Glory Train!*
> *That train is the only way I'll ever get to Heaven!*

The reverend came down from the podium to stand on the church floor, shucked off his elegant silver suit jacket like a fish slipping its skin, and tossed it over to an aide. There were no television lights, but a score of drugstore snapshot cameras flashed in his full, handsome, mahogany face with brightness.

"Now why should we register to vote?" he asked, leaving the question to linger for a moment. "*Only* 'cause you can change the world. Only 'cause you can change the world! You don't think that the world can be changin'?" Laughter rippled over the pews now. "Oh, are you wrong. You got up on the wrong side of bed this mornin' if you don't think the world can change. Things aren't perfect. But the last time I saw George Wallace, he was asking for forgiveness. Things are changing all the time. Read your gospel. It don't end on the cross. It doesn't end with Mary, weeping over her son. It ends with the son coming back. It ends with 'Come, Lord Jesus.' It doesn't end with the crucifixion, but the resurrection and the light. The gospel is the Good News. The gospel is little David bringing down Goliath with a rock.

"Our votes are rocks—just layin' around. *Rocks*—just layin' around. I tell you what. Get up off your knees. Get up out of bed. Roll your sleeves up, just like mine. Pick your rocks up. Grab your slingshot. Dry those tear-stained eyes. Say, 'Goliath: it's nineteen eighty-three now. These *hands* which once picked *cotton* . . .' " and the last lines of the reverend's refrain were outshouted by parishioners joining him word for word, "now gonna pick presidents. *Our time has come!*"

When the church organist began to strike up "We Shall Overcome," one of Jackson's aides sought me out near the rear of the church where I was holding my microphone up against a speaker. "Jesse," he said, "would like you to join him in the Amen Corner." The Amen Corner? "Right behind the pulpit," he explained with a smile, "locking arms with everyone else." A reporter who was more scrupulous about his ethics might have refused. He also might have been suspicious—that the Reverend Jackson was trying to pack photos with a few white faces. But in the quick consideration I gave the invitation I couldn't see anything wrong with lending my poor pale appearance to a rally to register voters who had never cast a ballot before. I was too young to have marched across the bridge in Selma, or on to Montgomery, too young to sit in at Greensboro, or, thankfully, to be beaten when the Freedom Riders' bus pulled into Anniston. So I was glad to have grown up enough to get pulled up out of my reportorial routine and be asked to stand behind Jesse Jackson at eleven at night in the swelter of a church in Jackson, Mississippi, and fold arms with strangers who had won a second American revolution while we sang and swayed to another national anthem. *Deep in my heart, I do believe, We shall overcome—someday.*

By the time the Reverend Jackson declared himself for president, I really was a Chicagoan Abroad, moving between assignments in El Salvador, London, and India. Walter Payton's determined march on a new rushing record proceeded. And Jesse Jackson ran better than pundits had predicted, winning conspicuous support among white as well as black voters. But then he tripped over his own redoubtable tongue, telling a reporter for the *Washington Post*, in casual conversation, about an upcoming trip to New York. "To see," quoth the Reverend Jackson, "the hymies in Hymietown."

I was in London when the story broke. More out of sporting than civic interest, I called a political reporter in Chicago who said that Jackson had appealed to some local journalists to explain the town's distinctly tough word-stock to their national colleagues in Washington and New York. "You know the way we sometimes talk here," my friend says Jackson told Chicago reporters. "You know how it is. You meet a man going to get a suit, he says, 'Gotta go up to Roosevelt Road, and see the Jew about a suit.' You know we don't mean anything by it."

There was a small nut of truth in that claim. London friends took me to a Chicago pizza restaurant, in which the featured foodstuffs were squishy facsimiles of home. The proprietor was also a Chicagoan Abroad. He had bedecked his interior with Chicago signage (ADDISON AV, O'HARE, STATE ST, CERMAK RD) and portraiture (Richard J. Daley, Ernie Banks, Al Capone, Georg Solti—and Hugh Hefner). The most gritty and real of American places had become another cutsey-poo marketing theme. "I can't make any excuses for Jackson," I explained to my friends, "but he has a point. As late as my days in high school, some of us kids from Jewish backgrounds still referred to Devon Avenue as 'Jew Town.' You brought laundry to the Chinaman, and ate lunch at the Greek's. *We didn't mean anything by it.*" Surrounded by such an assortment of Chicago props, I felt like the local shaman trying to explain the eccentric customs of his village to inquisitive visitors. "But listen," I persisted, "the Jewish kids and Chinese kids, Greek kids and Cuban kids, black kids and Korean kids, got to know each other in classes. We paired off for proms, married, and celebrated Christmas and Hanukkah, Greek Easter and Chinese New Year's." But that protesting phrase—"We didn't mean anything by it"—struck close to what my grandfather, the bigoted Chicago cop, would say when we asked him to *please* not use his station-house vocabulary at the Thanksgiving dinner table. "Hey," he'd protest, "I don't mean nothin' by it. Say, did I tell you? We had a couple of Polacks in lockup the other day . . ." Of course, my grandfather had never run for president, never been photographed playing kissy-face with Yassir Arafat, or demanded, as did the Reverend Jackson, to be acknowledged a world statesman.

There was a poster portrait of Walter Payton unrolled on an interior brick wall in the restaurant near to where drinks were picked up. In his navy Bears helmet, criss-crossed by a gray face guard, Walter had the look of some dark-faced, determined knight. I explained the importance of Walter Payton to my friend Ian. "Tell me," he asked, meaning his sarcasm to be only amiable, "in Chicago, is it like it is here, in Manchester or Liverpool? The people in all these second cities fixate on footballers because there is so little else in their civic lives?"

"Just about," I told him. "Except in Chicago, we don't smash in anybody's face or wreck railroad cars over a football game."★

Early in the third quarter of a fall game against the New Orleans Saints in 1984, Walter Payton took a short pitch out in the left side of the backfield and rambled over two tacklers for a five-yard gain. It put him at 12,314, or two yards ahead of the all-time rushing record of the great Jim Brown. The game was whistled to a stop. Photographers double-timed onto the field, snapping, snapping, Walter upholding the ball obligingly for the obligatory front-page photos: NEW RUSHING CHAMP and SWEETNESS! He then loped over to the sidelines and handed the ball off to Johnny Roland, the backfield coach—and then began to shoo civilians off the field. There was work to be done, a game to finish.

The Bears won their Central Division conference that year and defeated the Eastern Conference champion Washington Redskins in the first round of the playoffs, 23 to 19. The next week, however, the Bears ran aground. They played the San Francisco 49ers in Candlestick Park for the championship of the National Football Conference—the biggest Bear game in a generation. And they looked, as my stepfather put it in a phone call after the game, "like the little kids getting pushed off of the playground when high school lets out." The score was 23 to 0. It felt even worse. Chicago's defensive play had actually been out-standing. But Jim McMahon was injured, and the San Francisco defense had, with few other offensive weapons to distract them, focused suc-cessfully on Walter Payton. In the host of congratulatory handshakes players offered after the final gun of the game, Ronnie Lott, the fine, and ordinarily articulate San Francisco defensive back, had called out a compliment to Mike Singletary and his crew. "Next time, bring your offense." Lott said later that he meant only to encourage good players who looked bedraggled by seeing their best efforts unmatched by their own offense. But a simple, "Way to go," might have been more politic. Scoring zero points in a championship game is a special, high-level

---

★Europe was then abloom with football fan hooliganism. Thirty-nine fans at a football ground near Brussels died after being smashed against a fence by Liverpool fans. Britons were thereafter briefly banned from traveling to other games on the continent. But such a prohibition was impos-sible to police in Europe's free societies. ("No, sir, I ain't no football fan. Goin' to Amsterdam to see me Uncle Dieter.") Anytime European friends accuse Americans of being preoccupied with sports, I remind them that even the most menacing American fans manage to register their pas-sions without resorting to homicide.

variety of humiliation. Instead of ending the season with some resigned satisfaction, the Bears churned and burned, replaying the game like a stupidly lost love. By the time they gathered to begin the 1985 season, the Bears believed nothing short of absolute victory could assuage their absolute disgrace.

By the time the 1985 football season opened, I was in Washington, trying to create a new radio show called *Weekend Edition*. Jay Kernis, our founder, and I had tried to fathom a way to broadcast the program out of Chicago. National Public Radio was then under some criticism—from inside the network, as well as without—for reflecting an elite coastal attitude. I still don't think that critique proves out very well. But Jay and I became intrigued by the idea of creating a news program that carried a strong local stamp—something that sounded like it came from some*where*, and stood for some*thing*. Originating the show from Chicago each week turned out to be expensive and impractical. But Jay grasped that we could also make the blank stage of radio work to the same essential purpose. A show that *sounded* like Chicago could be created wherever we were. Many of our first staff members were Chicagoans Abroad.★ It was uncontrived for us to produce a program that imparted a Chicago accent, a Chicago outlook, to the news.

During one of our first weeks, Jay took a call out at our conference desk from a reporter offering a story on the upcoming Harvard-Yale game.

"No," Jay said after a brief consideration. "*All Things Considered* is Harvard-Yale. Our show is Northwestern-Notre Dame." Jay hung up the phone with a sly smile. "You know," he said, "sometimes, I'll be out somewhere, and someone starts talking about Chicago, and I'll join in excitedly. Then I'll suddenly remember: I'm from Bergenfield, New Jersey! *I'm not from Chicago at all!*" Under Jay's direction, Chicago became our program's Lake Woebegone—an improbable place populated by eccentric characters who sometimes seemed almost real.†

The rising success of the Bears became an important part of that early identity. By the time we began our pilot program in the fall of

---

★Producer Jonathan Baer, editor Ina Jaffe, technical directors Rich Rarey and Michael Schweppe, producer Maria Hinojosa, and later, Marta Haywood and Nora Moreno. Producer Neva Grant went to Northwestern. Our director, Cindi Carpien, had changed planes in Chicago.

†And Jay married a Chicagoan. How could he do otherwise?

1985, the Bears were becoming a craze of a kind. Mad Mike Ditka baying and barking on the sidelines, Sweetness Payton swirling through the lines, Samurai Mike Singletary slicing and dicing quarterbacks, and Mad Mac Jim McMahon swerving out of harm's grasp to complete a last pass. If football had swelled into a national metaphor, that metaphor had made it seem that America was becoming an increasingly corporate society. Tom Landry's Dallas Cowboys, or Bill Walsh's San Francisco 49ers, seemed to be pressed out of the same imposing but monochromatic mold. The Bears, with their burly bias toward defense, a quarterback who aggravated his coach by freelancing his own plays, and a coach who chewed clipboards while opposing coaches waited for computer printouts, gave some hope of breaking that mold and succeeding despite it; perhaps, in fact, because of it. One player in particular carried the weight of that hope, and a good deal more.

William Perry had been drafted in the first round out of Clemson, amid immediate confusion over his curriculum vita. He was listed as weighing 300 pounds; but that was palpably ridiculous—like trying to believe that Los Angeles was a village. The young man introduced to the press that day had a ready, gap-toothed grin and seemed shy and mild: a nice boy in the body of an overstuffed circus Bear. Buddy Ryan, the acerbic defensive coordinator, called Perry "a wasted draft pick."★ Ryan thought he was too fleshy and slow to compete in the National Football League—broad-tummied in a game that called for broad shoulders. His nickname became, for a time, just about the most famous in professional sports: *The Fridge*. At first, it was taken to epitomize his size. But it stuck because of the accounts of his heroic daily caloric intake—a dozen eggs, twenty pancakes, a sliced slab of bacon, biscuits, whole oranges, and half a loaf of buttered toast for breakfast. What happens to the other half? "I like," said Perry, "to save a little something for lunch." Perry's mother told reporters she had had to keep an extra refrigerator in her home, one for her son, another for the rest of her family. Fridge's girth was not carried trimly. He looked like what he ingested. Once, I saw him in the Bear locker room, pulling off a sweaty T-shirt. It looked—the phrase was not mine, but I can't find where it originated—something like a mud slide.

But where Buddy Ryan had seen a fat man trying to be a football player, Mike Ditka saw a football player who had allowed himself to

---

★It would be interesting to run a computer search to see how often "Buddy Ryan" and "acerbic" have appeared in the same sentence on sports pages over the years.

grow fat. Improbably, Perry had also played basketball at Clemson. There was videotape of the Fridge slam-dunking a basketball. The court seemed to quiver as he jumped, like the soil of Kazakhstan shuddering from the blast-off of a Russian rocket. But for many, William Perry was a figure who offered considerable hope—if, like a few million other Americans, he could stand to tuck in a bit here, tone up a bit there.

The Bears won their first two games, and in a surprising fashion for a team that still relied on defensive brawn to wear their opponents into a last-quarter daze. But the 1985 Bears began by coming from behind, with a burst of razzle-dazzle. They opened the season against Tampa Bay, the Buccaneers scoring 28 points in the first half, to the Bears' 17. But in the second half, defensive end Richard Dent tipped a Tampa pass into the grasping hands of cornerback Leslie Frazier, who took the ball in for a touchdown. Jim McMahon then ran for one touchdown and passed for another, securing the win, 38-28.

The third week of the season was the game that began to turn the Bears into a sensation. It was played in prime time, on a Thursday night, against the Minnesota Vikings. The Bears were down, 17 to 9, in the third quarter when an injured Jim McMahon was called in from the bench, screwing his helmet onto his head as he ran. "That daffy McMahon," suggested the announcers, "a world of talent, but doesn't always have his head in the game." As he called the cadence for the snap, McMahon noticed a lapse in Minnesota's defensive coverage and called out the signal for a change in the play he'd brought in from the coaches. Willie Gault, an Olympic-class sprinter (and only somewhat less convincing ballet dancer) the Bears had drafted as a wide receiver broke for a hole in the coverage. He was a length ahead of any defender when McMahon threw a pass that wobbled and wavered like a beanbag thrown into a high wind; but the ball came down true over Willie Gault's right shoulder and into his hands for a 70-yard touchdown. *That daffy Mac.* McMahon sprinted down to the end zone and butted his tender head against those of the tackles and guards who defended him—Jimbo Covert, Mark Bortz, Jay Hilgenberg, Tom Thayer, and Keith Van Horne. The Vikings got the ball back on the kickoff, of course, but fumbled deep in their own territory. McMahon, his head still woolly from his own congratulations, came sprinting back, sang out the signal for another play, planted his heels—and threw a 25-yard touchdown pass to Dennis McKinnon. Two consecutive passes, two touchdowns, in about two minutes. Not a bad productivity ratio, as a Nobel economist might put it. The Bears won their prime-time game, 33 to 24. Afterward, reporters surged into the locker room to gather around a Bear quarterback. McMahon, who suffered from eye sensitivity, had to put on a pair of sunglasses against the bright television lights. At that moment this was misunderstood as brash. But his words were strictly self-abasing. "Our guys on the line did it all," he said. "Willie and Dennis got free, made great catches. That's all." Mike Ditka seemed close to exultant over the play of a quarterback who was at once a punk, a biker, a Blues Brother, and a Bear. "He gets his uniform all dirty," said Ditka. "The players love him for that. And I like him, too." By the third week of the season, the Bears seemed to have been struck by a magic wand.

The next week, the Bears played Washington. I walked over to the commercial strip on Seventeenth Street near where I was living in the District to find a place for lunch and to watch the game. The territory was new to me, and I peered through several windowpanes and surveyed several menus before finding a spot with red-leatherette banquettes, steak sandwiches, and Bloody Marys on the bill of fare. *Black vinyl, red tablecloths, bloody rare meat, Bloody Marys,* I thought. *Good place to see a Bears game.* I took up a position at the bar, ordered coffee, and unfurled the Sunday papers.

"Will you be turning on the game in here?" I asked the bartender.

"Oh, wouldn't miss it," he said. "But I don't think the Redskins have a chance, to tell you the truth. Did you see the Bears that Thursday night?"

Oh, I had indeed, I allowed myself to share in some absurdly reflected glory. "As a matter of fact, I just moved here from Chicago. I'm a pretty big Bears fan." We fell into chatting: about football, the neighborhood, my network, the restaurant business, this and that. More solitary diners came up to the bar, a few more groups arrived and sat down at tables, the bartender graciously presenting me to each.

"This is Scott. He's new in the neighborhood. He works on the radio. He's quite a big Bears fan."

"Well," I'd laugh along with his smile, "I think that introduction covers all the important points."

Somewhere in the first quarter, while the Redskins sprang out to an early lead, it struck me that each person I had been introduced to was a man. The time was long past when women stayed home while men swarmed out to eat meat, drink beer, and watch football. When the Redskins scored, the chorus that went up from along the bar and tables was distinctly male. I turned around from the television screen. Men, in fact, more tastefully appointed, in slim black sweaters and tight black jeans, than most I'd seen soaking in a football game in a bar. I motioned to my new friend, the bartender.

"Maury," I asked, "have I missed a certain . . . a *theme* in this place?" His eyes glimmered with a smile.

"How could you miss it? It says, 'Steakhouse' right out front. But we have chicken, fish, anything you want."

"Yes," I said, "I know. You're very gracious. I just noticed that there seems to be a certain shared characteristic among the clientele." Maury shrugged.

"You mean, they're all Redskins fans? Washingtonians are crazy for their Skins. You'll have to get used to that." Maury wouldn't award me an inch.

"Yes, I know. I've heard. I guess I mean, have I walked in to some place I don't belong?"

Maury plucked a bottle of white wine from a tub of ice below the bar and topped off my glass. "No," he said, "you've walked into a friendly place in your own neighborhood. That one's on me, by the way." I felt foolish, of course, and not a little bit ashamed. "Been to many gay bars?" he asked.

"Just a few. On assignment. Once, with some friends, but it felt awkward." On the kickoff after the Skins' last score, Willie Gault nestled under the ball on his own one-yard line, looking up like a Boy Scout looking for constellations. He hauled in the ball and took off like a top spinning down a slide. A fake start left, a roll right, and then, loping like a gazelle across the plain, he launched himself into a straight run down the sidelines, 99 yards, for a touchdown. Maury and I turned to watch. Maury shook his head as I stifled a cheer.

"Well, they're certainly some wild ones," he resumed. "But they're getting quieter now, with this AIDS thing. Lots of straight people are even coming in, with the dinner crowd. Listen," said Maury in a confiding tone, "no man in here has asked me about you. But one of the waitresses has." He smiled. "And frankly, in this crowd, I like your odds." Jim McMahon topped off the Bears second quarter with three touchdown passes. A man came over and put an arm on my shoulder. "Tell me about Jim

McMahon, Mr. Bear fan," he said. "Is he really a Mormon?" The Bears scored twice more in the second half and won 45 to 10. Maury must have been only joking about the waitress. I bought a round for a group of four guys who had written out directions to a hardware store, a shoe repair shop, and a used furniture store. When I finally left, I exited to farewells calls of, "Bye-bye, Mr. Bears fan! See you again soon, Mr. Chicago Bear!" I walked home, half-a-glass over-the-line giddy, laughing at myself, at my new nickname, glad to have made new friends in the falling of a golden afternoon.

Next Sunday's game was at Tampa Bay. Walter Payton scored the 100th and 101st touchdowns of his career to lead the Bears to a 27 to 19 win. Our editor, Ina Jaffe, confessed the following workday that she had taken to drifting off to sleep by counting handoffs to Walter Payton: *McMahon hands to Payton, Walter runs left, Walter runs right.* By the time Walter had run the Bears down across the twenty, she said, she was usually asleep. I told her that sounded wonderful. "But," she pointed out, "if it works, you're never awake for a touchdown." Later that day, I was telling others on our staff about Ina's pre-dream reveries, and she interrupted. "I don't like what this means!" she exclaimed. "What does this mean? What does it mean when you no longer fantasize about sex, but the Bears running game?"

Before leaving the locker room in Tampa Bay, Mike Ditka cautioned his players succinctly, "Stop smiling. Get ready for war." The next game was a rematch between the Bears and the San Francisco 49ers, scarcely six months after the Bears had been so mortified. Again, the game was played at Candlestick Park. This time, the Bears packed along an offense. Walter Payton, running left, running right, was as reliable as he was in Ina Jaffe's dreams. He scored one touchdown, then another, and ran for 132 yards. Kevin Butler, their rookie kicker, and Jim McMahon's best friend (McMahon called him Butthead, which seems something only a good friend can do), kicked 4 field goals. I watched with some Chicagoans Abroad at the home of my friend and producer, Jonathan "Smokey" Baer, who thumped his fist against his sofa with each turn for the Bears.

"I can't *fucking*"—thumpthump—"believe it! Another *fucking*"—thumpthump—"score. I can't *fucking* believe it!" Smokey drew close, to share a secret. "I've been having some thoughts recently, doctor," he confided. "They seem crazy, I know. But do you realize," he asked, "that the *fucking* Bears could be the best *fucking*"—thumpthump—"team in *fucking* football?"

They won, thumpthump, 26 to 10. They were undefeated. The Bears flew back across the country after the game, avidly celebrating at 40,000 feet. Coach Ditka was stopped on his drive home from the airport and ticketed for driving while under the influence (he was also handcuffed, which seemed gratuitous; although, perhaps, not to someone who had ever seen him chewing a quarterback's head along the sidelines). Abashed, Ditka appeared to talk about his arrest the next day and apologized for any embarrassment to the team. When reporters pressed, he also imparted a startling admission for a Bear who had once nailed chairs into walls with his fists and broken a hand by bashing it against a steel trunk: *Mike Ditka had been drinking white wine.* One would have sooner guessed grain alcohol and anti-freeze. The embarrassing incident nevertheless underscored how modern a society Chicago had become. State troopers had become so incorruptible, they would give a ticket to the coach of the Bears even after a victory. And the coach of the Bears could manfully, close to tearfully, disclose that a gruff, tough Bear had imbibed too much white wine. One night, I brought a clip from the newspaper in to my new friends on Seventeenth Street.

"Oh, white wine, that's real sissy stuff," laughed Maury. "Tell your coach to come in here. We'll know when to cut him off."★

The next game brought new lore to the Bears' season. Buddy Ryan, the defensive coordinator, was still a hard sell on the usefulness of William Perry. Ditka, on the other hand, was impressed by what he had seen of the young man's discipline and progress. The two coaches had increasingly vehement quarrels, with Ditka invoking his authority to send in the Fridge for a play or two, Ryan using his to call him back out. Ditka, fuming and frustrated, hatched an idea intended more to show up Buddy Ryan than the Green Bay Packers.

Ditka had been thinking: when you have a man on your team that is so routinely likened to an earth mover, why not use him to move a little earth? In practices, Ditka called in Perry to line up as an offensive back. When Steve McMichael, Dan Hampton, Richard Dent, and other members of the defense that had become the most obstinate, unbending,

---

★Ditka, in fact, cut himself off, and did not drink until the playoffs.

and inviolable in modern football tried to stop a 350-pound Refrigerator running straight into their heads, they fell back. In fact, they fell like bowling pins. At first, they laughed; then, they dug in, ground down, made a last stand. And got run over. Staggered, almost for the first time that season, the Bear defense was dazzled. Mike Singletary, whose judgment was held highest on the team (higher, in fact, than Ditka's or Ryan's), walked across the divide between the offensive and defensive units along the sidelines to tell Mike Ditka, "Coach, they can't stop that kid for a yard or two."

Ditka, in fact, had determined that the Bears could stand to improve their performance at the goal line. They already had, of course, the most sturdy and storied running back in football in their backfield. But the very fact of Walter Payton's achievements caused defenses to fix on him at the goal line. Who could more be expected to get the call for a yard or two than the man who had already gained more than any other? For years, Payton had defied the deficiency of surprise by perfecting a stutter-stepped leap over the heads of defenders: step, step, then, a straight-up jump, bending his head and shoulders over like a pole vaulter's to bring himself to land across the goal line. However, even pole vaulters don't keep all the spring in their knees into their thirties. Walter could be brought down. But what team could stop the world's best running back if he was preceded by an earth mover?

The Bears went in to Green Bay. Packer fans had a hallowed custom of renting rooms in the hotel in which the Bears were staying, and convening an all-night party after the players' curfew, to distract and discomfit them, cause them to toss, turn, and stew instead of sleep. The practice was sometimes exercised with good humor. More than a few Bears had managed, over the years, to slip out of their rooms and join Packer merrymakers for a drink; Uncle Jack Brickhouse said that Packer backers even learned to have a pitcher of martinis waiting for Doug Atkins. Brian Piccolo had once enraged and amused the Pack pack by appearing at his room window in a helmet, his hands clasped over his ears as he called down, "I can't *heeeaaar* you!"

But the first Bear-Packer game of 1985 took place just days after Mike Ditka's arrest for drunk driving. There were signs, catcalls, banners in the street, and in the Green Bay stands. HEY, DITKA, THIS BUD'S FOR YOU (although, of course, THIS CHENIN BLANC'S FOR YOU would have been more accurate, and possibly funnier).

So when the Bears moved the ball down to the Packer goal line,

Coach Ditka turned to the Refrigerator along the sidelines. "William," he said, "*now*." There were gasps and giggles as the Fridge thudded into position, looking something like an oil tanker riding alongside a fleet of tugboats. At the snap, the pitchout went to Walter Payton, who held back for a moment, while William Perry ran into, over, and through Packer linebacker George Cumby. Cumby was a big man; but easily fifty pounds lighter than William Perry. It was like seeing a cement truck strike a baby stroller. *Oh, no! Sssssplat!* Walter Payton almost strolled in, on three easy steps. He could have walked in on his hands. The hole left by William Perry was as huge as—well, as a deep freezer holding a winter's supply of Salisbury steaks.

Later in the game, Ditka called in the Fridge with the ball at the three. This time, the handoff went directly to William Perry himself. The earth mover moved—with striking quickness. The Refrigerator scored his first touchdown in the National Football League, and the Bears won their seventh game of the season, 23 to 7. In the press conference following the game, there were questions about the two plays called to William Perry. Was it a prank? Some mockery of football? A special response to the insolence of those banners in the stands? Such questions aggravated the coach.

"Listen," Ditka said, his voice rising into a surprisingly high pitch, "I think that's ridiculous. He helped us score, didn't he? He can't be stopped, can he? Isn't the object of the game to score, to win the game? I don't understand why people would have a problem with that."

In the weeks that followed, the Bears defeated Minnesota, with the defense intercepting five Viking passes. The next week, another defeat of Green Bay. This time, William Perry caught a touchdown pass from Jim McMahon, raising rows of amazed laughter from the stands in Soldier Field. Ditka joked with reporters. "Maybe we'll see what William can do on punt returns next." And oh yes—Walter Payton ran for 192 yards, duplicating a personal record he had first set eight years before. The next week, they defeated the Detroit Lions, holding on to the ball for 41 of the game's 60 minutes of regulation play. When I went to the steakhouse on Seventeenth Street later that Sunday night, Maury poured out a Coach Ditka cocktail (cheap white wine, straight, water chaser) while we watched late highlights. "I don't think," said Maury, "that the Red Army can beat the Bear defense."

The next week, the Bears flew into Dallas. The Cowboys were a battered dynasty, but still considered the silver-starred embodiment of modern football: sports as a successful corporate enterprise, played by good Christian gentlemen (and, to be sure, the occasional hired heretic). Jim McMahon was injured once again, and the Bears were quarter-backed by Steve Fuller, a bright young man (a Rhodes scholar candidate) who had preceded William Perry by a year at Clemson. "Play tough on defense, help out the offense, and we'll win this game," Ditka told them.

Steve Fuller did just fine. He handed the ball to Walter Payton, who went over 1,000 yards in rushing for his ninth successive season. The Fuller Brush man—or Sir Cecil Rhodes—could have quarter-backed the Bears that day in Dallas. Richard Dent and Mike Richardson intercepted passes and ran them back for touchdowns. The Bear defense scored two touchdowns, which was two more than the vaunted Dallas offense could manage against them. The Bears dealt Dallas the worst defeat in Cowboy history, 44 to 0. For the first time, Ditka crossed the field with some chagrin at the final gun to shake hands with an opposing coach. Tom Landry, after all, had been the first football executive to evince any confidence in Ditka's coaching future. Ditka had put reserves into the lineup for the last quarter, but they scored twice anyway—subs eager to prove themselves. A group of our Chicagoans Abroad gathered at Ina Jaffe's apartment for a holiday dinner, and we raised a glass of white wine for Iron Mike, Mad Mac, Sweetness, Fridge, and Samurai Mike: "Once," I said, as Ina groaned and Smokey howled and Ina's husband, the writer Lenny Kleinfeld, scolded about pridefulness and heresy, "our people were slaves in the National Football League . . ."

With that victory over Dallas, the Bears not only clinched the Central Division title, but displaced, for a season, the redoubtable Cowboys (America's Team) as the franchise with the most avid national following. The Cowboys and 49ers, in their excellence, seemed to exemplify some of the colorless, corporatized values that were beginning to make sports drab. But the Bears were throwbacks in an age of instant nostalgia, "weathered" clothing, and "classic" music. Tom Landry, commanding the Cowboys in a trim, suburban Highland Park fedora, was famous for holding himself in. Mike Ditka became acclaimed for not being able to hold himself back. Bill Walsh of the 49ers seemed ever lashed into the headset by which he communed with coaches, scouting the game from on-high in the stadium. Ditka ripped headsets off himself in disgust, like a man who suddenly felt he was being strangled by his tie. A head-banging quarterback who tossed flutterballs, a coach who chewed up turf and spat it back, and a fat man who danced on his toes in the end zone—the 1985 Bears didn't have a personnel roster, but a cast of characters.

The week after winning in Dallas, they followed with another shutout, shutting down the Atlanta Falcons 36 to 0. The Fridge scored another touchdown (Ditka had him throwing passes in practice now, too, to prepare a possible surprise for the playoffs), and Walter Payton amazed with a 40-yard run. This lifted them to 12 victories, no losses, the first team since the Miami Dolphins of 1972 to go so deep into the season without defeat.*

Their national celebrity was cinched when the Bears took an off day to record one of the early music videos for a local group providing food to food banks in the city. It was, of course, strictly a novelty item; but with charm. An uncomplicated, post-disco beat plopped along obviously, while a company of robust, rapping Bears, their bodies looking strangely lithe without shoulder-pads, bounced on their knees, as if riding a bumpy stretch of subway track. As a music video, it was closer to burlesque than rap:†

> We are the Bears Shufflin' Crew
> Shufflin' on down, doin' it for you.
> We're so bad we know we're good.
> Blowin' your mind like we knew we would.

(At this last line, Jim McMahon is shown motioning at his own mind)

Stanza after stanza, the song confirmed the popular caricatures that were emerging among the Bears. The estimable Walter Payton got the first call into the dance line. Mike Singletary is shown in his glasses; after all, he had to read the lyrics off cue cards. It gave him a faintly owlish, scholarly appearance—Dr. Singletary, professor of applied geometry (the study of lines and angles as applied to a quarterback's body). Jim McMahon is in black sunglasses, his hair gently spiked as if afflicted with static cling. The last chorus belongs to William Perry; naturally, he'd wait around for dessert. And then came the refrain.

---

*A distinction they enjoyed for just a week. They lost the following Monday night to the Dolphins, 38 to 24. It was the only Bear loss of the season
†Copyright 1985, Red Label Music, Inc. Lyrics by R. Meyer, M. Owens.

When I tagged along with my mother into several Michigan Avenue stores that holiday season, the Shuffle seemed to play ceaselessly. Over the muzak in Marshall Field's and mingling with the Salvation Army bells wafting under the eaves of Water Tower Place. *We are the Bears Shufflin' Crew* . . . We stopped once, near a cologne counter, to watch a moment playing on a video monitor; I thought the Bears I could pick out in the front line, Steve Fuller, Otis Wilson, and Mike Singletary, rocked on their knees with the same sort of self-consciousness of a seventh-grade boy with braces at a bar mitzvah dance. My mother's voice gushed with delicacy. "Oh, look," she said, "it's our boys. Those darling boys."

Those darling boys won their first playoff game, against the New York Giants, 21 to 0. The Bears held the Giants to just 32 yards on the ground and overturned their fine quarterback, Phil Simms, behind the line six times. The next week, the Bears played the Los Angeles Rams in 20 degree weather at Soldier Field. The Bear linemen made a point of suiting up in short-sleeve shirts, standing along the sidelines pugnaciously without warm-up jackets, as if waiting for a question. *Cold? Frankly, I hadn't noticed* (of course a couple of heat fans were positioned to blow along the bench—for thin-skinned running backs and quarterbacks).

A fan in the Bear press office had fixed a field pass for me that let me stand along the sidelines, about twenty yards down from the bench. It was an honor, but just about the worst spot from which to try to follow a football game. Jim McMahon scrambled in 16 yards for the first touchdown; but the play escaped us until we saw him enact a celebratory head butt with his linemen. Linebacker Wilber Marshall scored the second, recovering a fumble then rumbling for more than 50 yards to score.

Review the game's statistics today, and the results seem preordained. But Bear fans had not seen enough good fortune to trust providence. With about six minutes remaining, though, there was a sign. Snowflakes, turning silvery as they seemed to shake down from the flat, slate skies, began to fall on the broad-shouldered Bears and glistened as they congealed against the Astroturf. The men from Los Angeles looked up, like condemned men hearing the snapping of the trap door of the gallows above them, and seemed to shiver under their long sleeves. Bear fans began to cheer—the first time since grammar school I have ever heard applause for foul weather. They chanted and clapped, as if finally exacting a Midwesterner's revenge for every unfeeling postcard of a sultry beach sent from friends in California, Puerto Rico, or Florida in the frigidness of winter: *70 degrees today. Went swimming. How's the snow? Ha!*

Chicagoans had built valuable lives in the kind of weather that had made millions flee for Los Angeles. Chicagoans who stayed had to tell themselves occasionally, *That which does not freeze me, makes me stronger.* The Bears snorted, laughed, and looked amazed along the sidelines, their breaths flash-freezing into pearly gauze against their hands, turning their hands and faces up to the sky. The stadium took on some of the same rapture as Harold Washington's headquarters on election night, a feeling that for once, between the snow, the score, and the chilled, silver sky, *all the instruments agreed.* Over the length of the field, I could make out Otis Wilson shaking his head as he laughed. "Bear weather!" he said over and over. "Don't believe it! Bear weather! It's ours now! Bear weather!" The Bears won, 24 to 0. They had kept two championship teams from scoring so much as a single point in two championship games.

The two weeks before the Super Bowl in which the Bears would play the New England Patriots was one of those periods in which commentators decide that something of a moment was occurring in sports; and the moment was sheer fun. Walter Payton shared the cover of *Time* with William Perry: the classic back and the archetypal cherub. "The Super Bowl Shuffle" went gold. Jim McMahon said his ass hurt, and he needed his acupuncturist. The Bear team physician resented the implication that some needle sticker was necessary to play pincushion on the rump of his quarterback and refused to bring the acupuncturist along to the Super Bowl. Mac, who had been cautioned by the NFL not to wear a headband with the manufacturer's name showing, because Adidas was not an official league sponsor, obliged by turning his band inside out—and writing ACUPUNCTURE across his forehead. He looked like a a captive in a fortune cookie factory sending out a message (the signal was received; the man and his needles were dispatched). During an outdoor practice one day, in Sewanee, Georgia, McMahon was vexed by a press plane flying overhead to take pictures of the Bear scrimmage, and of the effort Mac could make on a sore bum. McMahon took down his pants, and turned up his bottom—a Bear bottom, if you please, a blue-and-orange moon. By the time the Bears arrived in New Orleans and began to prowl the streets of the French Quarter, McMahon had become their clown prince. A television station reported that he had called women in New Orleans "sluts." A covey of club officials greeted him at breakfast the next morning by saying, "Oh, geez, Jim, what the hell have you gone and said now?" McMahon read through a newspaper account and pronounced it a fraud. "It says they interviewed me in a coffee shop at 6:30 in the morning," he said. "Since we got to New Orleans, have I ever been up and out for breakfast at 6:30 in the morning?" A persuasive point. "Jim and I have a strange and wonderful relationship," Mike Ditka told reporters. "He's strange, and I'm wonderful."

The mayors of Chicago and Boston made a bet: a dozen thick-crust Chicago pizzas versus a dozen Boston lobsters, to the chief executive whose team prevailed. Harold Washington's word on Chicago pizza was the product of devoted research. Every night, as he sat in his southside apartment plotting machinations, he would send his security detail out to pick up a thick-crust pizza, extra cheese, extra sausage, that no doubt was even more richly embellished when its makers were informed it would be consumed by the mayor.

"Lobster!" Harold told reporters with mock horror—for he knew the gustatory pleasures of lobsters, too—"Lobsters! Aren't they little red scaly things that eat trash on the ocean floor? Lobsters! I don't know as I'm looking forward to winning lobsters!"

During the playoffs, Mike Ditka had groused to reporters that the National Football League had not been even-handed in their off-field penalty assessments (McMahon was fined for wearing those headbands with Adidas visible; several defensive players had been fined for talking macho nonsense about "getting" quarterbacks). "There are teams that are fair-haired," said Ditka, "and there are teams that aren't. There are teams named Smith and teams named Grabowski . . . We're Grabowskis." His observation was lyrical without being logical. Between a Yalie, Gary Fencik, and Rhodes scholar candidate Steve Fuller, the Bears had their fair-hairs, too; and none in the league fairer than Walter Payton, who could untie a referee's shoelaces with impunity. The ascendance of the Bears into celebrity only delighted the NFL, which was pleased to see a revival of ratings in the nation's third largest market. Ditka's remark is mostly interesting today as some sign of the coach's motivational cunning. The Bears, after so many years of frustration, become national darlings and irresistible favorites, rolling into the Super Bowl on a tide of fourteen victories. But to keep their fires churning, Mike Ditka banked on resentment.

The Bears won Super Bowl 20 (I try to avoid the Romanesque XX designation of the NFL) with the most points, and by the largest margin, of any Super Bowl to that time: 46 to 10. I flew home to Chicago, where my mother had arranged to put on a Super Bowl party to watch "those darling boys." On the top of half-sized bookshelves framing the television, she laid out chili, corn bread, salad, and gingerbread Bears, on which she had used a pastry tube to embellish blue and orange frosting numbers: 34 (Payton), 9 (McMahon), and 50 (Singletary). She made one gingerbread Bear a half-size bigger, and more bulbous, than all the others—72, the Fridge.

In the Bear locker room below New Orleans' Super Dome, Mike Ditka heard the marching bands send a brass clatter through the cement bricks of their locker-room walls. He recollected for Don Pierson what he told his players:

> *This is out of love for each other. That's what the game is all about. Any other intentions won't be accepted. But you are going to win this game for each other. So let's go out there and play our kind of football. Heavenly Father, we are grateful for this opportunity and we thank you for the talents you have given us, the chance to prove that we are the very best. Father, we ask that you give us the courage and the commitment to use the talents to the best of our ability so that we may give the glory back to you. Father, we ask that you may protect all the players in the game so that they may play the game free from injury. Amen. Let's go.*

The Bears received the Patriots' kickoff. McMahon settled in over the upturned butt of Jimbo Covert, calling out the cadence for Walter Payton to run left. Mac took the snap, stepped into Payton's furious onward path, and flipped the ball into Walter's grasp, as he had on perhaps a thousand occasions. *McMahon to Payton. McMahon takes the snap. Hands to Payton. Payton gets the call.* But this time, on the second play of the twentieth Super Bowl, the game he had invested a decade of his life to reach, the greatest all-around running back of all-time was hit and fumbled. *Well, that'll happen sometimes.* The Patriots recovered and had the ball in their hands just nineteen yards away from the Bear goal.

Walter came off the field and onto the sidelines without a word—and he owed none. Fumbles are a fact of life. If you cared to weigh Walter's gains against his losses, his yardage against his fumbles, touchdowns against missteps, no runner would have a more favorable ratio. And it was, after all, only the first few seconds of the game. But when McMahon came into the sidelines, he told Ditka, "It was my fault, I called the wrong play. I should have known better." Meaning, he had misread the signals flashed to him by an assistant coach and sent Payton into the line on New England's strongest side, where he was likeliest to be hit. McMahon's avowal was partially true; and totally gracious. Ditka was impressed; and was reminded that McMahon was an easy man to misjudge. If you took in only what showed on the surface, you would see a premeditated punk, with self-promotion aforethought. But Mac was a man who combined the appearance of punk with the comportment of a gentleman. He was a hell-raiser, carouser, head-butting biker dude—who betrayed the instincts of an old-school patrician. One could imagine him saying, "Sorry, men, my fault, that bad bit of business back there, not Wally's." (And he was, by the way, the only player who could amiably call Payton by that name he so disdained.) Mad Mac was a blue-blood Bear. One could see why fierce men protected him.

The Bear defense, their backs against their goal, held for one play; another; and then another. New England gained no ground, but had one down left, still just twenty yards away. They set up for a field goal and made it—a chip shot, really, from so short a distance. New England 3, Chicago 0. The vaunted Bears were, for the first time in half a season, behind. *We are the Bears Shufflin' Crew. Shufflin' on down—eeeow! What the hell happened?*

Ghosts came to life in a fan's imagination. Don Young dropping a crucial fly ball, phantasms of fumbling Cubs, bumbling Bears, and stumbling White Sox, booting balls, whiffing at strikes, kicking wide, and passing long, stole into memory alongside Mrs. O'Leary's cow kicking over a barn lantern in a great wooden prairie town on a windy Saturday night. My mother, ever the attentive hostess, sprang to her feet as the suddenly back-pedaling Bears prepared to get back the ball. "All right, everybody," she announced, "you haven't *touched* the dessert yet. I want *evvverybody* to get up—" And, in one voice, my mother's friends and neighbors and the husband and son who adored her, barked out, *"Will you pleeeaaase sit the hell down?"*

But then the Bears began to resemble themselves. They drove down twice in offensive series, deep enough for Kevin Butler to kick two field goals. Richard Dent overturned New England's quarterback to force a fumble at the Patriot 12; Jim McMahon scrambled in to score. At halftime, with the Bears 20 points ahead, the network announcers acknowledged—it would have been absurd to try to sustain even a semblance of suspense—"If this were a prize fight, someone would stop it." The Bears scored three more times in the second half, with McMahon throwing a 60-yard flutter ball to Willie Gault, Reggie Phillips running back an interception for a touchdown, and William Perry trundling in for a front-page photograph: THE REFRIGERATOR RUNS—AND SCORES. As the final seconds ran off in the Super Dome, the Bears gathered Ditka up onto their shoulders and began to sweep him off the field. "Is that it?" my mother asked a little uncertainly, as we watched the clamor onscreen. "Is that *really* it, after all these years? Is this really *it*?" She leaned down to plant a kiss on my stepfather. "Did you ever think you would live long enough to see this, darling?" she asked him; and Ralph replied through a sleepy grin. "Hell, the way things were going, I didn't think I'd live through the first quarter." By the time I had taken the elevator down to meet up with friends, the clangor of car horns had overtaken the streets, and traffic had ground down. Friends and strangers were taking each other into their arms, without explanation, awkwardness, or apology.

The Bears spent a night celebrating along Bourbon Street, then flew back to Chicago for a welcoming parade. Had there ever been a parade so huge in a city so cold? Even in Moscow, they wait until May Day to strut their soldiery through Red Square. A million people turned out to see the Bears, nearly the same number who came out to celebrate mass with Pope John Paul in Grant Park; people will turn out for the possibility of miracles. I had been a reporter at that mass, but took in the Bears parade as a fan and spent most of it looking up at the flanks of a police horse; recommended for staying warm, but not for watching a parade.

The next morning, my stepfather decided to drive me to the airport and snapped on the radio as he pulled out of the spiral garage of their apartment building. I was waiting at the bottom with my suitcase; and when he reached the landing, Ralph looked shaken.

"Get in," he said, "and listen. The shuttle just blew up."

At the moment, I could think only of the hourly airplane that plied the skies between Washington and New York. "Oh my God. Who was on it?"

"The astronauts," Ralph said sharply.

"Astronauts?" I could still think only of Neil and Buzz, Al and Gus.

*"The astronauts,"* he said more firmly. "The shuttle. It blew up on takeoff." As Ralph drove on, I churned through the radio dial, searching for details. It seemed the best division of responsibilities. I have a clear self-interest in the supposition that every sort of story can be vividly conveyed over the radio; but that morning, we felt the need to see the catastrophe in television pictures. Ralph was a man who revered Abraham Lincoln, the Constitution of the United States—and Japanese technology. He was ordinarily the first in line to purchase something that *beeped* that was a marginal improvement over the something that *buzzed*. He took to what was new with such fluency I sometimes needed to remind myself that when Ralph was born, airplanes, radio, and even telephones amounted more to experiments than utilities.

"We got spoiled by everything working all the time," Ralph said as we drove on, listening gloomily. "People forget, it's flying through the air. It doesn't just happen. There's always losses. Wiley Post, Amelia Earhart, those two French guys who didn't make it before Lindbergh. There are always losses. We forget. Part of the price of life." It was an observation nothing in my life qualified me to make. But Ralph had lived long enough to see men and women die in a place in the sky that, when he was a child, must have seemed impossible to reach.

Sports abounds with *would haves, should haves,* and *could haves*—and probably *shouldn'ts.* The Bears who so dominated their season and won the Super Bowl on that day early in 1986 were favored to return for several more. But they couldn't manage to make it back even once. The cunning team of appealing characters that had shuffled into the Super Bowl began to fall apart. Jim McMahon seemed to be out with injuries three games for every one that he played. Walter Payton retired. Wilber Marshall, Richard Dent, and other pillars of the defense left as they became free agents and found other teams willing to pay more than the Bears for their experience. Celebrity could be distracting, especially after being disregarded for so long. And for the Bears' opponents, every Sunday was a chance to defeat the team that won the Super Bowl. Mike Ditka fumed, but his team missed catching fire.

The Bears turned in an almost equally imposing regular season record the next year, losing just two games. But they lost in the first round of the playoffs to the Washington Redskins. Ditka had signed the redoubtable Doug Flutie to play in place of McMahon. Most football scouts had cautioned that while Flutie was a daring and engaging player, at 5 feet 8 inches he was too short to throw over the upraised arms of mammoth linemen in the National Football League. Ditka, to his credit, discerned something of the grit and magic Flutie would later evince as the Most Valuable Player in the Canadian Football League, and later still with the Buffalo Bills. But that afternoon against the Redskins, Doug Flutie ran haplessly in circles around his own secondary, looking something like a small, gallant schnauzer trying to defend the family home. Washington won, 27 to 13, and went on to win the Super Bowl. The following year, the Bears improved—by 4 points. They lost to the Redskins 21 to 17.

In late January of 1987, just half a year after being reelected mayor with an electoral formula that seemed destined to endure into the next decade, Harold Washington dropped dead at his desk in City Hall at about five o'clock on a workday afternoon, his head plop-down on his desk blotter. It was a heart attack. He was sixty-five. Doctors said later that Washington was about a hundred pounds over playing weight; political observers added that he had withstood at least fifty times more political stress. I thought about those great, yeasty smiles that would rise on Harold's face when he would pop the top of a pizza carton, or stride with a boxer's step toward the microphone at a rally or city council meeting to rail against "these antediluvian forces that prey and prowl around this city like dinosaurs who don't know they no longer rule the earth." Harold Washington brought extra cheese, extra sausage, a thick crust, and exceptional spice into the city's political life. He died a Chicagoan's death—too much good pizza, too much bad politics.

During the fall elections of 1988, my colleague Linda Wertheimer was traveling along with Democratic presidential candidate Michael Dukakis when he departed from Boston to reach an afternoon rally in Chicago's Richard J. Daley Center. Linda, who cherishes political rallies with a collector's affection, found her heart rising over the sharp fall weather, the bracing bustle of the Loop, the political clichés striking and ringing the skyscrapers.

*"I just want to begin by saying,"* as Linda heard Governor Dukakis's

words bouncing back from the girders and braces of the Daley Center, *"that my dick is feeling fine!"*

"Well," Linda mused to herself, *"this* campaign certainly promises to pick up."

Mike Ditka had suffered a heart attack while Bearing down on his team at practice. When the candidate phoned the recovering coach at the hospital from his airplane, Ditka's condition had been relayed cordially, but concisely. "Fine, he's feeling fine."—which the governor then relayed to the rally. *I just want to begin by saying that Mike Ditka's feeling fine.* Certainly, better than Dukakis would soon feel. The governor of Massachusetts would be ground down to defeat by George Bush within two weeks. Coach Ditka returned to prowl the sidelines within a month, as if to say, *I don't get heart attacks, I give them.*

But after the 1992 football season, Mike Ditka was fired from the team he had come to embody. His sideline and press conference harangues and hysterics were becoming tiresome and embarrassing; and they were clearly not working. I was leaving the set of *Weekend Today* at Rockefeller Center in New York the Sunday morning after Ditka's dismissal when I was stopped by a security guard. "Hey, Scooter, Mr. Meyer just called down. Says you gotta get back up there." He paused because he could no longer swallow his smile. "Mr. Meyer says Mike Ditka is up there. Coach wants to kick your ass."

Ditka had come into town the night before to make a brief guest appearance on *Saturday Night Live!*, the show that still features a skit of a trio of beery Bear fans, clinking tankards and toasting "Da Bears!" He had stayed on to appear on a midday pre-game show.* By the time I arrived, Coach Ditka was sitting easily on the edge of a control room panel, holding court among producers and engineers, who were gracious enough to convey me forward. Bob Meyer, one of our producers on *Weekend Today*, made the introduction.

"Coach, I'm Bob Meyer. I'd like to introduce Scott Simon, one of our co-anchors. He's quite a Bears fan. He even did an essay about you

---

*I would come into our makeup room to have my face de-spackled after our program, just as an imposing assortment of colossal, limping former professional athletes and ever-expanding former coaches came in to be plumped and painted for pre-game sports shows. I saw Buddy Ryan, Joe Gibbs, Bill Walton, and Quinn Buckner, squinting and grimacing like kids while their faces were stippled with Max Factor. They are all nice men. But the friendliest—I wish I could say otherwise—was O. J. Simpson

this morning." Ditka smiled and held out his hand; and he shook mine firmly, but with consideration. He looked terrific, too, polished and lithe in Michigan Avenue Italian tailoring and hair styling.

"Coach." I found my voice catching. "Coach, I just wanna say, well, *thanks*. That nineteen eighty-five team? The *greatest* year *ever* for a fan. I mean, Sweetness, Mac, Fridge. My mother had a party. I flew back home. She even made Bear cookies. Seventy-two, Fridge, he was the largest . . ." I let my thin, strangled voice trail off, as I heard myself tediously trying to interest a man who had been carried off the Super Bowl field triumphant in the utter inconsequence of where I had been at the same time. Besides: I was finding it hard to go on. Tears sprang to my eyes, as I spoke into the face not of Mother Teresa, Nelson Mandela, or even Elizabeth Hurley, but *Mike Ditka*.

"Well, Coach, I guess what I'm trying to say is just, well," sniffle-sniffle-gurgle, "thanks so much for all the good times." Coach Ditka took my hand gravely and spoke gently. "Well, thank you, too, for all of your support. I really do appreciate it. Thank you, *Bob* (italics *mine*, as it resounded in my mind)." It was a comic and mortifying moment. Half a dozen people suppressed giggles and small, sarcastic mutterings ("Hey, the guy is obviously a big fan of yours!") as we hurried to squeeze through the sound lock leading out of the control room. When we had all stumbled out, and the thick studio door had softly fallen shut, our laughter began to clatter in the hallways. "All right, all right, that's okay!" I insisted. "If Coach Ditka wants to call me Bob, I'll change my name to Bob!"

I had worried, as my life again led me away from Chicago, that my sense of identity with the place I most cherished might begin to fade. But following the 1985–86 Super Bowl, the Bears helped reassure me that though my residence might move, Chicago would remain my center of gravity. My feeling for the Bears was part of a passion that both moved and shaped me: rapscallion pols, pungent pizza, brawny winds, and roustabout politics—what it feels like to blink lake snow happily out of your eyes. The city's character had become part of my own; as portable as imagination. Years later, I was in Sarajevo on a morning that the Serb bombardment had let up for a short cease-fire. People came stumbling out of basements and bathrooms, blinking and exhilarated, under a fine spray of snow fluttering in from the mountains where Serb snipers were, for a moment, holding their fire. The next day, many people would begin to grasp that for every old friend they could find, holding on, another had been lost. But on that first morning, the snow felt clean in our lungs; it made a wounded city seem soft and silver. We laughed as we made our way on foot through the center of the city, walking, for once, upright and increasingly, even foolishly, unafraid. "Bear weather!" I called out to the cold, encircling hills, to the bewilderment of my companions. "It's Bear weather."

*Chapter 8*

# FROM FATHER TO
# SON—TO STEPFATHER

One of the most vivid memories of my childhood occurred long after I had grown. While packing up my apartment in Chicago, I found half a dozen antique audio reels, wound tight with tape thick and black as licorice strips and labeled in my father's indistinct, scratching, script: Chez routines, Scotty Hallo, and Scotty X-mas. My father had bought one of the first tape recorders that had rolled out, a cumbersome brown steel suitcase of a contraption crowned by a small light bulb that blinked along with his practiced punch lines.

"I *keeesed* yuuu my dearrr," my father began one story with the accent he had learned serving alongside Free French forces in North Africa—or by listening to Maurice Chevalier. "I keeesed you, and yurrr leeeps were *seeeaaaring.*" Pause. "Sooo—sooo—*seeeaaaring.*" Pause. "You had furrrgotten to pooot out yurrr ceeegarrr *beforrre* keeesing me." I brought the tapes into our studios, where Rich Rarey determined they had been recorded at a speed no longer built into tape machines. So he rotated them gingerly by hand until the reels began to squeak with voices.

"The doctor says he's up to nine pounds now. Still below normal, but he's catching up." A young woman's dulcet voice, the sing-song of a schoolgirl in a plaid Catholic school skirt laughing with her friends on the afternoon bus home after class. My mother's sitcom sweet voice rolled on under Rich's fastidious fingers. "And he says that the little scar he has on his belly button? That will heal." In the b's of *belly button*, a listener might detect a faint trace of her theatrical intonation fighting off a signifying southwest-side Irish brogue. "Well, we're going to be signing off now," Ernie's voice rang in. "April twenty-second, nineteen fifty-two. Scotty's finally home. Mother, son, grandparents, Patti's parents. We're all here. We're signing off now. I'm the father," he said as my mother giggled along with their son's gurgling on his father's shoulder. "At least," he laughed, "*I think*."

"Who are these actors?" Rich teased. "They're great. They sound almost like they could be your parents. But the squalling kid," he added. "He gives the joke away." His josh hit at something serious. The couple on the tapes were clothed in some of the same characteristics as my parents. But they sounded more like actors portraying characters based on the people I had known and loved, rather than the persons we had all become. On the reels rolling under Rich Rarey's hands, Patti and Ernie were young, lighthearted, and manifestly in love. Play the reels through, wind them back, and for a few more minutes I could beguile myself into believing that their love, and their love's embrace that included me, had somehow outlived all our disappointments.

It was on the tape labeled Scotty X-mas that Rich and I heard the episode that encouraged us to try to make what we heard into a radio story. Patti, Ernie, and Scotty under the 1955 Christmas tree as my mother explained the manger scene:

"It was so cold at night that all the farm animals in the manger gathered 'round Baby Jesus to keep him warm," said my mother, her voice sounding seasonally tender and mild. "See? Here's the little lambs. And here's two camels, breathing on Baby Jesus to keep him warm. And here's two oxen. And they're all going night-night on the ground." In the background, you could hear my father peal forth with a vaudevillian snore. "Now, Scotty, it's the Baby Jesus' birthday. Would you like to sing happy birthday to Baby Jesus?" And so we sang:

> *Happy Birthday to you.*
> *Happy Birthday to you.*
> *Happy Birthday, Baby Jesus.*
> *Happy Birthday to you!*

And then, as mother and son sang the last sweet note, my father's voice broke in with British beer-hall ebullience: *"For he's a jolly good fellow, for he's a jolly good fellow . . ."* Rich roared with laughter—and quickly looked over at me, to confirm, I think, that his laughter didn't offend. Of course, laughing was encouraged—my father could still kill 'em from his grave. But I could only make myself listen to the affectionate and eccentric family bound to one another on the reels if I regarded the recorded fragments as scenes for a story.

In school productions of *Our Town*, I was almost always cast as the Stage Manager, directing the emotional freight of the work with a pipe instead of a microphone. My mother, the ingenue, had always played Emily. Over the years, we had sometimes called out lines with one another. "Oh earth," my mother would sometimes exclaim with wide, comic, Emily eyes when I was especially happy over a Cub win or a Bear victory, "you're too wonderful for anyone to realize you!" "Saints and poets know it maybe, Mother," I'd say back. "They do—some." But in listening to those tapes of times together I was too tender to recall, I had forgotten the Stage Manager's warning to Emily Webb not to go back to life to relive a favorite day—that you couldn't take pleasure in that day when you already knew the hailstorm of pains that were ahead. Hearing my parents on those tapes sound so delighted by their differences, so melodious in their mild and loving laughter, I wanted to reach back as a grown man to take hold of the boy I was and the kids my parents were to say, "Oh, look at us. For one minute, just look at us. Thirty years have gone by. Dad's dead. People hurt him, he drank too much. He hurt himself, he hurt us, he got lost, then he had a stroke in the shower of a small, crummy hotel room. We felt just terrible about it, don't you remember? But listen, just for a moment now, we're all together. For a moment, let's be happy. Let's look at one another!"

We aired a piece taken from those tapes on a Father's Day. Over the years, it has been replayed just twice; although many people have the impression it is played every year. But over the years, many people who have heard that mother, father, and son singing and giggling seemed to feel something tickled within themselves. There was something satisfyingly ironic in my mother and father, a mixed marriage, a broken couple, show folk, becoming for others a poignant portrait of the exquisite commonplace of family love—Lautrec sketches in a Rockwell scene.

• • •

By the time the story was broadcast, my mother had already been married for a decade to the Lincoln scholar, Ralph Newman. Ralph was a distinguished bookseller and civic figure. But his appearance, I'm sure he would not mind me observing, could also suggest something of an old vaudevillian. He had pearly bright hair, a full black floor mop of a mustache, pearlike proportions, and what he used to call, "my old second baseman's nose."

In the early 1930s, Ralph had played second base in semipro and minor league games in Arizona, Texas, and New Mexico. He was good enough, in fact, to acquire a nickname, Sparky. My mother could cajole him into undertaking small, unattractive errands, by saying, "Time to take the trash to the incinerator, *Sparky*," as she had once inveigled me to scamper off to bed by calling me *Billy Pierce*. Once, while playing for the Tucson Toros, Sparky had swung at a low curve from a Wichita Falls pitcher and sliced the ball wickedly along the seams. But the ball spun back, wickedly, and sprang up into Sparky's face. "Bang, zoom, right on my ol' schnozzola," as he used to tell the story. Ralph's father met him when he took the Super Chief back to Chicago, Sparky wearing a nose cast that gave him more than a vague resemblance to a bank robber, and waving a check for $500 signed by the great general manager Branch Rickey. "Look, Pop," he said, "look what Mr. Rickey gave me! Five hundred dollars!" But by the time the cast came off, Sparky had sufficiently recovered to grasp that the Toros had not given him $500 to secure his future, but to buy out the balance of his contract. Mr. Rickey wanted to cultivate players who could hit a curve ball, not chip them back into their own *schnozzolas*. When the cast was unwrapped, it revealed a nose that looked like something from Emmett Kelly's stage kit. Ralph decided to sprout a stout mustache to distract attention from his nose; which had the wonderful effect of stretching the semblance of a smile across his face in almost any aspect.

Ralph used Branch Rickey's bequest and a gift from his own father to set himself up as a bookseller. He began to specialize in Lincoln for the same essential reason he had become a second baseman—the field there was open. "Besides," he used to say, "I asked myself, 'What name would bring in more customers? Ralph's Bookstore—or The Abraham Lincoln Bookshop?'" In this calling, Ralph exercised the gifts of a showman and performer as much as a scholar. Mr. Lincoln, he used to remind customers and friends, was a mighty rail-splitter only for as short a time as possible. By his early teens, Lincoln had learned to evade the

toil and drudgery of splitting rails—plowing fields, or towing barges—
by telling stories. The real young Mr. Lincoln, Ralph used to say, was a
cool, complicated, commonly melancholy genius whose moral and
political precocity could be cloaked by an earthy, even goofy, sense of
humor. "Do you really think," he used to ask, "that Lincoln's friends
urged him to become a lawyer, to run for office, because he split such
good rails? Lincoln could hold an audience. First and last, he was a
superb raconteur. He could make 'em laugh, he could make 'em cry."

Ralph's traffic in the scholarship and commerce of Lincoln and
Civil War knitted him into a delightful filigree of scholars, lovers, fans,
hobbyists, and hangers-on that ranged from Carl Sandburg to Edna
Ferber to Mahalia Jackson—to Nathan Leopold. And Ralph was often
the link between. Among scores of stories, consider this: It was Ralph
who lured his friend Sandburg into testifying at one of Leopold's
parole hearings by promising to seat the writer next to an appealing
redheaded woman for the long drive down to Springfield. Whatever
Sandburg's incentive, he was ingeniously effective, the good, gray
Chicago poet, the Great Emancipator's biographer, urging commissioners to release, after three decades of incarceration, a man who had committed one of America's most infamous murders. "Your honors," said
Sandburg, shaking his shaggy, silvery, world-weary head in sorrow, "if
*this* life can now find a useful purpose, does it not mean that *no life* is
beyond redemption?" Leopold had been behind bars, but his family's
substantial bank account was unfettered. He had ordered Lincoln books
from Ralph. Rather more significantly for supporters of his parole,
Bobby Frank's murderer had also become a medical technician,
researcher, and subject for malaria research. He was ultimately released
from prison to spend his last years working at a hospital in Puerto
Rico. Ralph picked him up at the prison gate and then led reporters
on a *Front Page*–style chase. Sandburg had somewhat more success with
the parole commissioners than he did with the woman in the car. But
he continued to drop by Ralph's shop to browse through books and
use Ralph's phone to call New York, North Carolina, Tokyo, and Hollywood, trying to find Marilyn Monroe. Ralph once organized a birthday dinner for Sandburg at which his friends presented the poet with a
calfskin wallet containing an Illinois Bell credit card.

"This is great, how very touching," said the state's poet laureate.
"And this means," he inquired rather less sentimentally, "that I *never* have
to pay?"

"No, Carl," Ralph explained, "it means that you phone from wherever, and at the end of the month, they send you a bill." And Sandburg, said Ralph, looked blandly at the card and tore it in two. "What the hell," he asked, "do I need this for?"

In the late 1960s, Adlai Stevenson III came to seek Ralph's guidance on running for statewide office. "You knew my dad, Dad trusted you," said the younger Stevenson. "Do you have any advice?"

"Maybe just this, Adlai," said Ralph. "Don't change your name."*

A few months after the first time the story about my parents had been broadcast, Ralph and I were at a north-side theater to see a friend in a new production. During the intermission, a couple approached to chat, and I introduced Ralph to them as my father.

"Oh, yes," said the couple. "Your father, the comedian." I'm not certain Ralph ever heard the story about my parents; even the most self-confident of men should not have to listen to his wife make loving baby talk with a former husband. But Ralph knew his friends often relied on him for comedy, and so he told the couple, "Yes. That's me." They asked where he had played.

"Oh, out west," he said. "Arizona, Texas, Kansas." As the couple looked on quizzically, no doubt trying to remember what old vaudeville circuit had run through Tucson and Wichita Falls, the confusion finally came into focus for me.

"Actually," I intervened, "my father here is a Lincoln scholar." Which only compounded the verbal commotion.

"Oh, how fascinating," said the couple. "And when did you become a Lincoln scholar?"

"After I broke my nose," said Ralph.

"Oh, my word. Were you a boxer, too?"

"Boxer?" asked Ralph. "Hell, no. A baseball player."

"A baseball player, too?" they enthused. "When did you become a comedian?" Before I could uselessly intercede once more, Ralph responded with the obvious answer. "Well, all my life."

Mercifully, lights began to blink, calling us back into the theater. As we sank back into our seats, I tried to explain the confusion to Ralph.

---

*Ralph told this story for years. Former Senator Stevenson likes to tell it on himself—but tells audiences the admonition came from Mayor Richard J. Daley. Both Ralph and the late mayor were capable of borrowing each other's anecdotes. But perhaps the advice was so obviously wise, it was offered by both.

"They think you're my father," I said. "You know, my father, *Ernie*." Ralph received this with a twinkle.

"You mean," he asked, "they think I was in a Jerry Lewis movie?"*

"Must be," I whispered back as the lights dimmed. "Hey, laaady!" I squealed, Jerrylike. *"Nya-nya-nnnyyyaaa!"*

"Gee," said Ralph. "I like this role."

I didn't delude myself into believing that my father had somehow come to reappear inside of Ralph. But the two had certain inconsequential similarities. They both read, incessantly and indiscriminately, they both followed sports with intensity, they both had a self-educated man's fascination for gadgetry. They were both funny men, who had become self-made intellectuals. My father tended to be a reader among joke tellers, Ralph a storyteller among scholars. And of course—there was nothing inconsequential about this—they had both married my mother.

But Ralph possessed a power of personal discipline I envied; and wished that my father had acquired. He didn't drink to the point of danger, didn't pity himself to the point of depression, and (more or less) observed the orders doctors issued about how to increase his longevity. When my father had been told to cut out booze and curtail his intake of fried foods and desserts, he had bourbon, french fries, and a hot fudge sundae for lunch. "Just to get it out of my system," he said. As Ralph's health declined, doctors pruned his diet heartlessly (perhaps for the sake of his heart). "Gyros, no good," they said. "Scorn corned beef, blintzes, they'll blitz you." Ralph scowled but complied—he wanted to keep going. Once, we decided to go to an afternoon White Sox game and he suggested having an early lunch with a friend at Manny's delicatessen, one of his favorite haunts just west of the Loop. "Are you sure you want to go there, Ralph?" I asked.

"Why wouldn't I want to go to Manny's?"

"Oh, you know. Corned beef, latkes, the smell of new pickles. I don't want to feel—well—*taunted*." We went, and Ralph glowered comically as he lingered over a piece of cherry cheesecake. "It's like trying to have a good time," he said, "at an AA meeting in Dublin."

I did not confuse Ralph with my father. But at some point, I began to see and cherish in him a second chance to be a good and useful son. It was a painful time when, in 1975, Ralph was indicted and

---

*Ernie Simon was the golf announcer in Jerry Lewis's 1959 film, *The Bellboy*.

convicted for his appraisal of Richard Nixon's vice presidential papers.★ But I admired the way in which Ralph accepted responsibility and punishment without complaint or self-pity. I was too old and too recent a son to be idolatrous. Besides, Ralph had two older, accomplished daughters from his first marriage; he scarcely needed a new child. But I could offer an unconditional, unquestioning affection and fraternity, which, while perhaps short of an actual son's, was more intimate and involving than a friend's.

Ralph was convicted on a raw, gray day in November. He was released on his own recognizance, to return in a few weeks for sentencing. After a prolonged cry, our blended family clambered into an elevator that, disconcertingly, included one of Ralph's jurors. He seemed a nice man caught in a difficult place—again—and smiled without pleasure. My mother was warm. "Good morning, sir. Well, at least we all get to go home now, don't we?" When we came out of an elevator, I saw, for the first time, the face of my own profession turned against me: snapping cameras, harsh, sharp lights, yapping reporters barking slap-in-the-face questions: "Mr. Newman! Mr. Newman! Did you take a fall for Richard Nixon? Are you scared about prison? What do you think about Nixon now?" Ralph walked ahead grimly, saying nothing, no explanations, no excuses, DiMaggio striding back to the dugout after striking out. *Never complain, never explain.* For the first time, my mother's voice rang out as we tried to squeeze through the snarl and twist of all the entangling arms, legs, and television cables that had become lashed, like latticework, against the revolving doors. "How ever are we supposed to get out? I mean, my dears," she said to a television crew, "how are even *you* going

---

★Ralph was charged with backdating a deed that permitted Richard Nixon to take a substantial deduction on his 1972 taxes (the year Ralph had married my mother). Ralph pleaded not guilty. I accepted his word and we never discussed details. He also did not—as is the right of any criminal defendant—present a defense. Since any financial benefit Ralph might have gained from backdating the deed was small, the ordinary course for a prosecutor would have been to offer Ralph a deal to testify about those who profited most from the backdated deed—especially the man who took the deduction.

But by the time Ralph was indicted, Nixon had already been pardoned by President Gerald Ford. I never heard Ralph complain about the fact that Nixon's good fortune may have come at his expense. On the contrary: Ralph always said, "I don't want to see a president in jail." But he could get touchy about being mistaken for a Nixon associate. Ralph had begun to appraise official papers while working for an old client who genuinely was a close friend—Adlai Stevenson. It was Stevenson who recommended Ralph's expertise in Lincoln's funeral to Jacqueline Kennedy. Lyndon Johnson then retained him to appraise his official papers—he'd heard about the tax break—and Johnson recommended Ralph to Richard Nixon. The Republican with whom Ralph worked most closely was Abraham Lincoln.

to get out of here?" My mother's good manners broke a path. We tumbled out onto Dearborn Street, a few cameras giving chase. Only in movies do convicted men and their lawyers slip easily away in limousines; in the actual event, we had to flag down cabs.

We returned to Pat and Ralph's apartment for what Ralph commenced to call "my own wake." My mother broke out lunch meats, bread, tea, and coffee, friends brought in pastries—and the corpse himself poured drinks. Evening came on, but we avoided the custom of watching the evening news—after all, we were in it. Friends called to tell Ralph he had looked determined and dignified leaving the courthouse, while the reporters had yelped like small, mean, malodorous dogs. It was an early evening ritual for Ralph to stroll across the street to buy the afternoon papers and first editions of the next morning's papers. But callers had cautioned that front pages were paved with his photograph. The idea of Ralph walking back from the newsstand with a bundle of newspapers bannering his own conviction—replete with snapshot—was discouraging. So I went out.

*Daily News, plop!* under the arm, the early *Trib, plop!* and finally the early *Scum Times,* as we used to hail Marshall Field's tabloid. Ralph's uncharacteristically grim, cheerless face was stamped across them all. Riding the elevator back up to Pat and Ralph's apartment, I pointedly placed the backside of the *Sun-Times* on top, sports section showing. The Bulls were off to a strong start. Ludicrously, I thought about a joke my father had taught me: a reporter in Jerusalem, where tabloids open on the right because Hebrew reads right to left, runs out of an office building and drops a shekel in a pay phone to call his editor. "Chief, chief," he says, "I got a story so big, it'll blow this town wide open. Hold the back page!" A stanza from a song my father used to try to sing came back to me, imperfectly: *

> *And I believe that since my life began*
> *all I've had to give*
> *is a talent to amuse*

The son of a comedian—the stepson of a second baseman—ought to be able to throw out a line when his father needs one.

---

*Noel Coward's *If Love Were All.*

"Look, Ralph," I said presenting the pile of newsprint before him. "The Bulls aren't off to a bad start. Right behind Detroit."

"Thurmond," he said. "Nate makes a big difference." He picked up eagerly. "And Sloan and Van Lier. The Bulls just might put pro basketball across here.* Always been the college game, De Paul, and the high schools until now. You know," he inquired slyly of the group sitting softly around him on the sofa, "who's been the best professional basketball team in Chicago? Historically, I mean." A trick question, I knew; perhaps the others did, too. But we offered only a respectful pause.

"The Harlem Globetrotters," Ralph announced with a glint of his old delight. "Started in 1927 by Abe Saperstein, over on the west side. Stitched up their red, white, and blue uniforms at his father's tailor's shop on Roosevelt Road. Called them the Harlem Globetrotters because *Harlem* was a clever way of saying *Negro* in those days. Gave 'em national standing. And you know," he continued, "why they started all that clowning? Because the Trotters were so good, everybody was afraid to play them. They had to start the clowning to get bookings. Abe used to say, 'You can't get a lot of people to turn out if you say, "Seven tonight, a bunch of black guys run circles around our white guys." ' So they made it, 'Tonight, the fabulous Harlem Globetrotters entertain you!' " By the time Ralph flipped over the newspaper to see his face frozen in black and white by a bleak and unforgiving light, he could sit back with a small smile of quiet satisfaction. The historian at home.

Years later, when I had gotten back from covering the Gulf War, I went out to Chicago for a visit. After I unrolled a rug I had bought for a ruinous bargain in the smashed city of Basra and stood up to show Pat and Ralph that I had no holes in me, Ralph and I fell in to watching the Chicago Bulls and Detroit Pistons. It was the first weekend of the play-off series the Bulls would win on their way to their first championship.

"I think—I think—they're *just this close* to doing it," said Ralph, as my mother sat down on the sofa between us with cheese and crackers. "Pippen is playing much tougher."

"Laimbeer is getting shut out."

---

*And so they did. But that Bulls team of Jerry Sloan, Norm Van Lier, and Nate Thurmond lost to Rick Barry's Golden State Warriors in the 1975–76 playoffs. The Warriors went on to win the NBA championship, while Coach Dick Motta and the aging Bulls were broken up.

"Grant is blocking out Rodman."★

"MJ is drawing fouls."

"Foul him, foul him," said Ralph, "he's sinking the shots." Fan talk; father-son talk. After the game ended (I have had to look up the score—the Bulls won, 105-97; they would sweep the series against Detroit), Ralph rose to excuse himself on his way to the bathroom and turned around, haltingly. He was getting set to turn eighty, and his step was already beginning to slow, his bones growing brittle.

"I was just thinking. How old were you when your father died?"

"Sixteen."

"As I thought," he said with his face set full with consideration.

"Thought what?"

"Nothing really," he said, turning back around. "Just that, I guess by now, I've known you longer than he did, haven't I?"

Bill Veeck used to say that he had tried to rear his children with the refinement and enlightenment to wonder about the worth of what their father did. "I produce nothing, after all," he used to say. "No cars. No steel. No novel. No symphony. I don't deliver milk, or stack cantaloupes. The cure for cancer will be advanced not a whit by anything I do. All I can give to the world is the ephemeral idea that a few people have a good time." It was one of Mr. Veeck's best set speeches, and a bit of solil-oquizing that both Ernie and Ralph might have borrowed, word for word. With each, our talk of the show of sports was a way of reaching each other, a frequency we could tune in together in the emotional static of some new sadness or frustration. It was a way of sending out a signal: "I got you. Still with you. Still here."

---

★Dennis Rodman was then with Detroit.

# Chapter 9

# WAR AND REMEMBRANCE OF THE BULLS

O ver the years, as I saw several wars, I developed a particular repugnance for analogies between sports and war. Tellingly, I didn't encounter the practice among soldiers as much as politicians and reporters. I came to think of the trait as distinctly Nixonian—as when Richard Nixon tried to placate young protesters by talking about sports, rather than the war that had brought them to the national mall ("I think the Cubs are gonna make it this year"), or visited veterans' hospitals and talked about sports rather than the war in which the young soldiers had been wounded.

Of course, politicians are always trying to use sports to wage politics by other means. The mix of sports and politics is bipartisan and usually benign; or at least, laughably crafty—as when Hillary Rodham Clinton, planning a senate campaign in New York, welcomed the world champion New York Yankees to the White House and posed in a Yankees' cap. (When Mrs. Clinton was campaigning with her husband for national office she was pleased to be identified as a Cub fan, rooting for adorable underdogs. But when she needed to win her own votes in New York, she would be photographed only with top dogs.) One of the virtues of former athletes running for office—Jack Kemp,

Bill Bradley, Alan Page, or Jim Bunning—is that they don't seem to feel obliged to prove themselves regular guys by towing sports into politics.

Employing sports analogies in war seems especially pernicious because athletes and soldiers share relative youth, fitness, and competitive fire. The last test many of the soldiers faced was often on some kind of playing field. Parallels seem irresistible. And yet the stakes each face are gravely different. The parallels are irresponsible. Of course, we are always much quicker to recognize in others the flaws we carry in ourselves. I covered General Schwarzkopf's "left hook" around Iraqi troops during the Gulf War and cringed on hearing a sports term applied to war. But I have been culpable more than a few times myself.

When I first arrived in El Salvador in 1982, the young men and women who had run off from their villages and slums to pick up the gun with one of the rebel armies were called *los muchachos*—the boys. At first, I found something unexpectedly affectionate in that sobriquet. Even Salvadoran military officers used the term in briefings, as if to acknowledge that the people daring to try to bring down a brutal military regime were, after all, their own sons and daughters. But after just a few weeks of the war, I began to feel that the rebels were called *los muchachos* to diminish their magnitude in the mind of the public. The phrase fixed the guerrillas as implausible punks and vicious pranksters, not serious soldiers; much less a serious government. It would be a few more weeks before I saw a rebel soldier closer than as a blur or shadow. But I began to see the young—hauntingly young—Salvadoran government soldiers giggling boyishly behind sandbags at checkpoints as the *real* muchachos: smooth-cheeked kids dragooned out of villages and slums to carry a gun for a regime that would otherwise just as soon shoot them.

One of the first battles we saw occurred in the town of San Vincente, about an hour out of the capital. The rebels had taken over the town radio station before retreating, and mandated a brief format change. They played revolutionary anthems over and over again: *Venceremos! Venceremos!* We will win! We met Salvadoran soldiers walking out of the station who were bearing a tape cassette like a soccer trophy. Our producer, Kimberly Conroy, introduced us as radio reporters and asked to hear the tape they had liberated. They obliged by snapping the number one song on the rebel hit list into a machine, churning up a chorus of vigorous male voices: *Venceremos! Venceremos!*

Our engineer, Leo del Aguila, had an inkling and asked to see the cassette. It read, "Mitch Miller and the Sing-a-Long Gang." We thanked the soldiers and watched them walk away before raiding the radio station ourselves to see signs of the battle. As the soldiers walked off, I saw that they carried their rifles by threading them over their shoulders— the way other boys in the Americas often carry baseball bats.

The analogy is partly an illusion, of course. I have since also seen young soldiers, government and guerrillas, in Ethiopia, Gaza, and Bosnia—none of them baseball hotbeds—bearing rifles in the same manner. But the utter youth of the soldiers remains uniform, and unnerving. The most startling scene I saw during the Gulf War almost a decade later occurred when I stumbled out of a bunker one morning and greeted a group of young paratroopers eating breakfast while they lounged against piled sandbags. I peered into their plastic bowls and saw a kaleidoscope of colors turning mushy in the milk. *Froot Loops.* A kid's cereal, consumed by kids carrying lethal weapons, romping on sandbags like kids watching Saturday morning cartoons. Building bodies twelve different ways for war.

One night, some of the paratroopers took me along to a movie. *Bull Durham* was being shown on a video screen, Ron Shelton's rollicking and poignant story about life and love in the minor leagues. Any analogies between professional athletes and soldiers are a little more valid when applied to the Airborne corps. Paratroopers, like professional athletes, know that their careers are limited by the life of their knees. A few see themselves becoming commanders, coaches, or managers. But most paratroopers and players seem to see themselves as serving time in a passionate pursuit, then moving on when their limbs begin to tire. The temperament encourages irreverence, which can make both groups of youngsters fine companions during a war or a season.

Most of the soldiers had seen *Bull Durham* before back in North Carolina, where the real-life Durham Bulls are local favorites. For most of the film, the soldiers sat and reacted like the teenagers many of them were, hooting and snickering at the flash of a female breast or the out-loud utterance of *fuck*. But there is a scene in which Kevin Costner, seething with love, can no longer throttle his desire and sweeps aside a litter of dishes to take Susan Sarandon right there, *right there!* on the kitchen table, cornflakes crunching under their thighs. *Snap, crackle, pop!* The young men sat through this in sober, stifled silence. Suddenly, the overwhelming sound in the desert night was the silence of a couple of hundred young soldiers wiggling manfully in their seats. And when the sequence was over, a couple of hundred throats discharged . . . sighs. It was the soldiers' favorite movie. But I think sports and North Carolina only partially explained their enthusiasm.*

Frankly, I had a bad Gulf War. I lived through it, of course, which immediately mitigates a lot of grousing. And, remarkably, I saw not a single dead body, Iraqi, American, Saudi, Kuwaiti, or British, during the entire war; much less the appalling personal mutilation I had seen in other conflicts. In fact, after a while, it was the isolated, godforsaken, disinfected, inaccessible remoteness of the Gulf War's violence that began to repulse me. Back home, I knew, so-called smart bombs were the new stars of prime-time nightly entertainment. Once, I was able to call my old boyhood friend, Danny Zemel, now a rabbi in Washington, D.C.

"It all looks like a video game here," he said. "See the bad guy, *p-kow!* There's another—*p-kow! Got him!* I can protect my kids from certain video games, I suppose. But I want them to know what's going on in the world. What happens when the news gets to be a video game? Of course," he added, "it's all different for you over there, where it's actually happening." Just a couple of weeks later, some Marine intelligence officers took me along to see an artillery raid. They were proud of the way their service could coordinate air, land, and sea attacks simultaneously. Artillery raid—I guess I expected strong men with bowed backs and sinewy arms, hefting heavy shells into smoldering barrels. But no more, and for all the best reasons. The actual cannons firing were miles from the command center. The plan was if and when the Iraqis could fix a bead on the guns that had fired at them, so they could fire back, they would hit only steel. Some of the young men and women sending off the shells did, indeed, have brawny arms—but from pumping iron in gyms, not loading artillery shells. They sat at keyboards, calling out sequences and typing in coordinates, propelling thousands of pounds of explosives screaming and pounding into targets with the same essential flick of their fingers they might use to send an electronic Valentine. No, I told Danny, sometimes it wasn't that different over here at all.

The repugnance I felt over this kind of remote control, slaughter-

---

*A few years later, I got to meet Lawrence "Crash" Davis, the former career minor leaguer (he did play parts of three years for the Phillies) whose name had been borrowed for the film. He lived near Durham and had recently retired as personnel director for a major corporation. Mr. Davis would recite thoughtfully sanitized renditions of some of the movie's signature speeches for visitors. When I told him the story about the paratroopers, Crash Davis just shook his head. "Lemme tell you," he said. "That scene doesn't get any easier to take after you're all growed up."

by-keystroke was more a moral misgiving than disapproval. Saddam Hussein was a bad man who had made his own citizens the main casualties of his mad, immoral, imperialist venture. But it was difficult to root for all of the extraordinary instruments the U.S. military was dedicating to Saddam's defeat. One day, an Air Force colonel showed me the guts of the bomb known as the Bouncing Betty—a diabolical basketball in appearance, round and brown but studded. It was designed to be dropped onto the desert floor, then bounce up two and a half feet to explode a shower of shrapnel in all directions.

"And why," I asked the colonel, "is it set at two and a half feet?"

"Oh," he said without self-consciousness, "because they've calculated that two and a half feet is the height of an average Iraqi man's lower intestines, leading up to the heart and lungs. The weapon can do maximum damage in that neighborhood." I felt a rumbling in my own neighborhood. I had an image of bomb scientists at MIT, holding up tape measures against the torsos of mannequins and saying, "Just an inch higher now."

The first days of the air war that was designed to demolish Saddam's defenses before the ground war began coincided with the weeks leading up to the Super Bowl. The U.S. military was preparing some kind of vast, open-air Super Bowl–watching party for soldiers that, given the time difference between the United States and Saudi Arabia, would begin after midnight. They wanted to recruit reporters to cover the divertissement.

"Popcorn, Fritos, the works," said an exuberant young lieutenant who had been delegated to seek me out, sports fan to sports fan. He worked for a general who was always in search of opponents for his mid-morning, half-court basketball games. Reporters, as a rule, were not as fit as the general's junior officers; but they may have been less reluctant to block his shots and fill the lane against him when he drove in for a layup. *Oh, sir. Sorry, sir. Good drive, sir.* I was eager to be enlisted because the word was that after the game, the general invited you to use the hot shower at his headquarters. But the lieutenant was interested only in recruiting me to watch and report on the Super Bowl divertissement.

"We'll bring you out," he said, "there and back. Watch the game, talk to the troops, have a few dogs, and be back for breakfast."

"Oh, I dunno," I said. "I don't know if I want to be the guy covering a Super Bowl party when the ground war begins."

"Hey, my man, apply your brain matter. Do you think they're gonna begin the ground war when we got fifty thousand troops watching the Giants and the Bills?"

"Why not?" I asked. "Perfect cover, isn't it? Or, a great time for the Iraqis to attack. Like Washington rowing over to raid the Hessians on Christmas Eve, when they're all drunk on schnapps."

"Hey," said the lieutenant, "no schnapps out here in Saudi-fuck-ing-ay-Arabia, okay? But anyone you want to talk to. *Anyone.*" It was a continuing joke between us. "We deliver. Male, female, Southerner, New Yorker, Bills fan, Giants fan—Japanese fan." We spoke in the confidence and cadences of sports fans.

"What do you figure—Bills by ten? Their turn, it seems to me."

"Nah, Giants. We've been away, but Parcells has them kicking ass *awww*-some!" For once, the contemporary cliché was absolutely apt.

But in the event, I chose not to cover the Super Bowl party that the military had arranged. I saw videotape of the event later. Tens of thousands of exuberant soldiers were there, although, I suspect, more inflamed by the chance to clown for the attendant television cameras and meet members of the opposite sex in the middle of the night than to follow the Super Bowl.★ Eminently sensible thinking. But as someone who loves sports, it just felt jingoistic to help the army use the Super Bowl for crass political purposes. The Super Bowl is supposed to be used only for crass *commercial* purposes.

In the middle of the night during the middle months of covering the Gulf War, I often twitched sleeplessly in the sleeping bag on the bunker floor on which I was assigned to bed down. Outside, overhead, there was always the soft, smothered thud of bombs thundering into the earth just over the border in Iraq, shivering the shaving mirrors soldiers had tacked onto sandbags. Inside the bunker, the uncovered desert floor quivered with cold and quaked with each blast. The inside of my mind screened vexing and distressing visions. All the quaking, cold, and twisting produced the predictable result—I had to leave the bunker to relieve myself.

The U.S. Army had issued each soldier and reporter a camouflage-pattern slicker that pulled over the head. They were impregnated (the slickers, that is, although a few of the soldiers, too, as it turns out) with small silicon chips that were said to twinkle when picked up on long-range, infra-red lenses. The officers said any shape moving at night that

---

★Or, for that matter, members of the same sex. This was before the Clinton administration's Don't Ask, Don't Tell policy drove great numbers of gay soldiers out of the service. I had the impression during the Gulf War that a good many gays were serving, quietly, effectively, and without incident, in a good many strategic units.

did not so twinkle would be shot as a presumed intruder. This was war. Passwords were for movies. I didn't dismiss the admonition as theatrical. I had grown up hearing the story of Colonel Mickey Marcus, the first commander of the Israeli Army, who left his tent at night to relieve himself while robed in a billowing sheet. This lent him, lamentably, the appearance of a Bedouin—which was not a sight to reassure an Israeli sentry. So Colonel Marcus was shot by one of his own men. I doubted any allied soldier would be more favorably impressed by me.

One night, I awoke from a nightmare, and into the shrill whine of a sandstorm. Grains of sand banged like a drumbeat against the bunker tent tops, smacking like a cannonade fired by some Lilliputian army. *Damn, damn, damn,* I groused, *but when you gotta go, you gotta go.* Outside, the sand stung and the wind bit. Just a few steps from the bunker stood a serried rank of pipes, christened *piss tubes,* planted waist-high into the ground. In the middle of the night, in the middle of a war, in the grip of despondency, I sought solace in sports. *Dig in, Ace,* I told myself, and rooted my booted toes into the sand to try to stand against the searing wind. Reaching under the slicker, I used both hands to undo the bottom-most button of my flack jacket. Then, I raised the slicker up in folds, from my knees, to tuck it into pleats underneath my chin. Finally, fumbling in the stinging grit and scalding gusts, I lowered my fly. Up to bat again. Digging in at the plate. Two strikes, bottom of the ninth, fastball on the way, one chance to score. The great Ted Williams once said that the hardest athletic feat he knew about was to hit a pitched baseball. Ted Williams probably never tried to hit a piss tube in a sandstorm.

In the violet, violent darkness of a desert night, in the grim and gloom of a briny sandstorm, I began to relieve myself the way my father taught me. The language of baseball and boyhood combined. "Both hands now, Ace. C'mon now, you gotta shake hands with it! Keep your eye on the target! Way to go!" Strange, what will make a man proud. And then, in the instant I began to perform, I felt lonely, fearful, desolate. The sky ahead flickered with fire. The ground below rumbled with thunder. The wind stung my lungs with each breath. I felt too old for another war, too young to die at peace, too tired to cry. And then, it seemed, I didn't have to make the effort. Tears sprang into my eyes—except I knew I wasn't crying. *Damn, damn, damn,* I thought, *I'm sad, I'm sick, I'm trying to whizz in a sandstorm and now, it's raining in my face.* More drops splattered against my nose, and slid onto my lips. I licked. They had a sharpness I never suspected in rainwater. *Damn, damn,* I wondered, *has the enemy put something into the clouds over here? Have we?* Another sprinkle splashed against my eyes and lips. Then, I realized: it wasn't rain.

(So it's true: some reporters—certainly this one—don't have the sense not to piss into the wind.)

Back in my bag in the bunker, I rubbed a damp towel over my face and tried to gurgle back giggles. Soldiers were sleeping. Paratroops needed their rest. Again, it was thinking about sports that gave me a wave to ride back down into sleep. It was early in 1991. The Chicago Bulls were advancing on their first championship. I blocked out my own game inside my mind: Horace Grant, bug-eyed in bubble-lensed eyeglasses and his blunt, bald head, takes down the rebound. Clears it out to Scottie Pippen. Over to Michael, who passes off to John Paxson. He looks in from the arc: no shot. Back to Scottie, who charges in on his elegant Aztec legs, stops short, and bounds the ball back to Michael. The dream that—still—sometimes takes me from restlessness into sleep turns to stop-action here, with Michael Jordan, in full-limbed flight, rising toward the old red rafters rusting in the old Chicago Stadium: the house that nominated Roosevelt, and will be remembered as the main stage for Michael Jordan.

The soldiers and I used to joke, in the ease of camaraderie, about how little of life's circumstances we had in common. The differences were as plain as the official Red Cross identification I had to dangle alongside my dog tags:

*SIMON, SCOTT*
*(A Jewish family name; few of the soldiers were)*
*BIRTHPLACE: CHICAGO*
*(Big cold city; many of the soldiers were from small, sultry Carolina towns)*
*RELIGION: QUAKER*
*(Pacifist faith; not many pacifists among paratroopers)*

And then, perhaps most superfluously:

*HAIR: GRAY*
*(I had put "salt&pepper" on the form. But, as a young sergeant explained, the tag was too small to accommodate my vain insistence on precision.)*

But by the time of the Gulf War, Chicagoans and North Carolinians were already conscious of sharing a local hero: Michael Jordan. The tale was already being told, present tense, like a parable, in North Carolina and Chicago, with full stops for commercial opportunities.

Michael is born—well, actually in Brooklyn. But within a few months, the family moves to Wilmington, North Carolina, a wide-open town along the Carolina coast (Knicks' fan Spike Lee will never quite forgive the Jordans for the move). He grows up, a skinny stripling of a younger brother, fourth among five, in the obscuring but protective shadow of his older brother Larry. Larry, say the locals, was actually the predominate athlete in the Jordan family. Michael was the easygoing youngster who would sleep in, sloughing off family chores on his brother and sister by flashing an early low-watt version of his Wheaties smile. The brothers run against each other, hit and pitch against each other, play one-on-one in basketball, cards, and brotherly roughhousing. MJ will say later that no one—*no one*—not Gary Payton, Bryon Russell, or even Scottie Pippen in Bulls practices, ever guarded him as closely as Larry. When they hit their early teens, Larry continues to develop at the normal human rate. But Michael *grows*. An early sign of the hand of magic.

Still, at Wilmington's Laney High School, Michael is cut from his high school basketball team—and cries. As his tears dry, mortification hardens into motivation. One day, the team manager comes down with an adolescent virus, and Michael volunteers to haul the laundry. In practices, he plays his way back onto the team and begins to dazzle by seeming to brush the rafters with his jumps. MJ, as he's known by now, sends out letters to Virginia, to UCLA, seeking basketball scholarships, but they're not interested in an unscouted kid from the Carolina coast. A high school guidance counselor tells Jordan, "Son you can't play basketball forever, but you can get a good education at Chapel Hill, and with defense increases, GE should be hiring." MJ is sufficiently nervous over his future to take classes in cooking and sewing. His family is actually delighted—MJ bakes, by all accounts, a helluva an orange spice cake.

At the end of the spring season, he scores the last fifteen points in a last-second victory for Laney over rival New Hanover. When his name first appears in news stories, it's as Mike, Mike Jordan. The stories about the game bring MJ an invitation to the basketball summer camp run by the great and gracious coach, Dean Smith of the University of North Carolina, the man who integrated North Carolina basketball. He is impressed by the intelligent elegance of MJ's moves, the polish in his explosiveness. And, MJ's nervelessness—a trait to really stamp a bony, bouncy kid from the coast. Coach Smith is a bigger man in North Carolina than Jesse Helms; not to mention a more salutary influence.* Word about MJ has spread around the region, bringing registered letters under fancy seals from South Carolina, Charlotte, and even the lordly Duke. But James and Deloris Jordan are flattered that so fine a man as Dean Smith would have such regard for their son. The world seems to be opening wide for him. But he takes his first steps to Chapel Hill.

There, as a freshman, MJ plays his way onto a varsity that includes Sam Perkins and James Worthy. In March of 1982, Michael's first year in the livery of Carolina blue, the Tar Heels reach the NCAA finals against John Thompson's Georgetown. Sixty-three thousand fans clamor in New Orleans' Superdome. Dean Smith has taken teams onto that stage three times before, and without winning. Georgetown is anchored at center by the redoubtable Patrick Ewing. The lead lurches back and forth, back and forth, and with 32 seconds left on the clock, Georgetown is ahead, 62-61. Carolina takes the ball, brings it up court, and calls a time-out. Coach Smith figures that Perkins and Worthy will be closely guarded; and that Ewing will throttle any attempt to take the ball up the middle. The kid from Wilmington, after looking flustered in the first half, has scored a dozen points in the second. So Coach Smith sketches out a play that will wind down the clock and get the ball to Michael Jordan in the left corner. "If it comes to you, Michael," Coach Smith says gently but urgently, "just knock it in." As if it were beyond doubt. As if Coach had said, "And oh yeah, if you see my mail, just bring it in." Jimmy Black throws the ball in to MJ, back and forth, back and forth, the clock blinking down. Black passes to Matt Doherty, back to Black, sixteen seconds, Jimmy lashes the ball across court to Michael Jordan. Fifteen seconds left, sixteen feet out, 63,000 people watching over his shoulder, another few million in their homes. Is it possible to load any more pressure on the lanky limbs of an eighteen year old? But a composed and polite Jordan tells reporters after the game, "I knew I could

---

*Over the years, Jordan has been criticized for declining to support political candidates others have supposed should be important to him. Especially when Harvey Gantt, the mayor of Charlotte, ran against Senator Helms in 1990 and 1996 (Gantt is a Democrat and African-American). Jordan was quoted as saying, "Republicans buy athletic shoes, too." No doubt that explained some of his disinclination. But Helms, whom many liberals consider just about the last Confederate senator, is an astute politician who had sent fan letters to Jordan from the time MJ was a state basketball star. It was hard for Jordan to see such a discerning fan as an ogre. In any event, Jordan finally betrayed a political bent when he gave money to Bill Bradley's presidential campaign in 1999.

live with whatever happened because I had Coach's support"—praise that accented Dean Smith's gift to encourage his players to grow as men as well as athletes. The kid from the coast who, not so long ago, blinked back tears when he saw his name left off the varsity list at Laney High School, leaps, fires, and hits a cold-eyed, dead-on, championship *swish*: 63-61, *Carrrolllina!*

The boy next door, or, at least from just down the road, wins Dean Smith his first national championship. Two years later, after he has been College Player of the Year, pro teams pursue Michael like—well, no metaphor quite improves on *like the College Player of the Year.* MJ asks Coach Smith if he should stay at Carolina, which he loves, or put himself into the pro draft. Coach Smith gives him utterly fatherly, entirely unselfish advice—advice perhaps even more selfless than MJ's parents, who are set on their son not leaving without a college degree.* But if Michael stays, his coach cautions, he risks twisting a knee or jamming a toe before signing a contract that will make him rich; he risks losing a vocation—an art, really—he seems born to ennoble. "Michael," says Coach Smith, "I don't think there's much more you can do here. Give the world a shot." For the rest of his career, Michael Jordan will wear his Tar Heel shorts beneath his Bulls uniform. MJ will bear Chicago's name around the world. But next to his flesh and bones, Michael Jordan would keep Carolina close. And if God didn't love North Carolina, why did He make the sky Carolina blue?

Years later, some North Carolina friends would show me a bit of Wilmington. It welcomes the passing world over a stretch of Interstate 40 that has already been named for Michael Jordan. When he first came to Chicago in 1984,† reporters portrayed his hometown as something of a Mayberry. It is not. Wilmington is a port city, not a small town. It is a center of shipping, boat-building, manufacturing, and, more recently, movie-making. If they made a movie about Mayberry today, they might shoot it in Wilmington—but on a soundstage. Wilmington itself has grown too large.

---

*He eventually gained his degree after several years of summer school in the early years of his pro career. MJ loved Chapel Hill, after all, and actually welcomed the chance to return.

†Dumb fortune, really. Most teams were still trying to build around dominating centers. So Houston took the formidable Hakeem Olajuwon from the University of Houston while Portland chose Sam Bowie of Kentucky. Bulls general manager Rod Thorn actually half-apologized to fans for choosing Jordan saying, "We just wish he was seven feet tall."

There are beautiful, uncluttered beaches. But also gorgeously cluttered honky-tonk boardwalks, blinking with the neon silhouettes of bowling pins, fish, cocktail shakers, and sails, signs winking the particulars for Blue Martini Nights, Happy Hours, Ladies Nights, and Lottery Tickets. People in Wilmington, like those in Chicago, can get perturbed if admiring visitors seem enthralled with their town's outlaw lore and chronicles of roustabout corruption—they always want to tell you about the symphony and theater. It seems, at once, a leafy, beachy resort, a growing corporate and cultural center, and an old sailor's port of call. A salty place, in all senses, cheerfully vulgar, freewheeling, hard-working, wide open, and open all night. Which of course, sounds a good deal like Chicago, except smaller and with better weather (save for hurricanes). Even a brief tour lets you sniff some of the atmosphere that enlivened Michael Jordan's joy in hard work, his showmanship, his buccaneer's dash. You could see where a kid from Wilmington might grow up with a gambler's nerve.

The soldiers and I traded Jordan stories like playing cards: *What about this one? Did you see this? Remember that? I do believe the motherfucker can really fucking fly!*

"Didja ever see the game against the Celtics?"

Nineteen eighty-six, the Bulls made it to the first round of the playoffs. But their opponents were the legendary Boston Celtics of Larry Bird vintage. The Bulls lost, of course. But they once took the Celtics into overtime when Jordan sank two free throws at the buzzer. He scored 63 points on that day, but is remembered best for two: in the fourth quarter, he began to drive on Bird, the one player in the league he most envied and admired. Not for his physical gifts as a shooter and passer—MJ must have had few doubts even then that he had talents to match—but Bird's mental toughness, his basketball intellect, and his emotional durability in crucial moments over a long season.

"D'ya remember that?" asked a sergeant of about my age. "Jordan, the best slam-dunk artist of all-time, and he beat Bird with a shot Bird didn't know he had."

Indeed, Jordan had begun to move in the lane to drive on the basket. Bird blocked his path, and Michael pulled back. Then, MJ began to dribble the ball between his legs, daring Larry to grab in for a steal. But the Tough Old Bird declined, and thereby won again—nobody dunks on Bird. So with the shot clock ticking down, Jordan rustled his shoulder one way, twitched his hips another, danced back, leapt up, and shot as he fell back—two! two! two! Larry Bird couldn't block such a shot.

Magic Johnson wouldn't either. Paul Bunyan, possibly, but the list grows lean from there. Jordan, the young star, displayed tact as well as talent. He had scored on the game's reigning, fading, old star without beating him at his own game.

"Remember what Bird said after the game? He said, 'God came down to earth tonight disguised as Michael Jordan.' Hell of a compliment—"

"—and from a guy who doesn't give them."

"That's 'cause it wasn't a compliment," another soldier called from across the bunker. "It was a statement of fact." K. C. Jones, the Celtics' coach, had another. He said that during the fourth quarter, his players on the bench would look away from him, seeking to will themselves into invisibility. They didn't want their coach to see them and think, "Hey, maybe I'll send him in next. *Somebody's* got to stop Michael Jordan."

"But do you remember what Jordan said after the game?" I asked. Another soldier did. "Yep, he said, 'I would have traded all of those points just to win that game.'"

"What about that All-Star game in, oh, what was it, eighty-eight?"

I had watched it, in fact, because it was at Chicago Stadium. All-Star games are partly intended as exhibitions of flashy offense; playing genuinely tough defense runs a reckless risk of injury in a game that adds nothing to the standings. Still, it was captivating to watch Jordan's score climb that night, as he played in the intervals of All-Star games so that each player had at least a few minutes oncourt. Jordan had a dozen points at the close of the first quarter; 21 by the half; he was into the thirties by the third quarter and, a full two minutes short of the end, scored a basket to make it 40—which tied Wilt Chamberlain's record for scoring in an All-Star game. Isiah Thomas of the Detroit Pistons (also a local favorite—he had been a Chicago high school star) openly waved the ball toward Jordan from across the court, while his Eastern Conference teammates laughed into their sleeveless jerseys. "Take it, MJ! Take it!" Jordan shrugged him off with a smile. The crowd began to clamor, "Michael! Michael! Michael!" as Isiah seemed to offer up the ball like a crab puff at a cocktail party. But Michael still shrugged. Finally, MJ stepped up to be heard over the din and tumult. "What are you trying to do?" he called out to Thomas. "Tire me out for next Tuesday?" (when the Bulls would play the Pistons in Detroit). Michael Jordan would spring, leap, fade away, and fly. But he would not stoop to take an easy basket that would take a record from Wilt Chamberlain.

Jordan *flew*. That's what made him, at first, so fundamentally astounding. A player who seemed to come down from the sky, rather than jump up from the ground. It was a feat, like a home run or a knockout punch, that needed no translation to be understood. Other players could jump and dunk—a few, arguably, as well or better. But Jordan seemed to float; sometimes, almost to hover. There were a welter of serious scientific-sounding articles that sought to explain this sensation as a phenomenon of physics, genetics, athletics, or finally, aerodynamics. But I always believed his leaps and bounds had more to do with theater. When he reached the top of his arc, he held his pose, as great performers will. Olivier was once asked what made him an actor, and he seized a friend by his lapels to whisper fiercely, "Look at me look at me *look at me*." Jordan, too, managed to explode with poise. Soaring, sailing, scoring, he was the boy daring to fly at the sun. When sports reporters began to call Michael Jordan the most recognizable man in the world, other journalists cringed at the embellishment. What about the president—whoever he was at the time? What about Muhammad Ali? What about the pope? I remembered those street kids in Rio who were set off in a frenzy of running and leaping at just the sound of the word *Chicago*, jumping up from the teeming streets to throw themselves at the moon. "*Shee-cago! Shee-cago! Bools! Bools! Mie-cal Jordan!*" If I Could Be Like Mike. If he was not the most recognizable man in the world, he was probably the one who made the most guest appearances in dreams and reveries.

But as Jordan's image and reputation grew, so did a worry that works its way into the anxieties of most Chicago sports fans. Michael Jordan was acclaimed as the greatest player of his sport in his time. And so were, in their times, Ernie Banks, Gale Sayers, Dick Butkus, and Walter Payton. Is a pattern apparent here? Any joy in a second or third scoring title—an All-Star selection, a rushing record—begins to curdle when there is no championship in the bargain. Banks, Sayers, and Butkus never played in a championship game. Their reputations were huge, but their stages regional. Walter Payton played in a Super Bowl only years after his athletic prime. Imagine the historical event that might have been if Walter Payton had run his 275 yards on the international proscenium of the Super Bowl.

After a while, a chorus of admiring criticism is gently suggested by reporters and commentators. *So-and-so is a great player. Too good for the so-and-so team. But ya' know, the r-r-really great players, Joe Di, Joe Montana, Bill Russell, Magic Johnson, and Larry Bird, lifted up their teammates. Ted Williams won all those batting titles at Boston, but never a championship* for

*Boston. Maybe he worried more about swinging at a bad pitch than swinging to protect a runner. Maybe Michael Jordan worries more about leaps and dunks, making hi-light reels and McDonald's ads, than he does about winning championships. As the saint said, it is in giving that we receive.* Run through those psycho-sports clichés today, after watching Jordan lead his team to six championships, and such carping sounds ludicrous. Michael Jordan—and this is said *with respect*—would have considered selling his mother, not just a few scoring titles, to win a championship.

But in 1988, '89, and '90, the Bulls failed to get past the Bully Boys of basketball, the Detroit Pistons. Matched up player to player, the teams seemed equal. Add Jordan's transcendent will and skill, and the end would seem almost ordained. Except, of course, that's why they go ahead and play the games. Jordan, some smart people suggested, was both the glory that got the Bulls *that close,* and the ego that would keep them from a championship. Jordan even briefly injured his own image with an untypically unpremeditated remark. He called his teammates "my supporting cast"—which at once revealed his natural resort to theatrical terms, but infuriated more than a few of his teammates. They knew where their bread was buttered, but didn't care to have their noses rubbed in it. The conundrum over Jordan reminded me, absurdly, of what Indian politicians used to say about Jawaharlal Nehru: he was the giant banyan tree who grew so huge, surrounding trees withered from thirst in his shadow.

But Jordan was withering, too. He was used to winning at North Carolina. In fact, it was the revered Coach Smith who had convinced him, as no columnist ever could, that the supreme test of an athlete's skills was to inspire and elevate the play of his teammates—to work his will on others. I had a friend who worked on a photo shoot in the late '80s in which Jordan, the venerable Walter Payton, and Andre Dawson, the Cubs star of the time, posed in formal wear for the cover of a local magazine. She had two enduring memories. The first is that no one had to show Michael Jordan how to anchor his studs or lace his formal tie; he wore his tuxedo as comfortably as warm-up clothes. The second is that although Jordan was friendly and gregarious, he seemed a little wary of posing with a Cub—"as if," she said, "he could contract forty years of bad luck just by getting close."

When his contract came open for new negotiation, Jordan chose the security of a long-term agreement over sheer salary. He agreed to an eight-year contract knowing that if he continued on his course to become what a great many people were already calling him—the greatest player of all time—he would lock himself into a salary that would soon be surpassed by many lesser players. But Jordan had absorbed Dean Smith's anxiety about a sudden injury ending his career. (Of course, by the early 1990s, Jordan's second calling as a commercial star had already made him one of the highest paid performers in the world. He was scarcely working for salary alone.) Instead, he asked the team's new controlling owner, Jerry Reinsdorf, for an assurance: he would spend money to sign players to win a championship. MJ had put backsides in the buckets at Chicago Stadium and made the Bulls owners richer yet. Jordan had made himself rich, too; but that's not the only score he was keeping.

It was around this time—various accounts differ and contradict—that an assistant coach named Phil Jackson began to engage on different topics of conversation in the team training room with Jordan. One of Jordan's great talents has been his clarity. Not only what he can see, but what he can *see through*. Some players saw Jackson as a hound-dog-faced young former minor league coach with a cartoon mustache and a Grateful Dead grab bag of ideas. Jordan brought a different man into his focus. He saw a former reserve star who had been among the guts of great New York Knicks teams who had won championships in the 1970s with superior performance and guile. Jackson manifestly loved Zen, jazz, and rock and roll. But he didn't love *anything* more than basketball. Jackson's interests were wide and intriguing; but Jordan locked on to an *intensity* about the game that matched his own.

Jackson began to talk to Jordan about what he called the triple post, an offense that moves and roves by improvisation, rather than centers around a single strong player. The temptation to rotate an offensive in orbit around a single, blinding star—a Russell, Jabbar, or Jordan—was great, said Jackson. But wasn't Jordan frustrated by battling through too many games in which he scored mightily, only to lose closely? Score 63 points only to lose once, and you look heroic. Do it two and three times—and you begin to look hopeless. Teams knew that stopping the Bulls was as easy—or as hard—as stopping Michael Jordan. Put two and three defenders on MJ—it was about as obvious a defense as putting plywood over windows just before a hurricane.

A freewheeling, rolling offense, said Jackson, would free Michael, too, to make more shots. Jackson was a superb teacher. He appealed to Jordan's intelligence (Phil was the first person, serious with words, I ever heard characterize Jordan as a genius). When he chanced to make an analogy, it was not rock, Zen, or Native American spiritualism, but jazz.

A great jazz ensemble did not pretend that every horn player was as gifted or ingenious as Miles Davis. But every horn player who shared the stage with Miles Davis had to feel a sense of purpose in creating the sound that permitted Miles to soar—to make his leaps of genius. The beauty part of Jackson's presentation—and here, a Zen reference is inescapable—was that he revealed to Michael Jordan a way of becoming greater by enlisting the gifts of others. The scheme Jackson presented didn't shrink Jordan's role; it enlarged his sense of responsibility.

Jackson was too young to be perceived as fatherly by Jordan. But he seemed to carry himself with something of Dean Smith's composure, finding peace in the core of a storm. The Bulls head coach then, Doug Collins, was energetic, demonstrative, funny, fair, and young. When he roared and erupted along the sidelines, Jordan sometimes seemed to step away. Dean Smith had helped Michael learn how to bank his fires, to burn inside but stay cool to the touch. It was a cool touch he displayed from the time he was eighteen, wore baggy blue-striped Carolina shorts, and held the hopes of 63,000 people in his hands during a single leap in the Superdome.

Michael had won the second round of the 1989 playoffs over the Cleveland Cavaliers with a shot nearly as dramatic. Down 100 to 99 in the closing seconds, MJ had taken the ball into the foul circle and jumped up to loft a shot toward the basket. But Cleveland's Craig Ehlo was with him, inch by inch, his hand cocked to block. So in midair, Michael held back on the ball and drifted slightly to his left. Ehlo passed by, and started to come down, like a man in a silent movie who jumps out a window to land on the back of a horse who suddenly pulls away. Jordan began to fall, too—the law of gravity, finally, applies to Michael Jordan. It just seems to catch up with him last. On his way down, MJ released the ball. As the buzzer was blaring, it swished through. Game over. Bulls by one. They went on to defeat the New York Knicks in six games, but then ran again into the Detroit Pistons and lost in six. Four days after the team's defeat, the Bulls installed Phil Jackson as head coach. The team had the most scintillating player in the game; what they seemed to need now was a cool old hand who was in synch with Michael Jordan.

George Bush chose to end the Gulf War after one hundred hours. The coalition of countries that had joined to drive Saddam Hussein out of Kuwait was beginning to fall apart. Military intelligence people had told several reporters that Saddam's own military was enraged at their leader and emboldened to strike at his head. I assume they told President Bush as much, too. He could stop the war with the objective quickly gained and Allied casualties comparatively small, sustained by a certainty that just a month or two later, his adversary would be vanquished by Iraqis themselves, not an invading power. The people who criticize Mr. Bush for not *driving to Baghdad* did not have to hold thousands of lives in their hands as they made up their minds; their minds could be much lighter.

The night before the morning that the tanks were stopped, word had been passed among the paratroopers that the war would be ending before their services would be needed. A number of the young men had to bite back tears—at first, I thought, from sheer relief. But then they began to speak, sounding bitter. "*Fuckit.* We trained so hard. *Fuckit.* Wanted to kick their asses. *Fuckit.* Shit." A colleague and I, who had also covered a few wars, went from bunker to bunker, gathering quotes and bucking up their shoulders. "Relax, fellas. Try to be happy. Bless yourselves. Don't bitch. You're going to live. We're *all* going to live." The next morning, a master sergeant addressed the ranks, his voice fine and flinty as the Great Smoky Mountains. "Just because you didn't raise your rifle," he said, "and fire a shot doesn't mean you didn't make a contribution. You stood ready to lay down your life for your country. And I for one am proud to have served with you. For us, the worst is over. We are alive. We are healthy. We're going home. But there are hundreds of Allied soldiers who have died. And, let us not forget, thousands of Iraqis, who were soldiers, too, and who died for their country. Sometime today, I hope you make the time to say a prayer for their souls." I could see why good men would follow him.

I made a point of seeking out the sergeant to shake his hand and tell him it was the best speech I had ever heard in the field. He turned out to be a Vietnam veteran, an old paratrooper with knees that creaked in the rain, he said, like the floorboards of an old Buick. "Some of these boys," he said, shaking his head. "Good boys, now. Good boys. But some of 'em think war is a football game. They hear football games called wars, so I guess they think it goes both ways. Shit." He was from Beaufort, North Carolina, just up the road from Wilmington, due east of Chapel Hill. "Way I figure," he said, "we have thirty days to roll up here, another thirty before we're packed and out of the country. Playoffs should be beginning by then, right? Michael gets another shot at Detroit." I promised to call the sergeant's family when I got home.

"Is it hard," I asked, "after a war to care about something like basketball?"

"Oh, no," said the sergeant. "After a war, basketball is part of the life that's important to you." We agreed, as I recall—Bulls in six over Detroit.

In fact, it was just four. I was in Chicago, with friends at a tavern, when Dennis Rodman, then of Detroit, pushed Scottie Pippen in the back and sent him sprawling into the folding chairs just behind the basket, opening his chin. Rodman had a malevolent gift for choosing targets of opportunity. During the playoffs the year before, Pippen's father had died back in Arkansas. A couple of days after his funeral, Pip had to play in the decisive game in the series and came down with a migraine headache. All reporters who questioned his indisposition or his fortitude should, by now, be only ashamed of their doubts. But at the time, Scottie was an inviting pincushion for Rodman. Horace Grant rushed in to bring Scottie up off the floor by his shoulders. Horace was in a fury. He shouted—and not at Dennis Rodman, who had already danced away, but Pippen. "You play!" barked a towering, bug-eyed Grant as Scottie seemed to shake stars from behind his eyes. "You play! You play! You play!" He did. The Bulls prevailed, 115 to 94. Detroit's starters walked off the court during the game's last thirty seconds and did not stay around to shake hands and pass the torch. What was probably intended as the last possible insult became, in fact, the first sign of success. "In that moment," Jackson said later, "I knew we were going to become champions."

The finals that followed were what fans and advertisers had been hoping to see. Los Angeles versus Chicago, sun versus snow, Hollywood versus Second City, Jack Nicholson versus Bill Murray—Magic Johnson versus the magic of Michael Jordan. The Bulls lost the first game by two points. Michael had tried to sink a shot from eighteen feet out at the buzzer, but it banged the rim and bounced back toward Jack Nicholson, who may not have seen it through his sunglasses. Jordan told reporters after the game he had hurried the shot, and apologized for missing it (but not for trying it). To his teammates he said, "Maybe I was a little nervous. Okay? But we know now—we can play these guys."

The night of the next game, I was in Dallas, telling war stories to a group. One of my hosts slipped behind me during the question-and-answer period to whisper, "You know, your boys are playing now."

"Well," I told the assembled, "I don't want to take up any more of your time. If that just about wraps it up . . ." The host and some friends took me to a television set that was nearest a beer tap; in Dallas, never far away. The bartender sent over a beer when my friends introduced me as a Gulf War veteran. When they clarified my status as a veteran Gulf War *reporter*, the bartender said he wanted to call the beer back. "But he's a Bulls fan," my Texas friends shot back, "a *Bulls* fan."

"Well then" said the man behind the bar, "an order of nachos for Michael Jordan's friend." For most of my life, I reflected, being a Bulls fan had mostly brought on heartburn. We were watching when Michael leapt up for a slam dunk from the right side of the basket; there was a rise of breath in the room. But, MJ said later, he had quickly calculated that he had applied too much push, and might bang into the backboard. So Air Jordan made a midcourse correction. *Left shoulder, full rudder, down!* to begin to descend. But from the clutch of his upraised right hand, he let the ball drop down behind his back; and caught it in his left. Then, as Jordan passed below the basket he reached up with the ball and laid it gently up over the lip of the rim, popping it into the hoop like a balled-up napkin. *Oooh-aaah!* Gasps broke out at the bar. Old-style Texas whoops and hoots. The play was replayed, and replayed again; there was always some new feature to attend.

A woman at our table asked, "Is this like it was, watching Ali?" A man pointed out—a good point, too—that most of Ali's historic fights were never on television. Ali-Liston, Ali-Frazier I, II, and III, Ali-Forman, were all closed-circuit broadcasts. The number of people who actually saw Muhammad Ali float like a butterfly and sting like a bee was small compared to the millions watching Michael Jordan through every soar and swoop. "It's more like watching space shots used to be," said someone else; and when even I wondered if that wasn't bombast, he explained. "Space shots before they were routine. Space shots when everyone watched them because they expected to see," and with this we all followed the wave of his hand up toward the screen above the bar, "something amazing, right before our eyes." The Bulls won that night, and the next three games. Michael Jordan fell on the game ball in the visitors' locker room, hugging it close and keeping it in sight even as he showered before boarding the plane to fly back to Chicago as champions of the world.

Over the next three years, the success of the Bulls in winning three championships placed another symbol alongside cursive cola signs and humpbacked golden hamburger arches as an emblem of America: the snorting red countenance of the Chicago Bull. I saw bright red Bulls glowering from the brims of ball caps worn by bicycle riders in Beijing (where the team was known as the Red Oxen), and on T-shirts treasured by teenagers in Bosnia. Of course, the Bull was taken as a mascot for Michael Jordan. In São Paulo, street kids who got their heads shaved by obliging barbers in the slums, where they lacked the water to wash out snarls and lice, would rub a palm over their delicate bald heads and smile. "Bools! Mie-cal!" *Be Like Mike.* A sporting goods store on Ben-Yehuda Street in Jerusalem used to prop a life-sized cardboard Michael Jordan outside their door. Tourists would stop and pose for pictures, looking heavenward, at MJ's face. Just blocks away from the scarred stone streets that Jesus traversed in his last travails, and the golden spot from which Mohammad rose into paradise, people paused to have their portraits taken with a facsimile of a man who had only ascended above a basketball rim.

How entitled were Chicagoans to indulge a sense of identity with Michael Jordan? There's no reason to believe he would have amounted to any less of a performer had he been drafted by Houston or Portland; or traded to Boston, New York, or Los Angeles. But history may have worked to open Chicago for Michael Jordan in the same way the city had a place for Daniel Burnham, Jane Addams, Louis Armstrong, Frank Lloyd Wright, Saul Bellow, Gwendolyn Brooks, and Mies van der Rohe (and for that matter, Oprah Winfrey). There was opportunity for their ambitions. The Second City (a nickname awarded by a New Yorker, of course, A. J. Liebling; Chicagoans were simply self-confident enough to adopt it) always felt surrounded by too much sheer excellence to feel second-rate. It is a place of the first rank. But in sports, it rarely felt rewarded. Like New York or Los Angeles, Chicago was a large-scale city, not easily overwhelmed by a monumental star. Like Boston, Texas, and San Francisco, it had a sharp sense of local pride. But more than any of those places, Chicago meant the heart of America. Chicago was the place that had once been touched by fire; the place where they split the atom, winked at corruption, embraced newcomers, made music out of the blues, theater out of the ad-libs of real life, and built the city up to the sky. Michael Jordan *fit.*

Phil Jackson had told his players on the plane ride back home, "The hardest thing in the world to do these days is to repeat as champions. Everyone is out for you. Let's do something harder next year." With unprecedented opportunity, the Bulls learned about unanticipated problems. As the 1992 season began, they were invited to the White House to meet President Bush. Michael Jordan did not join them, telling teammates he did not want to deflect attention from them; which was true, but sounded smug. In a way, it confirmed that Jordan had a sane sense of proportion about himself. He had learned that his celebrity was some-times a gift he could best bestow on his friends by staying at home. (Also, an election was approaching. Jordan was reluctant to pose along-side any politician, including the president.) The Bulls issued a statement saying that MJ was tired; he wanted to spend the day with his family. Then, reporters spied him on a Carolina golf course. I wondered at the time—isn't the Soviet Union coming undone? Aren't there wars, famines, and fabulous corruption going on? What are reporters doing snooping after Michael Jordan on a golf course?

A month after the White House visit, investigators looking into the murder of a bail bondsman named Eddie Dow uncovered checks Michael Jordan had written to a convicted cocaine dealer named James "Slim" Bouler adding up to $165,000. Not, repeat *not*, to pay for cocaine or a rub-out, but to cover MJ's losses on the golf course that day. Inves-tigators emphasized that losing huge stakes in a golf game is no crime. Given Jordan's known wealth, it was not even much of a financial inconvenience. But for the first time, the press considered it fair game to report that in real life, Michael Jordan did not spend all of his spare time with the endearing youngsters who appeared in his Gatorade ads. For the first time, there was open speculation as to whether his high-stakes gambling was a hobby or a disease. His money was his own to spend. But even so devoted a fan as me found something troubling in what such losses suggested about Michael Jordan's values.

That season, though, there was another moment that confirmed how well Jordan wore the weight of his meaning to so many. As the sea-son began, Magic Johnson had announced he was retiring from basket-ball; a physical exam he had taken to satisfy an insurance policy had disclosed that he was HIV-positive. But Johnson was nevertheless selected, as he should have been, to the 1992 All-Star game squad. Some of the other NBA players groused that they were apprehensive over playing a contact sport on the same court as someone who carried the AIDS virus (to be gracious, there was a good deal less information and more myth about AIDS infection in those days). Magic's Western Con-ference team was ahead by more than 30 points as the final seconds clicked down. Johnson took the ball at the top of the key, and Jordan came up to guard him. As he did, the players from both squads began, softly, to drift away, leaving just Magic and Michael smiling at the scene on the court, beaming like the two best kids in the schoolyard, one-on-one, me and you, try me, try me. Johnson drove. Michael moved to block him. Magic faked to his left, dribbled over to his right, and twirled past

Michael to hang a last slam dunk into the basket. Jordan laughed, shook his head, and smiled—and for once, didn't try to get the basket back. The game horn sounded and Michael and Magic fell naturally into each other's arms. Maybe some other All-Stars were reluctant to get sweated on by a man with the virus for AIDS. Michael Jordan would embrace him. "It was the best way," he said, "for all of us to tell Magic thank you and good-bye."

The Bulls, meanwhile, had strengthened their hold on championship play. By the time they approached the 1992 finals, I was in Brazil, covering the Earth Summit conference, and was distressed to discover that I would host a public television special that would be aired at the same time as the first game.

"Hey, you and MJ, one-on-one," said the producer in New York. But I wouldn't be mollified.

"Bill," I told him, "I often host specials with audiences so small, only my mother is watching. But do you think even my mother will watch this one?"

"She can tape the game."

"She can tape the damn special," I told him. "The damn rain forest will be fine for two hours. I doubt that any species of snail-darter you can name will become extinct in two hours. But do you know what can happen over two hours in a championship basketball game?" My emphatic expression of priorities caused the producers to suspect the depth of my interest in environmental issues. Later, the game was rebroadcast in Brazil. You didn't need to speak Portuguese to follow Michael Jordan downing the Portland Trailblazers from the first moments, sinking six successive 3-point shots and shrugging as he passed Magic Johnson, on the floor broadcasting the game with NBC; shrugging as if to say, I dunno, sometimes it just seems like a hand from on high guides it in.

The Bulls were ahead 3 games to 2 when they returned to Chicago. They were stale and listless over three quarters in the sixth game, and sank 17 points behind in the fourth quarter when Jackson decided to bench his starters, save for Scottie Pippen. Perhaps fresh subs from the bench, playing to leave an impression, not protect a championship, might kindle a spark. Save for Scottie Pippen, of course, meant *including Michael Jordan*. MJ did not grumble. Instead, he rose gamely to his brief demotion, standing along the sidelines and grinding a towel in the air to cheer on Pippen, B. J. Armstrong, Stacey King, and a sudden star named Bobby Hansen. The bench closed the gap. Jordan came back in, rested, reinvigorated, and much obliged. As Jackson had insisted, the jazz and Zen of a roving, restless, ad-lib offense would set Jordan loose, too. The Bulls won, 97-93, their first championship at home. MJ lifted up their second gleaming gold trophy onto his shoulders and walked it out of the locker room back onto the court. The players breathed in the cheers and clambered up onto the scorer's table, fans and players waving, clapping, cheering, blowing kisses, rocking, swaying, and staying long into the night in the old Chicago Stadium. I would tell you that they had the time, the time of their lives, I saw a few men who danced with their wives—but that would be a preposterous cliché.

As the Bulls solidified their success, and Jordan his accomplishments and fame, the price of it all could seem onerous. Jordan began to be called a prisoner of his own fame (although, no reporter who knew how actual prisoners lived could accept that characterization). Prisoners don't tee off at Pebble Beach, romp around in Hilton Head, and enjoy vintage wines. Jordan's wealth could buy him fabulous comforts, amusements, lifelong security, and, sometimes, even seclusion. But his fame began to encumber him.

Once, it had just pinched occasionally, and intrigued him; as when he found that he couldn't buy toys for his children at Marshall Field's without stopping traffic on State Street. But as the Bulls accumulated championships, Michael's celebrity began to weigh on him in modest, unimagined, maddening ways. His teammates, who were pretty recognizable themselves (because of their height, even little-known basketball players are conspicuous), exchanged notes, wonderingly, on the life Jordan had to lead on the road. He couldn't be seen to be casual or unshaven coming into practice, because cameras were always near. He couldn't walk the fifty or a hundred feet between his vehicle and the locker room without security guards, because fame draws crackpots like moths to a flame, and nobody was more famous than Jordan. He couldn't go to movies, pick up a pack of plastic razors, stroll through streets, join teammates at dinner. He couldn't buy a souvenir for his kids without having someone in his office in Chicago get in touch with someone at FAO Schwarz's corporate offices in Manhattan, to see about keeping the store open late or opening it early or—hell, security, overtime, that's just too complicated. *Can you please just send something over?* He stayed in opulent hotel suites with sumptuous views—and then often couldn't part the curtains to enjoy them. Throngs would be below, looking up for a bald, brown head. "Michael! Michael! Spit on me!" He could rarely join teammates at great little Italian spots in North Beach, small east-side bistros, barbecue joints on Wilson Boulevard, or pizza-slice stands along the Santa Monica beach, because a glimpse of him would set off an armada of lights, cameras, and action, like the TV crews lying in wait for Marines to land in Somalia. It was hard enough for Garbo, Jackie O, and JFK Jr. to don sunglasses, scarves, or baseball caps to try to stroll privately about great cities. What does a 6 foot, 6 inch tall bald black man who is known around the world by his very silhouette do for a disguise? (In fact, Jordan suggested to writer Bob Greene that his minimalist hair style came about because it was impossible for MJ to get his hair cut in a public place—so he bought some clippers and sheared himself every nine or ten days.) In some of the great culinary capitals, he could only order room service. Waiters, bellhops, concierges, room cleaners, and maintenance people became conspirators to keep his privacy. They were flattered, friendly, and honorable—but always wanted autographs, T-shirts, souvenir caps. To make their collusion profitable, Jordan tipped profusely; $50 bills, $100 bills, nothing less, to receive a newspaper, extra towels, a room service pizza. "Thank you very much, my friend, a pleasure to sign the menu for your daughter. Please, take this. And I hope you'll help me get a little rest tonight." The world knew how much Michael Jordan scored, and how much he earned. He could not appear cheap in any aspect. "Hey, MJ," his teammates used to say, "I'll bring you some goddamn towels for just $20!" There were the reporters trying to track down his gambling debts, as if they were former wives owed alimony. And then, there were always sick children. Children in wheelchairs with shriveled arms and legs, children with Be Like Mike bald heads shorn by chemotherapy. The Bulls and Jordan's own foundation, very quietly, arranged for a sick child, often terminally ill, to meet Michael at most home games, sit behind the bench, and receive the shoes he wore at that game, smudged by greatness and signed. *Hang in there, buddy. Your friend, Michael Jordan.* He told teammates and other friends how much he grew to admire the children and their courage; how much it meant for him to see a light in their eyes. A man who could fly could feel in awe—and awe was the word his friends passed on—of the valor and nerve of children who had to persevere just to breathe. Sometimes, he called the kids and their families when he heard they were back in the hospital. "I'm rooting for you, pal. We'll have a big game for you tonight." Again, quietly, he helped out with some of their bills. But often, he got a grateful but sorrowful letter from a parent. "We just want to tell you, Michael, how much your kindness meant to our young child. Unfortunately . . ." How he hated losing. There were the thousands of desperate pleas, appeals, and solicitations he couldn't possibly begin to pursue. Prisoners who wrote, "I know they'll listen to you, Michael." Parents who implored, "I know he'll listen to you, Michael." Struggling community groups, clinics, and worthy causes all, who beseeched, "We know you must be overwhelmed with appeals, Mr. Jordan, but . . ." Overworked, overwhelmed people certain that surely the most magnificent person in the world would hear them out and help. To carry all of those hopes that people sent out from their hearts—not just to score gloriously, but live superbly, and never, never disappoint? *Be Like Mike?* Who could?

It was perhaps impossible for anyone else on earth to commiserate with Michael Jordan on the level at which he lived—not since Elvis. But pity was not called for. Besides, some of his teammates like to joke, Jordan's generosity was often only a recycling of their losses.

They liked to tell about the times when the team still traveled by commercial airliner. Phil Jackson gave "trip books" to his players—novels and nonfiction thoughtfully selected for their interests. Michael Jordan cherished the graciousness of the gesture, but rarely read more than a few pages. MJ would spend much of the flight in stakes poker games with friends on the team. Once, when the plane landed, men in coveralls from the flight service crew came onboard to meet Michael Jordan. MJ shook hands affably, plucked up some of his winnings, and pressed bills all around with his peerless Wheaties smile. "Thank you for your help, very kindly, thank you all." His teammates thought, *Awfully damn nice of Mike, he didn't have to do that. Part of the terrible burden of being MJ.* When the team arrived at baggage claim, Jordan slapped another bill down and said, "Okay, a pool on whose bag comes down first." Soon, a small pile of portraits of Ulysses S. Grant and Benjamin Franklin rose on the terminal floor. *MJ was the man! MJ wanted a pool! Get in! Get in!* Then, the rubber-strip curtain of the claim area parted. Jordan's bag came through. For almost fifteen seconds, it circled in solitary splendor. MJ picked up the pile of Grants and Franklins, laughing, and his teammates, faked out of their Air Jordans, had to laugh along. Sometimes, generosity is a sound investment in the future, isn't it?

• • •

$P$hil Jackson had said that winning any championship was arduous, and repeating was even more forbidding. How to rank the chance of three in a row? Good teams with bulging bankrolls, high draft picks, and frustrated ambitions spend mightily and precisely *just to beat you*. Bad teams with no prospects count the season a success just if they beat you *in a single game*. Success bred distractions as well as opportunities, resentment as well as recognition. While other teams changed and rearranged, champions got fatter with rewards and became bigger targets. A team with Michael Jordan had an offensive strategy that was as well-known as the Russian army's. Under Jackson, the Bulls had become a finesse team. They relied on execution, athleticism, and mental toughness (or, in Jordan's case, mercilessness). This convinced certain coaches—actually, I'm thinking almost exclusively of Pat Riley, then of the New York Knicks—to believe the Bulls could be put down the way they had been beaten back for so many years by Detroit: by a punch in the gut, a backhanded smack across the mouth, a few elbows in the ribs. The Bully Boys of Gotham.

By the time of the 1993 Eastern Conference playoffs, the Bulls and Knicks had become the most persistent and entertaining rivalry in professional sports. They had great ingredients. Two of America's ranking regional giants. Great arenas that had both nominated presidents. Michael Jordan had been born in Brooklyn and seemed to bloom in Madison Square Garden, from the time he had scored 42 points there as a rookie. Pat Riley wore slick Italian suits and had the game face of a shrewd, starved lizard and a defensive plan that might have been passed along from John Gotti. Phil Jackson had once been a Knick with sharp elbows, but was now taken to be at the right hand of the Dalai Lama. A face-off between finesse and thuggery, Manhattan and Midwest, class and brass-knuckles.

It occurs to me as I write this—I might even have been a small part of the media heat that put wind into such overblown metaphors. I was living in New York to co-host NBC's *Weekend Today* when the Bulls-Knicks series began. My loyalties were not obscure. In fact, I abused the authority of an anchor's seat by wearing Chicago Bulls sunglasses as I read the lead into our sports segment. "Last night, the world champion Chicago Bulls were mugged by a band of ruffians who claimed to be a professional basketball team called the New York Knicks . . ."

New York won the first two games, shutting down Michael Jordan with elbows, shoulders, and double-teams. He hit just 10 of 27 shots in the first game, only 12 of 32 in the second. In interviews after the game, MJ made a point of absorbing the blame. He was trying to deflect it from enormously sensitive Horace Grant, who scored just 2 points. Jordan told reporters, "It was my fault. I wasn't into a good rhythm and wasn't shooting very well." But the *New York Daily News* didn't know the difference between graciousness and garlic bagels. They pasted a stark picture of a dejected Jordan across their front page and adorned it with one word in bold, block type:

## GOAT

Every time I hear a New Yorker exclaim, "What a shame MJ didn't play for a New York team"—as if there, Michael Jordan might have become *rrreallly* famous—I think about the New York press. Time spent on a New York team, said Pat Riley, of all people, was time best measured in dog years—one counted for seven. If Michael Jordan had played in New York, tabloid paparazzi might have driven him to join the French Foreign Legion, where at least he could have shot back. After the first defeat in New York, MJ was dispirited, tired, bruised. What does a man from Wilmington, North Carolina, do when he's glum and marooned in a New York hotel room and can't so much as cross the street for a pretzel? Michael Jordan and his father, James Jordan, went to Atlantic City. At Bally's Casino, father and son played slots, shot craps, had a snack. They left, said the Jordans—if it was anybody else's business—at about 11:00 P.M. Some other gamblers insisted to the tabs that it was closer to 2:00 in the morning, although, as James Jordan later said persuasively, "Anyone who's there at that time has to be drunk and sees the Easter Bunny."

At first, Jordan tried to tamp down the press furor with his practiced charm. But reporters' questions soon got ugly. *How much of your poor performance was because you were out late gambling? How much did you drop at Bally's? Did you let down your teammates? Gambling late the night before a big game—do you think, Michael, you have a gambling problem?* When reporters began to ask about Slim Bouler, Jordan walked out, insulted. Phil Jackson stepped in to take the charge and told reporters he was not going to try to put a curfew on a mature, professional millionaire. *Are you seriously saying that Michael Jordan doesn't come prepared to do his job?* The Bulls flew back and, in Sweet Home Chicago, won the third game 103 to 83. But the Bally's furor boiled still. Jordan would not speak to the press; neither would his teammates. So James Jordan—Pops, as he was known around the team and pressroom—strolled outside the Bulls' training center, lit up a cigarette, and asked the assembled:*

> *Did you ever stop to think that Michael was just the same guy, and everyone else around him had gone crazy? . . . I mean, I talked him into going to Atlantic City. Just to eat a hamburger. Just to get away. We didn't go down there to win a lot of money. Hell, I lost $50, and found a way to turn around and eat it all back. Had a $42 meal, and with free drinks I broke even. The limo ride was free. If we'd went to an R-rated movie, everyone would say, "Michael's father carried him into a dirty movie." We should have taken the whole team with us. Maybe they would have played better the next night, too.*
>
> *Some demand him to be perfect. Every time he stubs his toe, someone is there to jump on him. He wants to live his own life, and he can't.*

The next night, Michael Jordan scored 54 points and the Bulls prevailed, 105 to 95, tying the series at two games apiece. Even the New York tabs began to joke, maybe the Knicks should organize a field trip to Atlantic City.

When the Bulls came back to New York, I was determined to see them up close. The closeness of the contest—the historic contention between two cities I loved—intensified and vivified for me the degree to which Michael Jordan's Bulls had become a devotion in my life. I was a reporter who had been around the world. I had lived in and loved other places. But across my heart, and clear down to my own shorts, I was an American, Chicago born, a Bulls lover, a Chicagoan Abroad.

During my year at NBC, various executives at NBC had always said, "If you ever want tickets to a Knicks game. Like, say, when the Bulls come to town . . ." With unapologetic self-interest, I finally called a few. Each of them said, "Oh, sorry, pal, any other time. But not this one." The night of that fifth game, I left Rockefeller Center and decided to stroll home by way of Madison Square Garden. As I lived on the east side, this was something like taking the Staten Island ferry to reach Brooklyn. *But*

---

*The most complete account of Pops Jordan's remarks appears in Mitchell Krugel's *Jordan: The Man, His Words, His Life*.

*I was drawn.* It was as if one great silver light had seized me by the shoulders and steered me to the Garden. I arrived about half an hour before game time. Ranks of people were turning away from the box office, muttering, "Nothing. Aww, shit, aww *nothing.*" But among the multitudes, you could pick out an occasional hard-eyed man in a slick leather jacket calling softly, "Tickets. Box seats. Tickets." Ticket-scalping, of course, is illegal. The police patrols outside weren't on the prowl just for pickpockets. I felt my face begin to flush. Is this what it feels like to buy cocaine? I had a brief photoflash in my mind (but notice, please, no moral qualms) of a seedy-looking Midwestern man being led away in handcuffs. "Listen, buddy, buying scalped tickets is illegal in New York. If you want to go to a basketball game, you plan ahead and pay the legal price, like everybody else." I envisioned a night-court judge with an Ed Koch intonation. "Oh, and you're a reporter? A journalist who doesn't know the law?"

But as I sweated through such specters, a man approached, a man from New Jersey in, as I recall, pharmaceutical sales. "The guy on *Today*, right? Bulls fan, right?" Uh, yes. "Hey, I bet you got good seats." I got bupkes, I told him. I'm just trying to figure out if I want to deal with one of these . . . gentlemen. Well, the man said, he and three friends had tickets. But one of their group was stuck at a late meeting; he wasn't sure he could make it at all. "We were just gonna wait another ten minutes and try to scalp the ticket ourselves." Really? "Well," I asked, "if your friend doesn't come—would you—ah, could you—ah, consider—ah—" He interrupted my fumbling. "Hey, you buy the beer. It's Take a Bulls Fan to a Game Night, didn't you hear?" We sat in seats rising up above some steel rafters and couldn't quite see the final-seconds flurry in which Knicks forward Charles Smith grabbed a rebound and tried to pop it over Scottie Pippen once, twice, three times. But then, we saw the ball fall to the floor past Scottie's knees; he plucked it up, dribbled down, and leapt as the last horn blared; 97-94, Bulls. On the way out, I thought my new Knicks-fan friends had absorbed their team's defeat with admirable equanimity. "Ah, well, that's Jordan," said one of them. "Always got to root a little for the Bulls with Jordan. You always feel that when he touches the ball, you might see something magic, right?"★

The next night, I went in to sit at the bar of an Italian seafood

---

★When the man from New Jersey told his friend later who had taken his seat, he said, "Why didn't you take Katie Couric?"

place around the corner from my apartment. The manager, Joe Terrio, said, "Oh fuckin' boy, Mr. Bulls Shit, do I have a treat for you tonight." He pointed out a tall man with a philosophy prof's beard, sitting with friends in the dining area. It was Bill Cartwright, the Bulls center, and a former Knick. The serving table beside him was festooned with drinks, melting down. "It began," said Joe, "when one guy sent over the first drink. Bill raised it up, like to say thank you, then set it down. I don't think he's drinking. Then, someone else sent over another. Then, another. Then, another. I guess," laughed Joe, "they want to get him drunk. But Bill won't give 'em the satisfaction." Cartwright was sturdy and steady when the Bulls won the next night, 96 to 88, closing down the New York Knicks and their Noo Yawk sharp elbows in six games.

For the finals, they faced the Phoenix Suns. But first, another furor. A San Diego "sportsman" name Richard Esquinas published a book on the eve of the championship series charging that Michael Jordan had lost more than a million dollars to him on the golf course and that MJ had been slow to pay. Esquinas said he regretted making the charge public—he considered himself a friend—but a million dollars was, hell, a million dollars. How else to get Jordan to pay?[†]

I thought—still do—that Michael Jordan's gambling is his own business. And yet, a boyhood friend who had become a financial counselor for athletes (no Bulls) said he was intrigued by reports that Jordan was slow to pay. It had to be at least occasionally embarrassing to confide to your financial counselors, your agent, your wife, that that million dollars in a monthly statement was to pay off a gambling debt. And remember this, said my friend: "Huge gambling debts are rarely owed to Mother Teresa." Jordan didn't bet on basketball—that is against NBA rules. But chances are, he had owed money to other gamblers who did. The worst scandals in basketball history weren't over throwing games, but shaving points. The commissioner of basketball investigated Jordan's gambling and found no violation of the rules. But could a Slim Bouler or Richard Esquinas say to Jordan, "Hey, MJ, win by six points, not eight, and we can do each other some good." And yet the idea that Michael Jordan could be tempted to compromise the sheer, Shakespearean mastery of his performance to save even a million dollars was preposterous—literally, inconceivable. You didn't have to believe that Jordan's integrity was impeccable to trust that his *intensity* was pure.

[†]Esquinas later indicated that he had settled for a lesser amount from Jordan.

The score was tied at 94 in the sixth game of the championship series at Phoenix with 14.1 seconds left when Horace Grant took a pass from Scottie Pippen along the baseline and cleared it out to John Paxson, standing just beyond the three-point line on the left. "It's the shot," said Paxson, "that I made about a thousand times as a kid in the driveway. You know, you start counting to yourself, 'Three, two, one ... ' " It hit. The Three-peat was won. Chicagoans Abroad on a foreign court, the Bulls took their trophy down into the visitors' locker room where Michael Jordan, slicked by champagne, beer, and tears, told reporters, "This was the hardest one. The least fun, sometimes. But the most satisfying."

About a month later, Pops Jordan drove the red Lexus his son had given him to the funeral of a friend about twenty miles north of Wilmington. He then set out for Charlotte, to catch a plane back to Chicago. It had been a long day, and he pulled over on Route 74 to take a nap—an old habit, perhaps, instilled in the time when blacks could not check into most motels in North Carolina. A few weeks later, state police found James Jordan's body in a creek near McColl, South Carolina, just over the border. The two young men who would later be convicted of killing him apparently didn't know that the man they murdered for his car, cellular phone, credit cards, and pocket money was the father of a rich and famous man who would have paid dearly for his life. In news accounts around the world, there was solemn and respectful reflection on the fact that even the greatest favor and fortune—and Michael Jordan had worked hard to win both—couldn't lock loss and tragedy out of anyone's life. There was also immediate, unsubstantiated but unsurprising speculation that the most obvious direction to take in beginning to investigate James Jordan's killing was within the underworld of touts, hustlers, and betting men to which, God forbid, Michael Jordan or his father might have owed some money.

I left NBC in the summer of 1993 and went off to Bosnia for National Public Radio to cover what I believed to be the most important story in the world. Covering the war in Bosnia would fundamentally change some of my principles. For the first time I saw, in flesh and blood, the most twisted result that pacifism can produce: all the worst people can kill all the best ones. The most vicious can kill the most gentle. Violence is a blunt club, a corrupt and unprincipled instrument. But when an alligator is chewing someone's leg, a blunt club may be more pertinent than principles. I still believed that pacifism had the power to pierce hearts, rock empires, and move mountains. But I didn't see how, by the summer of 1993, pacifism could turn back the methodical and pathological Serb massacre of Sarajevo. Reporting can capsize your convictions. So today, after seeing the strangulation of Bosnia and the rape of Kosovo, I am a highly hypocritical pacifist. I recognize the deficiencies of pacifism, but still believe in its capacities, too. Quakers have a phrase: "At least that's where I want to put my weight." In the meantime, I prefer being inconsistent about war and peace to being wrong.

I told Smokey Baer before I went off to Bosnia that I expected to be back by the opening of basketball training camps. I entrusted him, fan to fan, Chicagoans Abroad in the bond, with the continued prosperity of our cherished franchise.

"Four on the Floor next year!" said Smokey. "Four on the Floor! I got Kukoc in the fold already, didn't I?" Toni Kukoc, the Croatian Sensation, from the port city of Split, had signed with the Bulls but declined to leave while his family was still beleaguered by the war I was going off to cover. But by 1993, the war had moved out of Split; leaving Sarajevo besieged, but an opportunity for the Kukoc family to breathe, and for the most celebrated basketball star in Europe to play alongside Michael Jordan. Sports had become a currency in the world—and, among the least of the lessons I was to learn in Sarajevo was that the Chicago Bulls had become the most valued.

I was reunited on our first reporting trip into Sarajevo with engineer Manoli Wetherell. We first had to acquire credentials in Zagreb, Croatia. For all I know, Croatian border guards are funny, effervescent, and warm when not on the job. But during the war in the Balkans, they were famously, unremittingly, sour and grim, merciless and mirthless. They didn't like reporters, they didn't like Americans, they didn't like people bound for Bosnia who clogged their checkpoints with bales of inexplicable equipment. As Manoli and I were being sniffed over and patted down, she nudged me. One of the guards had unzipped our personal luggage and seemed to be helping himself to the contents, as if they were his own order of sweaters and socks from the Land's End catalog. "If I didn't know better," said Manoli, "I'd say he's stealing them." A day later, when we could unlatch the luggage ourselves, we realized that he had. Another border guard read my passport and other documents over and over, as if looking for anagrams. Finally, he pushed the pile back.

"Hmmm. Chicago," he said harshly. "Michael Jordan."

I took up the papers carefully. "Croatia," I said. "Toni Kukoc?" A little cajolery and overlooked larceny could apparently induce even a Croatian border guard to smile.

The safest place in Sarajevo when we arrived was also one of the grimmest. There was a cave carved into a slab of rock overlooking the Miljacka River downtown that some aspiring showman had once turned into a nightclub. But when the Serb bombardment began, *nightlife* took on a different connotation. The cave cafe was abandoned, and then discovered by roving, outcast refugees searching for shelter from artillery fire. Thirty-two families, more or less, were sleeping in the deep, dark, cold of the cave. Parents, children, and estranged souls who had been run out of their homes in an instant, like Pompeiians caught in the volcanic ash, frozen in the last clothes they had worn. They were laid shoulder to shoulder on the pool table, curled up beneath the pinball machine, and cramped into the wire mesh bins that once stored the club's beer. The stout rock that made the cave safe from bombs and sniper fire, though, also kept the cave achingly cold; and, even in the middle of the day, pitilessly dark.

A middle-aged Muslim man living there named Kaseem Livniak showed us around with a candle, carefully, moving with the step of an old man so as not to douse the candle flame. He had been an ad man before the war; a creative type, in an Italian olive-tweed sportcoat he had put on of a Friday morning more than a year before with the intention of leaving the office just after lunch to join his wife for a ski mountain weekend. But during lunch, Serb tanks had rolled into his apartment building; Mr. Livniak had been in that jacket ever since. He had lost sixty pounds over the year, and his Italian tailoring hung loosely off his shoulders. He looked like a small boy trying on his father's coat. Mr. Livniak insisted on taking us over to the spot where the light broke in on the cave's opening so he could fish his wallet out from a side pocket. "Please," he said, "you must see how my wife and I looked before the war." The wallet photo showed a handsome couple in a garden, sandy haired and fleshy with happiness. The man before us was gray as a shattered sidewalk and gaunt with want and fear. The photo he held out now looked like a portrait of two distant, younger relatives. Mr. Livniak's wallet had become an archive, holding money from a former world that could now buy nothing, pictures from a former life that had perished. We were moving on to another location when Manoli motioned that a lick of sunlight coming into the cave had caught the flapping edge of a poster that was still stapled onto a plank of the wooden bar. Number 23, in a red and white jersey, vaulting across an ethereal arch of stadium lights with a basketball in his right hand, as if he was moving the moon to a different place in the sky. "Look," said Manoli, "isn't that your friend?" And Kaseem Livniak smiled. He had told us that he was sure comfortable Americans could not understand people living in caves. "Like we are some kind of Neanderthals, you know? But I noticed you see the poster. Ah, yes. We're really a very sophisticated people. We know about Michael Jordan."

On a Sunday morning in the summer of 1993, we heard that electricity was to be restored for a few hours for the first time since the war began and rushed over to the Kosovo Hospital where a doctor had decided to stake those hours on an exacting operation to close the holes in the left side of a Bosnian soldier who had been blown up by a hand grenade. The soldier was smiling as his red wound was swabbed with yellowish antiseptic; and then, he shivered as it dried and began to sting. When the lights came on, the surgeon revved up a skin shearing device to take slivers of skin from the soldier's left thigh that they would try to suture over his ribs. The surgical team also plugged in a radio; incredibly, the song that came on was Sade's "Smooth Operator." But after so many months of disuse, the skin searing machine would not work. With their patient swabbed down and ready, the surgeons picked up some kind of hand instrument that looked like something stored in a kitchen drawer. It grated the soldier's skin off in small, irregular strips. Because there was no running water to sluice blood from the wound as they worked, the nurses instead sprinkled bottled drinking water onto crumpled tissues and squeezed water in dribbles onto the wound. Then, after only half an hour or so, the high hum of electricity shut down. The light died, the music stopped, and the doctors sighed. "There is only so much that improvisation can do," said the surgeon. "We must wrap our boy up and hope for a better day. We have been hoping for so long." Reporting opens instantaneous intimacy, then impersonally moves on. We never learned what happened to that soldier.

I had never before covered a war in a place that I thought I could recognize so well. The siege was a pitiless assault on city folks of mixed ethnic backgrounds, apartment dwellers, cigarette smokers and coffee sippers, sports fans, political skeptics, joke tellers, jazz lovers, pet owners, and night people. By the time we arrived, not a single window was without a gash; not a single building didn't lead down into rubble. The city skyline looked like a smashed smile in a broken jaw. Serb snipers sat in open windows in apartment buildings across the Drina River, so close that some Sarajevans said they could even see them squinting through rifle sights. At night, when the city was dark, the snipers seemed to fire at candlelights flickering in windows, at shadows, sounds, and stray dogs roaming the streets for food. Trash had been left to rot because garbagemen would be shot by gunmen for removing it; and in a city of so little, there was little to throw out anyway—so it was safer just to keep the trash. Most of the trees on streets and in city parks had been chopped down to be burned for heat. In one park, the grounds were being replanted—with grave markers. One day, Manoli noticed that several Sarajevans were out walking dogs on grounds known to break out with sniper firing and shelling. People straining on the end of a leash, waiting for a small dog to defecate, seemed an impossibly, wonderfully delicate concern in a dangerous place. We decided to do a story.

We were interviewing a woman in a fleecy white sweater on its way to turning gray who was walking a dog with a fluffy white coat also smudged by soot, grime, and the dearth of water for washing. The dog was named Arina. But we were unable to get the woman's name as clearly. As we asked, shots rang out and she turned to say, with exemplary consideration, "Excuse me, I must run." So did we. Shots trilled sickeningly around our ears and whistled in the weeds in front of us. Manoli, myself, and our translator, Miro Tedic, ran over an open stretch of ground toward the thin ledge of a shattered school building, the three of us bent so low we could have been contestants in a crab race at a summer picnic. People around us ran and fell to the ground, people in open apartment windows above us pointed at us and others scrambled, while shots clipped the ground around our ankles and toes. You run because you don't want to stay still for another shot; and you run wondering if the running only makes you a more enticing target in the scope of a sniper who is no longer fulfilled by shooting old ladies struggling across the street with heavy water cans and sagging bags of rice. A sniper makes you feel common cause with a bug caught crawling over a drain. Someone is about to die. What can you do? You can't do a thing. You send up prayers, promise in a burning wink never to lie to a loved one, fib on your taxes, or snap at a telephone operator. And while you wait, with your nose pressed into the scarred street, or your cheek jammed against a jagged brick wall, you find yourself getting as impatient as scared, convinced you need to move, confused about where, crazily indignant that a vicious kid with a rifle too big for his pants is making you cower like a lost dog in the street. It was scarcely the first time that Manoli and I had ever been shot at on assignment. But Manoli, her head tucked into her chin, muttered something with particular exasperation. "I do not want to get shot," she said, "doing a goddamn pet story."

Still, the story was almost worth it. We met a middle-aged couple named Nadya and Thomaslav, who had a dog and cat they had taken in from the streets in the first days of the war. Thomaslav was a sports writer for a closed Sarajevo daily, Nadya a nurse. He was a Serbian Orthodox, she a Muslim. The dog and cat, they said, were mixed breeds, too. Aki, the dog—who looked a bit like a German shepherd zipped into a greyhound's blue-gray skin—had been found sick, deserted, and cringing with flies in a garbage dumpster. Chula, the cat, a white and beige floor mop, came calling at their door after a bombing. Aki could hear the whine of grenades before humans and would bark when they pricked up his ears. "Thank you, Aki," said Thomaslav. "Now let's all get away from the windows." Chula seemed to sense the onset of artillery rounds and would fold himself into a furry ball on Thomaslav's lap. "Uh-oh, Chula is snuggling, here come the bombs." Aki licked our microphone as if it was made of liver. Chula was more discriminating: he preferred cookies from the emergency army rations stockpiled by United Nations soldiers—*French army cookies*, in fact, which Nadya and Thomaslav had to buy on the black market with cigarettes and toothpaste. "We need something to live around us," they said. "The animals don't know about war. Once, we didn't either. They remind us of peace. They take us out of the war for a few minutes. We get humanitarian aid, don't we?" asked Thomaslav. He took the term earnestly. "Human beings don't let animals die if they can help it. Someday, this war will be over, and when it is, we still want to be human beings."

Thomaslav had written mostly about basketball and soccer. As Chula and Aki settled down to be combed out, he heated a small pan of drinking water over a canned flame and pinched instant coffee into small cups for us. "A Bulls fan, yes? That's what my daughter tells me." Their daughter, a doctor at Kosovo Hospital, had volunteered her parents—and their pets—for our story. "So, how do you think Michael Jordan will like Toni Kukoc?" I asked about Kukoc, whom I had only seen play on the fabulous old Yugoslav national basketball team and against Jordan, Scottie Pippen, and other American Dream Teamers in the Barcelona Olympic games. Kukoc possessed what seemed to be a genuinely gorgeous, feathery touch in passes and shots. But he seemed too easily pushed off the ball and not much good at springing back to play defense. "Ah, you sound like you were reading our paper," said Thomaslav.

War was just beginning by the time of the 1992 Olympic games, but the immolation of the city was still incomplete. Kukoc had many fans in Sarajevo who would sneak out at night, as snipers were roosting, to hook televisions up to car batteries and watch their favorite old Yugoslav players contend against the United States. "I think, maybe he's better than what you saw. I think maybe, with so many people watching, and Toni knowing he is maybe going to the Bulls, he does not want to offend Michael Jordan or Scottie Pippen with his elbows. Toni is a nice boy. I am only thinking this now." Thomaslav said that during the first weeks of the war, Kukoc was playing a game for his Italian league team and it was broadcast on radio and television. That night, he said, for the first time in weeks, electricity snapped on briefly in Sarajevo, by surprise, and people braved paths up from their basements to take baths and hurl clothes into washing machines before the electricity quit. "Long about ten o'clock," he said, "bombs began to fall, and the snipers began to shoot. They like to shoot people running out from the rubble of buildings, you know, they are so brave, shooting at those people like we are bugs squirming out from under a plate. But this time, there were not many people running. We were all inside, huddled here and there, watching Toni and basketball. You get tired of running, and say, 'No, I will stay here and watch sane people play basketball.' So you see," he said, "I think you will agree: sports saves." Not since Chicago had I loved a place so deeply for being itself as Sarajevo.

Sarajevo was, like Chicago, a city with its own distinct humor, sharpened, deepened, and no doubt occasionally twisted by war. Less than a week into our stay, Miro Tedic arrived with personal news one morning. "Jesus," he announced with practiced comic blankness, "I saw Jesus, Scotty, walking down Snipers' Alley.* He was carrying the cross over his shoulder." For a moment, I wondered if Miro had really had

---

*The main street formerly known as Marshal Tito Boulevard that divided the city between Bosnian and Serbian enclaves. Serb snipers roosted in the apartment windows overlooking the street, and fired freely.

some sort of vision; Muslim exiles were as entitled as preteen girls in Fatima. "Did you say anything to Jesus?" I asked carefully. "Oh yes," said Miro in accomplished expressionlessness. "I saw the cross, and I said, 'My Lord, where did you get all that wood?' "

They had a score, if not a million of 'em, jokes, jabs, and stories that kindled a brittle laughter out of dread and rubble. That day, another Sarajevan we encountered in our rounds had another variation: "A man goes to his priest. He says, 'Father, forgive me, but last night, I fuck a chicken.' The priest says, 'Oh hell, that's all right. Fuck the chicken. Can I have the chicken for lunch?' " Some of the stories could make an admiring visitor wince. Sarajevens themselves said they recognized the ways in which the war had worn down not only their bodies, but their sense of what was precious, sacred, beautiful, or funny. So just as they chopped down the city's trees for fuel, rather than freeze, they made jokes out of the profane circumstances of their lives, rather than not laugh at all. The worst—the only one that risked genuine obscenity—went like this: "What's the difference between Auschwitz and Sarajevo?" What? "Auschwitz had gas." A horrified groan was considered the most gratifying response.

A comedy group called the Surrealists were holed up on the upper floor of a shattered old Tito-era state building. They had set up a type-writer and overturned a hubcap to serve as an ashtray, stepping down to sprinkle ashes as they spoke, like birds swooping down to sip water. They were manning what amounted to a rebel garrison of humor along Snipers' Alley, with Croats, Serbs, and Muslims among the players, along with Catholics, Jews, a converted Buddhist, and a Baha'i—show folk, after all. They reminded me of a Second City cast. Sometimes, they per-formed in small basements, holding flashlights up to their faces. In one sketch, an actress named Suzanna Jovic stood behind a man in a water line, waiting to fill a pail from an open tap. There is a terrible, audible, explosive *phhht!* But the woman does not run for shelter; she merely makes a face. It's not a bomb, just flatulence. "Oh, sorry," says the man turning to her, "I did not mean to do that." And the woman says, "Oh, that's all right. I understand. But tell me. Where did you get the beans?" In another sketch, Suzanna played Cinderella to a Prince Charming who is a blue-helmeted UN soldier, scattering chocolates and cigarettes to exhausted women on the streets. But Suzanna stumbles as she waltzes with the prince at his ball. Her feet are swollen from hauling pails of water up the stairs to her wicked stepmother's apartment. Cinderella runs away in embarrassment, while the prince plucks up her glass slipper. Of course, it is cracked by a bullet hole. He throws it over his shoulder, and the music resumes. "Find me a Swedish woman," declares the prince.

The Surrealists were trying to buy, borrow, receive, or purloin enough fuel to power a generator to run their lights so they could present a new show. They enjoyed telling the joke on themselves: how many liters of diesel fuel does it take to make a comedy show? About 800. *And at those prices, we're not surprised.*

As we were packing up our equipment, an actor and director named Boro Condic suddenly asked, "What happened to Michael Jordan's father?" It was about a month after James Jordan had been killed while napping along a roadside.

"I don't really know. It's being investigated. Looks like a couple of kids killed him in his car."

"Oh, shit, that is terrible," said Boro. "You know, we are learning so much here. Tragedy can hit while you are on the top of the world." I told Boro I found it odd and affecting that people in a city besieged by its own suffering were nevertheless intrigued and touched by the loss of someone who, no matter his grief, must surely be considered greatly blessed. "Oh," said Boro, "we have learned this, too. You should not weigh deaths on a scale, our side is heavier than yours." The comedian shook his head, gravely.

Back in Chicago, Michael Jordan was weighing his life on a scale after the death of his father. What had hurt him most about the press coverage of James Jordan's death was the suggestion that a stupid, savage murder might have somehow been set in motion by Michael's gambling. Knowing now that Pops Jordan's murder was the result of a roadside stickup, any other implication seems malicious. But the suspicion was inescapable at the time. Michael Jordan, after all, had just testified in a murder case about his golf course paybacks to a hustler. It would have been irresponsible for police to overlook the possibility that James Jordan's death traced back to gambling debt; and impossible for reporters to ignore their official interest. James Jordan himself—it was in the past, but on the record—had once pleaded guilty to taking kickbacks from contractors when he worked at GE in Wilmington. He was Michael's gambling pal. He was his son's dearest friend in the world. I thought about Pops, lighting up and enchanting reporters outside the Bulls' training center. "I mean, I talked him into going into Atlantic City . . .

Some demand him to be perfect. Every time he stubs his toe, someone is there to jump on him. He wants to live his own life, and he can't. It's scary. How the hell is this possible?" Pops taking the charge for Michael Jordan.

In late September of 1993, Michael Jordan came to see Coach Jackson with an idea about how he could reclaim his life from the strains of fame—declare victory and go home. He asked Jackson, "Do I have anything left to do here?" Jackson had discerned that some of Michael's joy in the game and his life was shrinking over the season. When James Jordan died, Jackson thought, *Michael won't be back.* Jackson had grasped the depth and character of Jordan's sorrow. People blessed with what looks like magic often worry about when their powers will run out—or, when magic will name its price. A man with Michael Jordan's exceptional sense of balance had to wonder if his astounding attainments, all the wealth, winning, and worship, was now calling him to make some sacrifice. He did not feel guilt in his grief over his father's death, but perhaps a sense of responsibility for what all of his success had brought. "For some reason," he said to Jackson, "I feel God is telling me to move on, and I must move on." The coach answered carefully, thoughtfully, tenderly, really. "You have nothing left to prove. You have done everything—*everything*—the world has asked of you."

The conversation continued, the talk of two men who would always figure in each other's lives. Jordan asked—more of a joke, really—"Is there any way I can just play in the playoffs?" Jackson was creative in response. Perhaps Michael could become a part-time player? But MJ had, of course, superb anticipation. "I'd just be criticized by the press for being a prima donna."

Phil Jackson did not implore or appeal. He simply and sincerely reminded Jordan that he considered him a genius. An artist on the order of Michelangelo or Picasso. A man who made masterpieces, who made the world look different.

"You might think about that, Michael," he said gently. "You don't walk lightly away from genius. You don't walk lightly away from this gift you have been given to make people happy."

But—at some point—*enough.* Jackson loved Jordan. He could see, in Jordan's hands and shoulders, the emotional freight Michael had taken on himself. Grief over his father, and the grueling grind of carrying so harrowing a load of hopes and expectations, crowds cheering, reporters peering, parents beseeching, the world clasping, grasping, clawing, *want-*

*ing.* It was not a time for a friend, a guide—*a coach*—to resort to a coach's tricks of motivation. *Man to man.* There had to be a special seat in a circle of hell reserved for a man who would try to trick Michael Jordan into thinking he had something left to prove. Hustlers were for golf courses. You could see how Michael Jordan would believe that God had taken a personal hand in his life when two coaches of the personal nobility of Dean Smith and Phil Jackson had been placed along his path.

*Chapter 10*

# THE INTERREGNUM

There are two intertwined myths about the year and a half Michael Jordan spent away from basketball. The first is that the Bulls collapsed. The second is that if Jordan had not retired after their third championship, the Bulls would have won two more in 1994 and 1995, before repeating three times again into 1998. An unbroken run of eight would have fixed them, beyond dispute, as the greatest team of all time. Their interrupted string of six leaves room for rational argument.

I can't accept either proposition.

The collapse of the Bulls after Jordan's second, and, presumably conclusive retirement may obscure an interesting fact. In 1994, the Bulls did just fine without Michael Jordan. They won 55 games, just two less than the championship year before. In fact, some fans and observers suggested that while the sport missed Michael's magic, his team had recovered a sense of balance. In 1994, Horace Grant, B. J. Armstrong, and Scottie Pippen were All-Stars—the first time three players from the same club were chosen as starters, and not one of them Michael Jordan. Scottie, in fact, was the All-Star game's Most Valuable Player. The Bulls swept Cleveland in the playoffs, but lost to the New York Knicks in seven games after a disputed call.* The Knicks went on to defeat the Indiana Pacers, but lost the title to the Houston Rockets.

Is it only a fan's phantasm to believe that: *if* that call had not occurred, and *if* the Bulls had gone on (as they did) to win the next game, that a practiced and confident Phil Jackson championship team would have outpaced the Pacers and then outshot the Rockets? (That's really only one iffy *if*.) The 1994 season had a frustrating end. It does not seem absurd to assume that Michael could have made more than a point's difference against the Knicks. But 55 wins and running the Knicks to the wire constituted a comedown, not a collapse.

The Chicago Bulls did not crash without Michael Jordan. But there is also no assurance that, had he stayed, the team would have won two more straight titles. Their opponents were building up to beat them, while various Bulls themselves seethed with annoyance and resentments that were only aggravated by championship spoils:

• Horace Grant was righteously indignant over what he took to be Jackson's favoritism toward Jordan and Pippen. When the duo had returned from playing on the 1992 U.S. Olympic Dream Team squad, they were exhausted, less from beating Burkina Faso than being celebrities. Jackson permitted them to relax through training camp, so they would be rested for the regular season. Grant felt that he was expected to carry more than his rightful burden, while Jordan and Pippen received more than their rightful acclaim.

• Pippen was insulted by general manager Jerry Krause's insistent claim that he had "discovered" Pippen. Central Arkansas was not a well-scouted basketball power. But word of Pippen's extraordinary physical gifts and developing skills had spread wide enough for Krause to trade for Seattle's fifth draft pick so he could select Pippen. Jerry Krause didn't "discover" Scottie Pippen Columbus-style, he just claimed him first. Pippen was also offended by Krause's expensive quest to sign Toni Kukoc. Krause would blandish millions of dollars on a man who, so far, had starred only against slow-footed Estonian centers and American

---

*Referee Hugh Hollins called a foul on Scottie Pippen, who had leapt in to try to block a shot by Hubert Davis. A replay showed no contact. But Hollins's call afforded Davis two foul shots, and he made them. New York won, 87 to 86. The league's chief referee, Darrell Garretson, later reviewed the call and confirmed it was bad judgment. Bad judgments are part of the game. The Bulls were understandably exasperated. But players should be reluctant to compare the bad judgments of referees and their own.

washouts. But Krause would not sweeten Scottie's contract, after he had shared Michael's burdens and helped beard Barkley, Drexler, and Magic.

• Krause, perhaps most grievously, was envious over the acclaim sports writers and fans awarded Phil Jackson for inspiring and refining the championship Bulls. Krause even managed to imply some deprecation of Michael Jordan, avidly admonishing reporters, "Remember, organizations win championships, not personnel." (Remember, water puts out fires, not firemen.)

• And Jackson—Jackson was already growing weary. "It gets harder every year to stay King of the Hill. Everyone gangs up to push you off— and sometimes, you just want to fall off yourself to get some rest."

I think that had Michael Jordan stayed, the Bulls would have won another championship in 1994. But not 1995. Too much was too close to boiling over, including Jordan himself. Instead, Jordan had a year-and-a-half hiatus, which humbled him as an athlete, deepened him as a man, and rekindled his joy in the art he had almost forgotten was a game.

The fortunes of the Bulls during Jordan's pause for refreshment is often dismissed as insignificant. And yet, one incident at least demands reminiscence for what it meant for the character of the team that Jordan would rejoin. In the third game of the series against the Knicks in 1994, Scottie Pippen sat down on the job. With 1.8 seconds left and the Bulls down by 1 point, Phil Jackson called a time-out and sketched out a play that called for Pippen to pass the ball inbounds to Toni Kukoc. The call was clever. Jackson knew that no other player had sunk as many last-second shots as Kukoc—albeit, they had all been in Yugoslavia and Italy. Jackson had been impressed by Kukoc's mettle. He might be a swinging door on defense and a rag doll about rebounds, but Toni Kukoc was a superb passer and a self-assured shooter.

Pippen was perturbed when he saw the plan. He thought his play over the entire season had earned him the right to try to Be Like Mike and get the call to take the last shot. Phil heard Scottie mumbling along the bench and could make out but one word. It said volumes: "Bullshit." Some of Scottie's wrath was residual. On the previous play, a slow-footed Kukoc had not cleared out of his zone, forcing Scottie to rush a shot that missed. "That didn't work," Phil told him. "Now we're going to do something else." He turned back to the pad on which he was sketching the play but caught a glimpse of Pippen glowering on the bench, shaking his head in disgust—a face Pippen's teammates didn't know he had.

"Are you in or out?" Phil asked simply. And Pippen said, "Out." The time-out was running out. Phil turned for advice to an assistant coach who said only, "Fuck him." With no time remaining for rancor, Jackson replaced Pippen with Pete Myers. The buzzer blared. Myers lofted a lovely pass into Kukoc, who took it smartly, jump-stepped, and cast a faultless three-point shot, as gorgeous as a rainbow, into the basket. The Bulls won, 104 to 102.

But Pippen's sit-down strike still smarted as the team came off the floor. Jackson, who loved Pippen as he loved, well, Michael Jordan, was—no Zen-aphorizing this one away—hurt and angry. And, amazed. Scottie Pippen was an unselfish player, who spent his energies selflessly on passing and defense. On Michael Jordan's retirement, Scottie Pippen had become perhaps the most talented player in basketball. He was having the kind of year that confirmed that. But his decision to sit was the kind of rash act that can end a career.* Who wants to play with a sitter? Scottie had broken the code. You might feel overlooked, undervalued, and unloved. You might be underpaid. But when the game horn honked—*you came to play.* If Jackson had stormed into the locker room, leveled a finger at Pippen and vowed, "You are never playing another minute for me, you sonuvabitch. And I will personally call every coach in the world to say you should never play for them, either," his reaction would have been beyond condemnation. Reinsdorf and Krause would have supported him. Scalia and Ginsberg would have supported him. *Michael Jordan* would have supported him. Jackson didn't demand dumb, rote obedience from his players. But he did ask them to play the game.

And yet, every great general knows when to do nothing. Jackson . . . took out his contact lenses. Bill Cartwright convened a team meeting. Jackson told the players he was leaving them to sort through their feelings while he struggled with his own in front of the press. In turn, each player told Pippen—who stood there, in his own tears, taking it all from them—that he was disappointed and hurt. Cartwright said, "This is our chance to do it on our own, without Michael, and you almost blew it with your selfishness." Scottie said he was sorry. A few times, he struggled to add something, then returned to that—"I'm sorry. I'm . . . I'm

---

*At least that's how it looked in 1994. In 1997, Latrell Sprewell tried to choke his Golden State Warriors coach, was suspended, then reinstated, traded, and resumed his career—with distinction—the next year for the New York Knicks. Next to choking, a sit-down strike seems civilized.

sorry." By the time Jackson returned, his players were sobbing and hug-ging—sensitive giants for the twenty-first century. The coach decided all that was left was to lead the team in reciting the Lord's Prayer. The next day, Jackson thought Pippen looked especially sharp in practice. Michael called his old coach to ask, "Can Scottie overcome this with the team?" And Jackson told him, "Michael, I think you can forgive somebody a lot, if you know their real intentions." Forgiveness seemed quickly rewarded the next day, when the Bulls defeated the Knicks 95 to 83.

Jackson's image as a wise man of the hardwoods rests more on that moment than any of his championships. Over the years, as his rep-utation as a Zen warrior grew, interviewers from outside the realm of sports would ask if he saw a lesson in the restraint he embraced when Scottie Pippen sat down. "Oh, not much," he'd often say, seeming almost embarrassed. "Sometimes it's wisest to let people discover their own solutions." As I was once writing his umpteenth expression of that into a notebook, Jackson filled in the silence. "I mean," he said, "I knew Scottie's heart. I still trusted his heart. People congratulate me on my patience. But all I did was to keep one of the best players in the game on our team." And, keep the one talent most likely to encourage Michael Jordan to believe that if he returned to basketball, he could pick up his place on a contending team. Holding on to Scottie Pippen kept at least a small hold on the hope against hope that Michael Jordan would one day be back.

Another, smaller myth about the interregnum between championships is that Michael Jordan was a bad minor league ballplayer. In fact, at times he was almost promising. Bad ballplayers don't run with Michael Jor-dan's speed (he finished fifth in the Southern League in stolen bases), or move with his grace. Truly bad ballplayers don't work as diligently as Michael Jordan, who came out to the park early, stayed late, shagged fly balls, and signed autographs (the last, at least, at a major league level). Of course, Jordan couldn't hit a curve ball. Most high school pitchers don't throw a curve, and most high school batters can't hit them; high school was the last time Michael Jordan had played organized baseball. Trying to hit the curve is the great leveler of talent in the minor leagues; those hitters who can learn will go on, those that can't don't. A gifted and dutiful player can spend a respectable three and four years in the minor leagues, learning how to pick up the spin on a curve in time to catch up with it. But by the time Michael Jordan might have learned, he would have been thirty-six (the age at which he would make his final retirement from basketball)—a real-life Roy Hobbes except, as he must have begun to sense, *no natural* at baseball.

The best record of Jordan's brief odyssey in the Chicago White Sox minor league organization, and probably the closest look of any kind at such an intensely guarded personality, is Bob Greene's book, *Rebound: The Odyssey of Michael Jordan*. Greene spent time with Jordan in the wake of his father's death, some of the lazy days of his minor league baseball career, and was finally along in the first days of Jordan's return to basketball. He became so trusted an intimate that once, during spring training, Jordan fell asleep on a couch in his own house in front of Greene, who let himself out the front door.

As Greene puts it in *Rebound*, Jordan discovered that he could retire from the Bulls and basketball. But he could not retire from being Michael Jordan. He liked many parts of minor league life, beginning with the fact that for once in his career as a professional athlete, Jordan got to play outdoors in the sun, rather than a frigid arena. Greene catches Jordan studying the small photos in the White Sox organization media guide—not just players, but clubhouse personnel, security guards, and equipment handlers. Jordan had learned that they might be reluctant to introduce themselves to Michael Jordan, and he wanted to be able to say hello to them by name.

But the crush of some of the crowds trying to encircle him to ask for his autograph, catch his smile, or—truly—touch the hem of his baseball uniform, jarred Jordan. Security at minor league ballparks is much more casual than in the NBA. Jordan could well afford his own security detail, but he did not want to surround himself at all times with off-duty cops. It was a bad way to live, and a bad way to look to the outside world—the billionaire in the bubble. Once, when his Birmingham Barons played a game in Memphis, Greene asked Jordan if he was going to visit Graceland. He answered with a sigh that corroborated Greene's notion that Elvis Presley was the last American personality to set off so much commotion. "It wouldn't be worth all the trouble it would cause to get it done," said Michael Jordan. There was another echo of Elvis-like weariness when Jordan told Greene, "Part of me felt like an old man when I was twenty-three or twenty-four . . . Whatever you're supposed to feel that makes you feel youthful, I've never experienced that."

In the middle of his minor league career, Jordan consented to play basketball once more: one last game that would close out the old Chicago Stadium, a benefit game organized for local children's charities by Scottie Pippen. Jordan was playing in the Arizona fall league at the time, and at first sent word that he could not appear.* He did not want to give the impression that his commitment to baseball was so casual, he could put it aside for a couple of days to play basketball. He did not want to fan any spark of a speculation that he would return to basketball. But ticket sales to the charity game were poor; Pippen appealed. It was just a few months after his 1.8 second episode, and Jordan also did not want his absence to suggest that Scottie had damaged his standing as MJ's everlasting teammate. Jordan had never had the chance to say good-bye to fans, his teammates, and the big, brick barn in which they had become famous. The cause, children's charities, was impeccable. The call went up again: *Mi-chael!* So Jordan played—and scored 52 points. With six seconds left on the clock, he embraced Pippen and began to walk off of the court, Michael Jordan's last steps on the floorboards of Chicago Stadium. He dropped down onto the floor, onto his hands and knees. For a single, frightful moment, some of the fans worried that Jordan, fatigued from a game so much more strenuous than baseball, had collapsed. Then, in the next second, they wondered if he was joking, joshing with Pippen and Horace Grant. "You take over—I'm a baseball player now—I'm too tired." Then, the crowd could see Jordan's bare crown poised just above the scowling red Bull face emblazoned, for one last time, on the center of the court of the old Chicago Stadium. Fans stood and wept as lightly, MJ leaned down.

> *Eyes, look your last!*
> *Arms, take your last embrace! and lips, O you*
> *The doors of breath, seal with a righteous kiss*

It may seem inflated to quote Shakespeare, *Romeo and Juliet*, Act V, Sc. III. Jordan's own words to Bob Greene are direct and affecting. "I was thinking," he said later, "about what you do when you know it's time to say good-bye to a good friend, and you know that words are not enough." The crying and the cheering went on for several minutes,

---

*John Starks of the New York Knicks, whose combative play had established him as a kind of Public Enemy Number One among Bulls fans, agreed to play. He is a tough, honest player, and a man of considerably greater geniality than his Chicago reputation. But even this kind gesture did little to improve his standing with Bulls fans. The show, for both the fans and Starks, was simply too good to close.

because Jordan's last act seemed not only beautifully appropriate, but poetically final.

A sequence of events caused Michael Jordan to return—a sequence far more concrete than the general impression of reporters and fans that Jordan simply tired of being minor league (and a mediocre minor leaguer) when he still possessed the talent and will to be the world's supreme athlete.

Life in the minor leagues seemed to renew Jordan's love of basketball as a game, not just a livelihood, art, or lucrative profession. Many of his minor league teammates in Birmingham and Arizona had been three-letter athletes in high school and enjoyed pickup games of basketball. Jordan would rent a gym, players would show up, and they would play *a game*—no crowd, no stakes, no obligations. Bob Greene tells about the time that a young front office staffer named Steve Gilbert was invited to join a pickup game with the Scottsdale Scorpions players and coaches. One of his teammates, wearing Carolina blue shorts, was Michael Jordan.

Gilbert told Greene that the other players on the court would take short breaks to catch their breaths—and pick up video cameras to record for posterity the night they played on the same basketball court as Michael Jordan. Gilbert, who was a well-conditioned amateur but no athlete, was left gasping after the game and could not catch his breath. The other players called the team trainer, who advised them to drive Gilbert to Scottsdale Memorial Hospital. There, as he lay prostrate on a hospital table and wired into oxygen tubes and heart monitors, Steve Gilbert said the doctors and nurses looked down and could only say, "What's it like, playing basketball with Michael Jordan?" Gilbert said he wanted to rouse all of his scarce breath to bark, "I'm in the fucking *hospital*, aren't I? What do you *think* it's like?" Gilbert was diagnosed with simple breathlessness, no heart attack. When he came into the clubhouse the next day, Jordan told him he would not play basketball with him again. "Because I can't have a good time out there if I've got to worry about you keeling over."

Jordan came to his second spring training in late February of 1995, just as major league baseball players were picketing the training sites in the first days of a strike. The baseball owners, led by Jerry Reinsdorf, who, of course, owned the Bulls as well as the White Sox, hired replacement players and sent them to training camp, too, where they shared practice facilities with the minor league players.

The major league owners had agreed that moving minor leaguers up would be bad for baseball. It could stamp the game itself as minor league. It could sow a blood rivalry that might flow for years, as major league players confronted the minor leaguers who had crossed picket lines to take over their jobs. Owners were horrified by the vision of games in which both union members and former scabs might be on the same field, armed with bats and fastballs—the high slides and bean balls that would fly. But replacement players were *replaceable.* Typically, they were former major league prospects who had once washed out and would not be much missed.

The baseball strike had suddenly made Michael Jordan the best-known name wearing a baseball uniform—the only player in organized ball that an audience, or television advertiser, might pay money to see. Jordan was in the additional extraordinary position of being both a minor league player and a member of the major league basketball players union. He did not want his celebrity to be used to break a players' strike. He was a union man, and he was also a businessman. He was certain Americans would not buy basketball shoes, hot dogs, and soft drinks from a scab. Jordan exacted what he thought was a personal promise from White Sox management: that they would not try to force him to cross the picket line and play in major league games. And so they didn't, exactly.

But White Sox general manager Ron Schueler decreed that minor league players could not park in the major league players' parking lot. For most minor leaguers, the edict was immaterial. They did not park in that lot. But Michael Jordan did because the White Sox knew that *he could not retire from being Michael Jordan.* Jordan was not only the most recognizable person on earth; he was the son of a man who had recently been murdered in his car. Jordan could not park his car on any street and walk two blocks to the ballpark without a reasonable expectation that his Land Rover, and perhaps his person, would be picked apart out of adoration, inquisitiveness, or mania. He did not complain or campaign for special treatment, didn't call Jerry Reinsdorf to say, *I thought we had a deal.* He didn't feel that he should have to. A team owned by Jerry Reinsdorf knew the special considerations that applied to having Michael Jordan on your roster. Jordan wouldn't cross a picket line for a parking space, or a major league spot. Instead, in a single afternoon, he simply packed up, left the White Sox training camp, and flew back to Chicago, where he phoned Phil Jackson to ask if he could come in to a practice (note that he called Jackson, and not Jerry Reinsdorf).

Minor league baseball, and a major league strike, had helped reawaken Michael Jordan's affection for basketball and his appreciation for what the game had given him. Years before, Jordan had told Bob Greene, "The basketball court is the one place where the rules say that no one can talk to me or walk up to me when I'm playing. During the game, for one of the few times in my life, I feel like I'm untouchable ... As loud as it is, it's almost a quiet time for me. I know that basketball games can be very exciting, but for me the game is one of the calmest parts of my life. No one can come onto the court. No one can cross those lines. It's a very calm place." But if Jerry Reinsdorf's management had even briefly congratulated itself on inducing Michael Jordan to come back to the Bulls—felicitations should be kept short. Jordan returned—renewed, but also newly suspicious of Jerry Reinsdorf as a man who would not stand by his promises. Michael Jordan might be the richest athlete in sports, but, like most Americans, he still had to occasionally work for sonsuvbitches.

Around the time rumor of Michael Jordan's return was being bandied about, I was scheduled to make a Sunday-night appearance at a synagogue in Indianapolis. My host phoned to say he had noticed that the Chicago Bulls played the Indiana Pacers earlier in the afternoon. The man who owned the Indiana Pacers was a member of the synagogue. Would I like to be his guest at the game? Then, the Thursday before the game, he phoned to say we would not be able to sit in the owner's box—those seats were being given to "someone else whose family needs them." But, he assured me, from any seats, it should still be a memorable afternoon.

"I can't tell you anything else," said David Leonards. "Just—you'll be glad you were there, believe me."

By the time we arrived at the Market Square Arena, there were already posters lining the railings, and bedsheets billowing in the stands:

WELCOME BACK, MICHAEL!
MICHAEL FOREVER!

(And this, of course, was at the table of mine enemies.)

The game was nationally broadcast, and news of MJ's imminent return was being pieced together from a ragbag of scraps and sightings. MJ's office said he wasn't in Chicago (true; but he could be playing golf or making a commercial someplace warm). MJ's agent was in Indianapolis (also true; but David Falk must have other clients on both teams). Other Bulls arriving at the arena had looked like they were stifling grins. And then, MJ himself arrived—6 feet 6 inches of sharp Italian pleats and creases, and a smile that suggested he hadn't come early just to watch. Ushers and the NBC road crew said they had seen him shooting warm-up shots and reported, "A little rusty on his release, maybe, but still sharp." My host and I were trading such preposterous bits of intelligence with aplomb when we felt a swell of noise rise out of the crowd—a literal gust from the force of 15,000 people suddenly, simultaneously clapping and gasping a bit at the sight of a famous bald head, bouncing light as he high-stepped onto the court in a white warm-up jacket. *Frrrom North Carrrolllina* . . . I saw the whole game without once realizing that Michael Jordan had changed the number he wore from 23 to 45. That night, I bored an audience and had a late, lardaceous snack of cheese sticks with some delightful people from the synagogue. I went to sleep in the cheap sheets of a desolate suburban motel, overlooking a vast, barren parking lot, a suety diner, and a cookie-cutter chain store. Michael Jordan had hit just 7 of 28 shots and gotten visibly winded and a bit rubber-legged in the last quarter. But the world still looked better.

# Chapter 11

# CHAMPIONS OF THE WORLD

Chicagoans can tell themselves their accomplishments in many fields are unrivaled. Still, nothing reassures more than a headline so signifying in the *New York Times*.

April 21, 1996, that newspaper's Sunday magazine carried a team portrait of the Chicago Bulls on the front cover. The Bulls were then closing in on the best regular season record of all-time in basketball. Michael Jordan was again the game's most valuable player. At the age of thirty-three, his leaps had been shortened, his step imperceptibly slowed. But he had worked hard and smart to invent a jump shot dealt with deadly effect as he floated back, a *jeté*—a ballet term—was for once probably exactly the term to use; although *fade-away jumper* seemed safer to say in polite company. The shot astounded less than a dunk in high-lights. But it was more difficult to defend against—and perhaps even lovelier to behold.

Scottie Pippen had improved and matured his talents so dramati-cally he had become perhaps the best all-around player in basketball; certainly the best defensive player. Jordan was as sagacious as gracious when he said, "This is Scottie's team now. I'm part of his supporting cast." And then—Dennis Rodman. He had put the old coach's metaphorical assertion, "I don't care if he wears women's clothes, as long as he can play," to the actual test. But Rodman's modern, meditative coach, Phil Jackson, saw Dennis, in whatever dress, as a talent to be enlisted, not broken. "Frankly," he said after Rodman's third change of hair color of the season, "I like Dennis as a blond." He likened Rodman to a *heyoka* of the Dakota Sioux, the cross-dressing clown "who brings change in everyone's reality."

The cover portrait showed MJ and Pip sitting at ease, arms folded in their laps, Alistair Cooke style. Toni Kukoc looked out wryly over an Eastern European poet's goatee. Steve Kerr was standing, to keep his smile at the same height as Kukoc in his chair; Steve could not quite keep the mischief from taking over his face. Luc Longley had to stand several steps in back of the rest, to squeeze his 7 foot 2 inch tallness into frame. Dennis Rodman had a mild, sedate expression on his face, softening against his Madonna-blond hair. Superman, Batman, Rodman, and friends. Giants-at-ease. Teammates. Mates. The headline below ran:

THE BEST. EVER. ANYWHERE.

Were they?

Other teams, in other epochs, merit being measured against the same claim. The New York Yankees of the Ruth-Gerhig era and Satchel Paige's Kansas City Monarchs were surely among the best teams of all time. But their times were segregated (which is why Bill Veeck always thought that an "*" should be placed by Babe Ruth's 60 home runs in 1927, not Roger Maris's 61 in 1961—Ruth never had to bat against Paige). The formidable Montreal Canadien dynasty of the Flying Frenchmen lacked the Russians, Czechs, and Swedes that quicken today's game. Pele's great Brazilian squads were all Brazilian.

But the Jordan-Pippen-Rodman Bulls ran in a time when basketball had become the global game, wired live around the world. Their roster included not only black and white Americans, but a Canadian, an Australian, and a Croatian. The New York Yankees of 1998 won a historic number of games and the world championship with Dominicans, a Japanese, a Cuban, and their own Australian on the roster. But the Bulls' 1995–96 record of 72 wins against just 10 losses is a slightly more dominating percentage (.878) than the Yankees' .714.

The noble Boston Celtics dynasty of Bill Russell, John Havlicek, and Sam Jones makes the most compelling case to be ranked above the Bulls. Even the most incurable Chicago partisan cannot find much to blemish a team that won, as the Celtics did, eleven championships between 1957 and 1969. But in every field of athleticism—ballet, marathon running, golf, soccer, or field hockey—advanced nutrition, scientific training, and year-round conditioning have made performers bigger, faster, and stronger. Michael Jordan is two inches taller and ten pounds more sinewy than his Celtics predecessor, Sam Jones. Toni Kukoc is six inches taller and carries almost thirty more pounds of muscle than the great John Havlicek. It's all in the statistics—and the vitamin supplements. The Bulls of the 1990s were simply bigger, faster, and stronger than the Boston team of the generation before.

And when Russell's Celtics dominated basketball, the game was smaller. It was barely a major sport (at least, outside of Boston; and even there, fan enthusiasm for the peerless Celtics could be eclipsed by the swashbuckling Boston Bruins). In fact, the Bulls were founded in 1966 because Roone Arledge, then the head of ABC sports, told the NBA they were not a national game, and could not hope to win a national television contract, without a franchise in Chicago. Pro basketball was still a sport that packed everyday crowds into modest arenas and got covered below the fold of Sports. In a small league, talent could accumulate; players had fewer options to improve their fortunes. Boston could build a dynasty and replenish it without worry about competitive bidding.

In the 1960s, a team won an eastern or western title, then played immediately for the championship. But the game has spread out. Teams today have to win three playoff series before reaching the finals. The season is longer, the attention more intense; the edge tested against more stones. If the Celtics had to battle the scrutiny and stress of three playoffs, I'm inclined to believe that Wilt Chamberlain's Warriors or Lakers would have captured two or three of those eleven titles won by Boston.

Stress is the great leveler among athletes of equal ability. Steve Kerr once said that there might be a thousand people of his general height (6 feet, 3 inches) who could sink the same number of free throws out of 100 that he can. But how many could sink a critical shot with 20,000 people watching in person and 45,000,000 on television? And how many could make that shot with wealth, reputation, and a world championship in their hands? The numbers begin to thin. I think that no team has played at a higher level—for longer and against greater stress—than the Chicago Bulls of the Jordan, Pippen, and Rodman vintage.

They were an interesting, congenial, international group. None were native Chicagoans. All became willing emblems of the city around the world. They were a working human enterprise of many colors and many flags. Their cosmopolitan quality—and their quality of competence—seemed an expression of the modern and accomplished city Chicago had become. Despite their isolation from the economic anxieties of the workaday world, several of the Bulls had known some of life's misfortunes; and even tragedies. Steve Kerr's father, the late president of Beirut's American University, had been kidnapped and killed by religious terrorists. Toni Kukoc's grand Yugoslav national basketball team was torn apart by war. Scottie Pippen had grown up in profound poverty. Ron Harper was a witty man, inhibited by a stutter. Dennis Rodman had been assailed by fag bashers. And all of Michael Jordan's deeds and fame could not keep his father from being shot to death along a roadside.

The Jordan that rejoined the Bulls displayed some marks of mellowing. The grisly and unexpected death of his father had encouraged Jordan to hold closer to what was precious to him—which included basketball, Jackson, and Pippen. Also, Jordan had been humbled. Not just by his .202 batting average in baseball, but by a glaring wearing down in his skills at basketball. In the 1995 playoffs, the first after his return, the Bulls were eliminated in six games by the Orlando Magic of Shaquille O'Neal, Penny Hardaway—and Horace Grant, who had left the Bulls on bitter terms. In the closing seconds of a close game, a young Orlando guard named Nick Anderson (from Chicago, to gild the embarrassment) had stripped the ball from Jordan's hands and pushed it out to Hardaway, who passed it over to Grant for a dunk, putting Orlando up by a point. A good play that was, for many Americans, an ugly moment—like seeing Joe Louis knocked through the ropes of the boxing ring. Then, with 6.2 seconds left, Jordan pulled up as if to launch a last shot, but instead passed it over to Scottie Pippen—who wasn't where Jordan thought he was. The ball, and the game, dribbled off of Pip's right foot. After the game, young Nick Anderson may have overplayed his moment, telling reporters, "Number forty-five doesn't explode like number twenty-three. Number twenty-three, he took off like a space shuttle. Number forty-five, he revs up, but he doesn't really take off." Jordan's reaction with reporters was frank and self-effacing. "I feel personally responsible." The next game, the team equipment manager hung both 23 and 45 jerseys in Jordan's locker; Jordan returned the 23 over his shoulders, scored 38 points, and helped bring the Bulls to a ten-point victory (although they would lose the series).

The Michael Jordan of the 1991 through 1993 championship

teams could remind you of James Huneker's observation that, "Genius never drops from the skies." Jordan found it hard to descend to understand talents below his own. But the Jordan who couldn't hit a curve and then was robbed of the ball in the broad daylight of a game, had to abide lesser talents—most prominently his own. React, but not accept. Jordan remained scaldingly intense in practices, and that's where Steve Kerr apparently won his respect. Steve stayed late each day to take one hundred foul shots; a trait to match Jordan. Steve also felt an unspoken empathy between them. Each had lost their father in a brutal, well-publicized murder. And yet, Steve felt frustrated when Jordan would be double-teamed and seemed to make no effort to find him; Steve let that be known. One day in practice, Jordan kept driving and pushing and flailing his elbows at Kerr's elbows and torso, as if to say, "You want the ball? Take the ball. What are you going to do with the goddamn ball?" Steve matched him, cheap shot for cheap shot. Then, as MJ asserted his superior height, his blows rose to strike spots on Steve's chest. And then, Steve Kerr stood up from the ball, as if ready to strike Bugs Bunny's *Space Jam* fwiend in the most weckognizeabuww face in da woowd. Their teammates intervened—"to save my life, and Michael's hands," Steve laughed later. Two conspicuously cool and clean players, the last two players they would ever pick to be brawlers. Kerr didn't apologize, really—didn't feel that he needed to. Later that night, though, Steve's phone rang. It was the great Michael Jordan, sounding sheepish, saying *he* was sorry. And thereafter, Jordan seemed to look for Steve a little more when Kerr came into a game—not just as a pair of hands to take MJ's passes, but as a man to step up to a three-point shot.

But the antagonism between the team and their general manager, Jerry Krause, seemed to grow worse. Krause is a short man with the basic silhouette of a diving bell. That alone distinguished him in the worst way in an athletic enterprise (most coaches, scouts, and general managers are former players at some level). The players hung a nickname on Krause that was said to be coined by Michael Jordan: *Crumbs*. Donut crumbs, cookie crumbs, hot dog roll crumbs, seemed to cling like lint to Krause's tummy. "Hey, Jerry," the players would call when he rode the team bus—they did not call him *Crumbs* to his face, deflating the idea that the nickname was in any measure affectionate—"Hey, Jerry, jelly donuts on the right!" (Players, of course, can develop indulgences more dangerous than donuts.) To an outsider, the ridicule smacked of childishly cruel schoolyard taunts, jocks tormenting the class nerd. But the players recognized a nerd's revenge in Krause's insistence that, "Organizations, not personnel, win championships." They heard it as the slur of a man who thought athletes were dumb, interchangeable parts.

Men who have to spend several hours a day refining their bodies into professional instruments can regard fat as a sign of slothfulness. But Jerry Krause's corpulence was the product of overwork, not indolence. He was so immersed in the long, irregular hours of scouting, tape-watching, trading, wheeling, and dealing that he malnourished himself with snacks; and proposed trades for exercise. At some point, Krause's sensitivity veered into vanity. He was never so shameless as to try to take credit for Michael Jordan. But when he boasted about "discovering" Scottie Pippen, or "rescuing" Phil Jackson from unemployment, Jerry Krause managed, in a single indignity, to both claim responsibility for their success and disparage it.★

But still: there could be something affecting about Krause. When he was introduced at championship rallies, he was booed—but stood up gamely to wave back. When the ribbing got rough on the team bus, and Jackson would smilingly intervene to try to tamp down the verbal assaults, Krause would shake him off. "That's okay," he said. "I can take care of myself." A few times, I left messages, asking to interview him. He never called back. "Secretive," said the players, "always very secretive. Won't talk about his work. He'll hold tryouts at midnight. Likes to whisper, talk behind his hand. Makes him feel important." The coaches and some players had seen a sign hanging in Krause's office: HEAR ALL, SEE ALL, SAY NOTHING. Perhaps not a bad credo for someone scouting and trading talent. But the line was originally the motto of Nazi Germany's Secret Service. Jerry Krause was Jewish; and no Nazi. But his intensity about basketball did not seem to promote a large view of human nature, much less history. Krause's dedication seemed to isolate and shrink his interests, while Phil Jackson's seemed to widen his circle of enthusiasms and friends.

Their differences were aggravated the more they were publicized. Reporters knew they could get the men to express conflicting opinions about proposed trades, draft choices, practice philosophies—and music,

---

★Phil Jackson was not unemployed as the term is generally understood. Coaches are like athletes, actors, directors, architects, sculptors, and migrant workers. Not *unemployed* so much as *between jobs*. Jackson was pondering law school and had taken an aptitude test to suggest future employment. He scored very high on the prerequisites for being a teacher, attorney—or forest ranger.

culture, and politics. The relationship between the philosophical coach and the furtive general manager began to resemble a bad marriage: you wondered not why the partners were coming apart, but how they had ever come together.

Once, I encountered Jerry Krause in person after a game and tried to make my case for an interview. His handshake was soft and brief. "Sorry, sorry," he said, "can't do that." I tried to avert my eyes from his paunch, but after all the stories—I had to glance. No crumbs. But there was a tawny blotch crusting on his blue oxford shirt between the first and second buttons up from his belt. If I had to guess, I'd say, mustard.

While Jerry Krause did not discover Scottie Pippen or rescue Phil Jackson, he did take a chance on Dennis Rodman. The Bulls' loss to Orlando in the 1995 playoffs had confirmed a weakness some coaches and critics had cautioned about in a team built around extraordinary shooting guards: the Bulls were getting beaten to, and therefore by, rebounds. Between Jordan, Pippen, Kukoc, and Kerr, the Bulls had better scorers. But Orlando was towering at the center. Shaquille O'Neal and Horace Grant plucked off shots that fell short and shoveled another chance back to Orlando, while keeping the ball out of Pippen and Jordan's hands. It was one of the essential equations of the game—rebounds gave a second chance to you, while keeping the game away from your opponent.

Any talk of rebounding in modern basketball introduced the name of Dennis Rodman. He had made himself, through ingenuity, hard work, and flair, the game's preeminent rebounder—and ranking screwball. In fact, the former may have slightly depended on the latter. Rodman radiated some of the same prospect of spontaneous, random menace as a great power pitcher with erratic control—he was the terrorist with terrible weapons, stealth elbows, and expeditious hands. And he had a personal story which, as much as Michael Jordan's, encouraged him to believe larger forces were at work in his life.

Dennis Rodman had grown up a wild, forsaken child on the outskirts of Dallas. His father—with the improbably apropos name of Philander Rodman—ran away from his family when Dennis was seven. His mother, according to accounts, was devoted but confounded and overwhelmed. Rodman did not play basketball in earnest as a teenager, though he had two sisters who were accomplished players. Dennis topped out at 5 feet 9 inches tall. He left high school for a succession of jobs—a car washer, an auto body mechanic, and a baggage handler at

Dallas–Ft. Worth Airport where, by his own account, he was also an occasional petty pilferer. People who remember him from the time he was unbending fenders and unloading Samsonites instead of hauling down rebounds recall him as shy. Then, at the advanced age of twenty, Dennis Rodman *grew*—eleven inches in a year. He was like the science fiction lizard who grows gigantic in the glow of an atom test. Suddenly, he couldn't fit more than his toes into his shoes and couldn't stuff his feet into his slacks past his knees. The only clothes that still fit were extra-large coveralls from the airport maintenance works. Rodman was not accustomed to the attentions of titanism. He found a kind of refuge from B-movie freakishness playing pickup games on basketball courts on the playgrounds of Dallas with players who could be five years younger, and five years more experienced. The games were serious and organized, stages for high school and college stars. Scouts came out to watch the kids—and sent back reports about the glandular baggage handler. A series of tryouts resulted in Rodman enrolling as a student at Southeastern Oklahoma State (he was adopted—literally, legally adopted—by a white farm family in the area after their young son brought his friend, Dennis, home to dinner). He was twenty-five years old by the time he was signed by coach Chuck Daly's Detroit Pistons in 1986.

His sudden growth seemed to stamp Dennis with a fundamentally different idea about his body. He saw it as a sudden, unaccountable gift, the one solid sign of providence in his life. Rodman bestowed care on his new, elongated torso that he had never shown for his old. Regular meals and professional training had given Rodman the frame of a champion greyhound: he was beautifully limber and balletic. He tested his new body to verify that it was real, making vast and imaginative demands on his fresh physique. On the court, he would hurl himself headlong after balls. After the game, he would hurl himself headlong into hell-raising rascality, all-night bouts of drinking, dancing, and copulation (a more romantic term really wouldn't seem to apply) that would turn an average man's mind into cotton gauze and his legs into rubber. But Dennis rebounded. His exceptional body became the source of all reward, and over the years Dennis embroidered, festooned, adorned, and embellished until it looked like a fresco in flesh and blood.

Rodman became a great physical actor: not for what he displayed, but what he concealed. While referees trained their eyes on the flight of the ball and the fight for position among players beneath the basket, Dennis would deliver a fleeting dig into a man's ribs with his elbows, or

hit his Achilles heel with a glancing brush from his toe. While they staggered, Dennis would often grab off a rebound. Occasionally, an opponent would strike back without Dennis's cunning subtlety. Rodman
would snap his head back and flop down in a wounded heap, like Buster
Keaton banged with a two-by-four board. More than occasionally,
Rodman's righteous retaliator would be called for the foul.

In the age of the specialist, Rodman became a virtuoso of
rebounding. A man who would one day be regarded as a wild, over-
ripened child with a five-year-old's span of attention had a disciplined
gift to pick up the spin and angle of a ball bouncing down from a missed
shot. He had the agility to pounce on the ball and perfected the touch
to be able to reel off a pass with sometimes stupefying precision. At
practices, Dennis would lie on his back and flick a basketball up from
the tips of his fingers, just his fingers, pop it ten and twenty feet into the
air, then flick it back up with another spin.

Rodman had won a place in the game at an age at which some
players were already washing out. He resisted the bridling that younger
players, scouted since high school, had learned to tolerate. He was indif-
ferent about diet, casual about practice, and careless about personal
safety, in play on the court and off. But Dennis was devout about exercise. Rodman might come late to practice, but would stay late in the
weight room, even after playing four quarters of basketball. His teammates would be scrubbed, slick-haired, slaked down with beer, and on
their way home, while Rodman was still curling barbells. Into his thirties, Rodman had a body with sinews that a younger player simply
could not develop; and a cunning most could not approach.

But this is the recollection of a Dennis Rodman fan. Dennis
helped Detroit win two world titles in 1989 and 1990, but fell to grief
with a new coach (as a matter of fact, Doug Collins) who had not yet
earned the stature that two championships had conferred on Chuck
Daly to indulge Dennis's infractions. Rodman was traded to San Antonio, where a new coach, John Lucas, had a wonderful reputation for
working with recovering drug addicts (which, by the way, had never
been among the plentitude of Rodman's excesses). Dennis won
rebounding titles in San Antonio, but the team faltered in the 1994
playoffs and Lucas was fired for being too lenient—and, perhaps more
seriously yet, for losing.

By 1995, Rodman's sly play began to be eclipsed by episodes of
seeming lunacy. He sulked, scowled, flailed, and fouled, skipped practices, and checked himself out of games with unconvincing

maladies. When San Antonio was defeated in the 1995 playoffs, Rodman sat on the bench barefoot, moping, and pouting, a living poster image of an athlete who looked unwilling to work for his millions.

Referees reviled Rodman. They considered him with the same contempt country sheriffs hold for moonshiners they can never quite catch with corn likker in their trunks, racing over moonlit Carolina back roads. *If that guy so much as smashes a taillight, I'm gonna run him!* Because Rodman slipped out of penalties they couldn't see, the referees slapped him down more severely for what they could detect. *Even if he didn't do that—he did* something! Coaches carried a set of mental calculations around about Dennis Rodman. He could give a team fifteen or more rebounds in each game. But it would cost his team six penalties. On the other hand, Dennis could also be counted on to commit and conceal three or four more fouls, which could assist in two or three scores. But he was insistently insubordinate—late to practice, late to games, inattentive to instructions, publicly contemptuous, perpetually in a state of imprecise insurrection. Most coaches believed in a domino theory of player insurgency—let one rebel, the rest will follow. The bottom line of the cost-benefit analysis coaches made about Dennis Rodman was: *He'll help you win games. He'll make you lose your job.*

Please note: I make no correlation between emotional instability and wearing women's clothing. When Dennis first began to exhibit himself in select pieces of lingerie, he was playing for the San Antonio Spurs. He told interviewers that cross-dressing made him feel liberated, in touch with his inner person, his feminine persona, and other pop clichés. Conspicuously, he wore gay pride T-shirts in the weight room and made friends in gay dance clubs. Over the years, reporters have speculated that Rodman's one-week stand with Madonna convinced him that sexual ambiguity could be a shrewd marketing strategy. If so, San Antonio, Texas, was not the best market in which to begin. Bigots sent death threats, slashed the tires of his pickup truck (Dennis was a good ole' Texas boy, after all—an ole' boy in drag), and spray-painted FAGGOT across his windshield. In response, Rodman appeared on the cover of *Sports Illustrated* in a lacy, black leather teddy, mesh hose, nipple rings, and a bird inexplicably perched on his forearm. I do not know where the latitude and longitude of Dennis Rodman's sexual orientation resides. But I have never had any cause to doubt that he genuinely just likes wearing women's clothing. I mean, nipple rings aside, his costuming *does* look comfortable. With his tattoos, teddies, rouges, powders, glitter, and spangles, Dennis Rodman painted a bull's eye for gay bashers onto his own head. His unblinking, unapologetic association with a gay identity seemed to give his life a larger sense of purpose.

As the days dwindled down to the start of the 1995–96 season, the Bulls had still not notably improved their ranks for rebounding. It was utterly obvious for Jerry Krause to be led to ponder the possibility of Rodman. But Krause often seemed more enthralled (too much so, said many of the players) with locating the nonobvious. Finding a talent like Toni Kukoc in the relative obscurity of Croatia conferred more attention on Krause—he saw to that. After Rodman had sat on the San Antonio bench with a hangdog frown and his huge, bare toes upturned in idleness, he was widely considered to be unemployable. He was daft, he was old, he was destructive. San Antonio tried to deal him away for months and found no takers. His agent was dialing up the Italian leagues. Teams demurred as if the Spurs were trying to sell off toxic materials, and in a way, they were. Trading for Dennis Rodman was deemed to be the same as placing a lump of kryptonite on your bench. He blazed bright, but robbed supermen teammates of their powers.

So Rodman was an outcast; and Krause asked to meet him. A simple request that had become scarce in times when athletes hired agents to block for them, and to burnish their best sides. But Dennis's agent knew his client possessed another important defensive ploy: charm. Jerry Krause, in his potato sack of a sportcoat, drip-dry white shirt, and skinny, spotted tie, discovered that he was touched by Rodman, from his marbleized hair to his nose rings. He found Dennis likable, shy, and remarkably knowledgeable about a subject that so baffled others—himself. Dennis told Krause it would be an honor to play for a team as talented, as classy, as the Chicago Bulls. He wanted to play basketball. He loved the game, and his love of the game had given him his life. Put him on the same team as Michael Jordan and Scottie Pippen, and he would play hard and with heart. All I want to do is lose myself in basketball, he told Krause. San Antonio, he said, the city as well as the team, would not let him play his game. The shoeless scene? His feet, Dennis said, suffered from a sweating problem. If the coaches had just let him be himself, he would have been ready to pull on his shoes and kick *motherluvin ass* with intensity. Intensity, he told Krause, was both his best attribute and worst trait. Sometimes, he boiled so fiercely inside, even he needed a break from himself; so he went off on binges. I'm older than other players, said Rodman, who was then thirty-five. Not one of those overpaid, coddled, candy-ass kids who've had scouts and agents waving scholarships and shoe contracts at them from when they had their first eruption of acne.

*I've come a long way, the hard way,* said Dennis. I know how to get up off my ass. Look at me, look at tapes of me, *just look at me*—have you ever seen anyone play harder to win? Talk to my old Detroit teammates. Talk to my old coach, Chuck Daly. *Talk to my psychiatrist.* Make me a Bull, Dennis Rodman told Jerry Krause, and I'll bring you another ring.

Krause was intrigued (he also made the recommended calls). He knew the Bulls could use Rodman's particular talent; and he suspected that between Jordan's illustriousness and Jackson's forbearance, the Bulls occupied a different atmosphere than other teams. Rodman's spark could catch fire in Chicago, without threatening to burn down the woods. But first, Krause would have to gain approval from Jackson, Jordan, and Pippen. The order was not arrived at alphabetically. Jackson's consent would count with Jordan. Jackson and Jordan's combined endorsement would make it difficult for Pippen to demur, and Scottie, of course, had the most specific and personal reason to disapprove of Rodman—he still carried a scar on his chin from the time Rodman had shoved him into a stanchion beneath the basket. There was also another, perfectly reasonable motive on Krause's agenda for approval. If the trio refused, Krause could not be accused of neglecting their call for rebounding talent—Jerry had even been willing to sign *Dennis Rodman*, for Chrissakes. And if Dennis joined the Bulls and drove them into exasperation, Krause could point out that Phil, MJ, and Scottie had said they wanted Rodman—*so what's their problem now?*

Jackson spent hours talking to Rodman. When they shook hands, Jackson asked, gently but insistently, "Please take off your sunglasses, Dennis. I would like to see your face." Rodman did, almost shyly; and met Jackson's eyes with his own. It was the first signal that Rodman could be reached with a human touch. Jackson was actually bemused by the idea that he, a man taken to be some sort of Zen master, could not embrace a master of deceit. Check my record, Jackson used to say, with a smile, I wasn't always considered some sort of holy man, I was a player with long arms. When I did look up Jackson's record, I think I discovered what he wanted: in 1975, Zen master Phil had led the National Basketball Association with 330 personal fouls. Dennis Rodman had never committed more than 292. Indeed, Jackson might have much to teach him.

Krause then turned to the two players. Jordan and Pippen had loathed Rodman when he was a Detroit Piston. But Jordan's reaction was shrewd and concise: he said he'd rather play with Dennis Rodman than against him. Krause finally came to Pippen, and Scottie's response was more complicated: if he can help us more than he can hurt us, fine. I won't pal around with him. But I'll play with him.

San Antonio was so eager to be rid of Rodman they traded him, even up, for a second-rank center, Will Perdue. Dennis presented himself in Chicago in a sleeveless denim shirt, studded with sequins. He wore a knit cap, he said, because he'd heard Chicago was cold. He was happy to be a Bull, said Rodman, pleased to be teammates with players he admired from the other side of the court. "As soon as Michael and Scottie get to see how I can help them out," he said, "I'm sure we'll get along fine." As questions began to flag, Rodman pulled off his cap slowly, teasingly—he was bringing up the curtain. There was a slight gasp, then a laugh: his hair had been dyed bright Bulls red. Dennis had the glowering Bull logo stippled onto the back of his head. *Rebound, Rodman!* Flat on his flowered, festooned ass, Rodman had reached up and hauled down new life for his career. Curtain up. Cue the lights!

With the addition of Dennis Rodman, the Chicago Bulls of history were created. Not just the winning basketball team, but the cultural emblem. Jordan, Pippen, and Rodman—his Royal Airness, the Prime Minister, and the Queen. Jordan was Michelangelo, the fine artist who made leaps of imagination real. Rodman was the performance artist, who leapt into flights of imagination. The breed of Bulls who won the first three titles had been champions. But the champions who won the next three created a pedigree. *The Michael Jordan Bulls.* They made Bulls fans out of opposing crowds, and sports fans out of people who knew and cared nothing for sports. People who found professional sports vacant and corrupt had to acknowledge a truth of the times—the Bulls were masters of a craft, Michael Jordan the practitioner of an art.

The Reverend Jesse Jackson ascended into the locker room to congratulate the team, black and white, straight and bent, Americans and immigrants, favored sons and refugees, all clasping together like the fingers on a human hand. "One finger can be broken. But put five fingers together"—and here, the reverend held up his own enormous old quarterback's grip—"and you have a strong hand. A hand that can pass and dribble. A hand that can write poems and pat children and slam dunk. A strong hand that can shake the world!" Coach Phil Jackson got a letter from a man who had gone on a spiritual retreat to Bhutan, in the Himalayas, at the top of the world. At a Buddhist monastery, the man pulled on a long cord to ring the doorbell and heard sandals slapping heels on a mud floor. When the door was pulled open, the man said he was received by a ruminative monk in a saffron robe—who wore a Bulls cap on the back of his bare head. Michael Jordan and the Red Oxen, emblems of harmony in a high country that belonged more to the sky than the earth. Jackson's correspondent had sent along a photograph of the monk in his cap, and the coach put the picture up in the Bulls' locker room to remind his players, as championships and honors accumulated, that they played for something more than mere honors. Street kids in Rio, swarming multitudes in Shanghai, monks, hermits, holy men, soccer moms, women CEOs, closet cases, punks, retirees, beggars, and stars, felt a fascination for Michael Jordan and the Chicago Bulls.

Their arrivals became events. The plane, ushered into a private gate, the bus parked beneath the plane, the police escort through thickened traffic, trucks and station wagons slowing down to try to peer through the darkened blue-green glass. *Is that them? Where's Jordan? Ohmigod, I think I see Jordan!* Aboard the bus, players would pursue their card games and punch out cell phone calls (each of them, after all, being principal income stream for a million-dollar corporation) while looking out wonderingly at the thickets of gazers and gawkers. The hubbub and the bedlam outdid even the excess of rock stars. When the bus reached the hotel or practice arena, crowds would be pent up behind police lines. Curious kids, criers, and squealers, men and women with faces reddening above their snow jackets. "Look at me, Michael, oh, God, please Michael *look at me!*" But frequently, Michael would be absent—whisked away in his own car by a separate security force and slipped in through a separate entrance. Ron Harper, who had a shaved head of a slightly lighter shade, would curl up the collar of his fur coat over his ears and face, peering through his folded fingers to step off the bus and sweep past the police lines, setting off small explosions of commotion and melodrama. "*Over here*, Michael. Look at *me*, Michael. My son, look at *my son*, Michael. *Michael!*" Once, in Los Angeles, MJ was working on his free throws in an early, unguarded hour at the Great Western Forum when a man rushed onto the court, threw himself at Jordan's feet and then . . . just stayed there, looking up, as if enraptured; until security guards who had been watching Jordan in solemnity stirred and scrambled out to remove the man. Another time, in New York, the Bulls had a team breakfast before departing for Madison Square Garden. A line of waiters in red jackets (and there seemed to be an unusually large number standing at the ready to pour out coffee and tea for twenty people) stood in the back of the room as the players filed in with their heavy, size-18 steps. As they settled into seats and Coach Jackson started to speak, some of the players saw tears spring up in the eyes of the waiters. Their faces were shining along with the silver service in their hands. They were crying, as if at a wedding, a graduation, some tender, hallowed, personal occasion that marked a passage in their lives. They were looking at Michael Jordan.

The 1996 championship season passed in mounting amazement. The Bulls began with five wins, Jordan scoring 42 against Charlotte on opening night, 38 against Toronto two games later. Jordan's imposing presence was now touched by poignancy. James Jordan's death, then Michael's precipitate retirement, his earnest blundering through the lowest rungs of baseball, and finally, his passionate return to basketball, had all reminded fans that his career was finite. Each new title, honor, and challenge rekindled the question: How long would he stay? What new moment would he choose to leave basketball for good? Each time Jordan stepped up to the foul line, a fusillade of camera lights flashed through the stands like a moving brushfire. The lights popped and rippled as the camera shutters snapped, stippling Jordan's form with small gnats of light that seemed to burst and die. Michael Jordan was before them in the flesh; they wanted to capture the moment, and take it home. *We were there. We saw him once—Michael Jordan.* The Bulls were losing just one game for every eight they played, an astonishing, and exhausting, rate. "This could be history," Smokey Baer said at the office one morning. "You heard it here first. This could be history!"

Jackson had said at the start of the season that his worst worry was what he called delicately, "the general age of the team." Rodman was already thirty-five, an age few players reach in the NBA. Jordan would soon be thirty-three. Scottie Pippen was thirty-one, but had played more basketball than Jordan; and paid for it with back spasms, spinal grinding, and foot problems.

Rodman went down with a wrenched knee for almost a month, just after the start of the season. He returned with his hair dyed green for the holidays (more fluorescent than ivy), and hauled down more than 60 rebounds in his first three games back. The Bulls, replenished by Dennis, would proceed through the holiday season without a loss, 18 straight wins, until the middle of February. As the wins tolled away, Rodman would change his hair color seasonally—from Bulls red to Yuletide green, platinum blond to Grateful Dead tie-dye, and, finally, a buff backdrop busily imprinted with a peace symbol, the red AIDS ribbon, and a pink triangle signifying gay pride. Dennis devised a curtain act for the end of victorious games. He would slip his thumbs under his 91 jersey, peel it off, teasingly, over his tattoos, and fling his drenched uniform into the crowd. *Dennis, Dennis, here, here, me, me! Dennis, I want your sweat!* He made a point of flinging one to Oprah Winfrey; another to Cindy Crawford; and another to Mimi, a man who was the prima diva (or is that donna?) at a Clark Street transvestite dance club. But an awful lot of sopping jerseys also flopped happily onto the upturned faces of car dealers, suburban matrons, pinstriped skirted lawyers, men in gray flannel suits, and their ecstatic children. There were those who found unfathomable the mutual attraction between the City of Big Shoulders and a player who wore lacy pastel halter tops. But as Rodman himself said after a game, "This is a city that works their asses off. I guess they respect someone else who does, too."

"What a showman he is," said my mother, in wonder and admiration, as we took in the end of a game on television. "What a showman."

"The bit with the jersey," I said. "Does that remind you of Frank Sinatra throwing his comb at bobby-soxers?"

"A little," said my mother. "But it's more like the diva plucking out one of the roses the crowd has thrown up, and flinging it back to thank them. That's what I see. He's not teasing the crowd, watching them faint over a pocket comb. I think Dennis is thanking them. I think he's saying, 'Thanks for accepting me for who I am.' What a showman," my mother repeated. "What a showman."

During the season, Rodman had organized a marriage ceremony in which he was both bride and groom, and brought out an "autobiography" in which he bared his buttocks on the cover.★ Most teams might complain that the resulting attention was distracting. But Michael Jordan's Bulls actually might have welcomed (most of) Dennis's distractions—they had the net effect of making Jordan's public burdens lighter. Why snoop for news about MJ's supposed golf course debts—or Scottie Pippen's publicized domestic problems—when Dennis Rodman was marrying himself at the corner of Michigan and Huron that afternoon? Sportswriters used to speculate that Rodman contrived his theatrics to call remarkable attention to average skills. But his play with

---

★*Bad As I Wanna Be.*

the Bulls suggested that Dennis's flamboyant touches actually obscured his athletic finesse.

However, late in the season, referee Ted Bernhardt called a questionable foul on Rodman in a game against New Jersey. Dennis tucked his hands into the belt line of his shorts, as if to say, "Well, I guess if you're gonna call them like that, I might as well not play." Rodman's character role aggravated the referee—surprise, surprise. It looked like disingenuous disrespect. So Bernhardt compounded one curious foul by calling another one against Rodman—this one for what amounted to bad acting. Dennis ran over to remonstrate—the way Britain remonstrated with Argentina over the Falkland Islands. He took Bernhardt by the elbows and pleaded without response. Then, Dennis nodded his head vigorously—until it butted up against the referee's chin. Suddenly, a small, silly, penalty had led to a stupid, malicious smack in the chin. Rodman was suspended. On his way off the floor, he upended a couple of folding chairs and felled a vat of Gatorade (see, athletes really *do* drink it). The libation ran bright orange as it sluiced and seeped into the floor—so bright, it could have been Dennis's hair coloring agent. But Phil Jackson could be seen along the sidelines, nursing a slow smile. He had been expecting some eruption from Rodman. He regretted that Dennis's target was a referee, but was also glad that it hadn't been, say, Joseph Cardinal Bernardin. It was Jackson's first witness to a real Rodman tantrum, and he felt unexpectedly relieved. His oldest player would get some rest, and perhaps some solace through his six-game suspension. Dennis was also fined $20,000 and called a press conference to apologize to the fans. More to the point, he called Michael Jordan.

Pippen had to miss ten games near the end of the regular season to rest his own wrenched foot—between the Bulls and Olympic teams, he had been playing intense basketball without surcease for nine years. Phil Jackson fretted over all the attention accumulating as the Bulls advanced on the 1969 Los Angeles Lakers record of 69 regular season wins. He was willing to trade finishing shy of that mark for a refreshed Scottie Pippen in the playoffs. Jackson, in fact, had begun to worry that his team might break the record, then break down with post-performance depression. He was willing to lose games, and miss the record, to prepare the team to win the championship. Jackson's lucidity caused some worry at league headquarters. They did not want the glorious season signaling Michael Jordan's return to the full strength of excellence and celebrity to be corrupted by any ugly innuendoes that the Bulls would drop a few games to improve their playoff chances. In the actual event, worry was gratuitous. When Rodman and Pippen pulled up lame, Toni Kukoc stepped in as a starter—and bloomed. He began to average 18 points a game. The Bulls advanced even as they went down. The best player of all-time, the best all-around player of the day, the best rebounder—and now, the best player from Europe, all on the same roster. Jackson decided that his worry about winning too much too soon was a trifling, coaches' caution. If the Bulls fell short of winning the seventy to set a new record, they would have begun the playoffs in disappointment. So instead, they won seventy-two. The most exceptional sight on the night they finished off the Washington Bullets for their last win was Scottie Pippen embracing Dennis Rodman. "I get along with Dennis very well," said Scottie. "We play very well together. We both work very hard for this team." I would observe that sports, like politics, makes strange bedfellows. But Dennis Rodman can make a common cliché singularly dangerous.

The Bulls defeated the Miami Heat in three straight games in the first round of the playoffs; then just dropped one against the nemesis New York Knicks, to win that seven-game series in five. Orlando, which had embarrassed them so much the year before, was next. Shaquille O'Neal was another year poised and experienced and, to say the least, no shorter, lighter, or less imposing. Horace Grant was another year motivated to win a championship against his old team. Penny Hardaway was hearing some of the same questions Michael Jordan had gotten at the beginning of the decade: how long can you really be considered one of the game's great players without winning a championship? And young Nick Anderson, who had gibed at Michael Jordan over his alleged declining speed? The kid was marked like a carton of expired eggs.

The Bulls swept aside the Orlando Magic in four straight games. The geezers routed the Young Guns. Rodman, who was eleven years older, six inches shorter, and eighty-five pounds lighter than Shaquille O'Neal, bedeviled, goaded, and goosed Shaq into stupefaction. It was like watching a woodpecker bewilder a bear. Luc Longley, the 7 foot 2 inch tall Australian the Bulls had signed for greater ballast at the center, would struggle for position beneath the basket, while Rodman unnerved Shaq from behind with love taps, trash talk, and entangling limbs. *Right here, Shaq. Oooh, right with you, baby.* O'Neal would try to lean back against Rodman, as if trying to keep the lid mashed down over a gargoyle; but Dennis would squirm away, reach around, and replant himself against Shaq's back. When a ball came off the board, the gargoyle was usually better positioned than the giant to bring it down. Dennis brought down 16, 18, 19, 20 rebounds against Orlando.

On the Saturday night following the end of the Orlando series, as the Bulls prepared to face the Seattle Supersonics for the championship, I got a small glimpse of Rodman's capacity to be, as Phil Jackson called him, the *heyoka*—the cross-dressing clown "who brings a change in everyone's reality." I had dinner that night at my favorite restaurant.* A friend and I were sitting at an outside table along Clark Street, on a block between the old Criminal Courts building and a transvestite dance club called The Baton. Among gay clubs, The Baton was practically the Old Vic. When I was a young reporter in the 1970s, police officers in the local district who may have been a bit light in their ticket books made a custom of going over to The Baton to, as they phrased it in the day before community relations workshops, *bust fruits.* There was always a patron or two who could be caught, unawares, with their pants down and written up for indecent exposure.

We lingered late on that Saturday night, chatting with our waiter about the Bulls. He was gay, and he told us about the ceremony of watching the Bulls-Magic series in a gay bar nearby. It was to watch, he said, the game within the game: Shaq versus Dennis, the son of a Marine drill sergeant trying to daunt and subdue the cross-dressing clown with his strength and size.

"And did you see? Did you see?" he asked. "The TV,† man, the TV didn't back down! Shaq thought the TV was some kind of weak girly-man, but the TV, the TV man, the TV *kicked his ass*, did you see it? He couldn't put Dennis down! Dennis made Shaq look like a moron! Like he was saying, 'Who is this queer? Why isn't this sissy *a sissy?*' But Dennis, man, the TV was *beautiful.*" †† Dennis Rodman as Jackie Robinson— a credit to his cross-gender. It was a busy spring Saturday night, and Chicago police were deployed a half block away around The Baton— but in the 1990s, merely to supervise an overflow crowd.

Suddenly, that block of Clark Street erupted in festivity, shrieks, laughter, and a high windstorm of smooches. A black, good ole' Texas

---

*Rick Bayless's Frontera Grill and Topolobampo, 445 N. Clark Street. 312-661-1434.

†In this context, a colloquial phrase for transvestite.

††While emotional and entertaining, this assessment is not fair to Shaquille O'Neal, who has always spoken with grudging respect for Dennis Rodman. They were briefly and cordially teammates on the 1999 Los Angeles Lakers.

boy pickup truck had pulled up to The Baton. Dennis Rodman and his friend, Mimi, stepped out. Dennis was stunning in a tight, sleeveless black leather halter, a studded collar, black mesh hose, and high-heeled dancing shoes; the pink triangle and AIDS ribbon in his hair seemed recently refreshed. From around his neck, Rodman unhitched a puce-colored scarf and stirred up the crowd by swirling it over his head. "Dennis! Dennis!" Chicago cops of the kind who used to crack heads among cross-dressers and bust men in bathroom stalls reddened and teared in their duty blues as they bellowed from the sidewalk: "We love you, Dennis! We love you!" In that moment, I was enchanted all over again by Chicago. The city's immense repertoire of human drama and comedy had now developed irony. The City of Broad Shoulders embraces all outlaws and outcasts—especially if they can haul down 19 rebounds against Shaquille O'Neal.

The championship that sealed the 1996 season was won in six games over a much younger team, the Seattle Supersonics. On game nights, a group of Chicagoans Abroad would gather at my apartment to watch and share something we believed to be momentous. This was the Bulls team that would not only enter the record book, but history. This was the team, Jordan, Pippen, and Rodman, whose profile would be struck into the skyline. Wherever Chicagoans Abroad went for a while, the names and notion of these Bulls would win recognition, open doors, summon up an image. *Chicago, you say. Like that crazy guy in the lingerie. Like that nice guy, what's-his-name's best friend. Chicago—Michael Jordan.* When the championship was won, Jordan fell on the ball onto the hard court in a heap, crying. Other players tumbled on top. Watching on that early Sunday night, we went around the living room with hugs and hoots, and even a few tears. At last, Michael was uncovered from the bottom, and an NBC microphone could be held up to his face. "I'm sorry I was away for eighteen months. I'm happy I'm back. And, I'm happy to bring a championship back to Chicago." Back in the locker room, Michael could not stop his tears, could not evade the cameras. He flopped out full, on the locker-room floor, half-under a training table, his 23 upturned. The little red silhouette on the collar of his shoes showed MJ stretched out in flight; the MJ who had just won the championship was stretched out on the floor, in relief, grief, and elation. "I'm glad—I'm sure," he said on rising, "I'm glad—I know—that my father was watching this." Then, he paused to swallow, time-out, catch his breath, bring up one last sentence that had to be said. It was the rare occasion when you wondered if Michael Jordan would complete a play. Then, he said, "This one was for you, Daddy." It was June 16. "Ohmigod," said Smokey. "I almost forgot. It's Father's Day."

Later that summer, the Democratic national convention was held in Chicago. It was the first convention to be held in America's most central city since 1968, when the police had, to put it far too politely, rather spoiled the city's reputation for hospitality. For almost thirty years, both major parties had been reluctant to return to the scene of those crimes. It would aggravate old quarrels. But by 1996, political reformers and old machine pols had more or less compromised each other. There was a reform-minded mayor in place; but he possessed the same name as the old Mayor Daley. Jesse Jackson still led the occasional demonstration; but now, more in the way that Ernie Banks still took a few swings in the batting cage on Opening Day—a beloved civic figure providing a photo op. Some of the people who had been protesters in the park were now on civic boards and planning commissions; even bank boards. When I made an early morning television appearance to reminisce about 1968, I encountered Mayor Richard M. Daley, who had been a guest in a previous segment. Change could be gauged in a thoroughly superficial way: this Mayor Daley's hair was longer than mine.

And by 1996, Jerry Reinsdorf and the Bulls had built the United Center, although, of course, it was really Michael Jordan. The building was surely built to hold a larger paying proportion of the following he had aroused. To build the United Center, they had demolished the old Chicago Stadium, which had hosted numerous political conventions. The United Center was centrally located in America's most central city, shiny, splendid surroundings for a national political convention. But by 1996, convention planners had a new sensitivity. They did not want to nominate candidates in a sports palace encircled by slum housing. It was a sensitivity that the Bulls and Michael Jordan shared, for their own political and social reasons. The team wanted to avoid summoning up the image of people cheering in thousand-dollar courtside seats while nearby, children squirmed in squalor. So, a number of the crumbling buildings on blocks near the United Center had been renovated with the help of a local philanthropic group—the James Jordan Foundation. Michael Jordan had been the reason for building the United Center, and one of the forces behind renovating its environs; and the enhanced surroundings enabled the Democrats to finally return to Chicago. Quite a three-point play.

During a convention session, I had been making my way across the floor when a group of delegates from Ohio stopped me. "Excuse me," said a Cuyahoga County pol, "but maybe you can help us with something." I said I'd try. "Where we're standing now," he asked. "D'ya think this is about where Jordan stands during the National Anthem?" I don't doubt—I confide a bias here—that no matter how many presidents may be nominated over its boards, the United Center will be better remembered as the main stage for Michael Jordan.

The Chicago Bulls had become, once more, the preeminent team in professional sports around the world, and also something more. But as acclaim grew, Jerry Krause got more aggravated at being overlooked. Phil Jackson was lauded for his "handling" of Dennis Rodman (a term Phil himself always resisted, saying, with all the authenticity of his Western roots, "You handle horses. Our players are men"). Krause, who kept careful accounts, felt scarcely congratulated for having the resourcefulness to sign Rodman. Krause had to look on, indignantly, while the tie-dyed Deadhead in scuffed sandals and droopy mustache that Krause believed he had salvaged from vagrancy became celebrated as a bearded metaphysician in fine Italian suits. Krause shared his diminishing enthusiasm for the man he had hired with snide remarks and gently uttered innuendo. Thank God for Michael Jordan, he said, or otherwise there would be no discipline on the team—that Jackson was such a flower child. All those Indian chants and loopy whoopy-doopy. Krause even implied that Jackson had shared the smoking of illicit substances with some of his players. In fact he had—Havana cigars, sent to Jackson by an admirer.

More rationally, Krause believed that the Chicago Bulls had won just about as many championships as they could before the aging team would break down in the stretch. Gamers all, they might eke out one more title with the same starring cast—Michael, Scottie, and Rodman, Luc Longley, Ron Harper, Steve Kerr, and Toni Kukoc. But then they would lose their chance to trade Scottie Pippen while he could bring in maximum value, swapping a depreciating set of limbs for fine young ones. Once, Krause had thought that Jackson would be a good coach for rebuilding a team suddenly bereft of Michael Jordan. But now he felt that Jackson had become tied too closely to Jordan, Pippen, and even Rodman; they were partners in concocting a magic formula called the Chicago Bulls. Krause worried that Jackson would keep trying to contrive the same magic, and that formula worked only because the first ingredient was Jordan. Otherwise, it was a prescription for Zen nonsense. Krause told Reinsdorf that the owner had to be nervy enough to perhaps sacrifice one more championship and trade-in his most success-ful team for improved options in the future. A true dynasty, he reminded Reinsdorf, didn't end with the demise of a king. It continued into the next generation.

Basketball's reigning monarch, Michael Jordan, was finally a free agent; but, of course, scarcely free. His estimated value to his team had gone from colossal to astronomical. Under the league's salary-cap requirements, the Bulls could pay Michael more than any other team—essentially, whatever they wanted to afford. That was the design of the game's labor agreement: allow players to make their own best deal every few years, but give incentive for stars to remain in the cities with which they were identified. After seven years, a somewhat larger proportion of the extraordinary wealth Jordan had brought to the Bulls could finally be awarded directly to him. It was useless for most any other team even to make a phone call—unless a Swiss bank wanted to start a basketball team. A team like the Charlotte Hornets could pay Jordan as much as the Bulls only if they intended to play with Jordan on the court alone.

But New York was—always is—a different case. Dave Checketts, the head of the Madison Square Garden corporation, which owns the New York Knicks, contacted Jordan's agent to say he saw a signal in the extraordinary performances Jordan seemed to save for the Garden—a New York native who bloomed under the city's bright, star-spangled lights. Now imagine, he said, playing *forty games a year* under those lights. If Michael ever wondered what there was left for him to achieve, Mr. Checketts had the answer: being a star in New York. "Now, we can only pay so much in straight salary," he essentially told Jordan's agent. "But we are prepared to be immensely creative in figuring out other avenues for compensation. Let me make this plain: money is not an issue. There is no need to negotiate about money. You can have any amount of money you name. The only question is: Michael, how would you like to play in New York?"

The reply from Michael's agent, David Falk, was delivered with surprising speed. It was, of course, no. *Thank you*, but no. Michael felt he could win several more championships with the Bulls. He wanted to be remembered as a star who spent a career building a string of cham-pionships for a city, not a hired gun who went to the highest bidder. Besides, he said to his agent, *I couldn't do that to Chicago.* Chicago's fans might understand if he chose to end his career with a year or two of curtain calls back home in North Carolina. But not in Gomorrah. Michael Jordan loved playing in New York—but he also loved being able to fly back home to Chicago. His children were Chicago kids, and Michael himself had become the face of Chicago to the world. What he loved most about New York was *beating* it.

It would be sentimental nonsense to read something noble into a man who has all the money in the world declining more. But the story does suggest that money was not Jordan's way of keeping score. MJ signed for somewhat more than thirty million dollars. But it seemed to cause him little exuberance. Just as Jerry Reinsdorf was adding his signature, the owner exclaimed in front of David Falk, "I hope I don't live to regret this." An owner of greater graciousness might have mustered the pluck to say something more like, "This is a great moment for me." But it was Jerry Reinsdorf. A player of greater magnanimity might have figured that any man paying him thirty million dollars has earned the right to express a little fretfulness. If Jordan turned an ankle in the shower that night, after all, the contract he had just signed would rank as one of the most expensive bad investments since Alexander Haig's presidential campaign. But Jordan was not the kind of man to shrug off an insult when he could *use it* to fuel his competitive fires.

Reinsdorf and Krause (*The Jerries* became an inevitable and inviting nickname) saw the Bulls as a club that, despite their title and attainments, had already passed a crest and were in decline. The 1996 championship season was impeccable. But in winning two games, Krause thought Seattle had tugged on the weakest seams holding the Bulls' lineup together. At times, Seattle had made the Bulls look old; another year would make them no younger. Reinsdorf and Krause worried that the Bulls' immense popularity would hamper them from trading several players—Pippen for sure, and perhaps Harper and Kerr—before they faded too much to bring in maximum value. Fans clamored for the return of Dennis Rodman. But how much money did the team want to tie up in a thirty-six-year-old rebounder?

At best, what Reinsdorf and Krause proposed was simply standard business practice in basketball; and in a sense, players had only themselves to blame. Free agency, which the players union had fought to win and had made so many players rich, was also what gave owners the incentive to trade their best players while they could still earn in return a player of equal or superior ability. If the team waited until good players ran out their contracts, an owner would be stuck with nothing to show for the club's years of investment.

Winning increased profits, but it also inflated the payroll. You had to reward your employees with pay raises, emolliments, and incentives, which, year after year, the Bulls met and exceeded. Pay raises increased operating costs, and *that* reduced profits. So while the Bulls won championships, year after year, they were paying more and more money to achieve the same result. This is not generally considered a sound business practice.

Professional athletics has become big business. But business principles are not always soundly applied to sports. Trading some of the members of a successful team may make sense for a club that's struggling to find the formula to win a first championship. But for a team in the middle of a championship run, the tactic sounds unsportsmanlike—even dishonest. Teams play to win, not lose. That certitude gives sports integrity. Fans cheer for victories, not profits. Ownership that tries to bust up a championship team that hasn't lost doesn't seem too distant morally from players who throw games for money. Imagine what would be said of a player who deliberately missed a critical shot and said, "I knew we were going to lose at some point. So I thought I might as well get it over with now, and start the rebuilding process." The Bulls' players knew the new math of sports. They were, after all, businessmen as well as athletes, rich men with investments who were conversant about assets and losses. But in the crunch, they were union, not management. The players had a fierce, sentimental desire to stay together until someone beat them. It was an instinct instilled from the time they had all played in boyhood pickup games—winners play again, play until darkness, play until they're all called home. Even as sly a buccaneer as Dennis Rodman, who had seen his career rejuvenated just in time to become a free agent, was guileless when asked, in the first ecstatic moments on the floor after he helped win the 1996 title, if he wanted to sign with the Bulls or move on for more money. The truly shrewd answer would have been, "We'll see." Instead, Dennis Rodman fixed his face in a hard frown, like a six-year-old boy who does not want to be peeled off the merry-go-round. "I want to stay right here," said Dennis. "I want to stay right here, with Michael and Scottie."

Jerry Krause's resolve to dismantle and remake the Bulls while they were still champions may have been composed of both sound reasoning and resentment. What's striking is what little regard he conferred on fans. Of course, fan appeal was not in Krause's portfolio. The fan of last resort was Reinsdorf himself, who ultimately paid to keep the team together past the point that Krause had urged. But Jerry Krause simply seemed to give no heed to how important the Michael-Scottie-Dennis edition of Bulls had become in our everyday lives. We saw more of the torments and triumphs of the Bulls, close-up, than we did of all but a few of our close friends and family. Not a day passed without some news of Michael, Scottie, Dennis. It was a little upsetting, as well as affecting, to realize that the Bulls had become family names in a city of disconnected, often rivalrous souls. Once, when Scottie was recovering from a foot injury, my stepfather, the atheist, wryly confided, "I've been praying for Pippen's health more than I ever have for my own."

I do not have much of a feeling for public opinion. I voted for John Anderson; I thought he would win. I actually liked the New Coke. I belong to a religious society with fewer members than the number of people who believe they have been abducted by aliens. And yet, I am sure that fans would have rather watched this group of men stay together, play, grow old, and eventually lose, than see a collection of young strangers in red uniforms try to live up to the name Jordan, Pippen, and Rodman had made for the Bulls.

But while management looked for an opportunity to take them apart, the Bulls continued to win together—maybe just to be contrary. In fact, Jackson and Jordan seemed to use the estrangement of management as an instrument of inspiration. The Bulls had beaten the Pistons, the Knicks, the Lakers, and the Sonics. They had won a place of esteem alongside the old Celtics. They had displaced the Yankees and perhaps even Mickey Mouse in universal appeal. But they had one last adversary. When players saw the banner that ran across a wall in their training site—WE WILL DEFEND WHAT IS OURS—they often made a mental, motivating addendum: EVEN FROM OUR OWN MANAGEMENT.

The Bulls began the first defense of their second sequence of championships by winning their first twelve games. They ended the regular season just three victories short of their historic total the previous year. If Dennis Rodman had not been suspended for eleven games for kicking a cameraman whom he blamed for being too close beneath the basket; if Rodman had not missed the last thirteen games of the season with a sprained knee, the Bulls might have done even better yet—a redoubtable achievement for an aging team that all other teams had devoted themselves to defeating. The Bulls were two games up on the

Washington Bullets* in the first round of the playoffs when the phone rang in my office and Luc Longley invited me to that night's game.

Number 13 had read that I was a fan and that I was a Quaker. He thought that meeting might promote my interest in the former while feeding some of his curiosity about the latter. The Bulls surged ahead in the last two minutes to secure the victory that would send them into the next round of the playoffs, and Luc slipped out of the locker room to meet and make arrangements for an after-game dinner. I was prepared, of course, for the fact that Luc was tall. Friends and I stood chatting on the ramp leading down from the stands, while Luc stood below on the level of the court; we were just about face-to-face. Reading about the Bulls had also prepared me for his famous amiability—the adjective *affable* usually seemed to trail *tall* and *Australian* in quotes. But I was not prepared for Luc's sharp, deadpan sense of humor, his lively mind, and a quality of friendliness that exceeded mere amiability.

I had been told that Luc preferred small places with character to the usual watering holes in which sports figures seemed to gather. I offered him options. There was an after-hours Italian place on Connecticut Avenue, I said, where the spy, Jonathan Pollard, used the pay phone to call the Israeli Embassy to set up drop-offs. Then, there was a late-night Salvadoran pupusa-and-margarita joint on Florida Avenue. "I was there just a few weeks ago," I told Luc. "The food isn't bad and I was almost shot to death by a man who said he thinks Scottie Pippen is a putz." Luc pondered for a moment. "Well, mate," he said brightly, "sounds like Salvadoran to me." When we arrived, a television set mounted in the corner was still tuned to the channel that had carried the game. Heads turned to see a figure on the screen walk into their real lives, more than seven feet tall.

The proprietor beamed, and scrambled after a stack of splotched menus. "Congratulations, Toni," he said to Luc.

"No, mate," said Luc cheerfully, "I'm the other white guy." When we sat down, he rubbed some scratches on his tremendous hands and talked about the business part of being a center. Much of it was the unglamorous application of blunt force—planting his 7 feet 2 inches on a square foot of prime real estate beneath the basket before someone else could. While Michael and Scottie danced and dazzled along the arcs away from the basket, Luc was slammed, bumped, and battered by simi-

---

*Now, of course, renamed the Washington Wizards.

larly immense players aspiring to hold down the same place. And if they did, Luc's job was to reclaim it. Trying to move a brick wall with your shoulder, inch by inch—that's what Luc Longley's work sounded like to an outsider. *Except that the brick wall often struck back.* He had an interesting background for such blunt work. His father, Richard Longley, was an architect of considerable distinction. His mother, Susan Hansen, was an educator. His uncle, John Longley, was a venerable sailor, a champion America's Cup skipper. Luc's size led him to basketball. Soccer and rugby are more popular games in Australia. Long legs (an early nickname was *Luc Longlegs*) in those sports can just lend an opponent more inches of opportunity for attack. But in basketball, extensive legs can be commanding pivots. If not for basketball, Luc thought he would have become a marine biologist. He was from Freemantle, near Perth, a sailing and surf, Indian Ocean city, and in the off-season would repair to a farm where he explored reefs, rode waves, and made commercials for Australian companies that exploited both his exceptional size and striking amiability (one took Quantas Airlines' claim to have more commodious seats seriously if the seats could accommodate Luc Longley). It was Luc's sturdy affability, as well as his size, that made him the best man on court to back down Dennis Rodman when he seemed set to erupt. Size, obviously, counted. But so did Luc's capacity for camaraderie, when he stepped in front of Dennis to walk him away from a showdown. *Awright now, Dennis, easy now, mate, laugh it off, matey.*

At dinner, I wanted to talk about the Bulls. Luc seemed more interested in Quakers. Graciously, he accommodated. Pippen was ailing, and Luc was concerned. Scottie, he said, was the flywheel that made it possible for Michael to drive the works so gloriously. Dennis? He wore you down with demands and distractions, and won you back with blandishments and charm—until the next time. Dennis would descend on his friends and urge them to fly off with him to Pearl Jam concerts and late-night revels. Most coaches would probably react with reflexive rejection and dread, and shout at his players, "Stay away from Rodman and his crazy schemes!" But Phil Jackson was actually encouraged by Rodman's instincts for gregariousness. He thought it knitted Dennis into the team's loving circle and may have even slightly restrained some of his most destructive inspirations. Dennis regarded restaurant, bar, and club tabs as rebounds—he got unhappy if one bounced away, unclaimed. Once, he had organized an outing to a gay bar and told the owner he wanted to pick up the check for all. When it was delivered, Dennis's companions were appalled—the owner had charged him for every customer of the evening. Let us help you out,

Dennis, they said, and Rodman waved them off. No, no, you guys are my friends, you make me look good. Well, Dennis, they said, not every son of a bitch in this place is your friend. Let us help. And Dennis replied, No, no, they're my fans. *They make me look good, too.*

Luc said the one question he got more than any other was—well, come to think of it, that would have to be, "What's Michael Jordan really like?" But that aside, since he had soared up in high school, the one question he got more than any other, often from shy, giggling girls (but not so shy they wouldn't ask it) was, "Are you . . . you know . . . *in proportion?*" Luc liked to stop a moment before answering. "Oh, no mate," he would say. "No way. If I was in proportion, I'd be *ten feet* tall."

I asked Luc if the enthusiasm of fans ultimately meant much to the players. Of course, he said. The applause and ebullience in a friendly arena created a kind of harmonic convergence. The happy hum lifted up all the home-team players. And on the road? Even more interesting, said Luc. You learned to use boos for the same fuel as cheers. There was a man in Washington noted for standing up in his $200 seat behind the visitors' bench and asserting his constitutional right to be an ass by bleating profane and defamatory remarks about the visitors. To borrow from A. J. Liebling, freedom of speech belongs to the man who can afford to buy season tickets. Was it really surprising that the man was a local lawyer and state legislator? But, Luc said, the Bulls blocked out his bleating like the blast of a burglar alarm. Or, they used the edge of irritation it gave them for a jolt of added determination. "It's gorgeous," said Luc, "to score and hear the cheers die in their bloody throats."★

Thanks to Luc, I was able to add some of that harmonic convergence myself, at close range. I attended the second game of the 1997 championship series, sitting next to Luc's mother and her husband. I took along my mother, telling her she should not live in the same city as Michael Jordan without ever once seeing him play basketball. We sat just behind a staggeringly beautiful woman and her two small children (their nanny, too, was staggeringly beautiful), who scrambled about in their seats during the happy clamor before the tip-off. The commissioner of basketball came over to pay his respects. The Reverend Jesse Jackson came over to offer his. Clowns, ushers, and the red-suited mascot, Benny the Bull, came over bearing small toys, noisemakers, and

---

★The next year, the Bullets began play in their new arena downtown as the Washington Wizards. The boor with expensive seats, attorney Robin Ficker, decided to give up his tickets; much to the relief of the Wizards' gentlemanly owner, Abe Polin.

candy. My mother was acquiring a highly favorable impression of professional basketball. One of the little girls turned around to introduce her top-hatted frog toy. She had Karl Malone's face under her pigtails—an unexpectedly handsome look on a young girl. It was, of course, Karl Malone's family. The Utah Jazz star, known as "The Mailman" for his all-weather reliability, had just won the league's Most Valuable Player award. He deserved it. But the decision was not well-received in Chicago, where Michael Jordan was held to have a lifetime lock on the honor. Each time Malone came to the foul line, the United Center stands roiled with derisive jeers. When he missed (and Malone missed quite a few in those first two games in Chicago; Scottie Pippen, a friend from the last U.S. Olympic basketball team, at one point whispered close to Malone's ear, "Mailman don't deliver on Sunday," and so, on that critical shot, he did not) the din grew greater. One of his little girls sat back in her front row seat, her eyes upturned, wide and shiny: old enough to know that it was her father being showered with unforgiving boos, but not old enough to comprehend that it was meant with no malice. I wondered what contemporary parenting book prepares you to reassure children that 30,000 people booing your father was not a thing to distress. Luc's mother had a more practical touch. With wise hands, she diverted the little girls with a noisemaker.

I won't boo. Well, maybe if Slobodan Milošević came onto the court, but no one in a basketball uniform. The worst player in any kind of game opens him or herself to an unmerciful exposure that earns at least a fan's silent respect. I admired Mrs. Malone's composure as she sat, pointedly unperturbed; and was vexed by my fellow fans booing so close by. At the same time, Luc's mother and her husband and Mrs. Malone traded small talk: about children, arenas they both liked or disdained, restaurants on the road to seek out or avoid, executives who were to be trusted or despised. Luc was a Bull, I was a Bulls' fan; Mrs. Malone's husband was one of the Bulls' most venerable adversaries. But Mrs. Malone and Luc's mother were on the same team. They were members of a company no fan could join. One day, their relatives might be teammates. But in a way, they already were—they knew risks and tests that were impenetrable to a fan. I was flattered to sit alongside Luc's family. But I did not flatter myself to think that being a fan, or even a friend, ran as deep as the kind of familiarity Luc could share with an opponent like Karl Malone.

The Bulls went out to Salt Lake City ahead in the series and riding a high tide of speculation about whether management would keep them together if they won. Reinsdorf took Jackson to lunch where the Bulls had holed up in the secular resort town of Park City, Utah. Reinsdorf told Jackson he respected all he had achieved and was grateful. But Jerry Krause had determined, and Reinsdorf had agreed, that it might be *time to go in a different direction*, as they all began to phrase it. Rebuild before they could be beaten. Shop Pippen, ship Rodman, swap the likes of Longley and Kerr while championships still swelled their trade value. Jackson's contract was running out. Reinsdorf said he understood that a coach with so many championship rings on his fingers might not want to stay around to preside over such diminished assets. Reinsdorf said he liked Jackson personally; he didn't want an aggravated round of negotiations that would only harden resentments. He said that he also appreciated the enormous popularity Jackson had earned in Chicago and didn't want Phil to feel he had to quickly accept another coaching offer in a rival city, just to make his house and car payments. If Jackson decided to step out quietly, to pursue some of his wide-ranging interests—write a book, repair to an ashram, run for office, tutor students on an Indian reservation, or just read, reflect, and heal—Reinsdorf was prepared to express his gratitude materially. A payment of a million dollars was mentioned—if Jackson agreed to keep it secret.

The offer alone was a measure of the eminence an old Deadhead now enjoyed among the ranks of coaches—Jackson was offered more money *not* to coach for a single season than all the money he had earned in thirteen seasons of actually playing basketball. But Reinsdorf's solicitude was clever as well as generous. Michael Jordan's one-year contract was due to expire, too. He had said he wanted to play only for Jackson. You might have to cast back to Neville Chamberlain in 1939 to find an example of how grave a miscalculation it could be to drive Phil Jackson away from the Bulls—and perhaps onto the bench of the New York Knicks or Los Angeles Lakers, who would welcome Jackson's staunch and unfailing friend, Michael Jordan. So Jerry Reinsdorf had a compelling interest in keeping Jackson on the reservation until Jordan was finally and convincingly retired.

Reinsdorf said he did not expect an answer by dessert. He merely wanted to exchange information. But both men knew that if the Bulls were defeated by Utah, no further exchanges would be necessary. Jerry Krause's doubts would be vindicated, and the dismantling of the Bulls could proceed without being diverted by another world championship.

The next night, Michael Jordan arrived for work at Salt Lake City's Delta Center walking carefully, like a man trying to step across a gravel road in his bare feet. He had a temperature, perhaps a stomach virus. The night before, he had ordered a room-service pizza, and the topping—clams, reportedly—had taken their revenge (one rule of the road: "Never order clams in a land-locked state"). Jordan had slept only in brief fits between bouts of nausea. Arriving for the game, MJ's bones felt brittle, and his skin, which usually shined with extraordinary tone of polished ebony, looked dull; it had the color of cooled ash. In the locker room, Jordan stretched out on a training table, a plastic bucket by his side. It seemed a night to suffer and sweat in a warm bed, not a basketball court. His teammates doubted he could play. Then, they took into account his extraordinary will, and decided, maybe he can play a few minutes. But no more. They had looked on while Michael took several minutes just to lace up his Air Jordans—one of the most graceful men in the world, fatigued just to tie his shoelaces. When the game began, MJ was sluggish, tentative, and tender. But he persisted for 44 minutes, although hitting less than half his shots. Utah surged ahead by 16 points in the second quarter; but Jordan led the charge back, drawing fouls, and sinking 10 of those 12 shots. With 25 seconds left, Jordan sank a three-point shot that put the Bulls ahead for good, 90 to 88. He scored 38 points in all, playing in spurts between waves of exhaustion, dizziness, and nausea. Almost more amazingly, he also hauled down seven rebounds. As the game horn blared, MJ finally faltered as he struggled to walk off the court, falling back into Scottie Pippen's embrace, and resting his head on Scottie's shoulder. *Hold me up, Scottie!* MJ declined the post-game press conference, but told reporters as he headed out, back to bed, "I feel better now that we won." And Utah coach Jerry Sloan, the old Bull, ran an eye over the printed sheet of game statistics and then asked the press, with more than a touch of acerbity, "Was he sick? I didn't know that he was sick. Was he sick? I couldn't tell."

The series returned to Chicago with the Bulls a game ahead. But the series was closer than what even that small advantage indicated. The Jazz were as mature in execution as the Bulls, and even as powerfully motivated. But for setbacks here and there that had turned them back from titles, Karl Malone and John Stockton might have won some of the same status as Jordan and Pippen. They were even as old and felt that their time to win had arrived—they had to claim their championship now. They began the sixth game in a storm of fast breaks that the Bulls could not blunt; Utah led by ten points into the second quarter. But then Pippen, Steve Kerr, and Jud Buechler began to ring in three-point shots. The game was tied at 86, with 28 seconds left, when Jackson called a time-out and sketched out a plan for a final possession that called for the ball to come in to Michael Jordan. You were expecting Jud Buechler? As the Bulls sweated and idled on the bench, waiting for the horn to call them back onto the court, MJ clasped a towel around his neck and gulped at a waxed cup of Gatorade. He was sitting at the end of bench just across from Steve Kerr; which seemed to give him an idea.

"This is your chance," he told Steve. "I know that Stockton is going to come off of you. If he does, be ready. I'm going to come to you." And Steve, a man who is usually comically modest about his abilities, looked over, locked eyes with Jordan, and pumped his thumbs back at his own chest. "I'll be ready," Kerr told Jordan. "Get the ball to me, and I'll knock it down." By percentage, Steve was the best long-range shooter in the league. But no other player in league history had sunk as many last-second shots under paramount pressure as Michael Jordan. Steve was the man they asked to rain down long-range shots when the Bulls needed to come from behind, not nail down a win at the end. Six seconds left, sixth game of the world championships—*a helluva time to begin,* thought Steve. As the Bulls trooped back onto the court, Kerr felt a twinge of rubber strike his knees. Suddenly, usefully, he wasn't worried so much about sinking the shot as disappointing Jordan's confidence. He thought, *This is the one thing Michael Jordan has ever asked of me.* Zenlike, Steve decided to stop thinking and give himself over to the moment. See how Zen can creep in, almost on little cat feet?

Pippen passed the ball into Jordan; sure enough, he was surrounded. MJ held up for a moment, dribbling, saw a flash of sunshine to the right, and began to drive. Bryon Russell stopped him short. MJ pulled back, as if to regroup for another drive and possibly try to draw a foul. Instead, he drew over John Stockton, just as he had imagined. Jordan held a stare on Stockton, but saw Steve Kerr floating just inside the three-point line, looking as unguarded and free as a traveling salesman out for an after-dinner stroll. Jordan snapped the ball over from his fingertips. Steve took it in his palms. With 5.9, 5.8 seconds tolling down, the hoop looming sixteen feet away, Steve Kerr wheeled around to leap and shoot. The ball sank as straight as an anchor pulling down an iron chain. Bulls by two. I was with a friend in stands high up in the third tier of the United Center, from which it was hard to see the shot hit home. But along the Bulls' bench, you could see tall men begin to bounce and embrace as the Jazz called a time-out and the United Center swelled with applause and cries. Bryon Russell tried to pass the back ball in for

Utah. But Scottie Pippen, sensing an unusual chance, launched himself at the pass and knocked it down while falling to the floor. With great presence of mind, Scottie then reached out and nudged the interrupted ball toward Toni Kukoc, who coaxed it up with his long fingers, passed it into his right hand, then hung the ball up over the basket, from where it dropped through the net as the game horn blared. 90-86—*gimme five!*★

A friend gave us a lift back downtown, and over his car radio we listened to Michael Jordan hold forth at the post-game press conference. There seemed more apprehension in his mood than exuberance. From the first, reporters wanted to know if he wanted the team back, all of it, for another run. Jordan answered like a victorious general who worried that politicians on high would give away what his men had won on the ground. He managed to be deferential, while implying defiance.

"Well, it's not up to me," he told reporters. "I can't tell you what will happen, or even what my plans will be. I have to sit down with Jerry, with others, and talk that out. But I feel, I think many of us feel, that we have earned the right to come back and *defend* what is *ours*, for the entire city of Chicago."

Strategically, it was a commanding response. It held Jerry Reinsdorf personally responsible for civic tranquillity. A bit surprisingly, Jordan then endorsed Dennis Rodman. Dennis had not had a distinguished series, which had heightened pressure on Jordan to spend some of his own leg strength on rebounds. Rodman's technical fouls, on several occasions, had put the Bulls down at disadvantageous times. But with victory gained, MJ said, "I like playing with Dennis Rodman.

---

★Sinking the shot that put the Bulls ahead made Steve Kerr a champion in the annals of Chicago sports. But it was the story he told about that shot two days later at the celebration in Grant Park that made Steve a civic favorite. As he told the story:

Coach Jackson called for a play that would, naturally, work the last shot into Michael Jordan.

"But, Coach," Steve told the crowd he cautioned Jackson, "I don't know if you've seen Michael's commercials, but he misses a lot of those shots."

(Indeed, Nike had run a commercial throughout the finals in which Jordan cited all the times he had taken a last shot—and missed.)

As the crowd—Jordan most prominently—howled, Kerr continued with his account of Jackson's reaction:

" 'Good point. Maybe Scottie should take the shot.' Well, we all looked over at Scottie, and he said, 'No way, man, I don't want to take a shot like that.'

"So, finally, I said, 'Well, okay, Coach, I guess I have to bail out Michael once again.' " Steve's shot got him onto sports highlights all over the world. But his story about the shot got him booked as a guest on David Letterman's show.

I don't care what kind of women's clothes he wears, or how he wears his hair, what kind of crazy things he does. There is no one who gives more on the court, who plays harder, than Dennis Rodman." A few days later, I was told that Dennis had returned to play in the playoffs and finals although he had not fully recovered from his knee injury. A man who had put his bare derriere in full color on the cover of a book had kept news of his sore joint to himself. Dennis had risked inflaming an injury that could cut short his career to come back to defend a championship. Underneath the indelible tattoos and lacy lingerie, Rodman had the kind of fortitude Jordan admired.

Reporters then asked what he thought about the concern of management that the Bulls needed to be rebuilt before they gave out.

"Rebuild?" said Jordan. "I don't understand all this talk about rebuilding. What's so great about rebuilding. I mean, haven't the Cubs been rebuilding for something like forty-three years?" Actually, it was closer to fifty. In my friend's car, we laughed as we heard Jordan's observation and cheered his bewilderment. In the Loop ahead, office towers had turned on crowns of red lights in the tops of skyscrapers. We saw people stopping in the streets, looking up, jumping, pointing—for a moment, I wondered if they thought they were seeing a UFO. Along Michigan Avenue, couples were stopping to gaze up at the lights like some new constellation. Fathers and mothers were hoisting amazed sons and daughters onto their shoulders to trace the necklace of red lights glistening against the silken black sky. "See it, pal? D'ya see it? That's for the Bulls. Every year, when they win, that's what they do. They say, Yea, Bulls!" Perhaps the city's skyscrapers should be lit up similarly every time another University of Chicago professor wins a Nobel Prize. But absent that almost annual event, the occasions for civic celebrations over sports had been so meanly spaced, you wondered why the men who ran a team called *The Best—Ever—Anywhere* would seem so eager to shut off those lights, dim the amazement, and hurry on back into normalcy.

Luc and his family spent much of the summer back in Australia. He made a few more commercials and helped lead a demonstration against clear-cutting in an old growth forest near his farm, spending the night on a platform up in an ancient tree—a sequoia in a sequoia. While Luc lounged among acorns, and Jordan, Pippen, and Rodman made a new round of commercials, Jerry Reinsdorf's other sports franchise, the Chicago White Sox, received the treatment Jerry Krause had sought to dispense to the Bulls.

The Sox were just three and a half games behind the Cleveland Indians in the Central Division when Reinsdorf traded away their best pitchers, Alex Fernandez and Wilson Alvarez. He declared, "Anyone who thinks we were going to catch Cleveland is crazy." The White Sox, he said, striking a familiar phrase, needed rebuilding. Perhaps they did. Cleveland was, year in and out, the most successful American League Central team of the 1990s. But to fans and players, Jerry Reinsdorf's trades violated the balance wheel of sports. You could no longer rely on the White Sox playing to win. To borrow a phrase, *Anyone who came out to catch their games was crazy.* I sent Luc newspaper clips to his farm in Australia and a note: if Jerry Reinsdorf wanted so much to rebuild something, he was welcome to rebuild my kitchen. A few weeks later, Luc called. "Get one of those French things," he advised—Luc owned a restaurant in New Mexico—"the stove with the bright enamel finish. I mean, if Jerry's footing the bill."

Jackson's contract had expired a month after they won the 1997 championship. He had taken the thoughtful precaution of cleaning out his office. But a few real-life Indian artifacts remained at the Bulls' training center while his agent jousted with Jerry Krause. Jackson had always gotten on better with Jerry Reinsdorf. They were two articulate men, in contrary ways, who disagreed so plainly about so much they could be amiable about their differences. Once, Jackson recollected, Reinsdorf had asked, "What do you think motivates men, Phil? I think it's greed or fear." And Phil spoke up in a soft, friendly way. "Jerry," he said. "I think it's love and pride." Jerry Krause was Jerry Reinsdorf's man, but Reinsdorf was his own. In the end, Krause was a payroll employee, too.

Reinsdorf agreed that Jackson was standing in the way of rebuilding the Bulls; but Jackson's absence would stand in the way of retaining Michael Jordan. Reinsdorf, who had made a fortune in commercial real estate, was shrewd enough to know when he had to meet another man's price. Jordan had taken the extraordinary step of letting himself be quoted on personnel, telling reporters that if he owned the Bulls (and someday he might) he would pay himself $50 million, Phil Jackson another $50 million, Dennis Rodman $25 million—and Scottie Pippen $75 million. Maybe they're all worth more, said Michael, "but I'm on a tight budget." Of course, the amounts were absurd. But they revealed the relative value Jordan placed on his colleagues, ranking Phil Jackson just alongside himself, and Scottie Pippen above all. The amounts *were* absurd, he acknowledged. But you know what was amazing? Reinsdorf could pay them all and *still* make money. *That's* how successful the Bulls were. *Check, mate.* So Reinsdorf flew out to Montana to see Jackson at his ranch.

Jackson appreciated the gesture; and was amused by Reinsdorf's opening. "Phil, don't you understand?" he said. Reinsdorf explained that each new championship sent him into Tiffany's, where he had to buy a new set of championship rings that had to bulge with more gold and glitter than last year's—or, the year's before. And then the wives and mothers expected matching pendants, because they had gotten them once or twice before. And then, a row of rank and file employees would stand outside of Reinsdorf's office to demand pay raises because they sold tickets and cleaned windows for the world champion Chicago Bulls. "So Phil," Reinsdorf said finally, laughing, "if you just lost once— just once, just one year—you'd save me a lot of money."

"Well, Jerry," said Jackson, laughing back. "You're the businessman." There was not much basis for small talk between them; Reinsdorf came quickly to the critical question. Phil, just tell me this, he said. "Can this team win another championship?" And Jackson said, "Yes, Jerry, I think they can."

Under duress and direct order, Jerry Krause re-signed Jackson to one more year. But, on the explicit understanding it would be Jackson's last. To prevent Jerry Reinsdorf's complaisance from being misread as warmth, Krause snapped at Jackson, "I don't care if you're eighty-two and zero—you're fucking *gone* from here next year." Jackson was more circumspect in explaining the understanding to reporters. "I assured Jerry (Krause) that I would walk out at the end of the season," said Jackson, "and he assisted me in that belief." Krause had already sent videotapes of practices to Tim Floyd, the coach at Iowa State he had been preparing to replace Jackson. It was an open cuckolding. Jackson considered practice something akin to confession: a confidential relationship between coaches and players, in which each was permitted to vent frustrations, share fears, and make mistakes. Sending those tapes to a stranger violated what Jackson considered a confidential, consecrated relationship between players and their coach. "Hey, what can I say?" he mused one afternoon in his office. "Jerry (Krause) falls in love with people. I know. He used to be in love with me."

Reinsdorf, Krause, and the Bulls were antagonists in what amounted to a casebook conflict between labor and management. The laborers (albeit millionaires almost all) believed that they produced the goods that created value. But management reminded them that, however exceptional their wages, the players were ultimately payroll employees who worked at somebody else's pleasure.

Jordan signed another one-year contract and reminded Reinsdorf of his thoughtless remark the year before; it probably earned the owner's unexceptional assent to a pay raise. Krause tried to shop Pippen once again. It was the last year of Scottie's contract, and the team's last chance to acquire something in trade for a talent they had helped develop. But Pippen had become *so* accomplished and experienced, there was no single or duo of players on any other team to match his value as Michael Jordan's co-star. So Scottie stayed; but he had foot surgery just before training camp and would miss much of the first part of the season. Rodman was even re-signed. He was offered a basic contract for just below a million dollars, but it was enlivened with incentives—extra money for winning another rebounding title, extra money for not drawing technical fouls—that could boost his pay to $9 million. The contract was a compromise, perhaps, between Reinsdorf's belief that men were motivated by greed, and Jackson's conviction that they were inspired by pride. Luc called just as training camp opened. "We got our team back, mate," he said. "We got back our team." I was a bit abashed to admit to myself how much I had begun to feel that way, too. Me, a fan; with no rights in this matter.

*Chapter 12*

# THE LAST DANCE

There will always be those who believe that Donald Duck could coach a team with Jordan, Pippen, and Rodman to a championship. Perhaps. But could Donald Duck bring them back again—and again? And then, again? There are coaches and managers who fire up a team for a season, two seasons, or three. But thereafter, the fires they fuel with rage and fulmination can scald—and burn out.

Mike Ditka may have been that kind of football coach. Less nobly, Billy Martin was that kind of baseball manager. Pat Riley may be that kind of basketball coach. Business groups pay him tens of thousands of dollars to talk about winning. But, coaching the Los Angeles Lakers, New York Knicks, and Miami Heat, Riley won only one playoff series against the gentler (in image, anyway) Phil Jackson.★ Does anyone deprecate Pat Riley's coaching by saying that Donald Duck could coach a team with Magic Johnson and Kareem Abdul-Jabbar to a championship? Accomplished coaches can coax episodic greatness out of players who are more commonly mediocre. Phil Jackson's achievement has

---

★Yes, the close one in 1994 in which Michael Jordan did not play.

been to inspire some of the best players in the world to achieve something more, year after year—to win when they have already won. Win not just to win, but to be something better.

Once, when I was interviewing Jackson, he quoted himself as having uttered a curse word. He asked me not to write it down. Growing up as a Pentecostal preacher's kid in North Dakota, he said, he had been urged at the point of a strap not to swear. His father took it as a sign of disrespect—not to himself, but to God. The coach still flinched on hearing himself curse away from the basketball court. Jackson said he had to teach himself how to swear, after learning as a statewide high school basketball star that coarse language was the poetry of sports. Polite, noncombustible language was his day-to-day prose. But he knew the importance of bursts of poetry. "For example," he said. "If I say to a player, 'Son, your deportment troubles me. To what do you owe it?' I'll get only a stare. But if I grab at his jersey and say, 'What the @!*&! are you doing out there?' they know that my intentions are serious."

(Jackson, by all accounts, has progressed from a student of profanity to a master. I once casually mentioned Jackson's reticence about swearing to Steve Kerr. Steve sounded stunned. "Phil had to teach himself how to swear?" he asked. "Well," said Steve, confiding a touch of his academic background, "he certainly applied himself.")

Jackson's fans admired his sense of proportion. He spoke openly of love and compassion, rather than blood and guts. He did not confuse basketball with war, religion, or even true love. Once, I told Jackson about Eugene McCarthy's old remark about football coaches—that they had to be intelligent enough to understand the game, but dumb enough to think the game was important. He laughed, and reached for a pad of paper. "McCarthy said that?" He picked up a pen. "What was that again?"

And yet, his fans should not underrate his intensity. As a preacher's son, Jackson had kept waiting for the Holy Spirit to move within him, take over, give speech to his skeptical tongue. Instead, by the age of twelve and thirteen, he felt *nothing*. But Jackson had already grown taller than six feet by the time he entered high school. 6 feet 1 inch, 6 feet 3 inches, then 6 feet 6 inches. Basketball gave an opening not only to his energy, but his fervor. He didn't reject faith, but found another. "I stopped going to services," he said, "and started working on my jump shot." Jackson's delivery into basketball had some of the signs of rapture.

Jackson declined to see personal affront in circumstances other coaches would take as a challenge to their authority. His refusal to treat

Scottie Pippen's sitting episode as a personal slap kept Pippen on the team. It might have even improved Pippen's performance, and enlarged his sense of loyalty. When I once tried to draw out Jackson to talk about locker-room speeches, he offered that most orations were routine and uninspiring—X's and O's. "But Michael, you know, I'm not really sure he's ever heard one of mine." Michael Jordan, he explained, suffered from a sensitive stomach. He usually spent the very last seconds in the locker room locked behind a bathroom stall—"centering himself," said Jackson; which may be Zen for bodily functions. Jackson said that many times over the years, he would reach for some ringing climax, only to hear some terrible biological blare from the most famous person in the world, centering himself behind the door of a bathroom stall. *Hey, Coach, I think Michael speaks for all of us.* Jordan, he knew, sometimes winked at the coach's meditation session—he would squeeze open an eye to see how many teammates were engrossed in meditation (actually, quite a few were). He needed a few absolutely unobserved moments just before the beginning of each game, when the eyes of the world would be on him as on no one else.

The Bulls began their last championship run with an October 17 exhibition game in Paris. I watched it late on a Friday night, with my twenty-two-year-old cat, Lenore, drifting away to death on my lap. I had projected, as pet lovers will, some of my own love of the Bulls onto Lenore. In this I was cheerfully assisted by a succession of friends and cat-sitters who had cared for her when I traveled, lifting Lenore toward the television screen during critical games (she did seem to follow the flashing figures), and propping a picture of Michael Jordan by her food bowl. Because Lenore's birthday was October 31, I had made an annual event of creating a character for her each Halloween. When an aging, intriguing Dennis Rodman joined the Bulls, his multihued hair and crabby pout seemed to almost eerily rebound in my aging Mexican cat, with her tortoise-shell hair and a cranky baby's howl. Some youngsters in my building took Lenore around for trick-or-treating one year. She was already in decline, so didn't bristle much at riding in a basket while swaddled in a red RODMAN 91 jersey. "Ohmigosh," people would say on opening their doors to Lenore's endearingly surly yowl. "Is that—what's that?—a kitty cat?" "Yes, yes," said the kids, "a cat dressed up like Dennis Rodman!" Unlike Rodman, Lenore scored.

The Friday night of the Bulls' exhibition in Paris, Lenore's eyes had become cloudy and swelled so much she could not completely close them. I held her lids down gently with my fingers, so she could rest; but her breathing came only in soft, small shudders. I called a twenty-four-hour animal emergency room, but they said they were too busy for the care she needed—the release she needed from the pain that racked her. Try and comfort her through the night, they advised; and don't be surprised, or sorrowful, if she doesn't wake up. Crying, I carried Lenore to her food bowl, laid her down on a souvenir Bulls rug nearby, and mixed some jalapeño salsa in with her beef and liver. There seemed no need to restrict her diet now. I tried to steady her on her squat little brittle legs as she picked up the scent of salsa and liver. Then, out of instinct and memories of great repasts past, Lenore tried to lurch forward. Her legs folded up below her, and she collapsed. It was a bit like seeing Muhammad Ali knocked down for the first time—my famously, gleefully omnivorous cat, Lenore Simon, falling before she could reach her food.

People who have pets in their lives, and then hold them close as they watch them die, often feel they must remind themselves that it's an animal in our arms, not an actual human friend or family member. But inside, where our bodies cannot lie to us, the ache is utterly real. I was a single man in his forties who doted on a cat—not an appealing picture. But I was glad to have grown up enough not to be defensive about feeling that I had learned a little something from a small Mexican cat with a brain about the size of a walnut.* As Lenore began to grind down, I was impressed by her defiant determination just to keep going. I won't put a human word, like courage, on the strength it takes an aging cat with aching limbs and wheezing lungs to walk, on four halting legs, down a long hallway to her food bowl. But I hope to have that plodding perseverance when I need it.

The following Friday was the Halloween that would have been Lenore's twenty-third birthday (the silly symbolism of that number was lost on me at the time). The Bulls, aging, unraveling, and absent Scottie Pippen, lost their opening game of the year to the Boston Celtics. I was in Flagstaff, Arizona, reporting a story on a federally funded Navajo medicine man. I had just concluded a swim at a gym when I saw a tele-

---

*After I broadcast a short essay following Lenore's death, I heard from several veterinarians and brain researchers who ventured that her brain must have been closer in size to a grapefruit. If so, I stand corrected. But she was a small cat, and her head didn't seem to me nearly large enough for a grapefruit.

vision set in the entrance area was tuned to the last quarter of the game. The Bulls had slipped behind by seven points.

"Here's where they come on," I told the young Navajo student behind the counter. "Here's where they are the Bulls."

"Not this year," he said. "Not with Pippen out. Jordan will get tired. Rodman is a flake. Not with everybody gunning for them. Get used to it." The former producer of our radio program, Cindi Carpien Gold, and her family had moved to Flagstaff; I went around with her daughters, Jessie and Michaela, for trick-or-treating. Both of the girls wore black tights, cut-out ears folded over headbands, and painted whiskers Cindi had eyebrow-penciled in over their noses. "We're kitty cats," Jessie and Michaela would announce to adults opening a door. Then, they dropped their voices to a whisper, so I would not hear them. "Because," they said hoarsely, looking furtively over their shoulders at me, "his kitty cat died."

"You don't have to drop your voice when you tell people about my cat," I finally told them. "Lenore had a good, long life. I really miss her. But I see you two dressed up like that and like to think that the memory of her is still giving us some fun." After hearing this minor league Mr. Rogers oration, Jessie and Michaela became almost boisterous as doors opened. "Trick-or-treat! His kitty cat died! We're kitty cats, too. Trick-or-treat!" Then, they would rattle their bags of candy, like misers shaking their coin purses. As a creature of public broadcasting, I admired their direct supplication. It was agreeably unadorned by the usual cloying appeal to the public good.

The next morning, I got a call. Ralph, my stepfather, had suffered a serious heart attack. I changed planes in Las Vegas, enroute to Chicago, and found a shop in the airport mall selling ties made from Norman Rockwell paintings. One was a Cubs tie, derived from Rockwell's famous depiction of Cub chagrin, Uncle Charlie Grimm's basset-hound frown tucked behind the forlorn batboy. I bought the tie for Ralph and imagined that he might wear it sometime soon, after he left the hospital. We could have lunch at Manny's, each of us no longer eating corned beef, but content to freeload from the trough of sharp green new pickles. "See this tie?" I imagined Ralph telling friends. "It's Rockwell's *Bottom of the Ninth*. Nineteen forty-eight, it was painted. That's Charlie Grimm, of course, and Hank Sauer. Walter Jacobsen might be the batboy, who knows? My son gave it to me, a couple weeks ago, when I was flat on my ass."

Under a thicket of tubes, Ralph was breathing heavily, irregularly, sounding like a dented, wheezing machine. I squeezed his hand carefully around a tube; he squeezed back, lightly. Occasionally, his eyes would snap ardently open, as if to take in enough to make up for lost time; then, his lids would fall back down. Ralph's daughters, a son-in-law, and one of his grandchildren, Dr. Suzanne Brandenburg, had all arrived. A heart specialist came in and announced, rather grandly, "Mrs. Newman, your husband has just aged thirty years." I suppose his admonition was meant to sober and prepare us. But I found the remark made me oddly optimistic. That would have made Ralph 116 years old.

The weekend following Thanksgiving, the Bulls came to Washington. I met Luc for lunch, and he seemed hugely depressed. The team was losing. Scottie Pippen had moved from dissent to disobedience, saying that though his foot would heal, his grudge against Bulls management was without remedy—he would never play for them again. Dennis Rodman was uncharacteristically sluggish on the court, arriving late in the locker room, suffering an apparent hangover from pastimes ordinary men might not be able to fathom. "He thinks he's some kind of rock star," Luc said gloomily, a celebrity famous for being famous; forgetting, perhaps, that his star status lasted only as long as he could haul down rebounds.

State troopers had formed a phalanx around the Ritz-Carlton hotel, where the Bulls stayed, to keep gathering crowds restrained behind thick nylon ropes set up in the parking lot. Hotel guests ranged around the lobby, looking for Bulls. At one point, three moderately large men, each of their limbs bedecked in an item of Bulls logo clothing— Bulls sweatpants, hooded Bulls sweatshirt, leather Bulls jacket, and Air Jordans—crossed the lobby with an air of sustained importance. They nodded down at Luc as they strolled into the hotel restaurant. *Luc, Luc, how ya' doin, my man?* I did not recognize them as players. Luc explained they were the official traveling friends of one of his teammates. The trio came along to carry the player's cell phone, punch out his calls, and run inconsequential errands that the star himself felt he could not manage because of the surrounding crowds.★ The star himself was taking a pre-game nap; his dependents were apparently feeling at a loss for a sense of purpose. "What they do," said Luc, "is keep walking around the hotel, hoping someone will think they're a Bull."

---

★Not, incidentally, Jordan or Rodman, who probably genuinely needed such insulation.

Michael Jordan, said Luc, felt that Scottie Pippen's anger was a fire that had to burn itself out. Maybe it would. Would Pippen really prefer that Jerry Krause engineer a spiteful trade that would send Scottie to Sacramento?★ But what happened if Pip returned to the team in chagrin, the second or third best player in the league (some, including Michael Jordan, even said *the* best), but still paid only as much as the 122nd best? Would despair douse his competitive fires? Would he say, to himself and others, "Well, if I'm going to be paid like the one hundred and twenty-second best player, I guess I'll just play like the one hundred and twenty-second best . . ."

It was a depressing prospect, said Luc. Maybe all the experts are right: we're too old, we're distracted, this is the beginning of the end. "But what an inglorious way for something so splendid to end, isn't it? It's sad. It's depressing." Luc began to shiver. "Is it cold in here?" It was not. "Oh, God, suddenly I'm cold," he said. Even a slight shiver is fearsome to behold in a man 7 feet 2 inches tall. He stood up to wrap a navy blue pea coat across his shoulders. "It's because it's so depressing, talking about this. I'm one of those people, everything registers right away. If I get depressed, I get cold." A huge, grown man, shivering like a small, blue-lipped boy by the side of a pool.

Both of us being travelers, we began to talk about restaurants. Luc was pleased with the progress of his own restaurant in Albuquerque, where he had played college ball. "We do a portobello mushroom sandwich," said Luc, "that's caused a lot of excitement." A young boy in a Bulls cap approached the table, shyly. "Mr. Longley?" he said, holding out a hotel message pad, his face shining. "Can I have your autograph?" I wondered if the boy had overheard the center of the Bulls—*Thhhe Mmman innn thhhe Mmmiddle!*—boasting not about muscling around Karl Malone, but grilling a piquant portobello mushroom sandwich.

That night, the Bulls helped the Washington Wizards close down their old Capital Center. I brought along a friend from Holland, an old photographer's model, who flinched with fascination every time Michael Jordan came to the foul line and flashbulbs boomed and bloomed. She didn't connect much with basketball (save for a reflexive tribal attachment to Rik Smits),† but understood the whistling and bristling of the flashbulbs in an instant. "Like you would take a picture of the Grand Canyon or the Statue of Liberty, yes?" she said. "You want to

---

★Nice city. But in 1998, an inferior basketball franchise.
†Of the Indiana Pacers. He hails from Eindhoven, in the Netherlands.

be able to show everyone, 'I was here. I saw this, that most people only see in the papers, or dream about.' "

The Bulls resumed their sluggishness for most of the first half. But in the closing seconds of that half, Washington's Calbert Cheaney leaned in on Michael Jordan and clawed furiously into the air, trying to take away the ball. Jordan fell back; he looked, in fact, as if he had begun to fall over. But as his legs began to swing up, seemingly out of control, Jordan let fly a shot that bowed over Cheaney's wild, flailing arms. The horn to end the half was blaring as MJ's shot—what amounted to the only *flop-away jumper* I have ever seen—found the net and fell through for two points. The Bulls won; their season seemed to pick up from that moment.

Ralph was shutting down—inch by inch, from his ears to his toes. His hearing was poor, his heart was faltering, his lungs seemed to boil up with fluid. His spine was fraying, his insides were turning against him. His mind was still sharp. But often, that only sharpened his sense of pain. Drugs seemed to dull every sense except hurt. He heard little, ate mildly, barely moved, and suffered without pause. On visits, I would arrive in his hospital room bearing the news under an arm. He would flip the *Tribune* open to the sports section, pull on his reading glasses, and look. *Whadtha Bulls do?* It was an encouraging development— seeing Ralph's eyes back behind his commanding black reading glasses. But over the weeks, my mother and I noticed that he never seemed to get much past the headlines. He would look for a moment, then a film of pain and dimness would fall back over his eyes. A couple of times, I would begin to read from a column; and stop within a few paragraphs, as he slipped back into a dazed drowse.

Pain—there is no comforting way to put this—became the prime sensation of Ralph's life. He would come out of the hospital for a few days, even weeks, until his lungs would fill, and his heartbeat would grow thick (and, by the way, his savings would begin to flatline); then he would be brought back. The hospital had a pain clinic, which checked Ralph from stem to stern and determined that nothing more could be done to ease his agony. His heart and lungs were just giving out. His spine was just grinding away. Heavier doses of narcotics would likely dull his senses so much he could not make use—this part was put a bit more subtly, but only a bit—of whatever time and liveliness he had left.

During our calls and visits, Ralph would describe the pain as *considerable*, *terrible*, or even *a bitch*. But he had to be asked about it; even then, he didn't complain so much as confide. I was walking back to his room one afternoon when I encountered one of the young doctors who would come in to look him over.

"Your father bears up very well under pain," she said with approval. "Rather like an athlete. Did he ever play sports?"

"Did he!" I said. "He used to be the second baseman for the Tucson Toros. He used to play on the same Great Lakes Naval Air Station team as Hank Greenberg!" The doctor was an Indian immigrant, and I think the specific names were rather lost on her. But she laughed. "Well, he's (got a) very stiff upper lip, you know. Lots of pluck." I thought about the young man who had taken the train back from the West during the Depression, brandishing a cast on his broken nose and trying to figure out how to make Branch Rickey's $500 check stretch for the rest of his life.

Luc had a holiday party. The Bulls were playing better, and the general mood was ebullient. Luc is an exceptionally thoughtful host and seemed to make an effort to steer his teammates into conversation with his shorter, civilian friends and neighbors, so that each of us might insufferably begin a conversation the following day. "You know, I was chatting with Steve Kerr the other night. You know, Steve Kerr, of *the Bulls*? Helluva nice guy. Anyway, Steve said . . ." In meeting some of the players, I tried to pretend to nonchalance. Several times, I tried to stand near Scottie Pippen to discover if I could overhear some hint of his intention to return or demand a trade. But he seemed to have a disappointing custom of talking mostly about cars. I stood on my toes to shake the proffered hand of Toni Kukoc, who was wearing a pair of black velvet slacks, and the effect was flabbergasting—like seeing a man walk out on black velvet tree trunks. There was more velvet tucked around Toni Kukoc's legs, I would wager, than the drapes of the curtains on the stage of the Metropolitan Opera. I told Toni that I had passed his name, desperately, to ingratiate myself with a Croatian border guard, and he laughed. He was a better-known man than Croatia's president, Franjo Tudjman (and certainly a much nicer guy). But Kukoc was clearly rueful about the breakup of Yugoslavia, and the Yugoslav national basketball team. "We were, you know, all of us, like brothers," he said. "Shit."

I made another circle near Scottie Pippen. I had not appreciated, until standing close by, the elegance Pippen now draped over the rawbones of his rural Arkansas youth. His fingernails shimmered. He was expensively perfumed. His shoulders were cloaked in exquisite Jordanesque tailoring (with his foot still mending, Pippen spent every game sitting conspicuously on the bench; I never saw him in the same sport coat twice). He spoke in a low, easy, refined-sounding voice; one heard that he had sought professional instruction to improve his commercial opportunities. He bent down with a shy smile to hear a small, elderly woman implore him to return to the Bulls when his injury had healed.

"Well, I want you to do whatever's best for you, Scottie," she said. "But I sure hope you'll be back."

"I tell you what, darlin'," he drawled disarmingly. "If I come back, it'll be just for you." And then he leaned down to lift her up in a smile and a hug.

"We all love you, Scottie!" she said into his shoulder, and Scottie patted her small back gently with his long fingers, glimmering with championship rings.

"I love you, too, darlin'," he said comfortingly. "I love y'all too."

At one point, Luc's wife, Kelly Longley, swept through in a great preoccupation. Guests were lining her hallways and winding up her stairs. "Do you know," she asked, "how to feed an eel?" Apparently, it was dinner time for one of the family pets: a slimy gray eel (but then, perhaps the eel thought that I was slimy, too) who lurked in the gravel of Luc's living room aquarium. I said I'd try. It turned out that eels do not survive on fish flakes sprinkled casually into their water. You have to put a small pellet of thawed raw fish into a pair of pincers on the end of a long rod, then slowly and deliberately troll the bait through the water until the eel shimmies up to snap at and swallow it. Eels are either famously fastidious, or notably nearsighted. They will not condescend to eat a fallen, gravel-flecked fish pellet. So I stood tiptoed in a small closet behind the aquarium, and tried to entice the eel. He sniffed at the fish pellet and opened his mouth, but I did not move fast enough to release the pincers. The fish spherule fell uselessly into the muck. The eel looked on, imploringly. I tried another. The eel snaked up to the pellet in the pincers, nose to nose. When I saw its small slit of a mouth pull open, I released the pincers. He took the bait. *Yes! Yes! Nailed it!* As I maneuvered a new morsel through the water, I noticed a chorus of famous faces looking through from the other side of the aquarium glass. Pippen, Bill Wennington, Jud Buechler were all looking on, watching me try to feed the eel. I allowed myself a small sense of identification with the players. Inducing the eel to snap at the pellet while Scottie Pippen looked? on, intrigued, felt a bit like trying to sink a foul shot in front of a crowd.

A while later, Luc began to shoot pool. When his teammates began to join the game, many stopped to slip off the heavy gold championship rings from their fingers. (Few of the Bulls were given to wearing flashy jewelry and would rarely wear their Tiffany hardware in public. But a holiday party among themselves allowed the players to wear their multiples of glittering rings with modesty—after all, everybody had them.) Luc cleared a small area on a bookcase for what amounted to a gold ring cloakroom. *K-thunk! That's the one for 91. K-thunk! There's 92. My agent has 93. K-thunk! 96, my favorite, yours too? K-thunk! 97, the one my son will get.* The pile of gold and diamond championship spoils sparkled like a pirate's hoard.

Right before the New Year, the Bulls played the Dallas Mavericks, whose coach, Don Nelson, concocted what must have sounded to him like a diabolically clever idea. Dennis Rodman was famously bad at free throws. He was sinking only about 39 percent. So Nelson instructed an eager rookie, Bubba Wells, to foul Dennis repeatedly to bring him to the free throw line. Nelson's reasoning (though trying to identify a reason in this thinking is like trying to fathom the reason behind invading the Bay of Pigs) seemed to be that fouling Rodman would undo the Bulls offense by making them rely on Rodman to score points. Bubba proved to be a trouper. Whenever Rodman touched the ball, Wells would touch Rodman—blatantly. *Foul! Wells! Rrrodman to the line.* Once, twice, six times, until Bubba Wells fouled out and had to take a seat. Rodman took two shots for each intentional foul, twelve shots in all. *And he sank nine of them.* Bubba Wells felt embarrassed by his coach. "I guess you call this taking one for the team. But it's not the way I play basketball." Rodman said, "Who knew?" At practice the next day, he lofted several shots from beyond the three-point line, as if to say, "And now, for my next trick . . ."

Right after the New Year, the old and improving Bulls had a chance to avenge their opening loss against Boston. The game was at home, but home was improbably festooned with pineapple balloons and facsimile palm trees. It turned out to be Hawaiian Night at the United Center, which is, I suppose, not a bad idea for a snowy January. I was standing for the National Anthem with Tish Valva, formerly one of our show's producers, who had become the producer in charge at our Chicago station,

WBEZ. Tish collects and creates palindromes—phrases that read more or less the same, backward and forward.* As the United Center organist began to roll into the first notes of the Star-Spangled Banner, Tish said, "Oh no—Don Ho." Oh yes, it was—the hardest-working relaxed man in show business, singing the National Anthem with his daughter. A few months later, we decided to profile Don Ho, whose professionalism I admired. He said it had taken a great deal for the Hawaiian Tourist Board to convince him to leave Waikiki Beach in January for a one-night stand in Chicago. A lot, as in money? "No," said Mr. Ho, who was himself a college basketball star. "A lot as in Bulls tickets. Meeting Jordan, Pippen, and Rodman." The Bulls won in a rout.

By January of the 1998 season, Rodman was beginning to reach form. There was a moment in the third quarter of the Boston game when a ball had gone bounding out over the line and seemed about to strike the seats. Dennis, however, launched himself at an angle to intercept it, heedlessly headfirst. Before the ball could smack into the courtside folding chairs, Rodman reached it and flicked it back out with his fingertips to Steve Kerr, who was standing alone, positioned to complete a three-point shot; which he did just as Dennis spilled his tattoos across the shoulders and laps of fans in expensive floor seats. *Sorry, darlin'. Thanks, babe.* It was an astonishing display of focus, precision, experience—and foolhardiness. A rebound that almost came at the cost of a smashed face. Yet it ended, as discussions about the balance between Rodman's talents and demerits often did in Chicago, in an admiring declaration: *Dennis gets the job done. Dennis pulls plays out of thin air.* Later, I began to ask Steve Kerr about the play, and he didn't wait for the question. "I know exactly what you're talking about," he said. "How can you not love to play with someone who will sacrifice himself like that to get the ball to you?" Rodman's abundance of annoyances probably didn't amount to much against the fact that to grab a rebound, he would throw his face into a line of folding chairs.

In the end, Scottie Pippen's foot mended, he banked his anger at management, and returned for the last running of the Bulls. Toni Kukoc, Ron Harper, and Michael Jordan in particular had stepped up in his absence. But there was a cost. Kukoc fretted at being returned to his

---

*Her most seamless, alas, was occasioned by misfortune. When word crossed the news wires that Tupac Shakur had been shot dead, Tish crossed wordlessly to our show board and wrote TUPAC KAPUT.

position as sixth man. Jordan was more fatigued. And yet, Pippen was fresher. When I asked Jackson one January morning for his cosmic assessment of the significance of Scottie's return, he philosophized, Jackson-like, about the greater harmony conferred by Scottie's presence. Pippen and Jordan by now complemented one another perfectly: two great players who gave 100 percent of themselves individually, 125 percent when they played in tandem. Scottie's long-limbed defense, said the coach, was ferocious and precious. His relentless roving would free other players to find new ways to make plays. "We're just," said Jackson, "a more orgasmic team with Scottie back." There was a pause. We were speaking over a cellular telephone, and I could not quite tell if Jackson was clearing his throat, or clearing his foot from it. "*Organic*," he continued on quickly. "We're much more *organic* with Scottie back. Oh, who knows?" He lapsed back into a laugh. "Maybe we're more orgasmic, too."

I was back in Washington on the morning that the *Post* ran the first story about President Clinton's relationship with a former intern named Monica Lewinsky. The story appeared the same day as an account of the arrest of Chris Webber of the Washington Wizards, who was stopped in his car with a small amount of marijuana in his possession. On the left hand side of the *Post*, twenty-four-year-old Chris Webber was assailed as a reckless, spoiled millionaire who did not take seriously his potential to be a role model for young children. On the right-hand side of the *Post*, twenty-four-year-old Monica Lewinsky was consoled as a feckless innocent who had been seriously taken advantage of by a man who should be a role model. If you were twenty-four years old, better to be on the right-hand side of the *Washington Post*.

I did not know until reading the *Post* that Monica Lewinsky lived in my apartment complex. I had never met her. Apparently, the elderly women who lived in my building no longer made it a point to introduce me to every young single Jewish woman in the complex. Well, it would have been hard to compete with a man who had his own jet. Still, I took some pleasure during the first weeks of the fracas in arriving home and shouting over to the troupes of reporters, producers, and camerapeople awaiting a glimpse of Ms. Lewinsky, "Jackals! Scum! Vermin! Colleagues!"

When the Bulls returned to town about a month later they stayed, as they ordinarily did, at the Ritz-Carlton right across the river in Virginia. Since their last visit, the hotel had become even better-known as the site in which Linda Tripp lured Monica Lewinsky for a wired chat.

The Bulls had many players who were intelligent, concerned citizens who followed the news. They might avoid the sports pages, in sake of their own sanity, but they knew the news. Steve Kerr, whose family knew from tragic experience what it was to figure in events, was in fact quite concerned at the time over increasing tensions between the United States and Iraq.* "I just worry," he said, "that all the attention focused on Iraq may destabilize our relations with the rest of the Arab world." I wondered how many NBA players laid their heads onto pillows each night with that worry.

I had left a jokey little gift and note for Luc "from" my neighbor, Monica Lewinsky. But it was clear that the Bulls had little interest in the story that was so saturating the news. At first, I thought their resolute lack of curiosity might betray the Bulls' insulation from real-life events. As the months wore on and the Starr investigation finally wore down the national sense of decency, the players' intentional lack of interest suggested they were more attuned to real-life values than reporters (Toni Kukoc expressed the idea that if a European political leader lacked a paramour, it would be considered a distressing sign of a lack of vitality. However, unless President Clinton intended to move to Zagreb, this argument was politically unavailing). The Bulls had raised sports into popular history, while much of the U.S. press and Congress seemed to be descending into gossip. If anyone wanted evidence of President Clinton's inconstancy, his irresolute policy in Bosnia was a better, fairer place to look than in his pants.

As the 1998 season progressed, so did public consciousness that each game played in an out-of-town arena might be Michael Jordan's last in that location. When a friend of Luc's and mine came down to say hello after the game in Washington's new MCI Center, some of the people gathered outside the locker room were chattering about seeing President Clinton in one of the sky suites. The president may not have made maximum use of his moment in history. But he had invoked the power of his office so he would not miss out seeing Michael Jordan play one last time in the capital. The players seemed honored without being exhilarated over the president's visit. After all, they explained, they had already met him at the White House after every championship.

---

*One of Steve's brothers had worked at the National Security Council. When reporters asked Steve, "What do you hear from your brother?" he enjoyed answering, "I could tell you. But then, I'd have to kill you."

A young suburban kid had cleverly picked up a blue stadium pass someone had let slip to the floor and been waved ahead by security guards. He was stocky, excited, and had Dennis Rodman hair—three or four colors streaking through his crew cut. He wore a souvenir stand RODMAN 91 jersey over a T-shirt. "Say," he asked us, "can I be here?" Yep, we told him, it looked as if he had outsmarted the system. "Rodman is my favorite," he offered superfluously, his eyes locked alertly on the locker-room door. Within a few minutes, Rodman himself came strolling out to board the team bus. He was conversing with Scottie Pippen. We looked over at the boy, who seemed buoyant and alight. A man should never miss a chance to see Michael Jordan play, or make a boy's night. Tentatively, I walked over to Rodman. "Excuse me, sir," I began. "Ordinarily, I wouldn't interrupt you. But there's a young man over there"—I motioned at the small throng now standing behind a rope— "with Dennis Rodman hair. It would really be the thrill of his life if you went over and said hello to him." Dennis looked back, blankly. He was wearing sunglasses at night in a darkening alleyway in an emptying amphitheater; I worried that I might have missed something wild in his eyes. Wordlessly, he walked over to the group. The suburban mini-Rodman reached up worshipfully with a souvenir program. "You know," said Dennis, looking down at the boy as he reached out for a pen, "you sure are a handsome dude with that hair."

It was beginning to feel, once more, like a championship season. But Ralph was unmistakably sinking. The details are disagreeable to remember now. When catastrophic illness strikes someone you love, you cherish them all the more; but even a love that fine and selfless adds a strain. Sickness becomes your sense of gravity, what holds you to the earth. If you're blessed, and we were, you have the chance to express your love in a thousand dear details. But as the weeks and months proceed, the advance of death can also deplete you of all patience, strain nerves, and drain away all the human and financial assets you had planned to have, but now see slipping away. The imprecision of the inevitable becomes maddening. Once, a doctor had sketched out for me the kind of care Ralph would need on returning home—medications, nurses, and all the accoutrements of home medical technology. Musing mostly to myself, I told the doctor, "I'm not sure how long we can afford that." His response was almost dismissive.

"Well, we're not talking about a long-term prospect."

"You mean," I asked, "he could be fine in just a few weeks?" The doctor's tone suddenly softened, as he realized that lunatic hope had clouded clear judgment. But his words stayed the same.

"No, son. I mean, we're not talking about a long-term prospect."

For decades, those closest to Ralph had tried to deter him from having that second Polish sausage, another scoop of butter pecan, a midday cherry blintz. "Oh, you don't want that, Ralph. You'll regret that, Ralph." Now, he seemed delighted but wise as to why all of us now stood by his bedside, ready to deliver his whims. "What about another scoop of caramel fudge, Ralph? Want some butterscotch sauce on it? That sushi place does takeout, you know. I could just run over." Immediate gratification seemed more pertinent now than pointless discipline. But Ralph's appetite was usually blunted by pain, weariness, and painkillers.

I arrived late one afternoon in his hospital room to find him unusually alert for the hour. He was watching the news.

"Glad you're back," said Ralph, shutting down the screen from his bedside control. I told him a bit about my afternoon. "I've been wanting to, you know, go over something with you," he said.

"Of course. I'm here." We had father-son talks of a kind over twenty-six years. But ordinarily about sex, money, religion, and baseball, not life and death. Once, Ralph had counseled me about sex; and once, memorably, I had returned the favor. We had counseled each other about romance—a man who has been married three times exchanging foolishness with one who had not been married even once. "At least," said Ralph, "you probably can't make a mistake I didn't make first. I've given you lots of room to improvise." I was a stepson, of course, not his actual son; a friend who happened to be the son of his wife. But over the years, we spoke several times a week, and during the last months of his life, virtually every day. Reporters learn to listen for the small, scratchy signals of intimacy. I began to think that with me, Ralph could review the blunders, embarrassments, and regrets of his life without feeling as personally implicated as he might with his wife, his ex-wives, or his two exemplary daughters.

"I'd be an idiot," Ralph said after I helped him settle painfully back onto a pillow, "not to consider the fact that I may not get out of this."

"You will. You'll be out in a few weeks."

"You know, *this*," he said with an impatient wave. "This little *bout*. Whether I'm here or home. A little while back," Ralph continued, "I worried that I wasn't leaving your mother with much. I've done what I can. I can't worry about that now."

"I know. She knows. You've had a wonderful life together." I caught myself speaking in the past tense; then noticed that I was only picking up on Ralph's own frame of reference. "You know what you can do now? Rest. Get better. Get out and kick the world in the old kazzazza." Ralph smiled dimly.

"Well, you know that old song," he said. "The spirit is willing, but the flesh is weak. Hell, sometimes even the spirit is weak." I had nothing smart or cheerful to say to that.

"Do you mind if I ask you something?" Ralph seemed to brace himself for some sort of corker—about fidelity, finances, or Richard Nixon. Instead I asked, "Has anything even vaguely *spiritual* happened to you through all this? I mean, with respect to your convictions and all that." Ralph let go of a smile.

"You mean, bright lights? A chorus of angels?"

"Spoken like a true atheist, God bless. No, no. Do you find yourself thinking there's got to be something over the next hill? Do you comfort yourself by thinking that"—I was taking some care with my tenses— "when that time comes, you'll be reunited with old friends? Finally meet Lincoln? Do you think you'll see Abe again?"*

Ralph paused before falling back on a shrug. "I think about all that. In my mind, I see all of that now. But *now* is all we know about. We don't know anything about what comes after. So, I think about things *now.* Friends. Your mother. The girls." (He meant his daughters.) Ralph then mentioned the names of several friends. "I think about things I've seen and done, places I've gone. When I think that way, I'm not such a prisoner in this bed. I can walk, I can hear, I can go places. I do more of that now. You know," Ralph said, "sometimes I find myself thinking about crazy things."

"Crazy?"

"Louis Armstrong. Paddy Bauler." An old, famously corrupt and captivating Chicago ward-heeler. "Sandburg. The Leopold thing." A new smile spread under his mustache. "Phil Cavarretta."

"Phil Cavaretta?"

"First baseman. Born in Chicago. Played for the Cubs."

"I *know* who Phil Cavarretta was," I said a bit too emphatically.

---

*Not Abraham Lincoln whom, all jokes aside, Ralph did not actually know, but an old cat of Ralph's.

"Played for the Sox, too, a couple of years.* But why in the hell are you thinking about Phil Cavarretta?" Ralph looked up with sleepy chagrin.

"I suppose you should ask the doctors that," he said, settling in. "I guess a man can't be held responsible for his dreams, can he?" I went off to buy Ralph some gum—his plenitude of prescription drugs left a tinny taste in his mouth—and by the time I returned, Phil Cavarretta's most devoted fan was sleeping deeply; perchance to dream.

On March 3, I watched the Bulls play the Denver Nuggets in Chicago. Joe Montana and his family were sitting a few seats in front of us, receiving the full share of Bulls hospitality. "Like some T-shirts, Joe? Can we get you and the kids some hats, Joe? Another beer, Joe?" With great, good class, the old quarterback demurred and assented just enough to be polite. It was an unexceptional, desultory Bulls victory until the fourth quarter. The Bulls were approaching 100 points. The team had a promotional deal with Taco Bell franchises: anytime the Bulls scored 100 or more points, ticket stubs could be exchanged for a free soft taco "at participating dealers all over greater Chicagoland." As the price for an average seat exceeded fifty dollars, the occasional gift of a soft taco seemed ever more urgently desired. With five minutes remaining in the game, the crowd began to stand and chant. Not *MJ! MJ!, Pip! Pip!*, or even *Dennis! Den-nis!* They chanted, "Ta-cos! Ta-cos! Ta-cos!" The silliness was a sign that the whole, restored Bulls had returned to a level of mastery.

The next night, I spoke at a dinner along with Dennis Ross, the special U.S. ambassador to negotiations between Israel and the Palestine Authority. Unencumbered by extensive knowledge, I was outspoken. Constrained by his own deep expertise, the ambassador was obliged to be guarded. However, we both talked happily about the Bulls. Ambassador Ross said that during breaks in negotiations, he had sometimes worked off sluggishness and frustration by shooting baskets on an outdoor court behind a hotel in East Jerusalem. His security guards would stand in a circle as the ambassador dribbled, jumped, and rattled off basketball shots. Late one night, he said, one of the Israeli cabdrivers who worked the hotel had called out as he chased down a jump shot that had missed even the backboard. "Mr. Ambassador," said the driver, "I

---

*Philip Joseph Cavarretta. Career batting average .293. Led the league in 1945, when he hit .355. Played for the Cubs from 1934 to 1953, and the White Sox in 1954 and '55.

think you are no Michael Jordan." A few minutes later, as Ross came in off the court to shower and return to the peace table, one of the Palestinian youngsters who played in the neighborhood had called after him, too. "Hey, Ambassador. Sir, you are not Michael Jordan." Ambassador Ross said it was rewarding to find common ground, even on so unexceptional a point.

The following weekend, the Bulls came to New York City for a Sunday afternoon game that was regarded as the last Michael Jordan might ever play in Madison Square Garden (at least, until he takes up hockey). Even the rancorous New York crowd seethed with red—swarms of kids roving over the Garden in red Bulls JORDAN 23 jerseys. When MJ was introduced, there was a strong chorus of boos, but also a mighty choir of camera clicks, and a cannonade of flashing lights. I had not yet noticed that Michael was wearing an original pair of red and black Air Jordans. They were, in fact, the very same pair he had worn as a rookie playing in Madison Square Garden fourteen years before—when he had scored 42 points. He said he had been rooting around in his closet to pack for the road trip and found the old shoes stored on a shelf as a memento. Jordan wore new shoes for each game (most players did, thanks to the largesse of athletic shoe companies, then gave them away) for a feeling of uplift. "You know," he said, "how wearing a new shirt or suit puts a spring in your step? That's how I feel about new shoes." So he slipped on the old ones, perhaps hoping to recapture something of his old spring.

I had forgotten how malevolent and chivalrous New York crowds can be in almost the same, overbearing breath. Several seats away from us, in seats glancing the rafters, one Knicks fan kept blaring a boisterous ridicule of Dennis Rodman. *Fuckin' fairy* was the most fathomable phrase I could pick out after the man had finished a mai-tai. "Rodman," he sneered, "gryurye e guddmn synbicht *fuckin' fairy!*" A New York friend I had brought along to the game announced, more than asked, to fans around us, "Does that jerk really think Rodman can hear him? Or that Rodman even gives a rat's ass?" When the fan wandered off and returned with a refill, my friend gave a rat's ass herself. "Oh, great, buddy," she said in the rising din. "Have another one. That'll really help." Drink, luckily, dulled his power of hearing, if not speech. And yet, every few rows, other Knicks fans had also raised up signs painted on box tops and bed sheets:

## THANKS FOR THE MEMORIES MICHAEL
## NYC § MJ
## MICHAEL FOREVER!

At halftime, the Knicks were ahead, 46 to 43. The Garden's interior camera found model Elle McPherson, John F. Kennedy Jr., and an assortment of more anonymous beautiful people waiting for the curtain to rise on the last act. In the visitors' locker room, Jordan seemed to pace more than usual, like a fighter between rounds who is convinced he can grab a thunderbolt out of the air.

"Hey, MJ," teammates would call over. "How many points you score here as a rook?"

"I don't know," said Jordan. "I don't count. One or two."

"Forty-two? Some kind of off night?"

"I was a kid," he laughed back. "Knucklehead kid."

After the game resumed, Knicks fan Spike Lee would leap up from his costly courtside seat and bellow at each Knick who came out to guard Jordan. "Guard him, goddamn," the director would yell. "You can't guard him. Guard him!" The gibes seemed to offend Jordan's professionalism and fraternity. At one point, he stood up from his dribble and beckoned to Lee with his left hand. "You want to try? C'mon out. You wanna try?"

With about five minutes left, Jordan began a drive to the basket, but had to back down from a block by the talented Allan Houston. Jordan's back bowed, almost alarmingly, like a bent straw. Knicks fans screamed as Houston, looming over Jordan, reached in for the ball. But before he could claim it, MJ managed to flick the ball toward the backboard. It hit. The ball banked in, almost crazily, for two points. The New York howls switched in a breath to resigned cheers. Playing Michael Jordan in Madison Square Garden was something like a backup on the George Washington Bridge. You can honk and honk, kvetch and moan, but in the end—just what are you gonna do?

The Bulls pulled ahead by 13. Jordan took down a Knick rebound and turned to churn a quick pass down court to Ron Harper. Harp counted down against the shot clock, dished the ball back over to MJ, who pulled up, leapt, shot, and swished the ball in for his forty-second point. Jackson called time. Jordan came over to the bench as a standing ovation swelled from the seats. Jordan took a towel from a trainer, hitched it around his neck, and sat down, breathing, gleaming, finished, and spent. With a minute remaining, he might have returned to score another basket or two, drawn a foul, sunk those shots, and surpassed his rookie total by two or four more points. But Jordan and Jackson both knew when a poem was complete.

As Ralph sank deeper toward death, I admired the way his atheism not only endured but even seemed to comfort. Some faiths fall apart under the duress of stress and skepticism. *If there's a God, why do little children suffer?* Ralph's atheism was unruffled by wise qualms. Even if atheism made eternity too mundane for some of us to contemplate, it certainly seemed to make sense of the here and now. If there was no hand of God to make the world gentler and better, we had to roll up our sleeves and apply our own.

Many times over the years, Ralph had corrected me after, in some aside, I had identified him as an agnostic. "No, I'm an atheist," he would say. "Agnostics don't know if they can believe. I *believe*. Just in something different, something a lot of people find difficult to accept." A number of times, Ralph congenially agreed to join my mother and me at midnight Christmas mass, flagrantly looking at his watch if the priest seemed to dawdle in dispensing the Eucharist. "What's wrong, dear?" my mother would ask in a stage whisper. "Do you have a late appointment?"

He told us that he wanted to have a sticker affixed to his driver's license, like those identifying blood and organ donors. Ralph wanted his to read:

I AM AN ATHEIST. IN THE EVENT OF MY DEATH, PLEASE DO NOT HAVE ME BAPTIZED OR BLESSED.

Ralph had a gadget-lover's faith in a future that would build better mousetraps, digital watches, and personal organizers. Even as he languished at home, his everyday world narrowed to sleeping, eating, and enduring pain, Ralph programmed a wiring box that would snap on the radio, douse lights, and swirl around compact discs (though he kept interrupting the sequence to play Louis Armstrong over and over) according to a schedule only he could recall. Ralph despaired of each new painkiller prescribed. But he was eager when doctors offered a new gadget. It was a device about the size of a cigarette pack with wires that a nurse would strap on his backbone. When the unit was switched on, it sent a slight, delightful jolt into Ralph's spine—not deadening the pain so much as distracting Ralph from feeling it.

One day, Ralph sat up and seemed alert while this unit was plugged into his backbone. "What's it feel like?" I asked. Ralph squeezed his eyes in contemplation.

"Imagine," he said finally, "that someone has this little, tiny, soft sable brush. And they can use this soft, tiny, sable brush, just to lightly tickle, tickle, tickle the delicate inside of your spine. That's what it feels like." I was deeply impressed by his vividness.

"You know, Ralph," I asked, bending down closer. "I just wonder. I mean, if it's as intense as you describe. Would you have to connect that thing just on your spine? I mean, there are other sensitive spots on the human form." For the first time in months, I saw his sly, confiding grin.

"Well I suppose," said Ralph, "that you could put it just about any-where."

My mother and I spent the night of my birthday as guests in a skybox at the United Center. From where we sat, the game was dominated by the flatulent red gas-ass of the Benny the Bull blimp that they kept trapped above the rafters between descents onto the court. A fine citizen and her husband had made a charitable donation for the dubious experience of sitting next to me at a Bulls game. She was a cantor and a chaplain at a local hospital who counseled patients afflicted with terminal illnesses. She accomplished far more for humanity in a week than I have achieved in a lifetime. But the cantor made me long to be sitting back among Knicks fans. Rodman would reel off a quick pass to Pippen, who would launch the ball on a line above the rim. *Alley-oop!* as MJ tipped it in. But the cantor would be saying, "If you ever want to profile a dedicated cantor who tries to bring wisdom and healing into the last, lonely hours of a human life, I want you to know, I'm available . . ." During the first half, I tried to divert her with half-witted logic.

"You know, Rebbe," I said, "tomorrow at the hospital, your patients are all going to ask, 'What was it like to see Michael Jordan?' You might want to pay attention, so you can tell them."

"Oh, Scott, *really*," said the cantor airily. "Anyone in the *world* can see all they *want* of Michael Jordan on TV. My people don't get a *big thrill* out of Michael Jordan." I thought of Ralph, tuned in from his own hospital bed. During halftime, my mother tried to take the conversational charge from the cantor and asked about her work in detail. But my mother could not put the cantor on the air; the answers I overheard sounded curt and dismissive. As the second half began I turned to the cantor with a suggestion I hoped might more agreeably enlist her occupational interests.

"You know, Rebbe," I said, "if you wanted to make a *brucha* over the Bulls for this half, I don't think anyone here would object." The cantor's voice rose, as if she was instructing a bar mitzvah student.

"Oh, Scott, *really*," she said. "I think that *God* has many more *important things* to worry about than basketball games, don't *you*?" I hoped not.

The Bulls ended the regular season tied with Utah for the league's best record, 62 wins over 20 losses. The Bulls had looked slow and felt lethargic for long stretches of the season, pulling out extraordinary resolve on defense to win games by a few points. Still—62 and 20; the very same record had made the Utah Jazz exultant overall.

Jackson convened a team meeting and reminded the players and coaches that they had all been running mates in an extraordinary lifetime experience—they would always be Bulls together. *The Best. Ever. Anywhere.* He suggested that everyone write out and share a short message, expressing what the season, and the association, had meant. No one demurred, no one smirked. They might almost all go on to other teams; a few would figure in more championships. Many, for they were a remarkably bright group of men, would one day retire and go on to rewarding enterprises. But they all had the sensation that in the whirl they had inhabited together, between so many late planes and close games, overwhelming acclaim, frightening fascinations, and championship blowouts, they had flown close to the face of the sun. They knew that the best part of their lives had been shared with those around them in that room. They were the Bulls of Bhutan holy men and Rio street kids—*The Bulls*, no matter who succeeds into those uniforms. Each player rose and read out his words. Overwhelmingly, they were gentle messages of thankfulness, not swaggering boasts. Michael Jordan wrote a poem. His teammates were gladdened, and a little flabbergasted—MJ was usually articulate without being transparent. His poem, they said, was personal and sweet. It even ended by confessing an anxiety about the future. The players then stood around in a warriors' circle with Jackson, folded the slips of paper into a pail, lit a match, and embraced as they laughed and watched their messages burn down.

• • •

The Bulls prosaically disposed of New Jersey and then Charlotte in the first rounds of the playoffs; they seemed to save their greater energy and passion for larger challenges. Finally, they had one, when they met the Indiana Pacers. The Pacers were veterans without being old. They had, in Reggie Miller, a player nearly as much a virtuoso as Michael Jordan in last-second shots. They had, in coach Larry Bird, a team leader nearly as cunning and nerveless as Jordan, too. And, they had a greater depth of quality in their reserves, which could refresh their starters.

It was with some surprise, then, that the older Bulls took the first two games at home. They shot poorly, hitting only 35 percent of their shots from the field. But Scottie Pippen's defense was peerless and insurmountable. With his long, strong arms and superior athleticism, he held up the Indiana offense like a sheriff's roadblock. For those two games, he scored less than 20 points and looked like the most valuable player in basketball.

Then, Indiana adjusted and rebounded to win the next two. Larry Bird decided to try to run the aging wheels under Jordan and Pippen down by rotating in fresh defenders. The fifth game was a phenomenon—a Bulls blowout of the kind they really had not had all year. Bulls 106, Pacers 87. Jordan scored 29, Pippen 20, Toni Kukoc 19. Selena Roberts of the *New York Times* wrote, "The gods of basketball hurled bolts of lightning . . ." But in the next game, the sturdy Pacers hurled them back—mostly at Jordan and Pippen. There were times when Chicago's unsurpassed tandem seemed almost to stagger over to the bench when Jackson called a time-out. The Pacers were ahead by 2 points with 5 seconds left when Jordan tried to drive in for a game-tying basket; and, perhaps, draw a foul to gain a shot that might give the Bulls the game. But a bolt of lightning struck. Jordan seemed to trip over defender Derrick McKey's left foot. He fell forward on the ball, which dribbled out of his hands. Pacers at the buzzer, 91 to 89. But a grim buzz settled on the court. *Michael Jordan had fallen on his face. Michael Jordan had lost the ball.* It was Joe Louis through the ropes, Muhammad Ali on the canvas, Michael Jordan on his knees. Once again, MJ had done the unbelievable; but this time, it was unbelievable feet.

Jordan, for the first time in memory, sounded defensive after the game. He declined to say that Derrick McKey had tripped him, but asserted the obvious: "I'm not clumsy, you know." At the same time, he didn't complain, didn't apologize. He had tried and failed—and would try again. "It still has to come through Chicago," Jordan told reporters and his watching opponents. "Indiana, Utah, they have to realize this still has to come through Chicago."

It was the first Game 7, win or lose for a championship, that the Bulls had played since becoming champion (which was itself a good measure of a remarkable run). When Steve Kerr and Jud Buechler drove in to the United Center early that Sunday afternoon, Steve had turned to Jud and said, "My God—do you realize—this could be our last ride to the game together? This could be Michael's last game? This could be—" Steve had several other soaring summations working, but Jud interrupted. "Stop it, stop it, *stop it!*"

A friend and I talked to Luc on the telephone before the game. His calm and confidence were striking. He was not convinced that the Bulls would win, so much as he seemed confident that they could play well and accept loss, if it came to that. His attitude bespoke something of his own character, and the character Phil Jackson had managed to stamp on the lives of the competitive men he coached. Losing was discouraging, but not a disgrace. They might be beaten by a better team, but never embarrassed by a classier one.

The national anthem was sung by a southwest-side Pentecostal church choir, and they were superb—a joyous, harmonious blend of black and white voices who soared as they mingled and rose:

> *God, He put a rainbow in the sky*
> *Children! God, He put a rainbow in the sky*
> *When it looked like the sun wouldn't shine,*
> *God, He put a rainbow in the sky!*
> *The sun grew dim and the days grew dark*
> *But God, He put a rainbow in the sky!*

It seemed an afternoon to send up huzzahs, impassioned shouts of gratitude, rather than desperate and parochial pleas for victory. That morning, Mary Schmich of the *Chicago Tribune* had written an admirable piece about the lasting gift Michael Jordan had bestowed, win or lose, on Chicago. It is worth quoting at length:*

> *He has been a bridge over troubled waters, spanning gaps in race and politics and lifestyle . . .*

---

*Sunday, May 31, 1998, edition of the *Trib*.

*The other night, I walked past a homeless man sitting on the Michigan Avenue sidewalk. From the radio he held to his ear, the bellow of the United Center trickled out in a low buzz.*

*Normally the man might have called, "Spare a dollar, Miss?" Normally I might have looked away. Tonight, we were friends and teammates.*

*"Who's winning?" I asked.*

*"Pacers are up," he said, "but it ain't over." We both nodded, residents momentarily of the same happy place in the universe . . .*

*Michael Jordan has become as much a staple of Chicago conversation as the weather. In some ways, he has been our weather, as reliable as the sun . . . Thanks to him, everyone in the Second City gets to feel first-rate.*

*And when he leaves, whenever that day comes, he'll leave us a little less talkative, and nostalgic for the time we could all agree on something.*

I'm inclined to say that day was the last time I ever heard Michael Jordan introduced in a game lineup at the United Center. Except—no one could hear it. From the moment introductions began, a wild wall of sound was sent up into the red steel rafters, a din of claps and cheers, hollers, prayers, and tears as physical and forceful as a windstorm. The sound surged up through the soles of my shoes and rattled the keys in my pockets. The vibrations thrummed on my ribs. Jud Buechler felt, more than heard, court announcer Ray Clay intone, "At right guard. Number twenty-three. Frrrom North"—full pause— "*Caaarooolllina . . .*"

"I'm thinking," said Jud, "this could be the last time. And we're wearing the same uniform, right? So I throw Michael a high five. It was so emotional, when it kind of hit me. It was so hard for me to believe we would lose this game and this would be the end of something as big as Michael Jordan."

The Pacers leapt out to an early lead. Bird went at the Bulls with the same thrust as a matador: make them bleed, especially Jordan and Pippen. Make them run, run them down, drain the blood and muscle from their legs and arms so that they are finished for the fourth quarter. At halftime, MJ berated his teammates for spending precious energy on disputing referees' calls. "We can complain. But who do you think controls the game?" he asked with composed acerbity. "Leave them alone. Don't make them take anything away. Every time we mouth off, we're just giving away free points and digging ourselves a hole. *Shut up and play.*"

They did. Kukoc scored 21 points and snapped back quickly on defense. Steve Kerr scored 11, including a 3-point rainbow that tied the game at 77 with 6:02 left. Joe Kleine, a reserve center who had been on the bench through the entire series, was so exultant he leapt up, flailing his arms like a man drowning—and inadvertently struck Steve on the chin. Kerr, ever the showman, staggered to the bench and sat down. "Hey, it's the playoffs," said Kleine, who was a friend. "Suck it up."

Indiana curbed Jordan's scoring. He hit just 9 of 25 shots from the field, 10 of 15 from the foul line. But he drew those fouls by driving, driving, *driving* with the ball through thickets of hard shoulders and elbows. He would get knocked down, get up, sink a foul, and then run back to begin the course again. MJ was staggered, stumbling, and utterly compelling. His will seemed to put steel into his legs. In the fourth quarter, he asked to guard Reggie Miller and played him so close that Indiana's sharpshooter could manage just a single shot over the final 12 minutes.

With 3:20 left, Luc Longley took a pass inside the key, turned to his left, and sank a last jump shot from fourteen feet out. It put the Bulls 5 points up and brought the fans to their feet to stay. The cheers became ceaseless, seamless, a perpetually renewing chorus. The Bulls finished with 88 points, the Pacers 83. Scottie Pippen said, "I can't say the best team won. Both teams deserve to go to the finals. I'm just glad it's us." Jordan was rarely so euphoric; he seemed to regain a touch of swagger along with his breath. "It's like I said," he told reporters. "Anyone who wants to take anything from us, they all have to go through Chicago. We're tired. But our heart isn't tired."

"Have we lost a little bit of our swagger?" Jordan asked in response to a shouted question. "Probably. It's hard when you're playing against the high standards we've set for ourselves. But we're still the champions. No one has taken anything away from us yet."

Outside the locker room, we saw Luc and embraced. A pair of shoes he had slung around his neck hit me on both sides of my face— quite happily so. I only regret that the toe imprint has faded. We stopped in for a drink in a room at the United Center, where a fine screen actor whose blue eyes are of great note began to offer Luc lessons on how to act hurt if he wanted to induce a referee to believe he had been fouled.

"Grab at your back, like he hit it. Favor a knee as you run down the court, just for a second. Put it in their mind, that's all I'm saying." Luc demurred, cordially. "Aw, no, mate, I don't give in for that kind of cheap stuff."

"All I'm saying, Luc," the actor persisted, "all I'm saying, you see, is that if you get all stoic and always show that stiff upper lip, the refs will never give you the benefit of the doubt." Luc (who has a younger brother, by the way, who is an actor) politely heard out the case a few minutes more until the actor went on to another tall audience. A couple of wives, mothers, and girlfriends of his teammates leaned in to ask what the famous blue eyes had been saying.

"Nice bloke," said Luc with a sleepy smile. "What did you say his name was?"*

Luc organized several carloads of relatives, teammates, and friends to run up to a Mexican restaurant on the north side. When he pushed open the backstage door on the United Center, a chorus of Luc-calls rang down from the fans overhead. *Luuuc! Luuuuuuc!* Luc began to climb into one car, his mother in another; but Susan suddenly tugged him back. "Oh, wait," she called, "I forgot something." Then, as the fans acclaimed more *Luuuc!s* yet, she kissed her son. No stiff upper lip among Longleys.

In the car, Luc cleared his throat and called back a question.

"Awright now," he said. "How many of you thought, back in the fourth, when they went ahead by three, that we had lost it?" A hubbub of denial ensued. *No, Luc. Certainly not, Luc. Not the way you were playing, Luc.* Luc laughed off the reassuring insincerity.

"Well, *I* bloody well thought we'd almost lost it," he said. For a fan to say that would sound faithless. But players earned their doubts with sweat.

The restaurant was preparing to close. But not for Chicago Bulls who have just won the seventh game of a conference title playoff. Pitchers of margaritas bloomed in cool pale green on the table. Platters of citrine green guacamole glistened suddenly within reach. Several actors who follow the Bulls arrived; a director, too. The conversation bounced without plan between basketball, children, Chicago, a new common European currency, and movies. My friend, Dr. Pauline Maki, urged me

---

*Oh, hell, why not? Aidan Quinn.

to stand and deliver a toast. Standing, at that point in the evening, was perhaps the hardest part.

"When Brigham Young was led to what we now call the Great Salt Lake by a flock of seagulls," I began, "he said to the Mormon pioneers, 'This is the place.'★ Well, tonight, Chicago was the place. And you," I ticked off the names of the players at the table, "were the people. And we send you off once more to Salt Lake City with the love and thanks of a city you have once again made proud and happy." No doubt I slurred my words and sounded sentimental and foolish. But I was actually glad to have the chance to speak into those famous faces what I felt was in the minds of a great many fans (it was also a cheaper expression of appreciation than, say, picking up the check). I have said a great many other things after a margarita that I have regretted a good deal more.

Ralph's days seemed to be shrinking into a few hours of awareness between longer periods of numbness and lethargy. He would apply the breadth of whatever energy he woke up with just to sip tea, eat a piece of fruit, say good morning, read a few lines, and fall back into exhaustion. Just to keep going into the next day required a hundred different daily acts of will.

The intimacy and urgency of his needs dismayed him. Ralph had always tried to carry himself as something of a big wheel. Among his circle of friends, colleagues, and acquaintances, he was the man who made plans, went places, captivated conversation, and reached for the check. Now, he needed help just to attend himself in the bathroom. It was demeaning and discouraging. A few times, when I was in the bathroom with him, a look of absolute embarrassment would tint and twist his face. It was so unlike any other countenance I had seen in Ralph, it made him almost unrecognizable. Every now and then, one of his nurses would wheel him out for a field trip. They would go to a bookstore, stop in at a popcorn and candy shop, then be wheeled back to the apartment or hospital room, where Ralph would be changed into pajamas and lapse back into sleep; surrounded by a happy bounty of books he might never read and candy to be taken by his visitors. Ralph's eyes would be closed, but his face was usually without peace. He would twitch and flash as if, behind his eyes, he had already found a freer place in which he

---

★I apologize for such a colloquial rendition of the historic Mormon trek to freedom.

did not have to fight so much to walk, hear, and breathe. Memories and dreams, I suspect, played on the same plane there, along with old war stories, ex-wives, fast friends, devoted daughters, fresh reveries, Louis Armstrong's trumpet peals, images of my mother, and—how could a man ever forget?—Phil Cavarretta.

*Chapter 13*

# THE LAST SHOT

The Bulls' flight out to Salt Lake City early the next morning had some of the same dizzy elation of George Orwell's observation that there is nothing more exhilarating than to be shot at without result. Jordan passed out fine cigars and then spent the flight repossessing some of his generosity by winning at poker. The Bulls felt reborn after beating the Indiana Pacers—as if they had slipped out of a noose, swerved to avoid a truck, outrun an avalanche. All the old clichés seemed fresh.

The Pacers had youth that the Bulls could not equal. But the Utah Jazz were as reassuringly old as the Bulls, man to man, almost to the month.* Utah was the team the Bulls most respected. They had a tandem of stars (Karl Malone and John Stockton, Olympic teammates of Jordan and Pippen) and toughness of execution that at times matched the Bulls' own. But they admired the Jazz without dreading them. The two teams had the same regular season record. Chicago had defeated

---

*Karl Malone is a month older than Michael Jordan. John Stockton is three and half years older than Scottie Pippen. Dennis Rodman, of course, is older than all of them.

Utah for the title just the year before, and both teams had stayed essentially intact. Had Stockton, Malone, and Jeff Hornacek somehow grown younger than Jordan, Pippen, and Rodman?

But Utah seemed to have greater depth on their bench, and certainly more rest in their bones. The Jazz had dispatched the Los Angeles Lakers in four straight games to win, once more, the Western Conference Championship. They had enjoyed ten restorative days at home while the Bulls spent themselves without restraint to bring down Indiana. Sports pundits advanced theories about the effect of a team so well-rested playing one so completely exhausted. No speculation favored the Bulls. The long rest might slow the Jazz by a step or two for the first half of the first game. But Salt Lake City's thin air would scarcely invigorate the Bulls. Malone, Stockton, Sloan, and company had never seemed stronger, more fiercely energized, or better poised to win a series.

Jordan, with equal parts craft, diplomacy, and even sincerity, had declined to predict victory. In fact, he had pointedly said, "We're the underdogs, but we're still the champions," adding, "I've had enough success to know you can't win every time. But at the end of the season, if you lose a game, that's it. It doesn't stick with me, keep me from sleeping. I can deal with losing." But privately, he urged his teammates to add it all up for themselves. Rodman would drive Karl Malone *crrrazy*. Luc Longley would lean on him. Scottie Pippen would loom over and lacerate Utah's play-making guards. Kukoc, Kerr, MJ himself, would rain shots in over their heads. Luc, with delightful directness, swept aside all the wisest projections. "Aw, *buwwwshit*," he said, curling his Australian *l*'s. "We know these guys. We know we can beat them."

The Bulls lost the first game, 88 to 85. But they took satisfaction in pressing the Jazz into overtime, on Utah's own court, at Utah's own altitude. Many analysts declared that the Bulls, bless 'em, had fallen just short of their best chance to steal a victory. Jordan, the furious competitor, sounded almost maddeningly serene, speaking not of winning or losing, but ying yang and Zen. "I've just decided," he said, "to use a little of that Zen Buddhism and relax, instead of being frustrated. Just smile and let it flow, channel my thoughts, my frustration in a whole different form." One wondered—had they built a golf course in Bhutan? "I'm going to enjoy this moment," MJ continued. "It may not happen again. This may be the last time, last dance, whatever. But maybe I'm taking it too serious. I should enjoy it. That's my mood from now on." Sometimes, you are reminded that an insight taken as a sign of maturity in real life can be regarded as a mortal lack of will in sports. But the entire team had not gone saffron. There was a small, cunning play with about two minutes left in the game that made the Bulls smile. Luc Longley and Utah center Greg Ostertag had fallen into a scramble on the floor for the ball. Neither man had a notably better claim. Dennis Rodman, who could always count on having the attentions of officials, quickly signaled for a time-out— which had the effect of awarding Chicago the ball. It was a small, legal larceny.

The Bulls respected Utah but detested playing in Salt Lake City. It was a clean, secure, congenial, and courteous place. But those are the kind of patronizing platitudes big-city types express when somewhere feels small-town.

Salt Lake City is growing. But not so much that it has become cosmopolitan. Even the white players were unaccustomed to roaming about a downtown that still looked so *white*. Team managements hoped that Salt Lake's lack of wicked diversions might enhance their players' concentration. But the Bulls believed the opposite: Salt Lake's tranquillity, insularity, and high altitude made them slumberous and slack. As they would joke, *how many times can you see Mormon Center?* Their disdain for Salt Lake's dryness could sound haughty. It's not as if you saw many Bulls, on road trips, strolling down the spiral of the Guggenheim or lined up for matinee tickets at the Shakespeare. Phil Jackson's Bulls were hardly incurious men. But they came to a town, they were road warriors, not tourists. A big bed, room service, extra towels, extra ice, ESPN, in-house movies, an adjacent shopping mall to buy Beanie Babies for the kids, a pleasant restaurant open late after the games—that's what players craved in a road town. By those measures, Salt Lake City was practically San Francisco (except, of course, for the restaurants).

But the city felt small and parochial; sometimes, oppressively so. From Seattle to Orlando, throngs of teenagers waited outside the Bulls' hotel for the barest glimpse of Michael Jordan and his gleaming head, or to see Dennis Rodman exhale an elaborate stage kiss from his glittered fingernails. But in Salt Lake City, a couple of outraged adults unfurled bedsheets in the parking lot of their hotel to decry Rodman as a biblical sodomite.

## Rodman: (W)NBA* Starts in June

Another showed a cartoon sketch of Dennis wearing a flower-print housedress of the kind, I daresay, in which he would never be seen:

Rodman

Best Wo-Man in NBA

(I wondered how many of the demonstrators knew that Rodman had set up housekeeping in his suite with the actress Carmen Electra.)

The aversion of visiting players for Salt Lake was no doubt inspired by their distaste for playing in the Delta Center. It was a very tough room to work—congested, oppressive, and deafening. Steve Kerr said, "Playing there is like trying to play the game with someone throwing snowballs at you. You can do it. You can even win. But it throws you off."

Most of the Jazz fans were courteous; at worst, a little boisterous. But a small number could also be baiting and bigoted (I count a sign that often appeared in the stands saying RODMAN=SODOMIST as bigoted). The arduous atmosphere aggravated and, in a way, inspired Rodman to some of his most creative displays—often to the greater aggravation of Karl Malone. Malone is manifestly a fine player and a fine man, professedly Christian. There is no reason to believe he is any more prejudiced against gays than most other athletes in the NBA. But when Magic Johnson announced that he wanted to return to play after retiring with the HIV virus, Malone was outspoken in his worries that Johnson might infect other players. Of course, the knowledge most Americans had about AIDS in 1993 was limited. Malone had probably heard more about the virus from churchly pontificators than scientists. But still, there was a contrast to be observed between Malone's resistance to Johnson's return and Michael Jordan's public embrace of Magic on the court of the All-Star game.

A man does not have to be homophobic to be irritated by Dennis Rodman. But Rodman knows how to poke at a man's sorest pressure points. Early in the first half of the second game of the finals, Rodman was sent out to guard Karl Malone. When Malone would step out on the perimeter to look for a pass, Dennis would make a point of pressing in close behind him, practically clapping his thighs against the back of Malone's thighs. He would bump his belly into the small of Malone's back and try to press his crotch, ever so lightly, against Malone's tailbone.

---

*Women's National Basketball Association.

Then, Dennis would murmur softly from behind Malone's back, "You sure are a fine-looking man, Karl. You're a fine-looking man." Which would help explain those occasions when Malone would suddenly, seemingly inexplicably, whirl around and slap at Rodman like a man trying to keep a swarm of mosquitoes off his neck.

The game was close until the last minute. With the Bulls behind by one with 48 seconds left, Steve Kerr launched a shot from beyond the three-point line and missed. The ball caught the lip of the hoop with an audible *boooiiing!* and bounded beyond the reach of Rodman, Malone, Ostertag, Longley, Jordan, and Carr, the usual suspects to spear a rebound. Steve saw a clear path of sunshine into the ball open up before him—after all, a defense doesn't worry so much about closing the lane to Steve Kerr. Steve rushed in. Karl Malone, who was moving toward the ball himself, looked startled to see Steve Kerr show up in his neighborhood. Kerr got there first. He seized the ball, dished it over to Michael Jordan under the basket, who tried to bring it straight up, got fouled, made the basket anyway, then was awarded a foul shot which, of course, he made. Suddenly, it was the Bulls by two, off an enterprising rebound by a man who spends most of his playing time farther away from the basket than fans in courtside seats. Steve then drew a foul himself and followed through with his more customary specialty for two more points. But his rebound was cited by no less than Michael Jordan as the key to securing the game. Steve Kerr—the Blond Hound of Rebound. The Bulls had seized an unexpected win in Utah, and now had a chance to return home and win another championship without ever seeing the Delta Center again.

Game 3 was an unrepresentative rout, a fluke, an impossible phenomenon. Scottie Pippen delivered one of the most brilliant defensive performances of all time. He ranged wide, he rushed in, he blocked, poked, and outright stole the ball and the Jazz's breath. It was a bit like watching a cougar run free through a chicken house. Phil Jackson said later, "Scottie was a one-man wrecking crew," and the image was unusually apt. Every time Utah began to set up a play, Pippen would run in and wreck it, as if smashing pottery with a baseball bat. When Karl Malone would lower his shoulder and drive into a lane to try to put up a basket, Scottie would be there to take the charge—that, of course, is a sports cliché, too, for *getting run over*—putting Malone off course and often drawing a foul. By the fourth quarter, Pippen, Jordan, and Ron Harper were sunning themselves on the bench; not only to spare their lungs and knees further gratuitous effort, but to try to hold down the score, and avoid offending Utah. By the fourth quarter, Stockton, Malone, and Ostertag were facing the world champion Bulls as embodied by Scott Burrell, Bill Wennington, and Dickie Simpkins.

But basketball is a hard game in which to hold down the score.* A team takes the ball, and a clock begins to tick. They have to shoot the ball within 24 seconds. A coach can conceivably instruct his players to miss. But shooting to miss is dishonest—it damages the basic principle of basketball. It demeans the integrity of the coach and players. The most honorable way to deliberately hold down a score is to bench the starters. But Jackson was unwilling to pull Jordan and Pippen when the Bulls lead reached 20 and 25 points. Chicago had made up that large a margin in the past; Utah was that good a team, too. So when the substitutes were summoned, into the fourth quarter of a finals game, they felt they were bounding into a precious opportunity to play before the largest audience that might ever watch them. Were they supposed to score points for Utah, just to be sporting? "What you saw out there," said Steve Kerr, "was a lot of guys who don't spend a lot of time out there having the chance to show what they can do." Steve pointed out that the Bulls had not even broken 100 points. "That's what's happened to the NBA," he said. "We don't even score a hundred and get accused of running up the score."

The final score was Chicago 96, Utah 54. It was the largest margin of any finals game in history. Utah's total was the lowest number of points scored in the National Basketball Association since the introduction of the shot clock.† Jerry Sloan, looking gray and grave, slipped on reading glasses to look over the official statistics report—a coroner going over a postmortem. "That's really the score?" he asked. "Frankly, I'm embarrassed. The whole league should be embarrassed." He charged that the Bulls had run up the score. In the home team's locker room, the atmosphere seemed to reflect officially mandated restraint. A Zen warrior does not exult in the humiliation of his adversaries. Phil Jackson, pointedly, refused to be photographed with a celebratory cigar. "Jerry (Sloan) said that? I'm surprised Jerry said that. He knows the game."

---

*Football may be the only major sport in which it is possible to sit on a lead by running the ball and punting it away to avert exorbitant scoring. Hockey has a possession clock, too. And baseball, by having no clock whatsoever, makes it impossible for a team to say that a lead is ever truly insurmountable.

†Until just the next year, when Jerry Krause's rebuilding Bulls scored just 49 points.

Jackson believed there must have been something wily behind Jerry Sloan's whining—he was trying to rouse the Jazz to dedicate themselves to revenge. But John Stockton, who needed no forged incentives to play with fervor, declined to sign on to his coach's protest. "I suppose," said Stockton, "we could have tried to play a little defense. That would have kept down the score, too." Within just a week, momentum had swung.★ When the series opened, depth, rest, hunger, and the high altitude of home favored Utah. But after three games, experience, restlessness, nerve, and an inheritance of championships seemed to assist Chicago.

Ron Harper was napping at home the next night when his daughter crept in to awake him. "Daddy, Daddy," she said, "look—Dennis is on TV." And so he was. On the off night between games three and four, Rodman had flown up to suburban Detroit to guest star (for a fee of $250,000) in a wrestling program as *Rodzilla!* Because Dennis was, so many excesses to the contrary, scrupulous about keeping his body intact between games, he didn't *wrestle*, exactly. Actual wrestling, even if carefully scripted, could have wrenched a wrist or jammed a knee. Instead, the burden of his performance as *Rodzilla!* was to bellow, bluster, and preen—and appear to smash a chair over the head of his opponents. Harper called Pippen. "You gotta watch it." Harp thought Rodman was actually rather good, considering his unfamiliarity with the form. "Made me laugh," said Harper. "Especially the bit with the chair."

Rodman was fined $10,000 by the league, and another $10,000 by the Bulls. Not for needlessly risking injury between games. Dueling scenes between actors on the stage of the Stratford Festival might be less carefully choreographed than *Rodzilla's* chair bash. Rodman was fined for missing a practice and an appearance before the working press.

Jackson took Rodman's flight as the act of a man who was eager for money, ardent for adulation, and anxious about the future. "It's our last year," said Jackson after practice the next day. "He's coming apart. It's pretty obvious. This is all finally coming to an end, and it hurts. It's something none of us want to go through. It's grief. We don't want to get caught up in the anxiety just yet, but this is what Dennis is going through." Luc Longley, whose towering affability had made him an unofficial Rodman translator, said that trying to change Dennis's behavior seemed a foolish chore in what might be the last paragraph in the last chapter on the storybook

---

★I had hoped to get through an entire book about sports without once using that phrase. But I have learned that is just not possible.

Bulls. "Either you embrace him or you don't," said Luc. "We embrace him. You don't want to distance him. Michael and Scottie have shown such patience and leadership, trying to understand and cope with him."

But practice, practice—wasn't practice where the team learned to harmonize their efforts? "Yes," said Luc, but Dennis was so good at running alongside as the lone wolf. "The fact is," he said, "I like having Dennis as a teammate. The things he brings us are far greater than anything he is taking away. Some of these long road trips, he spices it up a little. He's a good bloke to have around, really. Anyway," Luc announced with revivifying clarity, "shouldn't we be talking about basketball? I should think this next game is fairly huge for the Jazz, wouldn't you?"

The Bulls went back inside for a team meeting before the Jazz bounded out to shoot on the floor of the United Center. But they, too, talked about Rodman. "I just wouldn't have him on my team," said Jerry Sloan. "Winning just isn't that important to me." Jerry Sloan is a blunt, fair man who, should Rodman ever land on his team, might recognize the disciplined craftsman and good soldier in Dennis. But if winning *just isn't that important* to Sloan—what is?

College coaches have a responsibility to encourage good character; too many may neglect it. But there's something condescending about a pro coach who decides he has an imperative to elevate the demeanor and morality of his players. One of the reasons Rodman may have played with such perseverance for Phil Jackson is that Jackson's own well-known morals were taken as inspiration, not instruction. By accepting Dennis Rodman as he was, Jackson helped induce him to become something more. And really: What did Dennis Rodman ever do that threatened civilization and decency? He wore women's lingerie (sometimes, quite beautifully). He stayed out late. He decorated his body, and was indecorous in his behavior. He was insufferably ingenious about fouls. Once, he butted a referee with his head. And once, he kicked at a photographer who he felt had crowded him. Against other players who have abused drugs, beaten wives, and choked their coaches, Rodman wouldn't seem to be first in line for moral correction. On the floor before a practice on the day before the fourth game, Utah's Greg Foster may have been more discerning about Rodman than Foster's own coach. "As long as he (Rodman) gets the rebounds, I don't think anyone gives a damn. Maybe that's why they've won five titles and we haven't."

Just a few minutes before tip-off the next day, Michael Jordan told a watching national television audience, "Dennis Rodman is family. We care about him. We want to love and protect him." One wondered how long were the lingering effects of Salt Lake's high altitude. Jordan scored 34 points that night, Pippen 28. Rodman pulled down 14 rebounds and continued to bedevil Karl Malone. But most crucially, he rediscovered his fine touch with foul shots.

With three minutes left in the game, Jordan missed a turnaround jump shot and Rodman battled for the ball beneath the boards with Malone. In a mutual tangle and snarl, the two men went down. Malone's superior size may have given the referees an impression of responsibility for dragging down Dennis. Malone was called for a foul. If Utah had been awarded a vote about what Bull they wanted at the free throw line, it would have been Rodman. He had hit only half. Dennis stepped up to the line, bounced the ball once, twice, three times, exhaled, rubbed his rump, looked up at the basket lazily, as if watching a cloud pass by, and let fly. He hit the first. And then, the second. In the final three minutes, Dennis made 5 of 6 foul shots to help seal the 86 to 82 victory that put the Bulls ahead 3 games to 1; just one last victory away from a last title.

Phil Jackson was beaming in a set of braces festooned with small elephants. "Dennis," he said, "always redeems himself." Jordan shook his head with undeniable amazement. "I'll never figure him out," he said, "and I won't try. He puts pressure on himself, I guess, to excel in adversity."

"We need to get him through one more game," said Scottie Pippen, "then put him back in a trunk or something." Rodman himself suggested another potent motive for his performance. "I don't want to go back to Salt Lake City. Just don't wanna go back there."

In the analysis that followed, commentators suggested that Rodman's exceptional play had set as bad an example for young people as his disobedience. It suggested that misbehavior could be exonerated by accomplishment—that deeds redeem regardless. Some of those comments were satiric; but quite a few sounded serious. What does Dennis Rodman's success say to young people—break the rules and flourish?

Let's put aside the whole question about the desirability of making athletes exemplars of all values for youngsters. How many of the rest of us could satisfy such colossal expectations? Those athletes who do (and quite a few of the Bulls were notably principled, disciplined, and classy people) manage such virtues under incomprehensible scrutiny and temptation. Rodman's unaccountable accomplishments reminded me: clowns get the best roles. Karl Malone was a fine, religious man. You would want him as your brother-in-law, your neighbor, your friend. But in the fourth quarter, you wanted Rodman as your teammate.

After reporters left the interviewing area to file their stories, I dawdled to chat with a departing player in a runway near the locker room. Every few seconds, you could hear a rhythmic, solid metallic *clang!* in an adjacent area. The player parted open a door so I could see—Carmen Electra was in the weight room. She was keeping Dennis Rodman company—the cheerleader waiting for the class clown—as he put himself through a workout while his opponents and teammates were on their way home.

Despite their most energetic intentions, the Bulls and Rodman had to return to Salt Lake City. Utah was simply too good a team to lose four games in a row. Karl Malone had his best game, scoring 39 points, and beat the Bulls at home, leaving battalions of Chicago police idling, on overtime, in riot gear, waiting to staunch excesses of celebration in the streets.

The next morning, I stopped by to see Ralph. He was following the finals, but often forgetting the results the next morning—a good quality for a Cub fan to cultivate. He was sitting in a wheelchair, looking splendid: silver haired, pink-cheeked, well-knotted, and turned out in a blue blazer by his nurse.

"Did the Bulls win?" he asked. I told him no.

"As a matter of fact, Ralph, when I was walking east on Huron last night, there was a whole armada of police cars and cops in their blue crash helmets carrying around shields like chest protectors. But then the Bulls lost, and they had nothing to do, and four hours left on their shift."

Ralph absorbed the news and made a sly face. "Ha. All dressed up," he said, "and no place to go."

The next morning in Salt Lake City, Gert Burrell, Scott's mother, a schoolteacher in New Haven, Connecticut, put down a book in her lap to confide a dream. "I dreamed," she said, "that we're going to win tonight in the last few seconds on a shot by Steve Kerr."

"Any other particulars, so we'll know what to look for?"

"No, all I see is Steve," she said. "Steve, maybe taking a pass from Michael."

Three hours before game time, the Bulls were napping or pacing in their rooms while a company of family members and friends fretted for them in a lounge near the elevator. Most of us were wearing some signature of Bulls fealty—a pin, a kerchief, a discreet polo shirt. I signaled my standing as a fan with the excessive gesture of wearing a LONGLEY 13 jersey as a vest under my sportcoat. Luc's mother, Susan, wore just a simple knotted scarf. His father, Richard, an understated team shirt. Family members, after all, know their son or husband could soon be traded; they tend not to become as heavily invested in paraphernalia as fans.

A man wearing a gray suit, Air Jordan shoes, a Bulls muffler topped by a red-and-black Bulls Mad Hatter hat approached. "You folks Bulls fans?" he asked. The inquiry in reverse seemed redundant. His name was Ted Smith, from Libertyville, Illinois, and he was in Salt Lake for a medical products conference when he found it his great, good fortune to be booked into the same hotel, on the same floor, as the Chicago Bulls.

"I couldn't believe it. And I'm such a Bulls *fanatic*," said Mr. Smith, superfluously. Although the cartoonish hat and resplendent shoes lent him the look of some kind of fervent elf, Ted Smith had fine, sharp, silvery looks—Paul Newman playing the Cat in the Hat. He was in ostomy products. Ostomy products?

"For colostomy patients," he explained. "Colostomy bags and so forth." He proffered a card. "You folks from Chicago, too?" Yes and no, we explained. Some of us now lived in Washington and Baltimore. Some in Connecticut. This man here—I gestured at Richard Longley, an architect at work in Djakarta—just flew in from the South Pacific. And this woman here—Luc's mum, the educator, smiled in greeting—is from Chicago, but originally from Australia. We've come from all around to cheer the Bulls.

Mr. Smith looked from one tall, red-haired Australian to the other. A flash crossed his face. "Aw, gosh. I mean, aw, *gosh*. I mean—I mean—"

I interceded. "Mr. Smith," I said, "this is Luc Longley's mother." His reaction foreclosed further introductions.★

"Aw, gosh. Amazing," said Ted Smith. "You son. I mean, *your son*. What a class act." He told a story about bringing his daughter to a game for her bas mitzvah, standing in line from the early morning until late afternoon to buy tickets. Once, said Mr. Smith, he had taken his daugh-

---

★A good thing, too. The marriages and remarriages in Luc's immediate family circle can make introductions complicated—as it is in my own. His mother and father have both remarried. Both couples traveled to watch him in the finals, spending much of their time together. Their amity confirms that height is just one hereditary Longley family trait. Another is a gift for friendship.

ter to stand outside the parking gate of the Bulls' training center to watch the players as they arrived and left. "Your son," he said, "slowed down and rolled down his window. 'Luuuc, Luuuc,' I said, 'please say hello to my daughter.' And Luc put out that huge hand of his and tousled the top of her head. 'Pleased to meet you, matey,' he said. Gosh, I can't tell you what that meant to her." Luc's mother liked the story. It was a vignette that showed how some of her own graciousness now resounded in her son. When it came time to depart for the game, the Longley family realized that they had a ticket going unclaimed because a family guest had been delayed in flying in from Australia. Would Ted Smith like the ticket. "Aww, gosh. Aww, *gosh*. Aww, *amazing*. Would I? Would I? *Would I!*"

Over at the Delta Center, Scottie Pippen was ailing and inert on the trainer's table. His back was twisted and tender from standing up to so many assaults from the likes of Karl Malone. When Scottie walked, the base of his spine seemed to tremble like a bell each time one of his heels hit the floor. He had missed taking warm-up shots because he could not lift his arms or stand on his toes to shoot. A doctor pierced his back with cortisone shots, while a trainer warmed and stretched his muscles. Eight years before, he had been criticized for taking himself out of a game because of the pain of a disabling migraine headache. Now, he would try to play a championship basketball game with a precariously rickety back. His own play would be cramped. But the example of determination he might be for other players was expansive.

We were seated next to John Kerr, Steve's brother, an economist at Brown University. Gert Burrell, I told him, had this dream about Steve winning the game on the last shot. His response was more practical than romantic. "Oh, God, I hope not. Last second? I don't know if my heart can take that again."

Utah fans settled in around us. We noticed more than one fan wearing U.S. Post Office regalia. A member of our group said, softly, so as not to affront the good people around us, that you know you're in a small town when people wear U.S. Post Office T-shirts for special occasions. It struck me later that the provincialism was all ours. The mail carrier blouses and Post Office T-shirts must have been tributes to the Mailman, Karl Malone. Scottie Pippen played the first seven minutes; but the pain in his back made him flat-footed. Jackson had to take him out and send him back into the locker room for more massage and heat. With each Jazz score, the din in the Delta Center grew so deafening it rang your teeth. Pippen was down and absent, Jordan was overburdened, and the Jazz were uplifted by home. And yet, Utah was ahead at the half by just five points, 42 to 37. When the Utah cheerleaders sprang onto the court, John Kerr noticed that they danced in skirts long enough to wear without apology to an Amish barn raising.

Scottie Pippen, suffused by painkillers and consoled by warm massage, returned to the game; hobbling, he still drew off defenders. Jordan put up a fusillade of shots, hoping at least a few would fall. By the opening of the fourth quarter, the score had advanced to 66 to 61, Jazz. But the margin stayed the same. Five points, close enough to close with a single loss of the ball.

With two minutes left to play, Jackson called a time-out. The Bulls were behind, 83 to 79. It was a moment for cold reckoning. If the game was beyond winning, it was time to rest their best players, risk no further injury, and prepare for the final game. Scottie Pippen's lower back was brittle; his jump shots were falling like bricks off a short porch. Michael Jordan's jump shots were lame because his legs were limp; he would shoot, then lapse back on defense for rest. Basketball's two best, most complete players were reduced by injury and exhaustion to half strength. The Jazz were ahead at home. On the large screen hanging in the rafters of the Delta Center, the home team flashed a giant image of Karl Malone's dear mother, sitting in the front row courtside, while actor David Hasselhoff revved up a cheer that seemed to rattle the snow on the peaks of the Wasatch Range that was framed through the vast scenic windows of the arena. Utah was stronger, healthier, hungrier, more acclimated to the altitude—and ahead.

And yet, for all those advantages, Utah could put the Bulls down, but not out. The Jazz kept ahead by 3 or 5 points, but never so far that the Bulls could not catch them with a score or two. Along the sidelines, Jordan held his sides to catch his breath, deep, shuddering breaths that shortened what he told Jackson to declarative essentials. "We're gonna win this," said Michael Jordan. And Jackson said softly, evenly—after five championships, neither man depended on bravado for emphasis—"I know."

With a minute left, Jordan drove, drew a foul, made the basket, and sank his foul shots. The score was tied at 83. But then with 42 seconds left, John Stockton broke free to bury what bid to be the decisive 3-point shot for Utah, putting them ahead 86 to 83. If MJ drove in for another layup, Utah would probably stand back to avoid the foul and essentially award Jordan 2 points. Two were as useful—or useless—as none when you're behind by three. Utah would then get the ball back and run down the clock to win by a single point. If the Bulls lost, there would be a seventh game in three days. Three days in which the Jazz would relax and practice in their exquisite mountain surroundings, while the Bulls would stir and pace and feel pensive and cooped-up with small-town blues in a small-town hotel. They would not be a good bet to prevail. I am a foolish fan, but not always a fool. I was at the point of a Jacksonian embrace of the glory of defeat when I caught a wave from Ted Smith, the colostomy bag man in his Mad Hatter hat, who was sitting three rows ahead. Ted pumped his thumbs up with a grin of utter, senseless, touching and immaculate faith: "Hey, pallie!" he declared with a grin. *"We got 'em now!"*

Jordan sliced toward the basket for a quick layup. The Jazz laid back to avoid the foul. MJ got the basket. But Utah now had the ball. With 37 seconds left, possession was more precious than points. The Jazz could hold on while the clock ticked down, each tick tolling the death of a chance for Chicago to score.

John Stockton passed to Karl Malone—the Utah Overture usually leading to a score; one last score to secure a 3-point lead to put the Bulls down. But Karl Malone, impassive and composed, turned his back to Utah's basket and held up the play for an instant. The hesitation was smart. Each elapsed second collapsed a possibility for the Bulls. Jeff Hornacek sprinted to his right, to draw off Michael Jordan in pursuit. But Jordan lingered, almost softly, with a burglar's quiet. "Karl never knew I was there," he said later. So when Malone turned his gaze left to pick up a man to receive another stalling pass, Michael Jordan leaned below Malone's left shoulder and, like a man playing tag with a beehive, slapped the ball out of Karl Malone's huge and accomplished hands.

### 00:18.5

The seconds blinked bright red on the game clock, as Jordan bobbled and bounced the ball into the step of his dribble.

In full prowl and roar along the sidelines, Phil Jackson's first reaction was to worry—that Jordan or Rodman might call a time-out. A time-out would give Jackson the chance to hatch a final play. It might put an extra puff of breath into Jordan's winded lungs, and a last inch of spring into his ragged legs. But a pause would also give Utah the opportunity to compose its defense. Jackson preferred to see the Jazz scramble back from the disorder of a fractured play. Over whatever circuitry of intuition and Zen Jackson had soldered with Jordan over nine years, he now beamed an urgent signal: make your move *now*. But on the chance that telepathy might be dashed in the din and glare of the Delta Center, Jackson revved his arms against the air violently, like a man banging for rescue on a locked bathroom door. "Go!" he shouted. "Go down! *Go! Go!*"

Michael Jordan had not heard Jackson. In fact, he had barely looked over at his coach. Did Fred Astaire need to cast a glance at Ginger Rogers's feet? After all their trials and trails together, Jackson's and Jordan's wisdom and instincts were intertwined. Michael began to *move*. His course was as direct and remorseless as a gunslinger's. His bare head bounced light:

*00:17.0*
*00:16.0*
*00:15.0*

as he took the ball over the red stripe at the center of the court,

*00:14.0*
*00:13.0*
*00:12.0*

as he cocked an eye toward the clock clicking down in red numerals,

*00:11.0*
*00:10.0*

then a halt in place, as Jordan hovered on his heels at the left arc top of the circle, surveying—it was the indispensable cliché—his domain.

Steve Kerr was on Michael's right, Toni Kukoc to his left. Each had won famous, critical games with long-range, last-second shots. So they were covered closely. Utah did not want to risk the miscalculation that had defeated them the year before, when putting two men on Michael Jordan had freed Steve Kerr to take MJ's pass and loft the shot that will always sign Steve's career. Jerry Sloan was not going to lose two championships in the same way twice.

Of course, leaving Michael Jordan the space to take an open shot was probably the best-advertised risk since smoking cigarettes. But Sloan could also see that Jordan's legs were growing rubbery. A man needs something stronger in his knees than rubber to sink a fadeaway jump shot. Jordan had scored more than 40 points. But bone-weariness had slowed much of his fourth-quarter play. When he tried to snap into motion for shots now, he could look like a man trying to dance underwater. When he leapt, he fell back more quickly. *Michael Jordan was beginning to look earth-bound.* He had missed four jump shots in a row, clanged them, in fact, off the bottom of the rim so that they came off too sharply for Rodman or Pippen to pluck them off and punch them back into the hoop. During a time-out, Jackson told Jordan what had been excruciatingly evident in Jordan's own joints: his legs were all played out. *Drive, drive at the basket,* said Jackson, and hope that Utah would have to put him down with a foul.

Jerry Sloan could see the struggle between Jordan's will and Jordan's legs. He was willing to gamble for the chance that a toil-worn Jordan, slow-footed and wilting, would miss one or more of any foul shots he might draw. So Jerry Sloan sent out only Bryon Russell to guard Michael Jordan. In a way, it was an invitation—*take your best shot, MJ, we're ready.* But Sloan's insight was bereft of insider knowledge. Over on the sidelines, Jordan had agreed with Jackson. His jump shots were fading along with the string in his legs. But then, MJ advised, "I've got my second wind now." Driving to the basket seemed a duller weapon. Why play for a chain reaction of events—drive, draw a foul, sink one or two shots for a point or two—when the flag could be captured in a single stroke? Jackson said, "If you must take a jump shot, Michael, for chrissakes follow through, follow through."

I tried to catch a glimpse of Gert Burrell, sitting three rows behind the Bulls' bench, but lost sight of her behind a sign: RODMAN SODOMIST, with some kind of attached scriptural citation. Was her dream about to step out onto the stage? Beside us, John Kerr was beginning to rise out of his seat. "This sure would be a nice time," I murmured, "for one of your brother's—" But the sentence was cut off by a shout. John Kerr, faithful brother, joined a chorus rising even among the Jazz fans who bellowed as if calling out of a bad dream. "Michael! *Mi-chael!*"

(Months later, I asked John if even for a moment his heart had leapt with a hope that Steve would get the ball. And John Kerr answered with a brother's loving laugh, "Steve? Not Michael? Are you kidding?")

In that instant, I tried to imagine the millions of other places around the world sharing the suspense of that same moment. People sitting up with a squeak from vinyl recliners and congealing shards of take-out pizza in Vancouver, Metairie, and Miami, standing up from barstools and Cheez Doodles in Duluth-Superior, Durham, Appleton, and Port Arthur. In lazy, late afternoon front rooms, sick rooms, and Sunday license taverns, Portsmouth pubs and Ponce bodegas, rowdy kids and rapt adults, millions of people watching and listening, each sharing the same certainty at the same time, the worst-kept secret in the world since India exploded a nuclear bomb. *This just in, ladies and gentlemen: Michael Jordan is going to take the last shot.*

He drove right, crossing the dribble of the ball over from his right to his left hand. Bryon Russell reached in boldly to make his own steal. But suddenly, Michael Jordan stopped: as completely, as smoking-heels screechingly as a Road Runner cartoon. Bryon Russell kept on going, his momentum augmented by an emphatic tap on his tailbone from Jordan. The daring strike that Russell meant to seize the ball from Michael Jordan's dribble instead grasped nothing but the gap Michael Jordan had dug out for him. Russell's feet fell out below him, like a horse breaking down. He flailed gamely at the air above as he looked up into what must have been the living, leaping, wide screen, Technicolor nightmare of someone who makes a living in basketball: Michael Jordan with a clear look at an open shot.

The game clock blinked off breaths in tenths of seconds:

*00:06.0*
*00.05.9*
*00:05.8*

as Jordan stepped off from his left foot

*00:05.7*

as he lifted his right

*00:05.6*

as flashbulbs blared a bow of light around the court, and Michael Jordan measured off the last shot of his career. It was a cold-eyed, unsparing, unswerving dead-on shot that hit like a spike nailed into the heart of the orange iron hoop eighteen feet and four-tenths of a second away.

Steve Kerr once explained that a kind of memory in his muscles could tell him if one of his shots would hit from the moment it flew from his fingers. You make enough shots—and miss enough shots—and a spark or shiver in your bones can let you know if it will fail or fall in, rattle off or roll around into the hoop. Tennis player JoAnne Russell once urged me not to dismiss the squall of players who protest a call. Players practiced hours for years, she said, to learn how to slash a ball slyly and cleanly into the line. "Don't really good bartenders," she asked with a smile, "know when they've poured out a shot to the line without looking?" Players, she said, learn to trust their internal compass more than a line judge's blinking eyes.

Fans, too, develop mental muscles for powers of observation. A certain swing and ring resonating from the bat of Mark McGwire announces the takeoff of a home run. So it was only modest self possession when Michael Jordan said later, "When the moment starts to be the moment, you feel it. I knew it was the game-winning shot." Just two nights before, after all, he had stepped up into a last-second shot that fell short. But tonight, he pogo-stepped on the toes of his right foot; he held his right hand up high—posed it, really—for just an extra moment, like an exclamation point as his shot took flight from the tips of his fingers. *All the instruments agreed.*

Utah fans fell silent in their rows. The sound in the Delta Center died: absolutely, suddenly, as if someone had pulled the plug on a thunderstorm. As the game clock flickered

*00:05.2*

the noiselessness was so vast that a fan could convince himself he could actually hear Michael Jordan's last shot clip sweetly and neatly through the net of the basket: the net, the net, and nothing more.

For the first time that night, Bulls fans heard their own cheers. We hugged, we kissed, we shouted like kids on a camping trip hurling yells off the walls of a great cave. On the floor, Utah called for a time-out. In the seats to our left, a Jazz fan said with a sigh of resignation to her young son, "Well, we wanted to see Michael Jordan . . ."

Utah threaded the ball into John Stockton. Thirty-six years old, a short man among giants who often outplayed them; shrewd, slick, and famously nerveless: a Bull in Jazz clothing. Twenty-five feet from the basket, 00:01:0 showing on the game clock, Stockton rushed up to launch an audacious shot off the palm of his right hand. For an instant, a huge breath was bottled inside 20,000 throats. But the ball caught the fat side of the rim, hung almost like a dew drop on its lip, then bowled over the hoop without falling in, rolling out and away. When the ball bounded once off the floor, an outstretched Antoine Carr tried to hurl it back toward the hoop. But as the game horn blared against rows of exhaled breaths, the ball banged soundlessly and scorelessly into the expensive courtside seats. Dennis Rodman clambered in to claim a last, uncounted rebound, wrapping the ball in his long, ornamented arms and tucking it tightly to his chest as if it was, all metaphor apart, the most precious thing he would ever hold.*

Sweaty red Bulls began to bounce on the court. They tumbled onto one another, giants in a playground jumble. Before they could all find one another in the fog of victory, an NBA staffer with championship T-shirts flipped himself onto the floor and ran into Scottie Pippen—who took one to wrap around his head as he cried (if, God forbid, we ever hear air raid sirens screech in earnest, I expect the imminent end of the world to be heralded by men vending T-shirts saying, I DIED IN THE BIG ONE).

The three-peat was repeated, the sixth and most challenging championship won. Fans and reporters watched for clues in the way Jordan, Jackson, and Pippen embraced, as CIA analysts used to watch the greetings at Moscow's May Day parade. The trio enfolded one another in turn, abiding, tender, and sustained. Jackson already knew he would not return. Pippen, who had played with such bravery and devotion in the finals, assumed that he would wind up elsewhere, too; he was sobbing with such strength, he put his head into a balled-up warm-up jacket.† Jordan, judging by his later words, felt overwhelmed by weariness: certain he would not return, but disinclined to decide that out of exhaustion. He took Steve Kerr and coach Jimmy Rodgers into his arms at once, then awarded an extra moment of embrace to Rodman. *Hey man, I told you, we still got it.* Then, Jordan moved with outstretched arms through the rest of the team, Toni Kukoc, Luc, Bill Wennington,

---

*Dennis, in an act of uncharacteristic orthodoxy, would give the ball to a referee. Ron Harper, however, would ask the referee for the ball as he made his way off the court. The ball remains in Harp's house today. It is an artifact that could, to be vulgar about it, be sold for the price of a Van Gogh—the ball that scored the last basket for the last championship in the last seconds of the last game of the most famous player of all time. But Harper says he is merely keeping the ball for his good friend Michael Jordan; one of the few men in a position to disregard its commercial value.

†If the Bulls had won by, say, five points rather than one—if Jordan had scored more points in the stretch—he would not have needed to take the last dramatic shot that sealed the series. Pippen, after his daunting defense and gritty return in the second half, might well have been selected the Most Valuable Player of the finals.

Jud Buechler, and Scott Burrell. *Good job, man. Way to go, man. Hey, we did it, man.*

When Jordan got to Joe Kleine, the third-string center was crying. Kleine was thirty-six years old, a long-time sub who had been Jordan's teammate on the 1984 U.S. Olympic team. He spent thirteen increasingly humbling years with the meek Sacramento Kings, the collapsing Boston Celtics, Phoenix, Los Angeles, and then New Jersey before being signed by the Bulls to wait on the bench to spell Luc Longley and Bill Wennington. Kleine had played only a few minutes in just 46 games all year. But when he approached Michael Jordan with his arms spread wide to receive an embrace in the most marvelous moment of a discouraging career, Jordan instead jolted him. "Why are you crying?" Jordan demanded. "I did it all."

Jordan's teammates knew he could wound with words. It was part of the artillery of an articulate man who had learned that words, too, scored points. Jordan's teammates knew that the sweet-natured friend of Tweetie Bird featured in commercials was not an act, exactly, but an appealing personality Jordan kept packed away for children, his family, a few close friends, MCI, Gatorade, and McDonald's—*not* his teammates. But the teammates also knew something of the extraordinary pressure of expectation with which Jordan had to live; and how their own shortcomings could add to that. As Phil Jackson would tell reporters, "We all climbed on Michael's back, and once again he carried us home." So when Jordan lashed out at them in practice, ridiculed or mocked them, they told themselves that the man had earned the right to a little raillery among friends.

Some of Jordan's teammates later took his remark as a sign that Michael Jordan was finally weary beyond revival. In just a few moments, Jordan would find his better angels. He would be smiling and gracious before the watching millions, modest and generous to his teammates. Why assume that Jordan's sustained civility is some kind of pose, and his snapping episodes of pissy viciousness are real? Not even Michael Jordan's most ardent fans can contrive a clever excuse for his jab at Joe Kleine. But a man who had so often said *just the right thing* to reporters, referees, and sick children probably should be forgiven a slip with a teammate for whom he had just won a gold championship ring. It was a lousy remark to make to a nice man. But not inaccurate.

In the stands, we hugged, we kissed, and we worried how to make the journey down onto the floor. The Jazz fans sitting on all sides were so gracious as to bring a twinge—just a twinge, and it passed quickly—of regret that a team so game had once again fallen just a shot short. We shook hands all around and thanked them for their hospitality. I began to slip my sportcoat back over my LONGLEY 13 jersey, but a man who had spent the game sitting behind us caught me carefully on my right shoulder. "Hey, buddy, don't cover that up," he said. "You came a long way to be proud."

Trying to step down, row by row, was halting; we had to fall back a step for each three we could advance. By the time we reached the ropes of the courtside, the rostrum ceremonies had begun. Commissioner David Stern had handed the championship trophy over to Jerry Reinsdorf, who quickly handed off to Phil Jackson, who raised it aloft, and the cheering began. "On behalf of billions of Bulls fans all over the world," we could hear Reinsdorf say, "I just want to say, Michael, I hope that you and Scottie will return to defend this trophy next year." *Michael* and *Scottie*, it was impossible not to notice, but *no Phil*. Within a couple of days, Reinsdorf would tender a generous offer to Phil Jackson to return the next year, regardless of Jordan's plans or Pippen's desires. Jackson would find the offer sincere but unconvincing. Jerry Reinsdorf must have been rehearsing and revising his post-game podium remarks for much of the season. His words betrayed as much spontaneity as an Oscar acceptance speech, as if he had said, "I want to thank my producer, I want to thank my director, I want Michael and Scottie to come back. Whoops—did I forget to say Phil?"

Police and security guards linked arms to try to convey the Bulls into their locker room. But some of the worst fans were standing up on the most expensive seats. They rattled rancorous signs about Dennis Rodman as he tried to make it into the runway leading to the locker room. They booed and barked while a man standing over our shoulders had to catch his breath to keep up a verbal tattoo:

"*Fuck*you Dennis *Fuck*you Dennis *Fuck*you Dennis *Fuck*you Dennis"—gasp! "*Fuck*you Dennis *Fuck*you Dennis *Fuck*you Dennis *Fuck*you Dennis"—gasp! When the guards buckled back from the force of fans leaning in, their line gave way. Several of us were sent sprawling into the folding chairs set up for the high rollers sitting courtside. As the chairs fell over in rows, they folded, their forelegs snapping dangerously. Dr. Pauline Maki got a gash on her leg and said, "I took one for Rodman, and I'd do it again." But God truly watches over children and fools, so the fool continued his fanfare without hindrance: *"Fuck*you Dennis *Fuck*you Dennis *Fuck*you Dennis *Fuck*you Dennis . . ."* Dennis stripped off his shirt and turned up his smile, waving his shirt at the man, teasingly.

In the locker room, small white towels, swollen with beer and champagne, were thickening against the floor. Steve Kerr, his blond crew cut dampened by that locker-room cocktail, looked like a duck shaking off pond water as he stood with his brother John. When I stuck out my hand, he instinctively turned it into a hug. Then, a kiss. "Well," I confessed, "I guess I've already been kissing your brother."

"You wanna see the most amazing thing?" Steve asked. "See Carmen Electra over there?" The actress was standing near the showers, a slender tan leather tube top saturated by champagne shrinking against her bustline. "There's Carmen Electra over there, soaked by champagne. You can see her—well, you can see, right?" I could. "I mean, you can count the goose bumps, right? And you know what?" Mr. Kerr asked with a detectable twinkle. "All anyone still wants to see is Michael Jordan."

Luc, looking like a champagne-dappled sequoia, leaned down to pick me up as easily as other men might bring in the morning paper. *Mate, mate.* He set me down like a child, then overturned a bottle of champagne on my head. I felt grateful for the fellowship, but also chagrined—champagne baths ought to be awarded only to those who have had to bang heads with Karl Malone.* Leonardo di Caprio walked by. Anywhere else in the world, such an entrance might have touched off a riot of camera lights. But every other place in the world that night was empty of Michael Jordan. A cameraman barked in Leonardo's wake, mostly for the joke of it, "Who the hell let him in?" Antoine Carr, a Chicagoan playing abroad for Utah, came in to shake hands. Phil Jackson, wreathed in television lights, delivered another phrase carefully. "I think it's the best performance I've ever seen in a critical situation. Michael always comes through. How many times does he have to show

---

*Utah's drinking laws are widely misunderstood. A championship celebration in a locker room is a good textbook definition of a private party. Legally, there was no restraint on the right of the Bulls to quaff champagne. But the NBA was eager to avoid appearing to flout local liquor laws, erroneous as accounts of those laws can be (in fact, you can buy a drink in some licensed precincts of Salt Lake City at noon, even on Sunday). So reports persisted that if the Bulls won the title, they would have to splash about in Mormon champagne—sparkling grape juice. Jerry Reinsdorf was not about to be cast as an owner so pointlessly frugal he popped open grape juice for Michael Jordan and his friends. So with Gandhian commitment to civil disobedience, the Bulls laid in the bubbly. They were prepared to explain, straight-faced, that the champagne was for therapeutic bathing, not drinking.

us that he's a real-life hero? I don't know how you can avoid the word."

Cellular telephones may be manufactured for just such occasions. "I'm calling from the locker room . . ." I called my mother and Ralph. Ralph was drifting in and out of pain and sleep, but my mother said they had been watching. "Isn't Michael Jordan the most marvelous?" she asked. "Isn't he the most amazing?" Ralph was almost eighty-seven. It occurred to me that he had never seen the Cubs or White Sox win a World Series. If he had not been an atheist, he might have seen some divine reward for faith in the fact that at least he had seen the Bulls win six world titles (even though he may have nodded off for their last one).

Dr. Maki nudged me. "Hey," she said, "over there. By Phil's elbow. Isn't that Ted?" The colostomy bag salesman, in his red-and-black Bulls' Mad Hatter hat, was standing alongside Jackson, nodding sagely. *Yes, yes, Phil makes a good point there.* When Scottie Pippen crossed by behind him, slowed down by other shouted questions, Ted fell in step beside him, too. *Yes, Scottie's absolutely right about that. Who knows what next year will bring?* The Bulls' locker room was congested with celebrities: Michael and Scottie, Dennis Rodman and Carmen Electra, Gene Siskel, Bob Costas, Penny Marshall, Leonardo di Caprio—and Ted Smith, ostomy products sales manager, Libertyville, Illinois. We rushed over.

"Ted! Ted! Good to see you. How in the hell did you get in here?"

"Hey," shrugged Ted, "I'm a marketing guy!"

He straightened up to stand on his toes for a pose between Luc and Richard Longley, who then lifted Ted by his elbows up to their shoulders. "Hey, awright, Waltzing Matilda, maties!" A cluster of other players, Wennington, Buechler, Kukoc, and Kerr, clustered obligingly behind Ted Smith for another shot. "Oh, that one," I imagined him saying with elaborate informality to a client. "That's just me in the Bulls' locker room. Last championship. MJ's last shot. Nice group of guys. A real pleasure. Nice as they are tall. Now, let's take a look at your order . . ." The players didn't seem to resent a new outsider in their midst, but instead welcomed Ted Smith as a kind of Every Fan, a nice man and loyal fan they could flatter and thank for his devotion. A few players approached to pose and shake Ted's hand. I thought they were going to form a line.

"Hey, everyone!" Ted called out genially as he posed for another picture. "Colostomy bags for everyone!" It was time, obviously, to get back to the planes and go home.

First, for the Bulls' families and friends, there was a walk of several blocks back to the hotel where buses were idling, biding time to depart for the airport. Even in streets abounding with fierce Jazz fans, you could see children in red JORDAN 23 jerseys, holding on to a mother's hand or sitting on their father's shoulders. It was a crisp, brilliant mountain night, with the deep black sky swarming with stars that looked full to bursting. Kelly Longley began to sing to the stars:

> *Come on, oh baby, don't you want to go*
> *Oh come on, oh baby don't you want to go*
> *Back to that same old place*
> *Sweet Home Chicago!*

With our jerseys, our smiles, and our song—and our champagne-bubble breath—we were obvious outsiders. But the Salt Lake citizens smiled back and called out congratulations; a few even cheered. I wondered if Chicagoans encountering Jazz fans on their streets, if fortunes had been reversed, would have been quite so gracious. At the hotel, the players ascended to collect their luggage and check out while we now idled happily alongside the buses. When Kelly Longley came down, she was wearing Luc's game jersey, unrolled to her knees.

The buses pulled away for the airport, the streets now lined with people straining to look inside our darkened windows. Utah fans may have been disgruntled and disappointed; but they still hoped for a last glimpse of Michael Jordan. He wasn't on our bus. But as we passed through Salt Lake City's tidy, orderly, and handsome streets, there was a chorus of chaos outside the windows that could be heard even within all of our happy chatter: *Michael! Michael! Michael!* When the bus passed by the lissome, majestic lighted spires of Temple Square, the driver, a local man, piped up over the mike to say something—well, slightly disadvantageous about the local faith. Perhaps he was seeking only to put visitors from a famously heretical place at ease. But when the laughter faded, it set off a fresh chorus of the tune we had first struck up on the streets. Chicago blues seemed to ring with gratifying resonance off the white, white walls of the members-only inner-sanctum of the angel Moroni's temple :

> *Come on, oh baby, don't you want to go*
> *Oh come on, oh baby don't you want to go*
> *Back to that same old place*
> *Sweet Home Chicago!*

Margot Kerr, wife of Steve Kerr, struck up another number:

> *Sometimes I dream*
> *That he is me.*
> *You need a dream to keep goin' on*

A few more people chimed in, laughingly, for the refrain:

> *Ba-ba-ba-ba-bum.*

Most were a little uncertain of the lyrics that followed, so Margot led us quickly to the signature line:

> *Duh-duh duh-duh, Dah-duh duh-duh.*
> *Like Mike! If I could be like Mike!*

Then, the whole bus rang:

> *Like Mike! If we could be like Mike!*

Then again, louder, for good measure:

> *Like Mike! If we could be like Mike!*

Luc said he had hoped they would win the championship at home. But in the event, there was something poignant about capturing a title in an alien place, encircled by adversaries but succored by a small number of friends, and flying back home across the country alongside the stars. It suited the mood of men and women who sensed that in winning, they were about to lose hold of one another. On the flight back, there were a few cigars and tequila toasts; a few dark mutterings, among family and friends, about management; but mostly, quiet, tired, and unaffected conversation between men and women who would always mark the most important pages of each other's lives. They were sharing the last few hours of the last few years of an astounding ride that had brought them so high, it seemed they had put a hand on the moon. At some point, there was a spot of turbulence. The captain called for us to sit down and buckle up. I sat down next to Kelly Longley. Her eyes were dewy, starry, and sad.

"Everyone asks us," she said, " 'Which championship feels better?' This one, without a doubt. Because we all know each other. This is a business"—and Kelly left no doubt that it was *her* business, too—"where you're always moving around. Two, three years here, two years there, meeting new people, running in to some of the same old ones, never really knowing each other. But this is a *team*. We're best friends. We've shared so much. We're in and out of each other's houses all the time. Look, I know these years will always be the highlight of our lives. *For the rest of our lives*. Luc and I have had our children, we've won these championships. We have shared so much hard work, so much sheer happiness with everyone here. Let me tell you something. Aside from my family, most of the people in this world that I *love*," Kelly said with a catch, "are all around me. Right here. Right now."

Gert Burrell had fallen asleep in her seat, tucked in to her chin under Scott's red game jersey. We passed high over the blunt, open hand of America: the Tavaputs Plateau and the Sawatch Range, the North Platte River snaking just under the Sand Hills of western Nebraska, where the state is still dry, pure desert plains, and then rolls on east into fat farmlands and neat, honest towns you can pick up by tracing the train tracks with your eyes into the greening fields of middle Iowa, that lead on into the asphalt veins of northern Illinois. The small, soft lights of Rock Falls, Dixon, De Kalb, and Aurora seemed to lead like footlights into the brightness of Chicago, where they had lit the crowns of the Loop and lakefront towers with red lights. We looked down lovingly into the night, onto the red lights, the iron roof tops, silver street lights, smoky sidewalks, and the dark glints of the great lake: Chicagoans Abroad, coming home.

# EPILOGUE

I don't expect ever again to feel as devoted to a team as I was to the Chicago Bulls of Michael Jordan, Scottie Pippen, Dennis Rodman, Luc Longley, Steve Kerr, and Phil Jackson. In fact, I've promised as much. My fascination and attachment to that team became a token of the love I carried for Chicago as I made my life away from home. As I traveled, I saw red Bull faces blossom on exotic streets, rundown towns, and in high, holy places, home and away. Other sports teams, writers, artists, saints, politicians, crooks, and musicians had seemed to embody the city's ancestral image of sturdiness, style, and grit. But this championship breed of Bulls refined that reflection. They added Rodman's savvy, Satchmo-jazzy outrageousness and daring; Jackson's Jane Addams gentility and determination; and Michael Jordan's supreme, sky-piercing, Frank Lloyd Wright–like audacity and dominance. The years in which Chicagoans felt personally enriched by this acclaim were a rare and unrepeatable period—an era in which JORDAN 23 made the name *Chicago* a sign of magic for millions; as it had always been for me.

• • •

I would become a conscientious objector in the shortened 1999 season that followed. I could not bring myself to root for—or, for that matter, against—the Bulls who were bequeathed the name after Phil Jackson bowed out, Michael Jordan retired, and Scottie Pippen, Dennis Rodman, Luc Longley, and Steve Kerr were sprinkled over the rest of the league. Instead, I cheered for the old Bulls, wherever they landed, on a grateful fan's daffy conviction that I owed those players at least a year's more loyalty than what their employers had been willing to confer.

Comings and goings are the game itself in modern sports. Most players will shed one jersey for another every few seasons, with the regularity of reptiles. Part of what made the reign of the Bulls remarkable was not only the long partnership of Jordan, Jackson, and Pippen, but the fact that so many teams had tried to rework themselves precisely to defeat them; and failed. Yet it was the unbeaten Bulls who got broken up. Fans felt real grief—deprived of a tie that had given us a sense of wonder, oneness, and distinction.

But Jerry Reinsdorf and Jerry Krause seemed to feel left out of that tie; and, in a reflex that looked a lot like jealousy, they reasserted the right of an owner to wreck his own property. Building a team without Jordan, Pippen, and Jackson offered the owner and general manager the chance to win recognition that simply sustaining the national treasure of the Bulls had not.

Sports agnostics who remind fans that the games, after all, are just business perhaps don't know much about business. There must be a thousand better ways to make money than to own a sports team. Rich men and women tend to buy into sports only when they are willing to spend a mint to win some other satisfaction—an identity, a sense of purpose—that is not fulfilled by the fortunes they have already built.

Phil Jackson rekindled new reasons in his players to win, year after year. It was his surpassing talent. But the men above him who ran the Bulls seemed to run out of inspiration; and found none in Jackson's Zen incentives. *You must embrace losing to know the joy of winning* probably sounded like flighty, feathery stuff in an age that demands no-loss *exit strategies*. Jerry Reinsdorf and Jerry Krause seemed, in a way great players and faithful fans never are, scared of losing. It's sad that they couldn't enjoy the ride as much as the rest of us. The owner and his general manager looked for chances for the Bulls to surrender before they could lose. The players and fans wanted the game, and the team, to go on; however it ended.★

Six weeks after the Bulls won their last championship, and about halfway into the greatest baseball season of all time, Ralph Newman died. I don't believe that Ralph would have forfeited more than a day of the pain and incoherence he had borne for nine months. It was the cost of having the time to unreel a long, rich, cache of memories and say good-bye. But I also don't doubt that Ralph didn't want to stay on for a day longer. I flew back home. When I unfurled the living room sofa bed in their apartment, my mother apologized for an accumulation of books, papers, and bric-a-brac that had to be moved. "Now what are we supposed to do," she wondered, "with this big old popcorn tin?" The tin was the size of a snare drum. It was embellished on the side with the snarling Bulls emblem. She said Ralph had gone out on his last outing with his nurse just a couple of days before, and they had made the rounds between a bookstore, a gadget shop, and the popcorn stand. Ralph had returned with the Bulls tin tucked atop his lap.

"I said to him," remembered my mother, " 'Mr. Newman, what are we ever gonna do with that? How are we ever going to eat all of that popcorn?' But he was just like a little kid—he wanted the tin, didn't he?"

We held a public memorial for Ralph in the former public library building downtown. Several clergy were present, but as guests. Old friends, family, and fans formed the memorial chorus. Ralph's daughters, Carole and Maxine, invoked the personal privilege of flesh and blood to say Kaddish, the Jewish prayer for the dead. Ralph was an atheist; but as he used to joke, a *Jewish* atheist. Then Carole asked those assembled to sing the song Ralph had always considered the genuine National Anthem. "Beginning a ball game with the 'Star-Spangled Banner,' " he used to say, "is like beginning a honeymoon with your mother-in-law. You gotta overcome it." He preferred, of course, the "Battle Hymn of

---

★I believe that if Michael Jordan had stayed on with the Bulls, they would have won another championship in 1999. The shortened season would have favored their experience. More contestable, though, is my belief that if Jordan had retired, but the Bulls had retained Pippen, Rodman, Kukoc, Harper, then used money made available by MJ's departure to sign a discontented star, such as Penny Hardaway, they would have contended credibly for two more titles. Even if they had faltered, it would be an exciting team to watch—and a more noble way to succeed the Michael Jordan generation of championships than by playing to lose games and win high-draft choices.

the Republic." Especially the second chorus, which he considered an artful piece of poetry that sang not of faith as much as sacrifice:

> *In the beauty of the lilies*
> *Christ was born across the sea*
> *with a glory in his bosom*
> *that transfigures you and me.*
> *While he died to make men holy*
> *let us die to make them free.*
> *His Truth goes marching on!*

I had not seen Jack Brickhouse for several months. He had been recovering at home from surgery to remove a brain tumor. But he told me over the telephone a couple of nights before that it was important for him to "get up off my ass to say good-bye to Ralph." A man passed a microphone around the crowd for recollections; Uncle Jack was not about to let it pass. He held a hand on the shoulder of his wife, Pat, to steady himself as he stood. "You know," he managed to boom in a hale, Wrigley Field inflection, "we have a saying in baseball. 'Class will tell.' Well, it sure did. Baseball might have lost a mighty good player when Ralph left. But history got a real classy guy, too." Over the past year, I had learned a little about the exceptional effort it takes to get up off your ass when your body fights back for every inch. I looked over at Uncle Jack as he sat back down, heavily, and caught his eye. "Hey, Uncle Jack," I mouthed the words. "Hey-hey."

He chortled. Just a couple of years before, I had told Jack what a woman had told me: that men of my age who grew up in Chicago often exclaimed the words of his old home run call in the highest moments of romantic intensity. He was flattered to know that his personal motto would thus be enshrined for future generations. It became a covert little joke between us; something to say in front of his wife and my mother, just between us boys. "Hey, kid," Jack would say. "You keep saying Hey-hey now."

Champagne was served at the end of Ralph's service. When I reached up to hug Uncle Jack around his shoulders (he was walking on a cane and could not lift both arms) he tottered for a moment and spilled champagne on his shoes. "Now, slugger," he said, "there's a *real* tragedy." Then he leaned down close, comforting and consoling. It must have looked like a tender moment, my father's best friend, my stepfather's pal, soothing and advising me on mature new obligations. But what Jack was saying, in a low, sly voice, was, "You keep saying Hey-hey now, pal. Just keep saying Hey-hey."

Four days later, when I was just getting back to sleeping without fear that the telephone would trill with bad news in the middle of the night, I got a call telling me that Jack Brickhouse had died. The place of the visitation and internment, and even a good number of the mourners, were the same as just a few days before. The funeral director, a professionally sober man, could not resist joking that we should have inquired about group rates.

Jack's visitation and funeral, however, were also civic occasions. Fans came, clanking with Cub memorabilia and paraphernalia. The mayor and the governor sent mammoth flower arrangements—a floral baseball and a flowered bat, respectively—and a great number of florists managed to work in ribbons or vines that spelled out the phrase, HEY-HEY! My mother was remarking graciously on the ingenuity of the displays when an inveterate funeral-goer turned around to differ. "That's nothing," he advised. "You should have seen what they did for Cardinal Bernardin."

The funeral director set aside what amounted to a locker room for Uncle Jack's pallbearers. Ernie Banks came in, moving with silken conviviality. "Oh, it's a terrible day, God bless Jack. How are you, ol' buddy? Let's play two, God bless." Billy Williams, now a Cub batting coach, walked in sturdily, still looking like the club stalwart. He was the first man in the room to put on the pearl-gray gloves for carrying Jack's coffin—Billy, ready for the call. Ron Santo, his old ballplayer's frame looking like a bad fit in a black grief suit, tucked the pallbearing gloves into his belt, third base style, while we waited to be called out to the chapel. Johnny "Red" Kerr, the original Bull, was shucking off questions from the moment he entered. "I don't know if he'll retire. Only Michael knows what he'll do, and I don't know if he knows." Dan Ronan, an admirable young sportscaster whom Jack had taken into his heart, came over and asked, with wide, reddened eyes, "Can you believe this team?" Our pall-mates. Ray Meyer, the old De Paul University basketball coach, now in his mid-eighties, came in with a beery, robust look, but feigning chagrin. "Looking at all of you," he said, "I can see that by the time I go, none of you will be around to carry me." A sturdy looking man with silver hair stood up, and stuck out his hand.

"Do we know each other?"

"I don't think so. My name is Scott Simon."

"Bill Pierce."

*Billy Pierce!*

He was now in his early seventies, a solid citizen, husband, and father, retired from a second career in a west-side car dealership and making occasional appearances for the White Sox in clubs and schools. My rekindled adoration came out in a rush.

"Oh, Mr. Pierce," I said. "*Billy.* I used to think I *was* you, Billy Pierce. But I'm not left-handed, except when I talk on the phone. My mother—once, corn cobs hit me on the head. She asked, 'What's your name, what's your name?' And I said *you.* I said, '*Billy Pierce.*' So she knew I was all right. You taught me how to pitch. My father, Ernie, Uncle Jack, took me to the park. You tore off the corner of a sweet roll, and you *showed* me how to pitch." Finally, perhaps, I'd said something Bill Pierce could disentangle from the torrent.

"Aaah, the sweet roll," he said. "But they don't let you use it in a game." I had been using his joke since I was three years old. When we were finally called in to the chapel, instructed to walk somberly, I still looked up to catch my mother's eye, where she sat in a center pew.

"Didja see? Didja see?" I mouthed the words. My mother nodded back.

"Yes, I see! Billy Pierce!"

At the end of the day, after Billy Pierce and I had played, shoulder-to-shoulder, on the team that conveyed Jack's casket between church, chapel, and cemetery, we said good-bye and I gripped him in an impulsive embrace.

"Tell you what, pal," said Billy Pierce. "For the next twenty years or so, I'll pretend to be you."

I took my mother to dinner that night at Coach Mike Ditka's restaurant on the north side. "Billy Pierce," she said with a laugh. "What a nice man he seemed to be. Nice wife. Billy, Billy Pierce, after all these years." Together, my mother and I replayed highlights (the word may seem crass when applied to burials; but we are a show business family) from Jack's and Ralph's funerals. On the wall behind my mother there was a grainy old photo of a man in a leather-flapped helmet, high-stepping in caterpillar hops over the old sepia-toned muck of Wrigley Field in the twenties. "Hey," I said almost to myself, "I'll bet that's Red Grange." My mother turned to look over her shoulder.

"Yes. Yes, I think it is."

I did a quick calculation.

"You couldn't have been old enough to see him play—"

"Oh, no, not at all," said my mother. "I remember him from some club your father and I used to go to on the west side. They had a nickname for him."

"The Galloping Ghost?"

"That's it. Anyway," she remembered, "people used to come in, see him sitting there, and buy him a drink to get him to tell stories. 'Hey, Ghost, remember this?' That sort of thing. I used to think he was some nice old rummy grandpa. But then your father told me he was Red Grange, the Galloping Ghost, and got him to tell stories."

Once, my father and mother had wanted to join friends at a west-side Italian restaurant. But my mother did not want to leave their young German shepherd in the car. So, they concocted a story. My mother slipped on a pair of sunglasses. She was visibly pregnant. My father, mother, and our dog presented themselves in the restaurant vestibule, looking forlorn.

"I hope you can accommodate us," said my father. "You see, my wife here is blind." My mother stood alongside, one loving hand on my father's arm, another fixed rather more firmly on our dog's collar. "This is her seeing eye dog. My wife needs her at all times. I hope you can let us in."

"Oh, darling," my mother called out helpfully, "this place *sounds* sooo beautiful." A manager came over, manifestly moved.

"Oh, migod, Mr. Simon, yes, of course. Your lovely wife and her seeing eye dog are always welcome here." As they moved through the dining room, my mother remembered, you could hear people sighing at the sight of a beautiful young expectant mother—*lovely enough to be a model, isn't she? I wonder what her story is*—and her loyal, loving husband and devoted dog. But when they were seated, the staff began to set down effulgent platters of food.

"Oh, Ernest," cooed my mother, sneaking a peek through her dark glasses, "that platter *sounds* just *gorgeous*, doesn't it?" Our dog leapt up hungrily at the appearance of sausage and peppers.

"Down, girl," said my father over his own laugh. "Down, now. Remember what they taught you in seeing eye dog school! Behave, now, girl, or you can't have the veal scallopini." My mother remembered the story, forty years on.

"Well, I guess by that point no one was fooled," she said. "But the whole restaurant was laughing. Everyone thought it was so funny, it was kind of hard to throw us out. So they just let us stay. Your father had a knack for making people laugh and forget, didn't he?" I saw years disappear in my mother's smile, and a glimpse of my father when he was winning, impish, risky, and irresistible. My mother's eyes were merry, doe wide, and forest brown. She laughed like a lyrical brook in an Irish wood. Like my father and stepfather before me, I was out on the town with the most beautiful woman in Chicago.

I went down to Houston to watch the Cubs close out their season in the summer of Mark McGwire and Sammy Sosa shattering home run records. I walked through a warren of burrows and tunnels on the ground floor of the Astrodome until I saw a grove of gray and maroon ballpark jackets standing thickly around an open door. They were ballpark employees, ticket takers, vendors, and guards, each arrayed in a color according to their function; all of them looking out the door with faces turned up into the Astrodome's distilled sun. "What's everyone looking at?" I asked, and the answer came back in a chorus of Latin American accents: "Sammy. Sammy. *Sí? Sammy.*"

My old pallbearing mate, Billy Williams, the Cub batting coach, stood behind the screen as Sammy lashed out at batting practice pitches and explained that the snap in Sammy's stroke was what poked out so many home run balls.

"He's got a swing like a powerful mousetrap," said Billy. "Now look, when he swings now. *Thwaaap!* See? How quick his wrists come through? Like the mouse hits the cheese, and good-bye, Mr. Mouse. Bye-bye, hey-hey. Quick wrists, he's got. A quick, beautiful stroke."

The Cubs lost their game; but the New York Mets lost theirs; and so the Cubs thus fell down and stepped up into a one-game wild card playoff the next night with the San Francisco Giants. But first, in Houston, Sammy Sosa had to confront a reporting swarm. Mark McGwire had hit two home runs on the last day of the regular season, reaching 70, four ahead of Sammy. The Cubs conveyed him into a holding area, where he glistened under the lights and listened untiringly to a chorus of identical questions.

*Are you disappointed? Did you want to beat McGwire? Do you think you were playing for your team to win, not a home run record, and that hurt you? No, no,* and *no,* said Sosa. He stood between a tandem of American signs of success: two police guards.

"The way I see it, anyone who wants to beat Mark, they have to get through me."

*But just today, are you a little bit envious?* That question was the final straw that broke Sammy Sosa's smile.

"*No. No!*" he said firmly. "When you believe in God, you have no reason to be jealous of nobody. God loves us all the same."

Back in the coach's cluster in the locker room, Billy Williams sat with imperial elegance in a swirl of towels.

"Losing but winning," he said with a laugh. "Well, I don't mind. We don't get too hard on ourselves. Plenty of times in life, you play your heart out to win, and then lose. Only even when you lose, but you win. That's part of the game, too. See you up in Chicago tomorrow night?" I don't know, I told him; that's an awful lot of flying around, a long way to go for a ball game.

"Sure is," said Billy Williams. "But it's home."

Even in the days when I was striving to be a political radical, I was still a traditionalist about baseball. I supported Fidel Castro, opposed the military-industrial complex, and did not want to see lights installed at Wrigley Field. Each conviction was felt with equal ferocity. Today, I put my score as right about the military-industrial complex, wrong to be an apologist for Fidel Castro, and wrong to oppose lights in Wrigley Field. Perhaps that explains my enduring affection for a game in which being right 33.3 percent of the time is still considered an achievement.

Wrigley Field was ravishing that late September night in which the Cubs met the Giants. The last licks of orange, autumn light sputtered in the sky as the white stadium lights poured silver-plate over the infield and foul lines. Clamoring fans overstuffed the park, trailing signs and snapping up the top buttons of Cubbie blue windbreakers against lake gusts. *It's a beeeautiful night for a ball game!* Flocks of youngsters surged and clustered on the blocked streets running behind the left- and right-field walls, turning their eyes to the sky and staying alert for the sound of a Sammy *Thwaaap!* that would send a ball from on high into their midst. *Let's play two tonight!* When I walked down the concrete stairs leading down to the field, I glanced up at the manual scoreboard and noticed: just one game being played tonight. All the spaces and lines on the board were empty, save for a duo stretching across at the bottom left:

| 1 | 2 | 3 | 4 | 5 | 6 | 7 | 8 | 9 | 0 |
|---|---|---|---|---|---|---|---|---|---|
| SF | | | | | | | | | |
| CHI | | | | | | | | | |

The grid was waiting to be inscribed with the game's box score. The night had some of the same sense of gravity and delight as the seventh game of the World Series. The Cubs playing just one game, win or lose. If they won, they got to play on; if they didn't, they closed down in disappointment. There was an elegance and exactness to that which we didn't often get to see at Wrigley Field.

Mark Grace held forth in the locker room just before the game. The incumbent Cub, a sturdy iron rail of a first baseman, amicably gruff and compellingly profane, the team's favorite teammate. He had been a Cub for eleven years, his entire major league career.

"Yessir," he said, shaking his chop-top head with determination, "this is the greatest place to play *in the world.* Tonight, this is the *greatest place* in the world. Greatest *fans* in the world. Can you ever beat going to the office here? Look at this. *Look* at all those folks out there. Listen to this, goddamn, can you believe it? Win or lose. *Look* at this night. What a great group. What a great, goddamn night. Look as hard as you can, and remember. I just wish," Gracie added, "that Harry and Jack were here to see this."* The Cubs had made Ernie Banks a special dugout coach for the game, so he could wear a uniform and sit on the bench to call out encouragement. *Hey, Ernie,* players and reporters called out, *what kind of night is it?* "It's a beeautiful night for a ball game! But we're gonna play only one tonight! One to win!"

A tall man with an elegant stride made his way to the pitcher's mound to throw out the ceremonial first pitch. He was wearing a SOSA 21 jersey. During his first few steps, there was a suspicion. But when he tipped his Cubs cap, his most eminent bald bullet head was revealed for dead certain. Around the world, youngsters and aging children were wearing JORDAN 23 jerseys. But that night at Wrigley Field, JORDAN 23 was wearing a SOSA 21 jersey. The ceremonial pitch turned into an annointing: MJ throwing to Sammy, Jordan welcoming Sosa into the thin ranks of adulation. The two of them laughed and embraced like teammates on the grass just before home plate.

Steve Trachsel shut down the Giants for 6 1/2 innings. Gary Gaetti, the forty-year-old shortstop, hit a two-run home run. I didn't have a seat; the Cubs issued me a pass just to rove, and I was so roving when I caught a shout behind me. "Hey, Scooter!" Steve and Margot Kerr were sitting in second-tier seats on the third-base side. I think Steve went mostly unrecognized. In street clothes, he looks like a slim, bespectacled, sunburned teaching assistant who still plays pickup games

---

*Harry Caray, the longtime Cub announcer who succeeded Jack Brickhouse when Jack retired, had died just a few months before.

with undergrads at the Columbia gym. "Don't let that little guy fool you," the undergrads would say. "Killer long-distance jump shot." I waved up at them and called across the tiers. "You be ready, Mr. Kerr! They may be coming to you!" I was roving over on the first-base side in the top of the ninth inning, when the Cubs were ahead 5 to 3. Joe Carter of the Giants came to bat with a man on base and took a Rod Beck pitch on his wrists and popped it up high over the precincts of first base. Mark Grace looked up into the lights, locked his gaze onto the ball, and locked it into his glove for the last out. Gracie bent over from his waist for a moment, as if recovering from a long race; and then, a moment longer as the Cubs began to bound around him. When Mark Grace looked up, his eyes shined with tears. In the seats all around, fans began to call: "Good night, Gracie! Gracie, say good night!"

In my mind, I can keep the ball hanging for a moment between the moon and the stadium lights. Gracie is looking up from first. Sammy, smiling and tapping out heart kisses, is dancing in from right. MJ, beaming, looks on from the bench, while Mr. Cub stands up, clapping, on the dug-out steps—*Let's play two!*—and Steve Kerr stirs in the grandstands. *Be ready, Mr. Kerr, they may be coming to you!* Charlie Grimm, beaming chagrin, looks out with his basset-hound grin over first base. In the violet, velvet backdrop behind the brownstones and the porches over the left field wall, an El car twists in the turn from Addison toward Sheridan, shearing sparks against the steel night. Flashes fly and die. Falling, they light up Jack in the booth, *Hey-hey*, Billy Pierce in the bullpen, Gale Sayers scoring six in the muck, Sweetness sliding, Pic chuckling, *Can you believe this! Can you believe this?* Ralph and Ernie look on, admonishing, *You gotta keep the ball in front of you!* The ball slides against the moon. I inhale hope in my lungs and breathe it out, slowly, trying to hold the ball in the air against the stars.

# Selected Bibliography

I am particularly indebted to the following books and authors:

Bouton, Jim, with Leonard Schecter. *Ball Four.* New York: Macmillan, 1970, 1981, 1990.

Brickhouse, Jack, with Jack Rosenberg and Ned Colletti. *Thanks for Listening!* South Bend, Indiana: Diamond Communications, Inc., 1986.

Coleman, Nick, and Nick Hornby, editors. *The Picador Book of Sports Writing.* London: Macmillan, 1996.

Condor, Bob. *Michael Jordan's 50 Greatest Games.* Secaucus, N.J.: Citadel Press, 1998.

Ditka, Mike, with Don Pierson. *Ditka: An Autobiography.* Chicago: Bonus Books, 1986.

Durocher, Leo, with Ed Linn. *Nice Guys Finish Last.* New York: Simon & Schuster, 1975.

Early, Gerald, editor. *The Muhammad Ali Reader.* Hopewell, N.J.: Ecco Press, 1998.

Greene, Bob. *Rebound: The Odyssey of Michael Jordan.* New York: Viking, 1995.

Halberstam, David. *Playing for Keeps: Michael Jordan and the World He Made.* New York: Random House, 1999.

Hauser, Thomas, with Muhammad Ali. *Muhammad Ali: In Perspective.* San Francisco: HarperCollins, 1997.

Holtzman, Jerome, and George Vass. *The Chicago Cubs Encyclopedia.* Philadelphia: Temple University Press, 1997.

Hubbard, Jan. *Six Times as Sweet.* New York: HarperHorizon, 1998.

Jackson, Phil, and Hugh Delehanty. *Sacred Hoops: Spiritual Lessons of a Hardwood Warrior.* New York: Hyperion, 1995.

James, C. L. R. *Beyond a Boundary.* Durham, N.C.: Duke University Press, 1993.

Kruegel, Mitchell. *Jordan: The Man, His Words, His Life.* New York: St. Martin's, 1995.

Lazenby, Roland. *Bull Run! The Story of the 1995–96 Chicago Bulls: The Greatest Team in Basketball History.* Lenexa, Kansas: Addax Publishing, 1996.

Morris, Jeannie. *Brian Piccolo: A Short Season.* New York: Dell, 1971.

Pluto, Terry. *The Curse of Rocky Colavito: A Loving Look at a Thirty-Year Slump.* New York: Simon & Schuster, 1994.

Sachare, Alex. *Chicago Bulls Encyclopedia.* Chicago: Contemporary Books, 1999.

Vancil, Mark, Bary Elz, photographs. *Chicago Bulls: Portrait of an Era.* Chicago: Tango Publishing, 1998.

Veeck, Bill, with Ed Linn. *Veeck — As in Wreck.* New York: G. P. Putnam's and Son, 1962.

Whittingham, Richard. *The Bears: A 75-Year Celebration.* Dallas: Taylor Publishing, 1994.